# JOHANNES BRAHMS
## THE HERZOGENBERG CORRESPONDENCE

B. Miersch. pinx.                                    Druckmann. photo.

Johannes Brahms

Emery Walker Ph. sc.

# JOHANNES BRAHMS

## THE HERZOGENBERG
## CORRESPONDENCE

### EDITED BY MAX KALBECK

### TRANSLATED BY HANNAH BRYANT

### WITH PORTRAIT

## VIENNA HOUSE
New York

Originally published by John Murray, London, 1909


First VIENNA HOUSE edition published 1971


International Standard Book Number:
0-8443-0011-X


Library of Congress Catalogue Card Number: 78-163787


*Manufactured in the United States of America*

# PREFACE

*(Adapted from the Preface to the German Edition.)*

THE following correspondence between Johannes Brahms and Heinrich and Elisabet von Herzogenberg extends over a period of twenty-one years (1876–1897), and shows the gradual ripening into intimacy of a friendship the seed of which was laid some ten or twelve years earlier in Vienna, where Brahms had established himself in 1862.

Heinrich Picot de Peccaduc, Freiherr von Herzogenberg (b. at Graz, June 10, 1843), son of August Peter von Herzogenberg, an Austrian Court official, was descended from an old French noble family which had settled in Austria, taking the name Herzogenberg as the German form of Peccaduc. In 1862 he gave up his law studies and came to Vienna to study music under Otto Dessoff, director of the Opera and the Philharmonic concerts, and professor at the Conservatorium. His talents were of a wide order, and his tendency was to dabble in all the arts; but he soon recognized the necessity of concentrating his energies on one subject, and realized that in choosing music he would be able to turn to good account all the general culture he had acquired. In the same year (1862) Brahms left his birthplace, Hamburg, and came to live in Vienna. In him Herzogenberg promptly recognized his ideal. They probably became person-

v

ally acquainted at Dessoff's house, in 1863 or 1864, where Brahms was a privileged visitor. Herzogenberg had up to that time been strongly influenced by, first, Schumann, then Wagner and the New German school. He was now convinced that he was on the wrong path, and set himself with the utmost deliberation to conquer his native exuberance, and to shake off the effect of these influences by a severe course of theoretical study, taking Bach as his model. There is no doubt that his compositions lost in spontaneity and imagination in consequence, for his ruthless suppression of the natural instincts he had learned to mistrust made him almost a slave to form and technique. But his oratorios and the Church music to which, in later years, he chiefly devoted himself bear unmistakable traces of the Catholicism which was in his blood and had been fostered by his education at a Jesuit college, in spite of the fact that they were written strictly for performance in Protestant churches; and as these are the results on which his present fame rests and by which a future generation will judge him, it would seem a matter for gratitude that his system of self-repression was not entirely successful. Whether his whole attitude was a mistake or not, his long struggle with his own temperament was nothing short of heroic, and his unselfish, unwavering devotion to Brahms shows the natural sweetness of a nature modest almost to excess. In reading the letters, we realize what an occasional word of encouragement from his idol would have meant to him, and did mean, on the few occasions when Brahms was able to say that anything had pleased him. His respect for Herzogenberg's musical knowledge was most genuine, and he is said to have

exclaimed on one occasion: 'Herzogenberg knows
more than all the rest of us put together.'

Herzogenberg's studies with Dessoff ended in 1864.
On November 26, 1868, after a long courtship, he
married Elisabet, youngest child of Freiherr Bodo
Albrecht von Stockhausen—whose full title ran: Herr
auf Lewenhagen, Imbsen, Niedemjesa, Stane, Her-
mannsrode—at that time Ambassador at the Court
of Vienna, a descendant of an ancient noble family
of Hesse mentioned in the following of Duke Otto of
Bavaria as early as 1070.

Elisabet von Stockhausen was born in Paris on
April 13, 1847. In 1853 her father exchanged from
Paris (where he had been able to devote considerable
time to music, being, indeed, a pupil of Chopin) to
Vienna. His wife, Klothilde Annette (*née* Gräfin von
Baudissin), made literature her chief study, and to her
Elisabet owed not only her beauty and charm, but her
quick intelligence and remarkable powers of penetration, while her great musical talent was inherited
from her father. The home life was a very happy
one. Freiherr von Stockhausen was a religious man
and a strict Protestant, and the children were piously
brought up, besides receiving every educational advantage. The two sisters (Julie, the elder, was born
in Paris on February 25, 1842) were familiar figures in
Viennese society, and particularly in the concert-rooms
and theatres, in the middle of the 'sixties. Elisabet's
musical studies were made under Dirzka, an organist,
and later under Julius Epstein, at that time the principal
pianist and teacher in Vienna. Her progress was all
that could be desired. She had a wonderful memory,
fluent natural technique, a delicate touch, a quick grasp
of her subject and a true musician's temperament.

Brahms was at this stage of his career obliged to give lessons, to eke out a slender income of which the only assured item was his small salary as conductor of the *Singakademie*. A new pupil was consequently a matter of some importance, and he willingly undertook to give Elisabet von Stockhausen some piano lessons. After a very short time, however, he asked to be released from the engagement, the reason given being that Epstein must necessarily feel injured at being supplanted, and with justice. In vain was it represented to him that Epstein still taught the elder sister Julie, and had besides more pupils than he knew what to do with. Brahms persisted in his decision, and the lessons ceased abruptly.

The young married couple first settled at Graz, but removed to Leipzig in 1872, where they found more scope. Here Herzogenberg came more and more under the influence of Bach. On January 31, 1875, in conjunction with Alfred Volkland, Philipp Spitta, and Franz von Holstein, he founded the Leipzig Bachverein, and shortly after became president. The post brought him little beside honour; for although his salary was doubled with great regularity at each annual meeting, he received the same amount in the last year of his presidency as the first. 'Let arithmeticians solve the problem!' says a humorous chronicler of the society's doings. His wife rendered invaluable aid by rallying the lazier members of the chorus, encouraging the disheartened ones and leading the sopranos herself.

Once Herzogenberg had established a footing in Leipzig, his thoughts turned to a scheme for increasing the popularity of Brahms's music in that town. Some signs of improvement had already been felt. The

D minor concerto, played by Frau Clara Schumann in 1873, had not been hissed, as on the occasion of its first performance in 1859, while a performance of the *German Requiem* at about the same time had to a certain extent opened the eyes of the Leipzigers. The enthusiasm with which his works were being received in other places was also beginning to take effect. Altogether the time seemed ripe for a great effort, and the little group of Brahms's admirers, with Herzogenberg at their head, joined with Riedel and the Gewandhaus committee in arranging a 'Brahms week.' Brahms accepted their invitation, though with some reluctance, and arrived at Leipzig on January 29, 1874.

The week's programme included an evening given by a branch of the *Allgemeine Deutsche Musikverein*, a matinée of chamber-music at the Gewandhaus, at which Brahms played, a performance of *Rinaldo* conducted by him, and an extra concert given at the Gewandhaus, at which the orchestral *Variations on a Haydn Theme*, Op. 56, the *Rhapsodie* for contralto solo, men's chorus and orchestra, Op. 53, and three *Hungarian Dances* in manuscript, figured as novelties, while Brahms and Reinecke played a dozen of the *Liebeslieder* duets, Op. 52. The inaugurators of the scheme had every reason to be satisfied with the result. Brahms was the hero of the hour, his social success being hardly less marked than his public triumphs. It was on this occasion that the Herzogenbergs were drawn more closely to him. Elisabet wrote to her friend in Vienna, Frau Bertha Faber: 'I must tell you how much we liked your Johannes this time. He was not like the same person. . . . So many people suffer shipwreck on that dangerous rock called Fame; but we all felt that it had mellowed him, and made him kinder and more tolerant. He does not wear a halo of infallibility à la Richard Wagner, but has a quiet air of having achieved what he set out to accomplish, and is content to live and let live.' Three years later, when Brahms again visited Leipzig, he stayed with the Herzogenbergs, and the course of their friendship from that time onwards is traced in the letters.

Elisabet's death at San Remo on January 7, 1892, from heart disease, was a heavy blow, not only to her husband, but to Brahms, who had come to rely on her sympathetic judgment and absolutely frank criticism. Her personality seems to have exercised an unfailing charm on everyone with whom she came in contact. She had beauty, nobility of character, womanly tenderness, a passionate love of truth and justice, the courage of her opinions—every good thing, in fact, but health. Never strong, she overtaxed herself by nursing her husband through a long illness, and the strain told on her weak heart. After her death, Herzogenberg shut himself up in the house he had finished building just too late for his wife to set foot in it, and buried himself in work. His *Totenfeier*, a sacred cantata, is a beautiful monument to her memory. His great grief seems to have brought out the best in him, and his finest work, including the three great oratorios—*Die Geburt Christi*, Op. 90; the *Passion Music*, Op. 93; and the *Erntefeier*, Op. 104— was written in these last years of his life. As time went on he began to collect his friends about him again, and every year saw a group of fellow-artists and musicians assembled at the little house, *Zum Abendrot*, on Lake Constance. He died at Wiesbaden on October 9, 1900, having survived his wife by eight, and Brahms by three, years.

\* \* \* \* \*

In May, 1891, Brahms addressed to his publisher, Fritz Simrock, a document which he described as his last will. It was, however, too hastily drafted to fulfil legal requirements, and was subsequently declared invalid. In it Brahms ordered that all letters found in his house after his death were to be destroyed without reservation. But Dr. Josef Reitze, of Vienna, who became his executor, concluded that the will had been drawn up in a moment of irritation, and was not to be taken too literally. He therefore made a distinction, in sorting out the papers, between those of public interest and those of a private nature, placing the decision as to the advisability of publishing the present correspondence in the hands of Dr. Adolf Wach, of Leipzig, who had been an intimate friend of the three people concerned. Fräulein Helene Hauptmann, the possessor of the original letters from Brahms to the two Herzogenbergs, came forward with eagerness to help with the work; and thanks are also due to Herr Edmund Astor, Herzogenberg's Leipzig publisher, Herr Heinrich Buck, librarian to H.R.H. the Duke of Cumberland at Gmunden, Professor Julius Epstein, Frau Bertha Faber and Dr. Eusebius Mandyczewski, keeper of the archives of the *Gesellschaft der Musikfreunde* in Vienna.

The dates of the letters, when supplied by the editor, have been set in square brackets. Brahms seldom dated his letters, and the postmarks or, failing these, the contents of the letters had to be consulted.

H. B.

# CONTENTS

# CONTENTS

# CONTENTS

# CONTENTS

# CONTENTS

# CONTENTS

xix

# JOHANNES BRAHMS

## THE HERZOGENBERG CORRESPONDENCE

1. *Heinrich von Herzogenberg to Johannes Brahms.*

AUSSEE, *August* 1, 1876.

MY DEAR HERR BRAHMS,—I am sending you what I believe to be the first set of variations* ever written on a Brahms theme, thereby providing you with the nucleus of a collection of curios. To be first, for once, in anything was a great temptation, apart from that offered by your glorious theme. I have by no means exhausted its possibilities in my treatment, of which you will not, I hope, entirely disapprove.

I was unable to ascertain before leaving Leipzig whether you had finally decided to incorporate your arrangement of the cantata, *Christ lag in Todesbanden*, in our Bach - Verein publications. We should be delighted if you had leisure and inclination for it.†

You know we have the whole pack at our heels,

---

* Herzogenberg published his *Variations on a Theme of Johannes Brahms for Pianoforte* (two performers), as Op. 23, through Rieter-Biedermann. The theme is that of the song *Mei Mutter mag mi net*, from Op. 7.

† The Leipzig Bach-Verein, instituted in 1874 by Von Herzogenberg, Philipp Spitta, Franz von Holstein, and Alfred Volkland, published, through Rieter-Biedermann, pianoforte scores, with a supplementary organ part, of Bach's sacred cantatas. For these adaptations, Volkland, Herzogenberg and Wüllner were responsible.

and the closer we stick together, the sooner shall we silence them.* Also, if they still insist on dubbing Spitta an amateur,† and Volkland‡ and myself incapable enthusiasts, we could flourish your name in their faces. I would most willingly spare you the trouble of the pianoforte arrangement,§ and submit it to you when finished.

I am happily occupied in arranging the glorious Mass in F for our next concert. Last winter Volkland undertook the far from easy task of writing an organ part for the St. Matthew Passion-music. If only a good number of choral societies will take up the matter, we really hope to look back on some abiding results in the not too-distant future, always provided the firm of Rieter-Biedermann be not forced to bring the publication to an untimely end! If only our method obtains recognition, the rest of the enterprise does not matter.

* Refers to a heated argument on the treatment of accompaniments to older choral works which was being carried on at the time between Robert Franz (Julius Schaeffer), Friedrich Chrysander, Spitta, Hermann Kretzschmar, and others, through the medium of newspaper articles and pamphlets.

† Philipp Spitta (1841-1894), noted Bach biographer, was until 1875 Professor at the Nicolai Gymnasium, Leipzig. He was then appointed Professor of Musical History at Berlin University.

‡ Alfred Volkland (1841-1905), Director of Music at Basel, holding an honorary degree from the University, was conductor of the Euterpe concerts at Leipzig until 1875.

§ The arrangement of the cantata referred to was written by Brahms at the time when he conducted the *Gesellschaft der Musikfreunde* concerts in Vienna. He produced it there on March 23, 1873, as a novelty for the Viennese public, but did not claim the credit of the arrangement. Georg Henschel writes in his diary at Rügen in 1876: 'Brahms had the two first numbers of the Bach-Verein's edition of the cantatas beside him, and pointed out to me the unpractical setting. "A pianoforte score should be playable—written to suit the instrument," he said. "This is far more important than a strictly correct leading of all the parts."'

We lead a quiet, happy life here, out of reach of even the musical papers, with their reports from Bayreuth.* I hope the island of Rügen enjoys similar geographical advantages, and that Simrock† will shortly send us a voluminous package.‡

When you open my roll of music, you will think for the moment that you see one of your own—strangely unfamiliar—compositions! Our good Astor§ obviously accepted the piece with the sole malicious intent of frightening Simrock out of his wits with the title-page. Of course it sells all the better to the shortsighted visitors at Fair-time,‖ for they lose their heads so completely at the sight of JOHANNES BRAHMS, printed large, that the little notice underneath quite escapes them. It amuses me, of course; Astor too, I hope; so please take it as a joke yourself. But on reflecting that you will probably glance inside, I cease to be amused—while for you the fun begins, possibly?

With this grave query let me close, throwing myself on your mercy.—Believe me, yours very sincerely,

HEINRICH HERZOGENBERG.

* The first performance of Wagner's *Nibelungen-Ring* was held at Bayreuth in the summer of 1876.

† Fritz Simrock (1837-1901), Brahms's principal publisher.

‡ Brahms went to the island of Rügen on June 15, settling in the village of Sassnitz, where he put the finishing touches to his Symphony in C minor.

§ Edmund Astor, music publisher in Leipzig, son-in-law of J. Melchior Rieter-Biedermann, after whose death in 1876 he became head of the Winterthur firm, founded in 1849.

‖ The fairs, which are held three times yearly at Leipzig, still attract such a number of strangers to the town that the better hotels double their prices during those periods. There is usually a large proportion of undesirables among the ' Fair visitors ' (*Messfremde*), and the designation is used somewhat contemptuously.—TR.

## 2. *Elisabet von Herzogenberg to Johannes Brahms.*

AUSSEE, *August* 1, 1876.*

DEAR HERR BRAHMS,—Our friend Bertha† assures me that you sent us kind messages, and expressed, at the same time, a wish to see Heinrich's *Variations on a Theme by Brahms.* I am only too delighted to believe both her assertions. Heinrich did not want to bother you with the variations, thinking you must be so glad to hear nothing but the roar of the ocean and the lapping of the waves, that even printed, silent music must be unwelcome in your chosen solitary retreat. But your kindness in expressing the wish alters the case. I hope you will not entirely disapprove of the piece, but if it should have the misfortune to displease you, do not hesitate to say so. For 'as the hart panteth after the water-brooks,' so panteth Heinrich after honest criticism, be it condemnatory or flattering.

I hope you are keeping real, real well at Sassnitz, both for your sake and for ours; for the better you feel the more work you will do, and we obviously stand to gain by your diligence.

I remember hearing that, at Sassnitz, they give you nothing to eat but pale grey beef and indescribable, wobbly puddings, made of starch and vanilla. But you, it is to be hoped, are indifferent to such things.‡

* It is evident that the Herzogenbergs wrote on the same day, unknown to each other, each sending Brahms a copy of the work.

† Frau Bertha Faber, of Vienna, daughter of an evangelical pastor, Dr. Gustav Porubszky, and wife of Arthur Faber, had been a friend of Brahms since the time of the Hamburg Women's Choral Society (1859-1861).

‡ The writer permits herself a little irony here, as Brahms was known to be anything but indifferent to what he ate.

The person who told me her own bitter experiences was reduced to living on eggs, which she boiled or fried in the privacy of her own room. I tell you this so that you may adopt the same measure if driven to extremes. We are better off here. There is char and salmon in plenty—though the prices are so exorbitant that we never have either; on the other hand, cutlets and bacon-cakes are within our reach. Best of all, a certain B. F. of Vienna,* not unknown to you, sometimes sends us a wonderful meat-pudding for supper, and every time we go to see her she stuffs us with the unrivalled Aussee brand of *Lebkuchen.†* I go very often in consequence, and we chatter, as only women can, about a thousand and one nothings. I feel like an old woman beside Bertha, but we get on splendidly all the same.

The poor woman has suffered much just now in the sudden death of her father‡—a man as exceptional in the parental relationship as in every other respect; but she bears up bravely for her mother's sake, and devotes herself wholly to the task of consolation.

But how do I come to be writing you such a long letter? I hope you will not think it a liberty. If you do, please lay the blame on Bertha.

Last of all, let me ask if the idea of visiting Leipzig again ever crosses your mind? You did not have such a bad time before, and you know how many devoted friends you have here in spite of all the philistines—bother them!

In case you do come again, I have a real favour to ask: that you should stop at the Herzogenbergs' instead of at Hotel Hauffe. I promise you a bed at

* Frau Bertha Faber.    † A rich spiced gingerbread.—Tr.
‡ On July 17, 1876.

least as good, much better coffee, no very large room but two decent-sized ones, a silken bed-cover, any number of ash-trays, and, above all, peace and quiet; while, as a set-off against the gilt and stucco and all the glories of the Hauffe establishment, we would make you real comfortable, refrain from worrying you, and only make you realize the great pleasure you were giving us. Think it over! We live in Humboldtstrasse now, exactly behind Legationsrat Keil—so nice and convenient for you when you pay your visits to the Gewandhaus directors.*

But I must close, and that quickly. Good-bye, dear Herr Brahms. Give a kindly thought once in a way to

ELISABET HERZOGENBERG.

### 3. *Brahms to Heinrich and Elisabet von Herzogenberg.*

HAMBURG, *August* 20, 1876.

MY DEAR FRIENDS,—Most sincerely do I thank you for the gift, I might almost say the advertisement, of your Variations. It is really most gratifying to find a song of one's own absorbing another person's thoughts so effectually. You must have some affection for the melody you choose for a theme, I take it, and in your case the affection was probably shared by two.

But forgive me if my thanks begin, and my critical remarks end, sooner than you would like. How can I be disinterested, when, as I open the duet and play it in imagination, I have a distinct vision of a slender,

---

* Brahms was known to detest ceremony in any form, and probably never paid a duty call in his life.

golden-haired figure in blue velvet seated on my right ?*

If I say any more I shall offend one or other of you. But I will really make a point of *playing* the variations. Nothing is worse to read than a duet when the music is at all complicated. Then, when I have the pleasure of a chat with you again, should I have anything but praise to bestow, I will let you have my valuable opinion beforehand to bring you into the right frame of mind !† I might have something to say on the subject of variations in general. For instance, I could wish people would distinguish variations from *fantasia-variations*, or whatever we may choose to call the greater number of modern writings in this form. I have a peculiar affection for the variation form, and consider that it offers great scope to our talents and energies.

Beethoven treats it with extraordinary severity, and rightly calls his variations ' alterations.'‡ All the later ones by Schumann, H., or Nottebohm§ are very different. I am, of course, objecting neither to the form nor the music. I only wish for some distinction in the name to denote the distinctive character of each.

If I could enclose a few Sassnitz menus, your wife would be filled with surprise and envy ! We suffered

* Brahms had often played duets with Frau von Herzogenberg during his previous stay at Leipzig.

† Herzogenberg's work did not altogether please him.

‡ 33 *Veränderungen über einen Walzer von A. Diabelli*, Op. 120.

§ Gustav Nottebohm (1817-1882), a scholarly musician in Vienna, compiler of the thematic catalogues of Beethoven's and Schubert's works, and author of *Beethoveniana* and *Neue Beethoveniana*, was held in great respect by Brahms for his wide historical and theoretical knowledge. The reference is to Nottebohm's *Pianoforte Variations on a Theme by Bach*, which Brahms had often played with the composer.

nothing on that score, and pianos were all too plentiful.

I am not drawn to an arrangement of the cantata; it is so very difficult to adapt Bach for the pianoforte. Neither can I solve the problem : Is the arrangement intended for practical use in choral practices, etc., or for clever amateurs ? Rieter's attitude with regard to Peters * is incomprehensible to me.

I have heard of the charming party assembled at Lucerne. It is very alluring. You will have heard, either from herself or from Herr Volkland, with what delight Frau Schumann† plays your Variations.

Kindest remembrances to you both and to your neighbours of *Lebkuchen* fame. — Most sincerely yours,
JOH. BRAHMS.

### 4. *Brahms to the Herzogenbergs.*

[VIENNA] *December*, 1876.

MY VERY DEAR FRIENDS,—I am thoroughly ashamed of my clumsy breach of manners.‡ I had decided I ought not to presume on your kindness, yet my pen refused to write 'no'; and now your kind reminder quite confuses me.

But I shall arrive very, very early, and shall not leave until Saturday, you know. Also I fear your wife is counting on my having been chastened and hardened at Sassnitz, whereas the true conditions of Rügen

* Brahms considered that Rieter-Biedermann's edition could not be profitable, in view of the existing, more practicable, Peter's edition. This proved to be the case, and only five cantatas were issued by Rieter.

† Clara Schumann (1819-1896), wife of the composer and famous pianist, whose close friendship with Brahms dated from 1853.

‡ He had not replied to their invitation.

are quite unknown to her. However, *absit omen!* Three days before the concert I begin to perspire and drink camomile tea; after the fiasco (at the Gewandhaus) attempts at suicide, and so on. You shall see the lengths to which an exasperated composer will go!

But forgive this nonsense. I have written too many letters to-day. My best thanks, and please send me a card with your number—in case!—Sincerely yours, in haste,

J. BRAHMS.

### 5. *Herzogenberg to Brahms.*

LEIPZIG, *January* 3, 1877.

MY DEAR HERR BRAHMS,—We gathered from your letter, to our great joy, that you mean to try staying with us. You will at least be cosier and quieter in our well-guarded house, Humboldtstrasse 24, 2nd floor, than in any one of the hotels full of Fair visitors. Your rooms are so situated that you can easily refuse to receive, not only strangers, should their visits be inopportune, but also ourselves; we beg you won't use this privilege too freely with respect to the latter, though. Please let us have a card with the date and hour of your arrival, and to say which way you are coming—by Dresden or Eger. When will Simrock publish the symphony? Before the concert, I hope.*

* Symphony No. 1 in C minor, Op. 68, published by Simrock in 1877. Brahms arrived on January 14 for the final rehearsals of the symphony, which he conducted himself at the Gewandhaus on January 18. It was very favourably received. On the same occasion he conducted his orchestral *Variations on a Theme of Haydn*, and accompanied some of his own songs sung by Georg Henschel. Two days later he played the piano part of his Quartet in C minor, Op. 60, at the Gewandhaus Chamber-music Concert.

Please come as soon as possible (at once, if you like) and stay as long as possible.

If Frau Schumann stays with her friend, Frau Lepoc (Lepoque, Lepock ?), or with Frau Raimund Härtel,* she will be quite near us. The Freges† cannot put her up this time; we have discovered that much.

And now excuse this feeble letter and this superfine notepaper.—In haste, always yours sincerely,

HERZOGENBERG.

### 6. *Elisabet von Herzogenberg to Johannes Brahms.*

LEIPZIG, *January 23*, 1877.

MY DEAR FRIEND,—It is really quite too tragic! But that is always the way when you count too much on anything, as we did. *Es wär zu schön gewesen, es hat nicht sollen sein.* ——‡ is probably thinking the same. They say, by the way, that he could not face the terrific strain of deciding whether the finale led to heaven or hell.

Our first breakfast alone yesterday was a melancholy affair. The real good things of this life seem so much a matter of course when we have them that we feel unreasonably aggrieved when they are withdrawn. But we are grateful by moments, too, very grateful, and fully appreciate the fact that you were here, the manner of your being here, and the way you had of

* Wife of the head of the firm Breitkopf and Härtel.

† Dr. Frege's house at Leipzig was something of a centre for musicians (Mendelssohn and Schumann had been in the habit of going there). His wife Livia was a well-known singer.

‡ A certain member of the Gewandhaus committee had protested volubly against the proposed repetition of the symphony at an early date.

almost seeming to enjoy yourself here. That consoles me for many things. I am only too conscious of the many occasions when things went wrong. The conviction rose several times that I was mad to ask you to come at all, you spoilt creature, with your mock-turtles, your Prater* manners, and your constitution ruined by every conceivable refinement of luxury. The impossible was always happening, but you only smiled, as if it were quite possible, and so relieved all your hostess's fear and trembling. Thank you for that, you dear man, and for everything else. Only tell yourself repeatedly what those days were to us, for that alone can give you pleasure as you look back, and will be some small reward for all the pleasure you gave us.

And now tell me just this. Could you not go to Berlin now, to please Frau Schumann and others, and rest a little here on the way back?† We can't conceive of your going straight home to Vienna, and are counting so firmly on your passing through again, by some means, that your rooms are still untouched, and Heinrich does his writing at the standing-desk in my room. Minna seems possessed of the same idea, or else she would have been absorbed in a grand shifting and cleaning of everything available by now.

And now good-bye. Keep what is called a kindly remembrance of us, and please have the symphony printed soon; for we are all symphony-sick, and weary of straining to grasp the beloved, elusive melodies.

Kind remembrances from our adopted daughter.‡ Keep a little affection for

THE FAITHFUL

* The manners of the Austrian capital.—TR.
† After a performance of the symphony at Breslau.
‡ Mathilde von Hartenthal, a clever amateur.

## 7. *Elisabet von Herzogenberg to Johannes Brahms.*

[LEIPZIG] *January* 29, 1877.

DEAR HERR BRAHMS,—As Heinrich is buried in some work which *must* be finished, and as you were so kind as to ask for another letter, I am taking up my pen in his—Heinrich's—place. Although we were more or less prepared for the news on your card—how you must thank Providence for this invention of the post-office!—it depressed us all the same, for we had cherished some hope of seeing you here again. It was like leaving a little side-door open, through which you slipped in and out until the 25th, when it went to with a bang. Your little blue room was invaded by a horrid sewing-woman. Heinrich went back to his study, and the old, dull routine set in. . . .

Goldmark's rusticities* left us cheerfully unmoved, but pleased the general public very much. I turned quite faint in the garden scene, and was frightened to death in the trombone passage. This scene was called Bridal-Chorus on the programme, but no one realized the mistake; indeed, the critics discussed it as such. Goldmark was quite satisfied with his success, at which we were very pleased. One can't help liking the man.

Before I stop—which should in decency be soon, for you only wanted to hear about Goldmark—I want to tell you three things. (After a week spent in Leipzig, are you not in duty bound to take an interest in the local news?) Well, poor old Wehner† has had a

* Karl Goldmark (b. 1830), Viennese composer. His symphony *A Rustic Wedding* was produced for the first time at the Gewandhaus on January 25, 1877.

† Arnold Wehner, formerly Director of Music at Göttingen University, and Conductor at the Schlosskirche, Hanover, was one

slight stroke, which left him blind in one eye. The Brahms week, with all that drinking, did the mischief. He took cold, had indigestion, congestion of the blood, and finally this eye trouble. Hard lines, isn't it? The poor old man sits in a darkened room, day after day, with two grey tom-cats for sole company, who climb up in turn to paw his face, while Pauline's shadow hovers about him. You will admit that this is a tragic ending, whatever his faults may have been. My second item of bad news is that poor old Härtel* is being sent to Mentone on account of a bronchial catarrh. His wife is quite beside herself, and goes with him to-morrow.

My third has probably small interest for you, though all the more for me. The sketch you were so cruel as to tear up has been ingeniously pasted together, and looks all the more imposing—just like an old sword, covered with honourable scars, but quite serviceable. Indeed, I like it more than ever, now that I can feast my eyes on it again, after its—to me—inexplicable disappearance. Mathilde helped me with the bandaging, and you are going to be ironed out some time to-day, and now left in peace.†

Good-bye. Enjoy yourself. Remember us to all, and don't forget your less fortunate friends for those around you now. Heinrich, his wife, their adopted daughter, Paddock ‡—all send greeting.

Keep just a little affection for us, I beg.     L. H.

---

of Brahms's silent opponents. He had at first been very well disposed towards him when at Hanover (see Kalbeck, *Johannes Brahms*, i. 353).

* Stadtrat Raimund Härtel.

† Mathilde von Hartenthal had made a pencil sketch of Brahms.

‡ The dog.

## 8. *Brahms to the Herzogenbergs.*

[VIENNA] *January*, 1877.

MY GOOD FRIENDS,—It just happens that I have a sheet of paper at hand. It ought to be rose-coloured for shame, and ingratiating as an angel; but, unfortunately, neither my letter-paper nor my face can look as sweet and kind as Frau Elisabet's—and that no matter how I may exert myself. Otherwise I would do it to-day; for no one can have a keener desire to say real nice things.

It was so delightful staying with you. The memory is still warm, and I feel I want to keep it snugly buttoned up for a long time.

But these things are easier to express in music, and I therefore present this paper merely out of politeness to my hostess — an arm to take her in to supper. Afterwards I shall choose the most beautiful key and the most beautiful poem to write the continuation.

So —— is still friendly, in spite of my behaviour and my letter? Very bad for my morals! A little wholesome severity might be desirable in other quarters, too.

I am sorry about Wehner and Härtel. . . .

I discovered at Breslau* that it is a great help if someone else takes my first rehearsal. That clever young Buths† did it there admirably. I had only to take it up where he left it, and it went splendidly. The introduction to the last movement was quite

---

* Brahms conducted his symphony at Bernhard Scholz's Breslau Orchestral Concerts on January 23, 1877.

† Julius Buths (b. 1851), afterwards Director at Düsseldorf, had conducted the rehearsal in place of Scholz, who was ill.

different from the Leipzig performance—that is, just as I like it.

If you see Reinecke,* you might recommend Buths. He is a very good pianist, and has written a Concerto in D minor which is well worth a hearing, even at the Gewandhaus.

Would you be so very kind as to inquire for my symphony at Dr. Kretzschmar's?† I have not his address, and he did not go to Rostock from Leipzig. However, he will probably send of his own accord.

And now kindest regards to you all three, and a plea for remembrance, from

J. BRAHMS.

## 9  *Herzogenberg to Brahms.*

LEIPZIG, *February* 15, 1877.

MY DEAR HERR BRAHMS,—I hope you were not impatient with me for the delay in the arrival of the symphony. I confess my guilt, if guilt it was in your eyes, in having kept it back a few days, to learn it by heart. I had no time to ask your permission first, as of course I ought to have done. My little wife plays it accurately now, and is not a little proud of her feat in reading the score. But how shall I express our great admiration for the composer, and our thanks? My clumsy pen is, I feel, very inadequate. It seems to us an event of world magnitude, the absence of which is now unthinkable, enriching and ennobling our existence as only the greatest things can. As

* Karl Reinecke (b. 1824), pianist and composer, Director of the Gewandhaus.

† Dr. Hermann Kretzschmar (b. 1848), writer and composer, afterwards Professor at Berlin University, was one of the earliest and most persuasive apostles of Brahms' music.

a musician who has met with affectation and superficiality at every turn in his not inconsiderable experience, I count myself (and all earnest seekers) happy in this pillar you have erected—though with no thought of us—in our path. What matters the morass on our left, the sandy waste on our right ? It can only be a matter of indifference to you which road we strike. But if you will observe the Lilliputian migration (take a microscope, please !), you will perhaps find some satisfaction in the way the little folk have picked themselves up again, leaving here and there a boot in the mud in their anxiety to keep up, or shaking the dust from their garments (with quite a pretty colour effect), one and all determined to stick to the right path.

And that reminds me of Julius Röntgen's* *Serenade*, which we heard last Saturday. It is really his best work, and shows that he is not afraid to be 'tuneful,' unlike most other composers nowadays !

And now by way of farewell :

> For all that you've endured unvexed,
>    I am your debtor ;
> And trust that where you sojourn next
>    They'll treat you better ! †

We know, for instance, that Frau Faber makes 'dreams' of pasties. Remember us to the dear people. We so often wish we were near them.

---

* Julius Röntgen (b. 1855), pianist and composer, was from 1869 leader of the Gewandhaus orchestra, and afterwards Director of Music in Amsterdam.

† A variant of the well-known volkslied *Da unten im Tale*, set to music by Brahms. Herzogenberg's lines are as follows :

> ' Für die Zeit, wo Sie vorlieb nahmen,
>    Danke ich schön,
> Und ich wünsch', dass es Ihnen anderswo
>    Besser mag gehn !'

I have left no room for all the nice things I was
to say to you from my wife and 'daughter,' so
please consider them said.—Always yours very
sincerely,

HERZOGENBERG.

10. *Brahms to Herzogenberg.*

[VIENNA, *April* 23, 1877.]

DEAR FRIEND,—I hope my fat letter of to-day will
catch you in one of your leisure moments. You will
see at once that I do not mean this sheet—I could
never write a fat letter on ordinary paper—but something that will arrive an hour or two later. I really
felt I must send you a message or a greeting, and hear
from you in return.

Perhaps you may be induced to write and tell me
what you think of my green-stuff,* and *particularly* of
anything that has not the honour of pleasing you.

When you have had enough of the sweets, you may
turn to the study 'after Bach,' which should be
amusing to practise.†

I shall really write very soon to tell you where
everything is to be sent.

In any case, many apologies for giving you so much
trouble over my correspondence.

It would be nice if you had time and felt like writing
me *two* letters, and scolding me well.

Your 'daughter' ought really to send her sketches
to the right address!

---

\* Songs in manuscript from Op. 69-71.

† *Presto nach J. S. Bach*, from the Sonata for Violin Solo in G minor.
Two editions of this were published in 1879 by Bartholf Senff in
*Studien für Pianoforte von Brahms.*

If I were to tell how the drawing had been taken
for a portrait of one of my directors. . . !*

Won't you come to Vienna a little earlier this year?
I am not sure how long I may stay or where I may
go. It sounds like vanity—but you might spare yourselves the trouble of copying ; printing is so very, very
rapid.

But I must not give the lie to my opening remarks.
—With kindest remembrances to the trefoil, yours
sincerely,

J. BRAHMS.

### 11. *Brahms to Herzogenberg.*

[VIENNA, April 23, 1877.]

DEAR FRIEND,—Did you find them entertaining, and
was your lady pleased? Please pack up the whole
bundle now and forward them as soon as possible,
without losing a day, to Frau Schumann, Berlin,
N.W., In den Zelten, No. 11. I am, quite seriously,
ashamed to trouble you again, but it is done now.

Forgive me. I shall look for a reassuring word.
—In haste, yours very sincerely,

J. BRAHMS.

### 12. *Herzogenberg to Brahms.*

LEIPZIG, April 27, 1877.

MY DEAR KIND FRIEND,—Just my luck! I have come
home at last, tired and dusty, after being out all day
on concert business, without a moment's leisure for
writing. Thank you now most sincerely for your
very spontaneous sign of affection. It makes me

---

* The portrait of Brahms by Mathilde von Hartenthal mentioned
in Letter 7.

happier than I have been for many a day, first that
you should think of us at all, then your *knowing* how
pleased we should be (otherwise you would have sent
the parcel straight to its destination), and lastly the
beauty of the songs, one and all. We shall not
complain of the dream-like nature of their visit; it is
enough that they came our way at all. So indelibly
did they impress themselves on our consciousness,
that, even if we never saw them again and should lose
all tangible recollection, the impression would keep
its freshness, and we shall always like you the better
by twenty songs, counting from yesterday. To the
rescue, Samiel or Simrock,* and spare us this test!

We fetched Julius Röntgen, and sat at the piano
four hours. First he sang, then she; then she played,
then he; while I took prosaic notes of our impressions,
with the numbers and temperatures, on a slip of paper,
so as to be able to say the proper thing to you after
taking the parcel to post. This I did with my own
hand this morning, so Frau Schumann will have them,
and her delight in them, by now.

Our *special* favourites are: *Ei, schmollte mein Vater,*
*Ätherische ferne Stimmen, Silbermond, O Frühlings-*
*abenddämmerung, Es kehrt die dunkle Schwalbe,* and
*Sommerfäden.*† A curious thing happened with *Früh-*
*lingsabenddämmerung.* We had sung it through many

* Two of Brahms's publishers.—TR.

† The actual titles are : *Des Liebsten Schwur, Lerchengesang, An den
Mond, Geheimnis, Alte Liebe,* and *Sommerfäden,* from Op. 69, 70, 71,
and 72. Herzogenberg speaks of twenty songs; but, as the four
sets published by Simrock in 1877 include twenty-three songs, Brahms
must have added three. He seems to have attached particular
importance to *Alte Liebe, Sommerfäden, Serenade* (Op. 70), and
*Unüberwindlich* (Op. 72), as he noted the date of their completion
(May, 1876) with some care.

times with all possible fervour, when my conductor's eye, whose acquaintance you have not yet made, fell casually on the tempo mark. We were struck dumb, and exchanged conscience-stricken glances. I remember talking about tempo marks to you, and having the audacity to maintain that a decent musician could not go wrong in the time of any healthy piece. And yet, how slowly had we taken it, misled by that same fervour! *Sehr lebhaft und heimlich* runs the inscription—and we had wasted sentiment on every suspension in the left hand; we had lingered—with what delicious thrills!—on the two broken chords

$\sharp 4$       $7$

$2$ and $\sharp$ in the right hand, with the syncopated D

$d$       $d$

down below, and all wrong! I seemed to hear your satirical laugh in the distance. You may be right; you are, of course, and in future we will sing it with due 'vivacity' and 'secret' gratitude. All the same, the discovery affected us painfully, and we cherish a hope that Röder* made a mistake which you overlooked in the proof, and we may yet see it publicly inscribed *Langsam und heimlich.*†

There is nothing to be said about *Ätherische ferne Stimmen.* I only regret that the right hand should be balked of its evident desire to stretch 11ths and 13ths!

Words are never any good, but mine must be more futile than most people's; for I seem doomed to write you, of all men, the stiffest and worst letters. If you have seen in them hitherto the expression of my character, I must indeed have come off badly!

---

\* Music-engraver at Leipzig.

† *Cf.* following letter. Brahms changed the tempo mark to *Belebt und heimlich.*

The Bach arrangement is splendid, though we mortals can only manage it as a duet, and not easily at that.  Is it to be printed, or may we order copies of it ?  Piracy is, alas! one of the many forbidden pleasures, or we should have liked to copy out one of the songs in haste, to be preserved as balm for certain wounded female hearts.  But it has been dropped pitilessly into the treasure-chamber at the door of which that monstrous Berlin dragon suns himself.*

It would have been delightful to meet you in Vienna, but hardly practicable, even if you are still there, for we are not coming at all.  We are devoting the whole of May to my poor sister in Bohemia, who has just lost her husband.  After that I hope for a quiet time in the mountains.  We shall stay at Alt-Aussee until the end of September, working hard. You might really put in a little time there, too.  How nice for me to see you and Goldmark doing a climb together !

So Frau Schumann goes to Düsseldorf, after all.  Is she making a home for you, or what is behind it all ? I am not the *Wochenblatt*, and can hold my tongue.†

Once more—God bless you !

This is merely number one.  Number two follows close—to-morrow, indeed, when my wife has time to write.‡—Yours most sincerely,

HERZOGENBERG.

* Probably refers to Brahms's publisher, Simrock.—TR.

† Brahms had been offered the post, once held by Schumann, of Music Director at Düsseldorf, but the lengthy negotiations led to nothing.

‡ The letter was not written until May 5 (see Letter 14).

### 13. *Brahms to Herzogenberg.*

[VIENNA, *April* 29, 1877.]

MY GOOD FRIEND,—In return for your very kind letter, I must tell you at once that, although *Belebt und heimlich* is the tempo mark for *Frühlingsdämmerung* in the manuscript, I set it down practically in desperation, thinking the song very dull. But later on there is *immer langsamer*, *Adagio*, and at the end actually a pause ⌢ over the whole bar!

Frau Schumann has long had an idea of settling at Düsseldorf. I think it a great pity for various reasons, and am exceedingly sorry she has decided to go.

It has nothing to do with my invitation. The matter is at last (and only just) settled; for one thing, President Bitter* is going to Berlin.

I am very glad I was cautious enough to keep out of that wasps' nest.

Very best remembrances.—Yours in haste and sincerely,

J. BRAHMS.

Talking of manuscripts, I have not forgotten that I owe your wife one. She shall not be disappointed. It will be the tenderest thing I can find!

### 14. *Elisabet von Herzogenberg to Brahms.*

BERLIN, N.W. (!), *May* 5, 1877.

DEAR HERR BRAHMS,—Your birthday being the day after to-morrow, we shall celebrate it here with dear

* Karl Hermann Bitter (1813-1885), Prussian Minister of Finance from 1878, whose writings on J. S. Bach and his sons were well known, was then *Regierungs-präsident* at Düsseldorf, and President of the *Musikgesellschaft* there. In this capacity he had some correspondence with Brahms about the directorship.

Frau Schumann at her own house. How your ears should burn when we drink your health! Let me tell you it is a red-letter day for us, the day when you graciously condescended to visit this planet.

It was a delight to find your songs again here. It gave me almost as much pain as pleasure to have them at Leipzig, for to have such a selection there without getting to know them intimately, or having them at hand to pet, was too tantalizing. I have made up for it now, more or less, and know some of them so well that they are with me in my walks and everywhere. My prime favourites are: *Ätherische ferne Stimmen, Sommerfäden,* and the G-minor-y one in four-time with the dotted quavers (by Lemcke, I forget the name\*) and then the glorious *Mädchenfluch* and—*and —die dunklen Schwalben* (Henschel's)!†

Since you insist on hearing what we did not like, I will tell you, as I have a tiresome affection for home-truths. I don't like the *Tambour,* '*nicht ist da*' (No. 1, I think) or *Willst du, dass ich geh'.*‡ Particularly the latter fails to appeal to me; the words alone are enough. That kind of reproof is only possible in volkslied style. *Wer steht vor meiner Kammertür'* and the one before it in the Schumann book§ are so entirely different. The *tritt auf, tritt auf* in your duet‖ could offend no one, for instance, but this one has an unpleasant ring.

\* *Im Garten am Seegestade,* Op. 70, No. 1.

† Georg Henschel (b. 1850), singer, to whom Brahms had given the manuscript of *Alte Liebe* in 1876, when at Rügen.

‡ *Tambourliedchen,* Op. 69, No. 5; *Klage,* Op. 69, No. 1, and Op. 71, No. 4.

§ From Schumann's four duets, Op. 34, *Unterm Fenster* and *Liebhabers Ständchen.*

‖ From Brahms's duets for alto and baritone, Op. 28, No. 2.

But please don't mind my babble. Frau Schumann is asleep over in the other room, and the songs are on her piano; otherwise I could write another sheet or two about them—what an escape for you! Excuse the smudges. We have to fetch Joachim to go to Löwe.*

Good-bye, and we request that you will kindly live to be very, very old.

Elisabet Herzogenberg.

Signed : Heinrich von Herzogenberg.

Fillu.†

15. *Brahms to Elisabet von Herzogenberg.*

[Vienna, November 13, 1877.]

My very dear Friend,—You will no doubt think, when you see my writing, that I am going to drop on you again to go to Hauffe or Härtel or the Hauffe Hotel for me. However, you are wrong. I am coming to Leipzig in the beginning of January, but shall take my luck, or at a pinch can be guided by the stars (with which Baedeker decorates so many places in Leipzig).

But I have a request, and, what is more, one that hopes for an answer. Härtel is worrying me to help with the complete edition of Chopin. ‡

I should like to know whether your parents possessed any manuscripts, or, still better, copies of his works with any of his notes or corrections. §

---

* Probably an evening devoted to Löwe's ballads.

† Nickname for Marie Fillunger, singer, and friend of Frau Schumann.

‡ Brahms helped to revise the edition.

§ The father was a pupil of Chopin (see Introduction).

Could I see any there may be in Vienna? Or at Dresden * or Leipzig?

If I were a well-behaved person, my letter would be just beginning; or if I were sufficiently bold, I should be tempted to slip a practical joke on music-paper† into the envelope.

But I am neither, so merely send you—all three— my best remembrances, and request the honour of inviting you personally to the performance of my newest symphony.‡—Most sincerely yours,

J. BRAHMS.

VIENNA, IV. KARLSGASSE, 4.


16. *Elisabet von Herzogenberg to Brahms.*

[LEIPZIG] *November* 15, 1877.

MY VERY DEAR FRIEND,—I confess I thought something different was coming when I received your note, and was as delighted as a child to think that you were coming to see us. Instead of which—an introduction about Härtel-Hauffe and the stars in Baedeker, and

---

* Elisabet's brother, Ernst von Stockhausen, lived in Dresden.

† The practical joke was a copy which Brahms had made for Frau von Herzogenberg of one of his vocal quartets, *O schöne Nacht!* Op. 92, No. 1, first published in 1884. At the words '*Der Knabe schleicht zu seiner Liebsten sacht—sacht—sacht,*' Brahms left a space, and wrote across the score: 'Stop, Johannes my son, what's this? These matters are only to be treated in volkslied style; you have forgotten *again.* Only a peasant may ask whether he is to stay or go, and you are no peasant, alas! Don't offend that fair head with its glory of gold, but have done! Repeat simply' (here the song continues): '*O schöne Nacht!*' This was, of course, meant as a mild protest against his friend's objection to '*Willst du, dass ich geh.*' The original manuscript of this quartet was in the possession of Theodor Billroth, the eminent Viennese surgeon, and bore the date January 29, 1878. It was, however, composed in the summer of 1877. Both copies bear the name *Notturno.*

‡ In D, Op. 73.

after that the Chopin matter. Now you must admit it would have been much friendlier to begin :

'I am coming to you on January 1. See that you have good coffee, and fresh—not boiled—cream this time, since you have at last realized that I prefer it. Don't starve me, either, but give me a decent lunch (Emma Engelmann* will give you an idea of its dimensions). If these conditions are fulfilled, I will play you my new symphony at once without waiting until Stockhausen† comes,' etc.

Yes, that is how any nice, comfortable person would write. As for you, your letter really made me sad. You see, I knew long ago that you were coming in January with a new symphony in your bag—how can you write an elegant word like 'symphony' with an *f*?‡ —and yet I forced myself not to write, out of modesty, and with the idea that Brahms would write and invite himself if he wanted to come. And this is my reward! Hang modesty, I say!

I can tell you little about Chopin. So far as I know, my father has, or had, one single manuscript. This he gave to my brother, who has also my father's whole Chopin edition. He can best give you information. I believe Chopin scribbled a mark or two in some of the things. You shall certainly see all there is. I am writing to my brother about it by this post.

And now, fare you well—better than you deserve!

* Emma Engelmann, *née* Brandes (b. 1854), a pianist, pupil of Aloys Schmitt and Goltermann, wife of the Berlin physiologist, Theodor Wilhelm Engelmann, at that time Professor at Utrecht University. They were among Brahms's best friends. The Quartet in B flat, Op. 67, is dedicated to Engelmann.

† Julius Stockhausen (1826-1906), famous singer, and master of method at Frankfurt-am-Main.

‡ German modern spelling of the word, *Sinfonie.*—TR.

If you really wanted to be quite free this time and go to Hauffe (who has added a new storey, and grows more splendid every day), you might have broken it to me differently, so that I could glean a little comfort. That letter was horrid. You cannot go to the Härtels, because they are in Italy; nor to the Engelmanns,* who would no doubt like to have you, as the house will be broken up. Old Mrs. Engelmann has to be with Emma, who is expecting a baby, lucky woman!

So if you are not set on going to Hauffe's . . . write and tell your devoted friends,

THE HERZOGENBERGS.

17. *Brahms to Elisabet von Herzogenberg.*

[VIENNA, *November* 22, 1877.]

DEAR LADY,—Modesty is the most unpractical garb anyone can wear. Are you only teasing me, or did you really not see the insinuating way in which my letter pulled your beard—the beautiful one which adorns your husband's face? Your general information is, I may say, superfluous, and moreover untrustworthy. 'The good storks return'† in December, not January.

The new symphony, too, is merely a *Sinfonie,* and I shall not need to play it to you beforehand. You have only to sit down to the piano, put your small feet on the two pedals in turn, and strike the chord of F minor several times in succession, first in the treble,

* Wilhelm Engelmann (1808-1878), publisher and art-collector in Leipzig, father of Professor Engelmann.

† Quotation from the song *Alte Liebe,* Op. 72, No. 1. According to German legend, the storks bring babies.

then in the bass (*ff* and *pp*), and you will gradually gain a vivid impression of my 'latest.'*

But I must really apologize for doing nothing but contradict you. Here is some news to make up. Goldmark arrived yesterday, and will probably be in Leipzig in January with his opera.† This opera of his takes him away, not only from his studio at Gmunden, but from here constantly. I should like to keep him here. He is a delightful fellow, and there are too few of the sort in Vienna.

But how many letters have I written to-day? I really must stop. If I put this in its cover after all, it is only because I fear you may really have misunderstood my last.

It was, as a matter of fact, a begging letter. By the way, Epstein‡ led me to expect more from your Chopin hoard.

No more to-day.—With kindest regards, yours very sincerely,

J. BRAHMS.

### 18. *Elisabet von Herzogenberg to Brahms.*

[LEIPZIG] *December* 3, 1877.

MY DEAR GOOD FRIEND,—It was bad of me not to answer your last kind letter at once; but I had the Spittas staying here, and there was always something in the way. Thank you for wanting to come back to us. If you went to Hauffe's, I should be as sad as,

---

* An attempt to mislead her as to the character of the symphony, which was actually the reverse of gloomy.

† *The Queen of Sheba*, which was produced everywhere soon after the first successful performance in Vienna (1875).

‡ Julius Epstein (b. 1832), Viennese pianist and professor, who had taught Frau von Herzogenberg.

say, Simrock, if you published your second *Sinfonie* (since it must be !)* elsewhere.

If you would only express yourself a little more clearly, my gratitude would be complete. They say here that your *Sinfonie* is to be played in January, and not at the first concert, either. Frau Schumann tells me definitely she is coming back to hear the Brahms symphony, after having played at the New Year's concert herself. So please explain why the good storks (to which you evidently think you belong !) return in December. I must know, because I have practically no room in December, when both my little rooms will be full. It is an arrangement of long standing that I cannot possibly alter now, and I am therefore most anxious to hear that you made a slip the other day. Otherwise you would not be able to land at our house, though I hope we should persuade you to move across into Humboldtstrasse later. Your letter is so vague that I have just had a presentiment your sentence about the storks may be taken to refer to Frau Engelmann, in which case I am worrying unnecessarily about your visit. How I hope this may be so !

This sudden inspiration has quite dazed me, for the storks are flying about my head in their sphinx-like double character. Do clear up the confusion, and forgive these hurried lines.—Yours,

ELISABET HERZOGENBERG.

Tell us which day to expect you, so that we can look forward to it.

P.S.—On reading your letter over, I understand it perfectly, and see that I was a goose about the storks.

* *Cf.* Letters 16 and 17.

We may expect you in January, then; the earlier the better.  Both rooms are free from the 2nd.

### [*Enclosure.*]

About Chopin—my brother, I am sorry to say, confirms my conjecture.  He writes that my father's edition contains nothing that can be of use to you. Any notes there may be are not supplementary readings, but only corrections of glaring misprints, such as every musical person could make for himself. The fingering which is written in here and there might equally well be Alkan's.*  My father studied with him also.  Of the three manuscripts in my brother's possession, two are copies, the only genuine one being the *Barcarolle,* dedicated to my mother.  My brother would like to give you this, together with the personally presented copy of the G minor *Ballade;* but he must first ask my father, who made them over to him with the solemnest stipulations.  If you would still care to see the books, they are of course at your service, I was to tell you.

### 19. *Brahms to Elisabet von Herzogenberg.*

[VIENNA, *December* 12, 1877.]

MY VERY DEAR FRIEND,—I had a sheet of paper all ready for you, when there came a letter from Limburger,† inviting me to play my concerto at Leipzig on January 1.  I really don't know what to do, and have to think it over so carefully that you will have no letter.

* Charles Henri Valentin Morhange (1813-1888), known as Alkan, French pianist and composer.

† Dr. Limburger, Consul at Leipzig, was on the committee of the Gewandhaus concerts.

You can imagine the respect with which your last letter inspired me. It was a triumph of penetration, and read, I may say, like a page in one of Beethoven's sketch-books, where an idea is originated, developed, and—fill out the parallel for yourself.

But can you really stand a practical joke ? I wanted to make my peace by enclosing the Andante from my third piano quartet, which I still have, remembering that you liked it, and I hardly know whether I am keeping it back from vanity or a sense of delicacy. I will bring it when I come.

I will not insult your intelligence by offering to explain the little jest* I am sending, and need hardly say that I strongly advocate the exploitation of other people's motifs. . . .

But, as you see, my thoughts are with Limburger. To have the F minor† here on the 30th, and then play a piano concerto !?!?—Yours most sincerely,

J. Br.

### 20. Brahms to Herzogenberg.

[Vienna, December 13, 1877.]

My good Friend,—I forgot to say yesterday that, in case I do play at Leipzig, ‡ I should very much like to have a day or two at an hotel. I should be uncomfortable practising in a friend's house, you see, and yet I must practise. So if I am such a fool as to accept, I shall ask you to engage me a room at Hauffe's, or where you like, and order in a piano (an upright).

Then, when your rooms are at liberty, I shall be

---

* The manuscript of O schöne Nacht, mentioned in Letter 15. Brahms had used a motif of Herzogenberg's by way of a jest.

† He keeps up the fiction about his D major symphony.

‡ He was to play his Concerto in D minor, Op. 15.

free too, and can make a triumphal procession
through the town to your house.

N.B.—I expect to have a concert here on the 30th,* 
so shall arrive at the last moment. Are you on such
terms with Reinecke that you can ask him about a
concert-grand ? I shall come straight to rehearsal,
and should like to have the best possible piano.—With
kindest regards, yours in great haste,

J. Br.

### 21. *Herzogenberg to Brahms.*

[Leipzig] *December* 16, 1877.

My very dear Friend,—Since it has to be, I will
engage you a room at Hauffe's or 'where I like.'
Where I like happens to be the Palmbaum, a highly
respectable, clean, and sufficiently elegant hotel, which
is not far from us. You will thus be able to come and
rest from your labours, the finger exercises, in the
evening. Also we should like to invite you to dinner,
if not every day, very often, and altogether make your
necessary and voluntary exile as pleasant as possible.
It will also simplify matters when the blissful moment
comes for you to move into Humboldtstrasse. So, unless I hear from you again, I will ask you to consider
yourself booked at the Palmbaum, and make your
arrangements accordingly. You will, I hope, let me
know the day and hour of your arrival soon.

I will order you an extra-magnificent piano through
Reinecke. I think I can get you a full-sized Blüthner
(Aliquot), or, if you like, a fine Bechstein (from your
friend Robert Seitz, who will at worst only request

* The D major symphony was played at the Vienna Philharmonic,
under Dr. Richter, on December 30, 1877.

the manuscript of a symphony in return!). Or, if you like Grotrian, Helfferich and Schulz, I can try for one of theirs. Blüthner is certain.

My best thanks, by the way, for taking my egg into your cuckoo's nest.* History will not be able to say in our case that a pupil has robbed his master. Writers such as Emil Naumann† and others will be so flustered, if this sort of thing goes on, as to be reduced to classifying Brahms as the Epigonus of his most faithful disciples. And it would serve you right!

But why did you keep back the part which divides us ?

Would it not have been better to fill this serious gap‡ with something nice and non-committal than to exercise your fatal memory for certain conversations ?

I am copying out this exquisite song, and want to have it sung here, so please send what is missing.

The youth steals along a familiar path to his beloved,§ but what matter, if he does it melodiously ?

I have a Bach concert to-day. Counting backwards, how many have there been ? Who could guess ?

Our kindest regards, and we hope soon to hear about the hotel, the piano and the date of your arrival.—Ever yours sincerely,

HERZOGENBERG.

*(P.S. from Elisabet von Herzogenberg.)*

I have to thank you for the manuscript, which would have pleased me better without its strong flavour of sarcasm, aimed at my poor feminine scruples. You

---

* See notes to Letters 15 and 19.

† Emil Naumann (1827-1888), composer and writer on music at Dresden ; author of an *Illustrated History of Music.*

‡ See Letter 15, note.      § See *O schöne Nacht !*—TR.

think me prudish, and it is useless to defend myself,
although nothing could be more unjust. If you only
knew how many lances I have broken for your
Daumer songs, even the much-abused *Unbewegte laue
Luft.**

But one gets hardened to ingratitude. It is just the
way in which the question is put—May he stay?†—
that makes all the difference, and Lemcke is not, to
my mind, the man to put it.‡ Now, this E major piece
might say or ask what it would; it is so beautiful, one
would put up with anything. What a distressingly
good memory you have! Please exert it to remember
the promised manuscript from the C minor quartet.
You will not grudge it to the misjudged

WIFE OF THE ABOVE.


22. *Elisabet von Herzogenberg to Brahms.*

[LEIPZIG] *December* 26, 1877.

MY DEAR FRIEND,—Your rooms will be ready on
the 31st, and you will be so good as to come straight
to us, and not go to the hotel first for twenty-four
hours. What good would it do? You would only
have a pitiful couple of hours for practising in any

---

* Op. 57, No. 8. Georg Friedrich Daumer (1800-1875), author of
the exquisite German version of Hafiz, and the collection of songs
*Polydora*, was at one time unjustly decried for the sensuality of his
poems. His *Frauenbilder und Huldigungen*, in particular, brought
him much adverse criticism. Brahms, who used several of Daumer's
poems, had taken the words for the song in question from this
collection.

† The particular point in the song to which Frau von Herzogenberg had taken objection (see Letter 14).

‡ Karl Lemcke (b. 1831), poet and writer on æsthetics and
literature, held posts at the Universities of Heidelberg, Munich,
Amsterdam, and Stuttgart.

case,* and you certainly would not make use of them without someone to look after you  Once here, I shall be that someone, seat you at the piano, and then depart lest you should feel shy. If we only knew whether you really were coming on the 31st! You will not write, and we are so looking forward to your coming, especially if you don't mean to be horrid to me any more. Mind you don't forget my Adagio. I think it is quite fair that you propose to give me that, for I love it so very, very dearly. And now be good, and come to

YOUR DEVOTED HERZOGENBERGS.

### 23. *Brahms to Elisabet von Herzogenberg.*

[VIENNA, *December* 29, 1877.]

Impossible to discuss hotel, puddings and piano at this distance. I hope, however, you will not make any fuss or burn up the dishes.

I am to arrive on Monday at 12.45, and go straight to the rehearsal. Your husband would perhaps like to ask if I cannot have a change and a wash in between, but it's no good.—Ever your unwashed

J. BR.

The orchestra here play my new symphony with crape bands on their sleeves because of its dirge-like effect.  It is to be printed with a black edge, too.†

* Brahms was to play his D minor concerto on New Year's Day at the Gewandhaus, where on a previous occasion (January 27, 1859) it had been very badly received (see Kalbeck's *Johannes Brahms*, i. 352).  He conducted his second symphony at the following concert on January 10.

† This is in keeping with his jest about the 'F minor' symphony (see footnote, Letter 17).  The symphony was, in fact, well received in Vienna, some parts with enthusiasm.

24. *Elisabet von Herzogenberg to Brahms.*

[LEIPZIG] *January* 16, 1878.

DEAR, GOOD, MUCH-MISSED FRIEND,—Here is the only press notice I have been able to lay hands on so far. But you shall have them all, no fear! including the ——, which declares with some finality that your latest lacks inspiration. You will have to get used to all these things, and cultivate a ' superior attitude,' as Frau Pastor says. But when you write (we do not expect to hear until you are in Vienna),* do tell us ' why and to what extent you are above criticism.' We will see to it that the little essay is widely circulated. As you know, I never tire of upholding your good name, and always assure people that you are the politest, most sociable and polished creature in the world; that you took lessons in deportment from Frappart† in Vienna; and that it is only the grossly ignorant who fail to appreciate the elegance of your bows.

I can't think of anything more to-day. Nothing has happened except that *notre maître, notre enfant* departed on the evening of the 11th, leaving two very sad Herzogenbergs behind. One grows accustomed to delightful visitors with such fatal ease. Thank you for the eleven beautiful days you vouchsafed us. It was so good of you to give us so much of your time. I was really touched every time you spared an evening from the Beethoven table.‡

* From Leipzig Brahms went on to conduct his new symphony at Bremen, January 22 ; at Amsterdam, February 4 ; and at The Hague, February 6.

† Louis Frappart, principal dancer at the Viennese Opera.

‡ In a certain restaurant.

You did forget your liqueur-flask, after all. My state of mind on discovering it was much like my small nephew's, years ago, when he discovered that Mathilde Hartenthal had gone away without the nut-crackers he had given her. 'What will she do, poor thing?' he exclaimed feelingly.

It is more important that you left a nightgown; I shall send it on to Utrecht, laundried a snowy white. Here in Leipzig we go on just the same. I am studying the D major duet* with W——, the tenor, and take immense pains to get it nice; but W—— can't manage the B♭-E-A-D at the end, in the Chamber scene, which makes singing together very difficult.

But goodbye, goodbye. I can't have you saying: Talkativeness, thy name is Woman! etc.

I hope you will thoroughly enjoy the C minor,† though I question whether you can enjoy your own music half as much as we do? Pity us a little that we cannot be there too, and think of us occasionally anyway.—Your most faithful admirers,

LISL AND HEINRICH H.

### 25. *Brahms to Herzogenberg.*

[HAMBURG, *January* 18, 1878.]

DEAR FRIEND,—This is, to all intents and purposes, a post-card, whatever it looks like; a short, hasty scribble, with no allusion to the delightful days I spent at your house.

Well, I think every day what a good thing it is I am not entertaining you here, for the weather is vile as only Hamburg weather can be—and is, on 360 days in

---

\* Op. 75, No. 3.
† The C minor symphony at Hamburg and Utrecht.

the year.    (It is difficult enough to hit the other five.)
Not an hour, the whole time, when you feel inclined
to go out, or even look out of the window.

But I shall enjoy doing the C minor.   The orchestra
are so enthusiastic that I am really looking forward to
this evening.   To-morrow I go to Bremen (Karl Reinthaler);* Wednesday to Utrecht (Professor T. W.
Engelmann).   I have promised to give them the D major
in Amsterdam on February 4.   The Utrecht address is
quite right for letters.

And now you have the post-card revealed.   Would
you kindly send the parts of the symphony to Amsterdam?    Address to J. A. Sillem, Heerengracht,
478.

I expect you know Simrock's agent, though, and
only need to hand the packet over to him.   You may
also—in sober truth—call the other parcel a duet, and
give it to him to send to Utrecht.

I wrote to Wüllner† the first day I arrived, but do
imagine our poor friend's torture‡ when she hears
that the programme consists of the D major symphony,
Phantasie with chorus, Beethoven, and—*Feuerzauber!*§
I will of course write and urge her to come, though the
whole thing is so comic that I shall find it difficult to
be serious about it.   I can't think that anything will
induce her.

---

* Karl Reinthaler (1822-1896), composer and conductor at Bremen,
an enthusiastic admirer of Brahms.   He was the first to give the
*German Requiem* in full at Bremen Cathedral on April 11, 1868.

† Franz Wüllner (1832-1902), conductor at Munich and Dresden.

‡ Frau Schumann, who was to play the Beethoven Phantasie at
the same concert with the Brahms symphony at Dresden.

§ Frau Schumann's antipathy to Wagner was so great that
Brahms feared she would not play with *Feuerzauber* on the programme.

And now, thanks for—everything, and also for your
very kind letter.  Rest assured, however many you
write and however kind they are, I shall consider it a
loan, and repay it with interest.  Greetings to all the
little brothers and sisters, and to Bernstorff.*—Ever
yours,

J. BR

### 26.  Elisabet von Herzogenberg to Brahms.

[LEIPZIG] *January* 19, 1878.

Your welcome letter has just arrived, giving the
best of flavours to our breakfast, and we thank you for
all the nice things you say or imply.  But you must
really make Wüllner change the programme.  'It
takes many hounds to kill a hare,' but one *Feuerzauber*
would be Frau Schumann's death.  It is inconceivable
that she should play.  There really is a want of delicacy in the arrangement.  How can any audience be
expected to appreciate really artistic work and a
piece like *Feuerzauber* on one and the same evening?
O Wüllner, Wüllner!  I always thought you a gentle-
man, but this programme betrays the impresario.
The glittering 'fire-piece' will excite everybody, of
course, and the palm of the evening goes to Wagner.
'O, how far, how far above,'† etc., are the gentle
D major, breathing beauty, dropping balsam into the
soul; and the *Phantasie*, written for the elect—and to
have on top of these, a *Feuerzauber!*  Why is he so
impatient, our good Wüllner?  Are we not to have
all Wagner's enchantments let loose in our theatres

---

* Eduard Bernstorff (1825-1901), the anti-Brahms critic of the
musical paper *Die Signale für die musikalische Welt.*

† First line of the duet *Klosterfräulein* (Brahms, Op. 61, No. 2).

soon enough, and is it not the right, the only place for them ?

> ' Fire is mighty when watched by its master ;
> When fire is master itself—there's disaster.'

Frau Schumann will do quite right in refusing to play, but surely you can influence Wüllner to a change of programme? Shake off your indifference for once— for the sake of your dear, dear symphony, too—and make him understand that it is inartistic to appeal to our higher and our lower natures in one evening. What would Wüllner say, I wonder, to a picture exhibition with a Raphael and a Makart hung side by side ? But here I am repeating myself over and over in my rage. Would that you had a spark of indignation and less humour in your composition, and had written to Franz as well as to Wüllner !

Heinrich is sending your parts to Amsterdam, and packing his excitement in with them. By the way, our dear Frau von B. has taken away my nurse* again, and sent her off to Frau Emma at Utrecht with the birth-day presents. But they are addressed to you, for you are to have the amusement of handing over the nurse to Frau Engelmann, accompanied by all the appropriate witticisms. Give my love to the dear thing, who can do so much : play so incomparably with those tiny white hands, laugh like a bird, bewitch everybody—and bring children into the world, which is surely the best and most wonderful thing a woman can do. Please assure her of my sincere, ungrudging admiration.

* * * * *

How glad I am that you are doing the D major in Amsterdam ! Dear old Julius† will hear it, and will be so pleased.

* Probably a doll from the fair at Leipzig. † Julius Röntgen.

Good-bye. Send another 'post-card' soon, and *work Wüllner.*

Do this—and accept my devotion; or decline—and cause me much pain.—Yours,

ELISABET HERZOGENBERG.

27. *Elisabet von Herzogenberg to Brahms.*

[LEIPZIG] *January* 31, 1878.

Here is your Eduard* again. I have taken the liberty of falling more and more hopelessly in love with him. You have no notion what a gorgeous thing it is. Please correct the chord in the accompaniment on p. 7, second bar, where it should surely be F, as before; not F flat.

I am not enclosing the bundle of press notices, in spite of your orders, for we conceived a sudden loathing for the stuff. It is a shame to waste a quarter of an hour over it. I am putting the precious pile in with the music to go to Vienna, where you have at least a waste-paper basket into which it may be some slight satisfaction to hurl it. I hope *Eduard* will arrive in time for Emma to see. Please point out all its beauties. Show her the amazing variety in the accompaniment to Eduard's replies—the 'vulture' verse where it is so subdued, and the right-hand part is simple and monotonous; the change when you come to the 'roan,' where the subdominant is introduced, and the D flat in the tenor (which was the ninth before) has the effect of something quite new; then the exquisite passage in the right hand up to G flat and down again —you can hardly believe it to be the same melody

* *Edward,* ballad for alto and tenor with pianoforte, Op. 75, No. 1.

as in the beginning; and again, when the mother's
questioning comes, it is the same and yet quite different,
with the gradual rise in pitch by three degrees up to
the splendid climax in B flat minor. . . . Oh for the
gift of words to describe this masterpiece! And how
natural, how necessary and exactly right it all is! . . .
Just as if Eduard's excitement and his mother's must
inevitably have had that note from the very beginning,
and could have no existence apart from the music.
And to think that the poem has lain there so long, a
dumb thing, until someone came along, took it to his
heart, and gave it to the world again in F minor—his
own!

But ours too; for enjoyment is possession. Or have
you any objection to raise?

Well, good-bye. Don't think me unkind, but—have
you written to Dresden? I challenge you with my
best tragedy voice!—Kindest regards,

ELISABET H.

### 28. *Brahms to Elisabet von Herzogenberg.*

AMSTERDAM, *February* 3, 1878.

MY DEAR FRIEND,—If I send these few hasty, whis-
pered words, it is with the full consciousness of their
inadequacy; and I wish I could do anything better to
thank you for your—in part—admirable, but wholly
kind and charming letter.

It was the *Feuerzauber* dissertation which was so
admirable.

I had written to Frau Schumann, hoping to persuade
or soothe her. But the spectre has no terrors for our
friend. She writes, quite casually, that of course she
need not listen!

I have not written to Wüllner—my pocket is stuffed full of unanswered letters—but I was tempted to send him your dissertation. However, we can let the matter rest now. Unless Frau Schumann changes her mind, I shall go to Dresden, and hope you will go too!

Holland is really charming; I lose my head over it each time. Number 2* takes so well with both musicians and public that it is not spoiling my stay. We do it at Amsterdam on the fourth *and* the eighth, at The Hague on the sixth; besides which Number 1 is being done at a sort of people's concert at Amsterdam on the fifth!

But you rather exaggerate my communicativeness in thinking I wanted *Edward* (I beg your pardon: *Eduard*)¹ back.† When I read the kind things you say about it, for instance, I feel distinctly annoyed, and say to myself: 'Why did you not take more trouble? It ought to have been much nicer.' I must be mistaken of course!—but it is a curious sensation.

I leave on the ninth. Have you nothing else to send? By the way, I have not yet thanked you for anything, not even for the amount of trouble you took over that 'more important' article. But the best of all these parcels is that they bring letters with them, and these deserve more thanks. For to-day, however, only kindest messages to you both and a few others.— Always yours most sincerely,

J. BRAHMS.

¹ Heaven help me if I should write *Eduard* for *Edward* or *sinfonie* for symphony!

* The D major symphony.

† That is to say, he was in no hurry to publish it. It appeared in the autumn of that year, however.

*Elisabet von Herzogenberg to Brahms.*

LEIPZIG, *February* 5, 1878.

MY DEAR FRIEND,—Please don't jeer at my poor little
epistles, or I shall be afraid to go on scribbling, and
that would be grievous. I do get a little something
in return—as witness your last from Amsterdam. We
were quite resigned to having Julius Röntgen's account
for our first, so imagine our shame and surprise at
receiving your letter. We had heard from the Engelmanns how you were being spoiled in Holland; how
men and women, leaders of the orchestra and chorus,
were all fighting for the honour of crowning you with
laurels. The Dutch are evidently by no means so
cold-blooded as is commonly reported. It would be
amusing to start an inquiry as to why the Middle-
German pulse beats so feebly, and consoling to discover
some ethnological solution. But I did not mean to
touch on this sore point; I set out to thank you, for
I do think it so very kind that you found time to speed
a message into our quiet Humboldtstrasse in the midst
of these exciting times, where you go from triumph to
triumph. But you knew how grateful we should be.

Heaven preserve *me* from writing *Edward* wrong
again to incur your mockery! I had better write
Brahmst for Brahms!*

\*          \*          \*          \*          \*

Indeed I do not consider you 'communicative.' If
you were, that evening when you fetched one duet
after the other out of your box would not be such

* The name Brahms is still written with the final *t* by some of
the composer's relations in Holstein, and his father was sometimes
addressed in that way in Hamburg. Brahms had himself a peculiar
aversion to it.

a *fabulous* event in our memory. But you really did ask to have the duets back.

Yesterday you unconsciously performed several deeds of mercy. You raised the sick, healed the broken-hearted, fed the hungry, and gave drink to the thirsty. We went to see poor Holstein,* and played him the C minor† in our best duet-fashion, which is, as you know, exemplary. He lay on the sofa, bright-eyed, nursing the score, and drank in the familiar sounds, this being the first time he has been permitted to refresh his memory. You can do many things, my dear Friend, and this power to gladden the heart of a poor sick fellow and charm back the colour into his cheeks, the brightness into his eyes, is not by any means the least of them.

Heaven's greeting to you; and please greet, in your turn, Julius Röntgen from us. Poor boy, how hard both he and his parents found the parting!

Good-bye, good-bye. Make many others happy, and be happy yourself.

Give us a thought now and again.—Your

HERZOGENBERGS.

Kirchner‡ has been playing us his arrangement of the E flat variations. It is quite excellent; only an enthusiast could have done it.

---

* Franz von Holstein (1826-1878), composer of opera, was then on his death-bed.

† The first symphony.

‡ Theodor Kirchner (1823 - 1903), composer and pianist, who arranged several of Brahms's works. He arranged the variations in question (Op. 23), originally written as a duet, for pianoforte solo.

## 30. *Elisabet von Herzogenberg to Brahms.*

[LEIPZIG, *February* 19, 1878.]

MY DEAR FRIEND,—It would be nice to hear from you again, if only a line. Do tell us at least whether you have decided to go to Dresden for the D major. We should love to go, and, as luck will have it, we could arrange it nicely. Julius Röntgen made us waver by saying you intended to stay in Vienna and work. But surely you will not fail Frau Schumann on the top of her other trials—poor *Feuerzauber* victim! Julius Röntgen has some amazing stories of the way people lost their heads in Amsterdam. Would that anyone here would do the same; but we shall never live to see that!

\* \* \* \* \*

Rubinstein\* will be sent off to-morrow in the bad company of ——† and the Leipzig press notices. This note is merely their passport. My poor Heinrich has a nasty cough, and is quite knocked up. The worst of it is, he must go through with the rehearsals until the concert‡ on Saturday. But 'Abide with us, for it is toward evening,'§ is such heavenly music that it ought to make Heinz well again.

Good-bye for to-day. Kindest messages to the Fabers.

And don't let your pen go rusty! By the way, if you are ever at a loss to know what to write, please do some solfeggi, with or without words; there are so

* Probably a new pianoforte work of Anton Rubinstein's.
† Pieces by a Leipzig composer.
‡ One of the Bach-Verein performances which Herzogenberg conducted, while his wife accompanied and sang.
§ An Easter cantata by Bach.

few of these elaborate vocal pieces.* I now sing
Bach's organ sonatas, which give me intense delight ;
but how nice to have anything as elaborate written
actually for the voice—at least eight quavers to every
word! That would be glorious. Julius Röntgen, on
the other hand, hankers after finger exercises from your
pen, with the hand in ' fixed ' position. It seems that in
Amsterdam the very tiniest damsels want to play
Brahms, you Pied Piper!

My poor dear joins me in all kind messages.

ELISABET HERZOGENBERG.


31. *Elisabet von Herzogenberg to Brahms.*

[LEIPZIG] *March* 1, 1878.

You know the delight with which we in Humboldtstrasse hail every shaving from your workshop ; how
much greater our delight over this thrilling witch-
duet,† which is one unbroken flow of inspiration.
That nice old weather-worn manuscript paper suits
, too.‡ The words seem to me quite blood-curdling,§
and I was furious with an enlightened professor to
whom I lent the poem the other day. It only struck
him as intensely ludicrous, poor fellow! *He* was not
brought up on Grimm's fairy-tales. I am glad to say
the duet sends cold shudders down my back every
time I play it, although I know quite well by now that

* Brahms did not respond to this desire, perhaps considering her
complaint unfounded. He was better acquainted with the old Italian
writers of solfeggi.

† *Walpurgisnacht*, duet for two sopranos, Op. 75, No. 4.

‡ Brahms had a predilection for old manuscript-paper, which he
bought as waste-paper.

§ By Willibald Alexis.

the mother has flown up the chimney. I am going to
practise it with the youngest Röntgen girl. Her
innocent childish soprano is the very thing for the
witch's daughter, and I intend to distinguish myself as
the witch. And how delightful it all is again! The
whole situation is so clear from the very opening, and
I like the way the bass doubles the voice in *''S ist heute
der erste Mai, liebes Kind,'* and, farther on, the introduction of the frightened daughter's motif into the accompaniment to the mother's replies (let anyone with a
desire to shudder and shake come and listen), which
makes that part as much a duet as if the daughter's
voice were heard. Of course the answer is the question inverted—that one would expect! And how it
works up to a climax at the end—there is a family
resemblance to *Edward* there! All this you know so
much better than I, that it is absurd for me to go
on chattering; I feel quite ashamed of having let my
pen run on thus far. But you are so meek!

Do you mind if I sing *Ob im Dorf wohl Hexen sind?*
with *ob* on the strong beat (D)—in deference to Herr
Kipke,* let us say! It fits in quite nicely. Old Herr
Engelmann† was here to-day, and read out with pride
your fine panegyric on the infant.‡ What a farce,
when the indignant grandmother told us that you
hardly deigned a glance at the new arrival!

Our Bach concert, which took place a week ago,
went off brilliantly, although our organist was taken
ill on the very day. Amanda Mair, the pretty
Swedish girl, came to our rescue, and acquitted her-

---

* Karl Kipke, a music critic, who accused Brahms of faulty
declamation.
† The father of T. W. Engelmann.
‡ Brahms's letter of congratulation to the family at Utrecht.

self admirably. Women are not always to be despised, you see.

Good-bye now, and thank you again. Whenever you feel moved to give me a *great* treat, send me some more. Shall I have to pass on the Witch to someone else presently? (Fear-motif in D flat!) And *are you going to Dresden?* And Frau Schumann, and the *Feuerzauber? 'S ist heute der erste März, liebes Kind*, and we are still in the dark.

Herr Simrock* was inquiring anxiously as to your movements to-day; but you are going to let poor 'Toggenburg' Astor† have the duets, are you not?

> 'Good deeds do make us like unto
> The blessed angel train;
> And at the last, if so we do,
> The heavenly realm we gain.'

*Auf Wiedersehen* in Dresden.—Your most grateful
E. H.

32. *Elisabet von Herzogenberg to Brahms.*

HUMBOLDTSTRASSE, [LEIPZIG] *March* 10, 1878.

MY DEAR FRIEND,—I must absolutely write and tell you with what delight we look back to those days in Dresden.‡ The beloved D major haunts us waking or sleeping, and we don't know how to thank you enough for a happiness such as seldom comes our way. But I am also impelled to write for another reason. I am going to quarrel with you! I hope we are on a footing which permits of an occasional word in earnest as well as in jest, and you must please take it

* Brahms's publisher.
† Head of the firm of Rieter-Biedermann.
‡ The D major symphony was performed by the Dresden Court Orchestra on Ash Wednesday, March 6, at the Royal Opera House.

meekly from one of the most assiduous of your crowd
of incense-burners.  On this cheerful assumption I
venture to proceed.

   You were so sweet and good at Schillerstrasse,
and I can't tell you how much I enjoyed hearing you
talk in the window-seat (after spilling all that liqueur),
and setting my good brother's little paradoxes to
rights with your convincing logic.  Then the name
of that worm —— cropped up, and, sure enough, you
treated us to the old story of his praising Heinrich's
quartet* and, in the same winter, dismissing yours
(the B♭)† with contempt—all this with a certain com-
placent irony, as who should say : Of course the man
has made a fool of himself for all time.  Now it was
no impartial third person to whom you were speaking,
but just the one man whom you know to be the first
to laugh at such an ignoramus ; no puffed-up creature
intending to make England the centre of his activities,
whose opinion of himself needs modification, but one
who does not think himself worthy to unlace your
boots, a seeker, a humble learner, who is a thousand
times more vexed by such over-rating than by the
most withering adverse criticism, simply because he
learns nothing from it.  I cannot understand how you—
you who ought to be quite indifferent to such incidents
—could twice be guilty of such ungenerosity (I can
only call it that), and it hurts me even more on your
account than on Heinrich's, sad as it is that you should
so misjudge him.  I was quite ready to pick this
quarrel with you last year, but Heckmann‡ happened

   * One of the three published later as Op. 42 by Rieter-Biedermann,
and dedicated to Brahms.
   † The Quartet in B flat, Op. 67.
   ‡ Robert Heckmann (1848-1891), violinist and leader of a string
quartet.

to be there, and I could not find a suitable occasion. Also I was a little afraid of being suppressed by some cool witticism, though I should not fear that now. But let me tell you straight out that it was neither kind nor just in you, and therefore so unlike you that I can only hope it was a drop of alien blood, which you may now get rid of by opening that particular small vein without the least danger of bleeding to death!

The worst that can befall me is to have you say again pityingly, 'Poor child! poor child!' while you think: If one had to consider one's words to that extent! But, don't you see, it is really rather a different matter when the person you misjudge and wound is just the one who would lay down his life for you, who loves you as a poodle or a child loves, or as a Catholic loves his patron saints, even though he may not have the gift of showing it. But it is I who suffer most in this case, and I assure you he knows nothing of this audacious lecture, but goes to sleep with a good conscience, assured that it will all come right with sunrise. His wife is a bit of a firebrand, however, and cannot resist flaring up in your face. You deserve it this time, too. But I feel sad as well as angry; for nothing distresses me more than to bear a grudge against one on whom I should like to heap kindness without reserve, respect without measure.

I know you don't *mean* to be cruel at such times. It is a kind of 'black dog' (no intimate acquaintance, thank Heaven!) on your back which prompts these speeches, so deadly in their power to wound others. If you knew how deadly, you would give them up; for you are kind enough at bottom, and would never consciously throw scorn on true affection.

So do pull up this weed in your garden, and, above all, don't hate me for this interminable letter. Women never can be brief, you know.

Until I have just one kind short line from you (you will then be absolved for a whole year!), I shall soothe my *Herzeleid* with your *Choral-Vorspiel,** which I am happy to say I know by heart, and can play to myself in the dusk.—My profound respects to Johannes Brahms, and—a hearty shake of his hand.

ELISABET HERZOGENBERG.†

### 33. *Elisabet von Herzogenberg to Brahms.*

[LEIPZIG] *March* 13, 1878.

\*      \*      \*      \*      \*

. . . Well, in future I will take no notice of your most cutting remarks. It would, however, be better if you reformed a little. . . . Very many thanks for the *Herzeleide-Vorspiel.* We are so fond of it that it gives us quite a peculiar pleasure to possess a morsel of it in the living form of your handwriting. I drummed it through to Kirchner when he was here with Astor, and roused him to great enthusiasm. I can't get over the way everything is *expression* in this piece. You can sit down and revel in it without ever having enough, and all the art in it seems designed solely to heighten the pathos. . . .

Herr H——, the high-priest of Dresden critics, is of course at a loss to understand why the first part of the

---

\* *Choral-Vorspiel* and *Fugue* for organ on '*O Traurigkeit, O Herzeleid*,' which was published as a supplement to the *Musikalisches Wochenblatt*.

† Brahms's answer to this letter is missing. It is obvious from the following letter that he did reply, and succeeded in appeasing Frau von Herzogenberg.

first movement of the D major is repeated. He also inquires why you don't confine yourself to chamber music, in which you have done some really good work, and incidentally try your hand at musical drama, that main stream into which all currents must inevitably flow ! You are aware, I suppose, that the theme of the Adagio is slightly contrapuntal ? They made a lot of charming discoveries about you in Dresden, but they admit the great success. I wish they would abuse you instead, the idiots ! Fancy classifying Riese's* singing as refined, sincere, and in the spirit of Beethoven ! After all, public performances are horrid. Who are all these people, I should like to know ?—Good-bye, you kind person. Do *really* reform ; it is well worth while.

ELISABET H.

If I only knew what you had scratched out at the bottom !

### 34. *Brahms to Herzogenberg.*

[VIENNA, *March*, 1878.]

MY DEAR FRIEND,—Here is the Nottebohm† document, which I prefer not to keep back until the spirit moves me to letter-writing.

. . . I will just add many thanks for the quartet.‡

A mere glance through it has done me good, and I am looking forward to a pleasant hour with it this evening.—In great haste, yours sincerely,

J. BR.

---

* A tenor from the Dresden Opera, who sang Beethoven's *An die ferne Geliebte* at the same concert at which the Brahms symphony was performed.

† See note, Letter 3.  ‡ The quartet mentioned in Letter 32,

### 35. Brahms to Herzogenberg.

[VIENNA, April 3, 1878.]

The undersigned begs to inform his esteemed patrons that letters addressed *poste restante*, Naples, will find him from April 14th to 20th.\* From the 20th onwards—Rome. He travels with Billroth,† and requests orders for writing letters, amputating legs, or anything in the world. Orders carefully executed by himself and companion. Further plans—none. Will probably be back in Vienna by the middle of May.—Etc. Kindest regards,

J. BR.

### 36. Elisabet von Herzogenberg to Brahms.

[LEIPZIG, April 9, 1878.]

MY DEAR FRIEND,—It was very nice of you to give us a sign before leaving for Italy. I hope you will thoroughly enjoy viewing the] Promised Land through your own eyes, not those of Adolf Staar‡ and his

---

\* Brahms started on his first Italian tour on April 8, accompanied by Billroth and Goldmark. Goldmark stayed behind in Rome to superintend the final rehearsals of his opera, *The Queen of Sheba*, while the other two went on to Naples, Billroth being anxious that Brahms should gain a thorough impression of Italy. 'I should be quite content to have seen Rome,' wrote poor Brahms to Ernst Frank. 'On the way back we shall see it, and anything else that turns up, with thorough desultoriness.' On the return journey he stayed for some time at Pörtschach, where he found his Viennese friends, Dr. Kupelwieser and Dr. Franz. 'The first day was so delightful that I had to stay one more,' he wrote to Arthur Faber. 'But the second day was so delightful that I have settled down altogether for the present.'

† Theodor Billroth (1829-1894), the famous Viennese surgeon, a passionate music-lover, and an intimate friend of Brahms since their first meeti з at Zurich in 1866.

‡ Adolf ꭒtaar, a well-known writer on Italy.

æsthetic followers. I must confess I have not read them. Swallowing impressions second-hand, when one would so much prefer tasting them oneself some day, is too maddening. I can't conceive of you as a tourist—that is, as a person setting out to enjoy things —your usual function being to provide enjoyment for others. Now you suddenly forsake the passive for the active rôle. How fresh it all will be, and how greedily you will absorb all the beauty at which you have had up to now the rare good sense not to nibble!

We heard yesterday from Frau Schumann of your Italian journey, and should have written to congratulate you to-day even without your card. We think, all the same, that you are having a prodigious spell of idleness. What in the world will become of us if you give your pen too long a rest?

Unlike you, we are not having a gay time—at least, I am not. We have just returned from my poor old uncle's funeral at Dresden. . . .

You will be wondering why I am writing on these scraps of paper. I left the key of my writing-table in Dresden, and am condemned to sit before locked drawers, cut off from pens, ink and paper, and all that makes life worth living. My only resource is a small copying-case which my brother has given me. It has the advantage of registering double everything one writes, but to appreciate that one must be writing lists for the laundress or be a celebrity. Happy you, who are out of reach of my double letters! Otherwise I might have sent you the first movement of the D major, written out from memory, which I want you to be so good as to look at some day. Frau Schumann goes so far as to call it quite a possible pianoforte arrangement, but I can't altogether trust the dear woman, who is too good for this world. Well, as it happens, you escape this infliction, a further cause for congratulation. So dear Frau Schumann has decided on Frankfurt.* I only pray she may be anything like as happy there as she deserves. . . . And Arthur ?† Is he there ? You do not mention him any more than the chamberlain of the Queen of Sheba.‡

And now accept all our good wishes. We really are *very* glad that you are having such a good time. I hope the sunny Italian landscape will smile on you as effectually as did the Carinthian, so that you bring home as rich a store of melodies as last year. The critics will know so well how to account for them all !

Good-bye. Be happy, and send an occasional postcard our way.—Yours sincerely,

ELISABET HERZOGENBERG.

### 37. *Herzogenberg to Brahms.*

LEIPZIG, *May* 13, 1878.

MY VERY DEAR FRIEND,—Our poor Holstein§ is sinking fast, and can only last three or four weeks at most. He is in constant agony. The doctors diagnosed it first as hardening of the stomach, then as cancer ; no cure is possible. His mind is quite clear, however, and it is touching to see his thoughtfulness for all around him. He is all consolation and courage. I never saw a more affecting end. If you could see how the poor fellow's eyes light up at every sign of

---

\* Frau Schumann left Berlin to settle at Frankfurt in 1878, where she was Professor at Dr. Hoch's Conservatorium until a few years before her death in 1896.

† Arthur Faber.          ‡ Goldmark.          § *Cf.* Letter 29.

affection from far or near, you would send him some last message yourself. He has always been so devoted to you. Won't you write him a friendly line or two ? He is worthy of being mourned by the best of us.

We see him nearly every day, and have watched the dreadfully rapid development of his disease, the germ of which he must have carried for years. His appearance changed quite suddenly. Up to yesterday he was inclined to talk, easily amused and interested in everything. His unhappy wife* broke down entirely after the consultation three weeks ago, when his danger was first recognised, and even lost her self-possession before him, after bearing up so long in a way that astonished us. Now she is as if transfigured by his touching attitude. The whole house is like some beautiful church where it is good to rest awhile. Pain seems less in evidence, and there are gleams of inspiration which pierce one to the very soul.

We know what an interest you took in him, and will write again soon. In a few days we leave Leipzig, unwillingly enough, and only because we are needed elsewhere; but we shall have news every day.

My dear wife joins in kindest regards.—Ever yours sincerely,

HERZOGENBERG.

### 38. *Brahms to Herzogenberg.*

[PÖRTSCHACH, *May* 17, 1878.]

MY GOOD FRIEND,—Your sad account of poor Holstein was so unexpected that I was as much shocked as

---

* Hedwig von Holstein, *née* Salomon (1819-1897), whose fine character Helene von Vesque has immortalized in her novel *Eine Glückliche.*

pained. I find it hopeless to write to him, or even to
her. Were I in similar case, I should not expect it
from my best friend. Yet I know that women demand
such consolation ; and I therefore ask you to act as
my interpreter for the moment. She is bound to feel
your departure very keenly, poor thing! Personal
sympathy is the greatest comfort after all, and a real
help ; but writing to inquire for news, when you know
it can only be bad and have no hope of improvement,
is tragic. . . . I seem to remember your telling me
you were going to stay with Dr. Oberhofer in Vienna ?
I met him in Rome and was reminded of it.

I should be able to see you in Vienna, unless I had
to go to Düsseldorf after all.*

Give my love to the poor invalid. What will his
unfortunate wife do when it is all over ? Who will
help her over the first terrible days ? Is Frau Dr.
Seeburg† there ? Kindest regards.—Yours,

J. BRAHMS.

* Brahms was to have gone to Düsseldorf at Whitsuntide to
conduct his second symphony at the Fifty-fifth Lower Rhine Festival,
but gave it up, nominally on a question of clothes, actually because
he could not tear himself from his work, being in a productive mood.
On May 20 he writes to Arthur Faber : ‘ They want me to go to
Germany for the Festival, which means a dress-coat and *décolleté !*
I must think it over.’ In July he writes to Frau Bertha Faber :
‘ First your husband fails to send me an old coat ; then, instead of a
nice waistcoat, he sends one that could only have been left hanging
in the cupboard by an oversight. I should have been obliged to buy
a new one at Düsseldorf, and have *on that account* declined to go—the
only thing to do in my circumstances.’ Obviously, these excuses are
not meant to be taken seriously. Joachim conducted in his place.
The symphony was enthusiastically received, and the third movement
had to be repeated.

† Frau von Holstein’s sister.

## 39. *Elisabet von Herzogenberg to Brahms.*

[ARNOLDSTEIN IM GAILTALE]

HAUS SAMEK, *August* 10, 1878.

MY DEAR FRIEND,—The worthy bearer of these lines is also taking a hat to Pörtschach, which you will be so kind as to appropriate for your own use. It is own brother to that hat of Heinrich's, to which you took rather a fancy, and will press less heavily on your forehead than your dark felt. My mother had another in her trunk, and is quite delighted to present it to you. Knowing your taste, I should like to have sewn a ribbon round it, but it would spoil the style, and therefore cannot be done ! . . .

We still feast on those happy hours when we were rain-bound at your house. I am so glad you allowed me to bring the motet* to Arnoldstein, for my stupid eyes are slow at taking in anything of that sort right down to the smallest details. First I have only a delicious vague impression, such as one receives on entering the nave of a cathedral, at sunset, say; all is light and colour with just a hint of the glorious art which must have conceived the whole effect. But to see it all with understanding eyes takes leisure and daylight. Once I am imbued with the spirit of it, I can single out each separate feature, each beautiful line, for the object of my devotions, and I know of nothing more enjoyable.

Our little English friend† has just written me that

---

* *Warum ist das Licht gegeben den Mühseligen?* from two motets for mixed chorus, unaccompanied, Op. 74, No. 1, published by Simrock, 1879.

† Ethel Smyth, pianist and composer, at that time studying with Herzogenberg. Her compositions include three operas : *Fantasio*, produced at Weimar in 1898; *Der Wald*, on the Continent and at

she has drilled three entirely unmusical singers so thoroughly in the alto, tenor and bass parts of the *Liebeslieder*,* that they are now able to sing them with her quite satisfactorily.  She is going to 'inoculate' the folks in her neighbourhood, as she puts it, with Brahms, by means of a small concert to include the *Liebeslieder, Mainacht, Von Ewiger Liebe,*† and the Andante from the pianoforte concerto!  She is convinced she has the most suitable possible programme.

And now for a favour.  My mother is so afraid that, if anything happened to our little one‡ here, we should not be able to get a doctor.  Are there none in Pörtschach?  Do tell us the name of one.

Farewell, and let me thank you again for all your good deeds.—Yours most sincerely,

ELISABET HERZOGENBERG.

Be sure you come to Arnoldstein!

### 40. *Brahms to Elisabet von Herzogenberg.*

[PÖRTSCHACH, *August* 12, 1878.]

MY DEAR FRIEND,—There is only a young consumptive doctor here who is undergoing treatment himself, and would certainly not be able to go and see your sister.

Let me save up all the rest for my visit to Arnoldstein: my thanks for your visit to me here, a long

---

Covent Garden; *Strandrecht* (The Wreckers), at Leipzig and Prague, 1907—concert performance under Nikisch in London, 1908 ; besides various chamber-music works.

* Waltzes for pianoforte duet, with vocal quartet *ad lib.*, Op. 52.

† Two songs from Op. 43.

‡ Frau Elisabet's sister.

argument about the hat (which is really much more suitable for H.), and so on.

Your exchange of the motets* was a surprise— unpleasant in so far as your possession of mine goes; pleasant, on the other hand, because it gives me an opportunity of looking through the other more carefully. It both demands and repays study.

Please tell me the name of your house, and whether there is a hotel in the place, or which out of many I should choose.

In haste—as you see; in sincerity—as you know.— Yours,

JOHANNES BRAHMS.

### 41. *Elisabet von Herzogenberg to Brahms.*

[ARNOLDSTEIN] *August* 15, 1878.

MY DEAR KIND FRIEND,—This is what happened about the motets. When you gave us your gracious permission to bring the dear songs here with us, I said, half to myself, 'And the motet?' As you made no reply, I took it for silent consent, and slipped it in with the rest. But it has been well taken care of, and is returned to you herewith in good condition after being thoroughly petted by us. Don't, don't be angry. I am wholly responsible for the theft, but I really thought you winked at it consciously. 'Why, why'† should you grudge me this incomparable pleasure? I cannot get over my delight in the first movement. I will say nothing of the first page‡ or the second right down to the '*Why?*' but,

---

* She had sent Brahms one of her husband's motets in place of his own. Four of Herzogenberg's motets were published by Rieter-Biedermann as Op. 103.

† The motet opens with the words *Warum? Warum?*

‡ P. 7 of the score, bars 8 and 12.

oh, the *glorious* setting of the words 'and cometh not'!
The syncopation in the alto, especially the suspended
E, is too adorable.   Then the crossing of the soprano
and alto—but I will spare you an exclamation mark
after every single bar.

We are staying with the innkeeper Grum, but he
has only one other room beside our two.   However,
there are not many visitors, and this one is almost
certain to be empty.   There is another inn—but it
would be best to send us a line before you come, so
that Heinrich can arrange something.   We find Arnoldstein very pleasant and 'very cheerfully situate,' as
your trashy old book says.*   As drawbacks we have
so far only discovered swarms of flies and ducks,
and a detachment of cavalry stationed here, which
seems out of place in so peaceful a landscape.   The
advantages are many : luxuriant vegetation, extraordinarily fine beeches, sweeping firs, air clearer than
at Velden, and the fascinating Gailtal hills in the
distance, with Dobratsch sharply outlined in the fore-
ground.   It is a very good place to vegetate in.   But
there is no fish, alas for you !   Delight the hearts of
your faithful Herzogenbergs with a message before
long.

### 42. *Brahms to Herzogenberg.*

[PÖRTSCHACH, *September* 7, 1878.]

DEAR FRIEND,—I expect to arrive at Arnoldstein
to-morrow, Sunday, at 11.21.   If my note arrives before
me, and should you be inclined for an expedition to
Tarvis, Weissenfels, or anywhere, be at the station
and take a ticket for me with yours.   Otherwise I

* Valvasor, *Chronicle of Carinthia.*

shall stay at Arnoldstein, for you cannot have left for good yet.—Yours,

J. Br.

(This is for H. and El. of course.)

### 43. *Elisabet von Herzogenberg to Brahms.*

ARNOLDSTEIN, *September* 12, 1878.

MY DEAR, GOOD FRIEND,—In case you have not had a letter, I write to say that I have just heard from Eugenie.* Her mother is not at Kiel, of which there seems to be no further question, but at Rüdesheim for a few days, hoping to cure her arm† in the more bracing air there. She goes to Frankfurt at the end of the week, where Marie,‡ meanwhile, has been moving in. Felix's§ condition seems to be very critical. One lung is past saving, Eugenie says, while there is 'just a possibility' of curing the other. They propose now to take him to the Home at Falkenstein close to Frankfurt. Eugenie is to go over with him the end of this week to inspect the place, and will leave him there if he takes to it.

I must thank you again for your very kind visit to us. You know we can't be wildly demonstrative, but it is to be hoped you can see without that how happy

* Eugenie Schumann, fourth and youngest daughter of Robert and Clara Schumann.

† Frau Schumann suffered from nervous rheumatic pains in her arm for several years, and was sometimes prevented from playing. Dr. Esmarch, of Kiel, treated her for this.

‡ The eldest daughter.

§ The youngest and most promising son, born when Schumann was in the asylum at Endenich. He provided the words for Brahms's songs, Op. 63, Nos. 5 and 6, and Op. 26, No. 5. He died of consumption in 1879.

it makes us to have you. Walking out with you, Herr Doctor, is not only an honour and a pleasure, but a heartfelt delight for us. Since your train steamed away, we have gone back to our quiet life. Hildebrand* has not put in an appearance yet, so our one distraction in the midst of our communion with nature and our work in this shabby little room is the very precious memory of the days you spent with us. You were so very good to my Heinz. He is sitting bent over his quartet paper now, and thinking, as he makes tails to his notes for the new theme and variations, that a word from John the Baptist's lips is worth more than a hundred essays on 'Style in Composition,'† even were they written by the Almighty himself!

I am suffering from an intermittent fever in three minor keys—B, F♯ and A‡—a fever for which my old cookery-book has no remedy.

Oh yes, there are all sorts of ghosts haunting our rooms, and we are superstitiously concerned not to scare them away. . . . But good-bye for to-day. Send us your address to Hosterwitz, near Dresden, or to Leipzig, will you? And keep a corner in your affections for us. It makes us happier than almost anything to think you do.—Always your sincerely,

ELISABET H.

* Adolf Hildebrand (b. 1847), the sculptor, who executed the Brahms monument at Meiningen, the relief figures on the tombs of the two Herzogenbergs, and the bust photographed in this book.

† Richard Pohl (1826-1896), the voluble Wagner apostle, was bringing out a series, Æsthetic Letters to a Young Musician, in the Musikalisches Wochenblatt, with the title In which Style ought we to Compose?

‡ The keys of three pianoforte pieces, published in 1879 as Op. 76 (Nos. 1 and 2 of book i., and No. 7 of book ii.), which Brahms had played to them when at Arnoldstein.

*44. Brahms to Elisabet von Herzogenberg.*

[PÖRTSCHACH, *September* 14, 1878.]

*Frau Puck,*
*Tradesman's wife,*
*Klagenfurt*
*Burggasse*
*(at Emperger's, the Baker's.)*

This is the address as I have it from our postmistress.\*
Kindest regards, also thanks for your letter and for my
pleasant visit (I am thanking the young lady in the
same breath).

'Miss Post-Office' has just volunteered, to my
horror, that the tea is not considered good now.
Well, you can but try Frau Puck, and don't blame
me if it's bad.

J. BR.

*45. Herzogenberg to Brahms.*

LEIPZIG, *October* 4, 1878.

DEAREST FRIEND,—How easy it would be for me
to appropriate your motet† now, for the only proof
of your authorship is the royal leonine touch. And
where is the court of arbitration that could settle the
matter? Being an honest fellow, however, I propose
that you should often give me your things to copy out.
You could then feel secure, and sleep in peace without
rummaging among your piles of manuscript paper.

We are all on heaps here, and smothered in dust.
I am porter while my wife cooks. But we begin to
see daylight, and shall soon settle down to our comfortable old routine.

---

\* Frau Werzer, manageress of the hotel and post-office at Pörtschach, with whom Brahms was on excellent terms. 'Miss Post-
Office' was the name he gave her daughter.

† See Letters 39-41.

5

While you were at Leipzig* we spent one day in Vienna, and now it is just the other way round. It is almost like the fairy-tale in which everyone wants to change places. But the memory of our meeting in Carinthia and the prospect of seeing you in January and hearing your violin† keeps us up. A man here, who is too clever by half, told me you had written a third symphony; it was in G minor. Did *you* know? Kindest regards from us both.—Yours most sincerely,

HERZOGENBERG.

*(P.S. from Elisabet von Herzogenberg.)*

Guess who has perpetrated a symphony? You can't?—Richard Wagner!‡ So we shall have it at last, the long-looked-for model which is to 'deliver' us from the repetition of the first part, and unfold to us in a series of arabesques the mystic form without form. We are looking forward to the unholy din and the chatter of the so-called critics, although it is rather a case for tears. All the philistines are wild with delight over *Siegfried* and *Götterdämmerung*, and of all the attractions the Fair offers this is the most popular. They hardly know whether to admire Wilt§ or Fafner more.

We found much to depress us on our return. Poor

---

* Brahms had been invited to the Hamburg Musical Festival (September 25-28), on the occasion of the Golden Jubilee of the Philharmonic Society. He conducted his second symphony on the third evening, and called at Leipzig on his way back.

† The Violin concerto, Op. 77, and the Violin sonata, Op. 78, were commenced in the summer of 1878, and finished late in the autumn.

‡ A symphony composed in 1832, and performed in the following year at Prague and Leipzig, which was revived in 1878 for a short time.

§ Marie Wilt (1833-1891), prima donna at the Court Theatre, Vienna, who ook the part of Brünnhilde at Leipzig.

Engelmann is seriously ill, and his illness has a ghastly
name. But he seems to be improving, and his wife is in
better spirits. The dear old man lies on the sofa, without a suspicion of the real nature of his illness, fretting
over his helplessness and finding his chief amusement
in a charming little Venus and Cupid which he has
had painted.

Our little English friend* is staying with little Emma
at Utrecht, where she is blissfully happy and can hear
the Horn trio and the C minor quartet ;† but we shall
be able to deliver your messages to Limburger‡ very
soon. When, oh when, are you coming to Humboldtstrasse ? We want you badly. We often feel ourselves such fish out of water among the philistines
here.—Kindest regards from

THE WIFE.

### 46. *Elisabet von Herzogenberg to Brahms.*

[LEIPZIG] *October* 18, 1878.

MY DEAR FRIEND,—Are you really conducting at
Breslau on the 24th ? I can hardly believe the report,
and am convinced you will turn up here next Thursday
through some trap-door or other. Your presence
would be chief of all the pleasures that have been
devised for Frau Schumann§ and you surely would

---

* Miss Ethel Smyth.        † Brahms, Op. 40 and Op. 60.
‡ Director of the Gewandhaus committee.
§ The jubilee to celebrate the fiftieth anniversary of Frau Schumann's first public appearance (at a concert given in the Gewandhaus
by Caroline Verlthaler, a pianist from Graz) on October 20, 1878. A
concert in her honour had been arranged at the Gewandhaus on the
14th, consisting of Schumann's works, at which a golden laurel-wreath
was to be presented to her. Brahms was not able to be present, as
he was conducting at Breslau on the 22nd (his second symphony),
and playing in his A major quartet on the 24th.

not hurt the dear woman by staying away on this
occasion.　Please send me a line, so that we can enjoy
the prospect of seeing you, and get the coffee roasted.
Unfortunately, we cannot put you up this time; that
pleasure is reserved for January.　One of my spare
rooms has measles, and is at present peeling, while
Filu* is in posession of the other.—Yours in haste, but
very sincerely,

ELISABET HERZOGENBERG.

### 47. *Elisabet von Herzogenberg to Brahms.*

[LEIPZIG] *November 17, 1878.*

Ach! . . . ha - ben Sie Er - bar - men
ein . . mal doch . . mit mir Ar - men
und . . . . . schik - ken Sie - - mir end - lich

*stringendo*

* Marie Fillunger.

die . . er - sehn - ten In - ter - mez - zi !*

E. H.

### 48. *Brahms to Elisabet von Herzogenberg.*

VIENNA, *November*, 1878.

This is all I can send for the moment. The *Romanze* you sing so charmingly† is not there, I am sorry to say, for my copyist has no time. So if you wish to keep either of these, you will have to bespeak a pen in Leipzig and send me back my copy in due course

What a pity I have no long letter to answer! I should so enjoy it.—Yours most sincerely,

J. BRAHMS.

### 49. *Elisabet von Herzogenberg to Brahms.*

[LEIPZIG] *December* 13, 1878.

MY DEAR FRIEND,—I wonder if you set me down as the wretch I am conscious of being for keeping the

---

* 'Oh, have pity on my misery, and send the longed-for Intermezzi!' Brahms had played some of his new Capriccios and Intermezzi (Op. 76) to the Herzogenbergs on his visit to Arnoldstein in September, and the above is a reminiscence of the Intermezzo in A minor, second part. It may be taken as a proof of Frau von Herzogenberg's remarkably quick ear and retentive memory.

† Refers to the song in the previous letter. Brahms sent this particular piece later, with the inscription *Romanze für 2 zarte Frauenstimmen und 2 zarten Frauenzimmern gewidmet.*

longed-for pianoforte pieces without a word of thanks. I assure you, I am as ashamed as any poodle, and as terrified as — what shall I say ? — lest you should refrain from sending me another line to the end of your days. Of course I could reel out yards of excuses to justify myself, but I prefer not, for there could be no *adequate* excuse for such neglect. You see, I am at least conscious of my guilt, and I implore your forgiveness, indulgence, pardon, and all the rest.

And, do you know, the dear pieces are still with the copyist—our Leipzig copyists are such slowcoaches—but I will really send them off to-morrow. The one in B minor,* which I kept back because it gave me such untold pleasure to practise it, is now being copied out for me by our little English friend.† Please note, however, that I have only *one* very nice little English girl.

And now, do tell me, is the violin concerto really not finished ? We heard a wail to that effect from Utrecht, but refuse to believe it. It looks so unlike you to promise more than you can carry out ; and you *did* promise us the concerto at Arnoldstein—dear old sleepy Arnoldstein, where we had so much time for counterpoint ! Here I am cook and charwoman by turns, have a terrific weight of housekeeping on my shoulders, and only sit down to the piano in an occasional breathing-space. For many reasons do I look forward to January, therefore ; I shall have a person who can cook, and hope to become a normal being again myself. You will come in any case, concerto or no concerto ? But I must stop. She gives me no peace, the B minor copyist. If you want to see something beautiful, look at the last eight bars. We play

* Capriccio, Op. 76, No. 2.      † Miss Ethel Smyth.

them over and over, and can never have enough of them.

I am going to play them to the Utrecht Engelmanns shortly. What a triumph to forestall Emma for once!

My favourite, now and for ever, is the F sharp minor.* I flatter myself that I really appreciate it, and should play it exquisitely if I were any sort of a pianist.

But good-bye. I know I shall not get the *Romanze* now, for my sins, any more than the C sharp minor.†

Heinrich sends messages (he is working very hard), and Ethel Smyth too. She does the prettiest gavottes and sarabandes. Write and tell us when you are coming, so that we can look forward to it.—Your devoted

HERZOGENBERGE.

### 50. *Brahms to Elisabet von Herzogenberg.*

[VIENNA, *December* 15, 1878.]

MY DEAR FRIEND,—I really only wanted to know whether you had received the music, as it would have been awkward if you had not. You will certainly have forgotten to pepper the *pâté de foie gras* over your many excuses. If Utrecht Engelmann is over, how would it be to offer him the B minor for his Emma? You either can't or won't believe that I am too modest to ingratiate myself by these delicate attentions.

But I have a particular request, and should be glad to hear, by post-card, whether you will undertake to fulfil it in its entirety. Every day I try to get a letter written to Consul Limburger, but I should prefer it so much if you or Herzogenberg would go and see

* Op. 76, No. 1.          † Op. 76, No. 5.

him, and make him understand that I would rather *not* come at New Year. Joachim is coming here, and I should have a chance of trying the concerto through with him, and deciding for or against a public performance. If we do that, and are fairly satisfied with it, you can still hear it afterwards. The Consul also invited me to conduct the C minor,* etc., and I am not inclined to do that either. What is your conductor there for, after all! There is some sense in conducting one's own works before they are printed, but only then.

Joachim is very busy, and we, like you, suffer from overworked copyists. He will get his part, properly written out, to-morrow for the first time, but he has a big concert on hand for the 29th, and so on. Tell the Consul all this, and *pile it on.* In any case, it is my earnest request that you will see Limburger without delay, so that I can feel as if I had, in a way, given him his answer at last.

\* \* \* \* \*

You might, after all, take a sheet of paper instead of a post-card, and tell me whether the University vacations have begun in Holland, or whether there is anything worse at the back of Utrecht Engelmann's visit to you.

Grieg† was in Leipzig, too. How did he get on? I read a bad account of him in Rieter's paper‡ just now—which looks hopeful!

* The first symphony, which was to be performed again at the Gewandhaus on New Year's Day.
† Edvard Grieg (1843-1907), Norwegian composer.
‡ The *Allgemeine Musikalische Zeitung*, published by the firm Rieter-iedermann, was founded in 1866, and withdrawn in 1882 ; edited from 1869 onwards by Friedrich Chrysander.

But I am letting my pen run away with me to-day. Many apologies; it is too late to alter anything now.— Yours in haste and sincerely,

J. Br.

### 51. *Elisabet von Herzogenberg to Brahms.*

[LEIPZIG] *December* 15, 1878.*

DEAR FRIEND,—Most regretfully do I return your beautiful music. If you will signify my restoration to favour by sending me the C sharp minor and the *Romanze* after all, I shall be your devoted slave, and I promise to return them within twenty-four hours. . . .

I have just had bad news from the Engelmanns. They were quite cheerful a few days ago; the Professor thought it quite possible his father might recover for a time. But there has been a sudden change for the worse, and he seemed to fear yesterday that the poor old man might not last the night. The womenfolk know nothing of this, and the invalid is still buoyed up by various consoling delusions. I am just going there, and will let you know of any change.

Good-bye, and keep us in your thoughts. I suppose my letter and photograph, sent shortly after our return, never reached you, as you reproach me (who am a confirmed babbler) for not writing. Thank you again for the piano pieces, which are my greatest joy. Remember us to the Fabers, who have not forgotten us, I hope.

ELISABET HERZOGENBERG.

Your photographs went like anything at the bazaar for a pound apiece. The girl who sold them asked quite innocently whether the inscription were not a piece of satire!—In haste,

THE SAME.

* The note-paper bears the motto: 'Postponed is not abandoned.'

52. *Brahms to Elisabet von Herzogenberg.*

[VIENNA, *December* 21, 1878.]

You really take everything far too seriously. If Herzogenberg has not committed himself irrevocably with the Consul, I may say that Joachim is quite keen on playing the concerto, so it may come off after all. I am against having the symphony\* on the same evening, because the orchestra will be tired as it is, and I don't know how difficult the concerto† will prove. I expect to be in Berlin by the 28th to rehearse it on the piano with Joachim—though I can stay here if you don't approve! The concerto is in D major, which should be taken into consideration in arranging the programme. *Indeed* I received your photograph, ungrateful wretch that I am!

J. BR.

\* *Cf.* Letter 50, note.

† The concerto for violin, for which Joachim had provided fingering and bowing marks. Brahms had written in the autumn saying that his first impulse had been to 'offer his fingers' for Joachim's concert in Vienna, and keep back the violin concerto; but his disinclination for concert-playing was too deep-rooted, and he had grown used to playing with himself as sole audience. Yet he hated to think of Joachim's playing in Austria, while he 'stood there doing nothing,' and the only alternative was to conduct the Violin concerto. Would it be true hospitality to send him the score with a proper copy of the solo part? The middle movements had been discarded ('they were the best, of course'), but he was putting in a 'feeble adagio.' 'We might as well give them the pleasure at Leipzig,' he adds; 'we could hold a consultation here at the piano.' The result of the consultation was exceedingly favourable, and the new work was able to be included in the concert programme for New Year's Day at Leipzig. Brahms went to Berlin on December 18, and from there to Leipzig with Joachim.

### 53. *Herzogenberg to Brahms.*

[LEIPZIG] *December 23, 1878.*

MY VERY DEAR FRIEND,—I was just about to sit down and write you the result of my talk with Limburger, when to our surprise and delight your post-card arrived. I wrote off to Limburger without a moment's delay, but have had no reply up to now. He was going to meet the committee to decide upon the programme the following afternoon. Fortunately, he had telegraphed to Joachim earlier, and secured him for the first of January, so we have come out of this exciting time fairly well on the whole.

I almost think you have put off the journey to Berlin too late. The rehearsals, the final rehearsal at least, will in consequence fall immediately before the concert. Would it not be better to go straight there immediately after Christmas, say on the 27th, and to come on here for the first rehearsal ? I will inquire and let you know the exact day for which it is fixed. You will only want five first violin parts, five second, three violas and eight basses (or, if these are copied separately, five 'celli and three double-basses). Let me at this point formally invite your trunk to stay with us, for you will probably like to be in its immediate neighbourhood—possibly in our spare room.

I am not going to bother about the keys; the concerto may be in G sharp minor, for all I know! But you will surely write to Limburger yourself? I didn't exactly promise that you would, but I let it be taken for granted.—With kindest regards from us both, yours sincerely,

HERZOGENBERG.

*(Postscript by Elisabet von Herzogenberg.)*

December 22.

Poor old Herr Engelmann died this morning at three o'clock very peacefully. It was like falling asleep. And he was just one of those who cling to life!

I am going there this afternoon, and am dreading seeing those poor women in their trouble. What a blessing Utrecht Engelmann is there!—Kindest regards, dear friend, from yours sincerely,

E. HERZOGENBERG.

### 54. *Brahms to Heinrich von Herzogenberg.*

[BERLIN, *December 29, 1878.*]

DEAR FRIEND,—I expect to send off my trunk to-morrow, Monday, at two o'clock. Arrival in Leipzig timed approximately for 5.30, 5.15, 5.7½, or 5.20. I shall also see that it is sent to the right street, so mind you are near at hand!—Kindest regards,      J. BR.

### 55. *Brahms to Elisabet von Herzogenberg.*

[VIENNA, *January,* 1879.]

MY VERY DEAR FRIEND,—I don't know what sort of an opinion you have of my tidiness, but don't form one on the strength of the question which I have to ask.

Did your brother ever entrust the manuscript of Chopin's mazurka, Op. 41, No. 2, in E minor, to me?* A pile of the various editions and manuscripts of this mazurka has been accumulating here for ages, and

---

* The manuscript was the property of Messrs. Härtel (*cf.* Letter 16).

yesterday I really tackled it seriously. There is the printer's copy of Op. 41 from Härtel, but besides that the original manuscript of No. 2. I am not inclined to think it belongs to Härtel, for I have a habit of marking such things, usually with a faint pencil-mark. In the bound volume of mazurkas, for instance, there is your brother's name. . . . I might multiply excuses and pleas for justification, but why trouble about a little untidiness when I know to my sorrow how severely you judge me on other scores ?

My concert tour was a real down-hill affair after Leipzig ;* no more pleasure in it. Perhaps that is a slight exaggeration, though, for friends and hospitality are not everything on a concert tour. In some trifling ways it was even more successful; the audiences were kinder and more alive. Joachim played my piece more beautifully with every rehearsal, too, and the cadenza went so magnificently at our concert here that the people clapped right on into my coda. But what is all that compared to the privilege of going home to Humboldtstrasse and being pulled to pieces by three womenkind—since you object to the word 'females'?

I wish you would not go to Norway. Come to Carinthia instead, or go to Baden, where I could meet you. We might profit mutually by each other's company—it need not be all on my side !—In haste, but with kindest remembrances to the whole party, yours very sincerely,

J. Br.

* Joachim played the Violin concerto on January 14 in Vienna. He then went to England without Brahms, and played it twice by request at the Crystal Palace. Meeting Brahms again, they played it together at Bremen, Hamburg, and Berlin.

*56. Elisabet von Herzogenberg to Brahms.*

LEIPZIG, *April* 13, 1879.

MY DEAR FRIEND,—My conscience reproaches me vaguely with treating you badly, and, indeed, my post-card* was but a shabby return for your somewhat enigmatical letter. I might fill four pages with excellent excuses, but am restrained by my consideration for you, so don't be too hard on me.

The Volklands† spread a rumour that you might be persuaded to call at Leipzig on your way back, and this note is an attempt at the said persuasion. People who know geography insist that it is the natural route to Vienna. I who know no geography can only say how delighted we should be to see you again. It seems to me, too, that we have some right to expect you, after your cavalier treatment of us in January. So please be nice, and do your utmost to arrange a peep at us. . . .

I wonder if we shall meet in Carinthia? We are going to Austria, after all, and not to Norway, but shall hardly get away before the middle of August, when we may go to the Carinthian Alps, in the shadow of which I suppose you intend to stay.

My husband would write and add his petitions to mine if he had not just hurt his right hand. As it is, he can only send greetings, and say that he endorses everything I have written. *Auf Wiedersehen* in Humboldt-strasse then, in my blue room?—Yours very sincerely,

ELISABET HERZOGENBERG.

* The post-card is missing.    † *Cf.* Letter 1, note.

### 57. *Brahms to Elisabet von Herzogenberg.*

[BERLIN, *April* 15, 1879.]

MY DEAR FRIEND,—The news contained in your letter enables me to pass through Leipzig with the greatest placidity. It is excellent hearing that you have given up the North Cape, and are going to Vienna and Graz. I shall see you much more comfortably there than now in Leipzig, when I am anxious to get home But I shall come to Graz and over hill and dale in Carinthia, wherever you like.—In haste, yours sincerely,

J. BR.

### 58. *Elisabet von Herzogenberg to Brahms.*

LEIPZIG, *April* 21, 1879.

MY VERY DEAR FRIEND,—Forgive me for bothering you, but could you send back the green volume of Chopin, which you routed out the other day, to my brother in Dresden, Kaiserstrasse 5 ? I wish I could spare you the trouble, by offering to burgle your house when we pass through Vienna, and pack it up myself, but my brother is keen on having his green book at this moment.

We can understand your passing through Leipzig in that mean way, but it was a great disappointment. We had foolishly counted on your coming.

The prospect of meeting you in the mountains is consoling, however. I have more faith in Carinthia, as you are sure to have left Vienna, when we pass through at the end of May, and what should take you to Graz ? I should have nothing of you there either, though the Thieriots* would—and I ought not to grudge it them.

I am enjoying the piano pieces† all the more since I made the blissful discovery that the C sharp minor and the C major are not so difficult as they look.

Best love from Heinz, who is beside himself with joy at the thought of Carinthia and you. I hardly see him all day, he is so frightfully taken up with some short sacred part-songs,‡ which will certainly be inflicted on you this summer. He has also written a second string trio,§ which sounds extremely well, and, what is so very desirable, *reads* well.

We were invited to the Kirchners the other day, and I was sorry for the rest of the party. He and I played duets for over an hour and a half! It was *all* Kirchner, of course, and really duets, especially when played at sight, are only entertaining to those directly concerned. Dear old Kirchner! He is a wee bit offended every time, because I am always provided with something new. 'I don't know why we play the things at all,' he says in an injured tone; 'you take no interest in them.' Yet he is always so ready to sit down at the piano, poor lonely fellow! The duets really interest me, too, while I am actually playing with him. There are many delightful touches, and all his work bears the real musicianly stamp; but as to sitting down to master these miniatures, so sentimental for the most part, playing them over and over

---

* Ferdinand Thieriot (b. 1838), composer, and at that time 'artistic director' of the Steiermark *Musikverein* at Graz. He was a country-man of Brahms's, and, like him, a pupil of Eduard Marxsen.

† Op. 76 had now been published by Simrock.

‡ Twelve German sacred folk-songs for mixed chorus, Op. 18.

§ Second Trio in F for Violin, Viola, and Violoncello, Op. 27.

to oneself and bringing out the middle voices on the
keyboard with one's thumbs—who would do it ?

Kirchner has been giving an organ recital here in
the Paulinerkirche—by announcement, not by invitation, for the first time—with an eye, we think, to the
approaching vacancy at the Thomaskirche. It was a
pitiful performance : not one item of real organ music,
but just odd scraps, mostly from Schumann's Pedal-
piano Studies* and *Paradise and the Peri*. He steered
clear of pedal passages, but would hold one pedal
note for a quarter of an hour while he played shimmer-
ing modulations on the 'echo'. He never began nor
ended anything properly, but made convenient bridges
between one fragment and the next by hanging on to
the notes in a disgraceful way. Really, it was almost
like hearing an amateur coquet with the stops. One
or two Bach themes cropped up, only to raise vain
expectations, for they lasted about three bars, and
were taken from the *Wohltemperiertes Klavier*† at that.
We were much disappointed, for we had thought the
organ was plane sailing for him.

But I have something on my mind. What is the
Vienna Conservatorium like? Could one advise a young
student, who is taking up composition, to go there ? . . .

There are one or two poor fellows here who would
like to try a change, and have asked Heinrich's advice.
If it has to be a conservatorium, which should you
recommend? Berlin, Frankfurt, or Vienna? Another
thing : Is Nottebohm dear for private lessons? One
of these young men would prefer that, but is afraid it
may be beyond his means. I am ashamed to importune
you in this way, but it is no use going to any but the

* Op. 56.
† That is to say, pianoforte, not organ, fugues.—Tr.

6

best for advice. . . . Besides, you can answer all these
questions on one page.

You are now released with kindest regards, a jubilant
*Auf Wiedersehen*, and the assurance of my boundless
esteem.—Your chatterbox,

ELISABET HERZOGENBERG.


### 59. *Brahms to Elisabet von Herzogenberg.*

[VIENNA, *April 29*, 1879.]

MY DEAR FRIEND,—Forgive me if I only manage to
reply to your questions. I dare not wait until the
letter-writing spirit moves me to answer your kind
and charming letter as it deserves. Briefly then :
our conservatorium is in a terrible state as regards the
teaching of composition. You only need to see the
teachers, and not—as I often do—the pupils and their
work.*

I should not recommend Frankfurt either, just now ;
Berlin and Munich, possibly, if it has to be a conservatorium at all—you know I am not partial to them !
Nottebohm charges three *gulden* a lesson, so far as
I know, and we can hardly expect consideration
from him, as that would imply that he needed it
from us !

* Brahms was for over twenty years a member of the committee,
formed in 1863, for distributing the stipends granted by the Austrian
Government for the education and support of young musical talent.
He had in this capacity ample opportunity of judging the masters
and students of the Vienna Conservatorium. His conscientiousness is
shown in the opinions expressed in his marginal notes, some of which
Hanslick reproduced in the *Neue Freie Presse* of June 19, 1897. In
1884 he complained : ' It is really disgraceful and inexcusable year
by year to ruin beyond repair the little talent we have.' But the
circumstances are now considerably improved.

I can strongly recommend him as a teacher.  I send him everyone who comes my way, and have often had reason to be delighted with his results.

Be sure you let me know when you are coming to Vienna.  I should like to run over from Pörtschach for a week, and would fit it in accordingly.  I have engaged my seven beds* again, and might have been there by now, but for the Festival week† and the uncertain weather.

Don't laugh over the newspaper descriptions of the Festival procession.  It was beautiful beyond expectation and beyond description.

Your description of Kirchner at the organ is delightful.  He produced for your benefit all the little tricks which used to entrance the good Swiss ladies ten or twenty years ago.‡  But the Leipzig churchwardens may not have such keen — and pretty — ears as yours!

Can you, between ourselves, tell me anything particular about the post of *cantor*§ at St. Thomas's ?  I have to decide, practically without knowing anything about it, though I don't think it matters much.

Excuse this hasty scribble, and accept kindest remembrances for yourself, Heinrich, and our little friend,‖ from yours,

JOHANNES BRAHMS.

* Brahms sometimes took a whole house in the country for the sake of privacy, although he only used two rooms.  The summer was his best working time.

† The silver wedding of the Emperor and Empress.

‡ Refers to the time when Kirchner was organist at Winterthur.

§ Brahms had been offered the post of *cantor* at St. Thomas's, once held by Bach.

‖ Miss Ethel Smyth.

### 60. *Elisabet von Herzogenberg to Brahms.*

[LEIPZIG, *May* 6, 1879.]

DEAR FRIEND,—I am touched by your kindness in replying so minutely to my questions. We imagined the state of things to be such as you describe, and Heinrich had strongly advised the young man not to try the Vienna Conservatorium. We have considered the *cantor* question and made some inquiries. It would be tempting indeed to paint the position in glowing colours if there were a chance of getting you here; but, alas! you have probably given up the idea again.

The *Thomaner* have got into slack ways lately, and do everything mechanically. There is no temptation to go and hear the Saturday motet* nowadays. But, of course, the late director† was much too old; anyone able to infuse new life into them would find good healthy material enough, and be able to do great things. There is every possible facility offered for securing good performances, as, for instance, *carte blanche* in the way of orchestral rehearsals, of which Richter took no advantage. Röntgen trembles even now to think how often he may be summoned, once a proper *cantor* comes who will insist on his privilege as regards the town orchestra. But we can only think of the possibility of having you here among us as a beautiful dream, for we cannot conceive of your really accepting the post, although it would have its advantages. But what would become of your delightful

---

* The motet sung at St. Thomas's by the famous choir every Saturday is an old-established and very popular institution.—TR.

† Ernst Friedrich Richter (1808-1879), a distinguished theorist, follower of Moritz Hauptmann, was *cantor* at the choir school from 1868 until his death.

summer holiday, your beloved Pörtschach, with its lake from whose waves there rise D major symphonies and violin concertos, beautiful as any foam-born goddess! No, we cannot imagine you here, however desirable it may be for us and for Leipzig to have you descend on us like a whirlwind. By the way, it was common knowledge that the cantorship had been offered you before you wrote about it. To think of having you for our *cantor!* What could be more splendid? . . . Good-bye now, and forgive this hurried scribble. Many thanks again for your most kind letter. Are you really going to Holland for the Festival? Our 'little' friend is one of many who hope you may. Heinrich joins her and myself in kindest remembrances, and we wish with all the fervour of our concentrated selfishness that you would come here. There are such nice sunny apartments in this neighbourhood!—Yours ever,

ELISABET HERZOGENBERG.

### 61. *Herzogenberg to Brahms.*

GRAZ, *July* 25, 1879.

MY DEAR HERR BRAHMS,—We have been tied here since the beginning of June for double family reasons, and shall not get away to our dear mountains until the beginning of August. We should have liked to go to Carinthia again, but fate has decided otherwise. Frau Schumann goes to Gastein at the end of July, and, as we have no other plans, we shall do ourselves the pleasure of joining her there, as we have told her. We shall be at Bockstein, half an hour from Gastein, from the 7th to the 14th of August, staying with relatives, and shall visit the mineral baths virtuously. My original plan was to look you up at Pörtschach on the way, proceeding to Gastein by way of Spital and Mallnitz (Hohe Tauern). But I can't expose my wife to the fatigue of an eight-hour ride on horseback, and must therefore give up Carinthia altogether. You need not be angry, for it hits us hard enough. You are sure to pay Frau Schumann a visit, however. How would it be if you arranged for us to meet you at Gastein? Do think it over, and give us the pleasure.

Don't leave us in the dark as to your decision, either, but write soon and tell us you agree, and will do it.— Ever your faithful          HERZOGENBERG.

### 62. Herzogenberg to Brahms.

GRAZ, July 31, 1879.

MY VERY DEAR FRIEND,—As you intend coming to join us, and are not afraid of the twelve hours' train journey, I am bound to provide entertainment for you on the way. When you get into the carriage at Pört-schach, take out the music enclosed in this cover and abuse it to your heart's content—always provided you have nothing better to do or to read, and are tired of looking out at the green landscape. The melodies and the words are taken from F. M. Böhme's Old German Liederbuch.* Except for some slight variations, I have kept to his version, and am making him responsible for

---

* Franz Magnus Böhme (1827-1898), theorist, published his Alt-deutsches Liederbuch, a collection of songs and melodies, in 1877. This was followed in 1893-94 by a new edition of Ludwig Erk's Liederhort in three volumes. Brahms had not a good word for either collection, and the German Volkslieder in seven numbers, which he published through Simrock, may be regarded as an artistic protest against Böhme and his method. Herzogenberg's arrangements are those mentioned by his wife in Letter 58.

its accuracy. My concern has been purely with the *composition*, and that I thoroughly enjoyed.

We leave on Monday, August the 4th, arriving at Gastein on Tuesday. We shall hardly stay there more than three or four days, as lodging is sure to be scarce bad, and dear. From there we go to Berchtesgaden, where dear Frau Schumann is to join us about the 14th of August, if I understood her aright. You have doubtless written a regular 'Gewandhaus piece,' since you speak of the winter. We shall take you at your word. Good old Thieriot has gone, with his usual happy imperturbability, to stay at the most hideous spot in Steiermark. He *passes through* Venice on his way back to Graz—a place I shall have much pleasure in turning my back on this time. *Auf Wiedersehen.*—

Yours,

HERZOGENBERG.

### 63. *Brahms to Herzogenberg.*

[PÖRTSCHACH, *August 2*, 1879.]

Best thanks for your package, which takes me back for the moment, with an ominous sigh, to certain tricks of my own in the old days. Your plans, and Frau Schumann's, strike me as so varied and uncertain that I don't know what to do myself. For the present I place my hopes on Berchtesgaden. It would be charming if we could all be lazy together there for a few days.—With kindest regards, yours,

JOHANNES BRAHMS.

### 64. *Elisabet von Herzogenberg to Brahms.*

LEIPZIG, *November 24*, 1879.

MY DEAR, GOOD FRIEND,—You have, I am sure, quite forgotten us, but all the more do we think about you.

Many are the thoughts that speed silently toward you
in your blissful unconsciousness, and here is one—
chosen because it needs no answer—of which, set
forth in writing, you must endure to be made aware.
You remember I took the liberty at Arnoldstein—of
blessed memory!—of copying one or two songs without your kind permission. You graciously allowed me
to keep the copy, however, and to show it to anyone
possessed of a pretty face or any other recommendation.
It so happens that a very nice girl, an alto, who is
staying with us for the Bach concert, has sung and
pored over the glorious *Todessehnen** until she longs
to have it and be able to sing it—in public as well. It
sounds so splendid, you see, that one yearns to share
it with a multitude of people; it is so divinely vocal
that—well, I will only say she will fade away altogether
unless she is permitted to have it. But permit it you
must; let us be conscientious at all costs! So please
say yes (or no!) on a post-card to seal Fräulein Fides
Keller's fate. She sings the ' Mussel 't charmingly,
too, and would like to have it to put in her cupboard.

And when are we really going to see you here,
pray? You are coming in January for certain; we are
counting on that, and looking forward to it immensely.
Seriously, the thought of this refreshing annual visit is
the one thing that enables us to put up with, and
swallow, certain things here. I prefer to say nothing
about your sonata.‡ What a lot you must have had
to listen to already—to the point or otherwise—on the
subject! You must be aware that it appeals to the
affections as do few other things in the realm of music.

---

* Op. 86, No. 6.                † *Therese*, Op. 86, No. 1.
‡ The Violin Sonata in G, Op. 78, which was completed in the
summer of 1879.

You interpret it this way, that way, lose yourself in blissful dreaming as you listen to it, and become an enthusiast of the first order. The last movement in particular holds you enthralled, for the soul of it positively overflows, and you ask yourself whether it can be just this piece in G minor that so moves you, or something else that has taken possession of your inmost self, unknown to you. And then there is that dear ♪♪ ♪ which almost deludes you every time into thinking that Brahms 'discovered' the dotted quaver.

Here I am chattering away after all, poor dear man! Please send a post-card, and let it say you are coming, won't you? When shall I receive the something dedicated to me, which is my due after ignominiously relinquishing the other to Herr Allgeyer?* I call it base to promise anyone such a Christmas present and then snatch it away again.

My greeting to you. When I play the last page of the *adagio* in E flat with the heavenly pedal note,† getting slower and slower to make it last longer, I always feel you must be a good sort after all. Prove it by coming to visit us poor Leipzigers.—Ever yours sincerely,

ELISABET HERZOGENBERG.

Do you know, by the way, that your fiddle sonata is 'somewhat free in construction,' and that every movement is 'written straight on' without repeats! (If one could only make these people say what they mean by 'written straight on'!) But the last movement

---

* Ballads and Romances, Op. 75, dedicated to Julius Allgeyer, painter, engraver, and photographer, also Anselm Feuerbach's biographer, whose friendship with Brahms dated from 1853.

† Op. 78, p. 20, bar 5.

is 'so rich in material that another composer might boldly call it a first movement.' Isn't it amusing of the *Kölner Zeitung* to be so wise!

### 65. *Brahms to Elisabet von Herzogenberg.*

[VIENNA] *November, 1879.*

MY MOST HONOURED AND DEAR, OR MOST DEAR AND HONOURED, FRIEND,—I will confess, though with some constraint, that your letter was a real act of charity, for I was beginning to think you had some grievance against me. Apparently not? As you are inclined to think me a good sort, and I can vouch for its being the case, I beg to suggest that it is a pity to drift apart on account of side-issues. We meet with little enough that is good and few enough of the good sort in this short life.

Therefore I thank you again, with meaning, for the cordial which your kind letter proved to be. Please don't suppress any nice things you have to say about my music. A little flattery is always sweet, and the generality of people are dumb until they find something to cavil at.

Indeed I want to see your beautiful name on the most beautiful possible piece, but at the crucial moment it never seems to be just that! I did think of the sonata,* but you remember we were none of us quite satisfied with it at Salzburg?†

But I am forgetting your singer. You had better give her what she wants, with the usual elaborate

* Violin and pianoforte sonata, Op. 78.

† Brahms had visited Joachim at Aigen, near Salzburg, in August, and had played through the sonata with him, the Herzogenbergs coming over from Berchtesgaden for the purpose.

formalities.  But I don't want the word 'manuscript' on any programme, as it might offend other singers.

Let me finish as I began, with some timid remarks. The tricky passages in the new trios* are charming, but I am reminded of the trickiness of the volks-lieder,† to which I cannot reconcile myself. I am hardly at liberty to say much on the point, as I am forced to remember the innumerable tricked-out volkslieder I myself have perpetrated.  One specimen still exists, unfortunately.‡  We must have a chat about it all sometime.  I am inclined to think Herr Heinz will not be pleased later on to know his are in print either, besides which they seem to me peculiarly difficult—and so on!

Any letter that is finer than the average—or more idiotic—is liable to fall into the market and become public property.  Take warning by the first instance and—don't you think the enclosed a fair example of the second?§  Yes, D major is certainly an easy key.

I have still one blank page, so will write down a jest of Mosenthal's‖ which is going the round here.  He was complaining that I was too sober for anything in my art.  I protested that I could be gay on occasion, and he admitted this, but added: 'Yes, when you are really worked up and feel hilarious, you sing: *Das Grab ist meine Freude!* '¶

* Herzogenberg's *String Trios*, Op. 27.

† *Cf.* Letter 62, note.

‡ *Deutsche Volkslieder für vierstimmigen Chor gesetzt*, published in 1864 without opus number.

§ A letter from some member of the committee.

‖ S. H. Mosenthal, author of the poem *Deborah*. Brahms met him sometimes in society and in the Viennese restaurants.

¶ 'The grave is my delight.'

I am quite curious to know what sort of cantatas you do.*  I should like to come and listen !

Kindest remembrances to you both and a few others from yours most sincerely,

J. BRAHMS.

Please tell Kirchner his *Davidsbündler*† are quite safe.  He shall have them back all right ; it is only my laziness which has made me keep them so long.

### 66. *Elisabet von Herzogenberg to Brahms.*

[LEIPZIG] *November* 28, 1879.

My DEAR FRIEND,—I can return your thanks with interest—compound interest.  It is long since anything gave us so much pleasure as your letter.  You see, we ordinary mortals can't help thinking sometimes that a man like you must accept all the tribute of love and respect paid him as a tribute merely, for which he is vaguely grateful in the mass without realizing very definitely the share contributed by the individual.  This being so, it is particularly heartening to find we do matter a little after all, and your charming way of putting it is worth more to us than I can say.

The letter you enclose is really classic, but I could not think of taking it for my collection of autographs ; you must keep it in your own possession. . . . I should like to chatter on, but have some parts to correct for the concert to-morrow, and have various sad visits to pay.  ·Our poor old Klengel died yesterday at the age of sixty-one.  His six children are quite overwhelmed with grief, for they adored him.  They

---

* At the Bach-Verein.    † *Neue Davidsbündler Tänze*, Op. 18.

are now like lost sheep. It seems to us there is more trouble than usual this winter.

Heinz sends greetings, and thanks you for your kind words about the trios. He still hopes you might judge the bulk of the volkslieder more leniently if you heard them. We really found them easy to sing, and everything worked out satisfactorily in practice. One or two of them he admits to be too tricky.

Fräulein Keller thanks you for the songs. She has an extremely sympathetic alto voice and is thoroughly musical. I wish she could have a chance of singing in Vienna. Remember me to Artur Faber. He is a splendid fellow, and I shall not fail to assure his wife of the great pleasure it gave me to have this glimpse of him. Well, good-bye, and again many thanks. What could make you think we had a grievance against you? It is a mystery to me, and yet, what matter? You are well informed now at least. Don't let us lose you, dear Friend.—Yours ever,

ELISABET HERZOGENBERG.

### 67. *Elisabet von Herzogenberg to Brahms.*

[LEIPZIG] *December* 1, 1879.

DEAR FRIEND,—I am returning your precious manuscript, having first hastily committed it to memory. I also send the programme of our concert for which you so kindly asked. The performance was, as usual, a great pleasure to us, and an ample reward for our pains. It is one of the proudest moments of our life when the chorus show their grasp of the thing and rise to the occasion. They forget themselves and their nervousness, and exchange happy looks in all the beautiful parts, while the basses are really affected by the passage *Ich aber werde traurig sein*, and sing it exquisitely. One realizes the collectivity of this mass under the power of one great personality. Such moments are precious indeed! Our chief pleasure is to watch the enthusiasm of the singers grow with each rehearsal, and we count it our chief glory to have aroused that enthusiasm; for there are very few who have it in them to begin with—the real thing, that has nothing in common with the rank and file conventional admiration of 'good old Bach.'

Radecke* is a capital organist, who does not merely sit and pull out the stops in due order.

But no more of that. There is a more important matter, which I forgot to mention last time. For heaven's sake don't come just at Christmas, for we shall be away ourselves—unfortunately, for we should love to stay at home. But you will come some time, won't you?

We buried Klengel to-day, and sang Bach over his grave as well as we could.

Good-bye, dear, dear Friend. Heinz the good sends kindest regards, as does his faithful

ELISABET.

## 68. *Elisabet von Herzogenberg to Brahms.*

[LEIPZIG] *February* 4, 1880.

MY VERY DEAR FRIEND,—You rejoiced my heart by sending those glorious pieces.† They were the more unexpected as I never dreamed you would have time to think of it before your concert to-day and the

---

* Robert Radecke (b. 1830), violinist, pianist, organ virtuoso, musical director, etc.

† Two Rhapsodies, Op. 79.

triumphal tour through Poland.* At best I only looked forward to receiving the coveted treasure some weeks from now, and was thankful to find—after a G minor night† I spent recently—that I remembered more than I thought at first. But a night like that is terrible, and the Almighty ought really to be more merciful—if he is musical. Scraps of the glorious whole pursue you, and you try vainly to connect them. All at once one bar shines clearly through the fog, then another, and you feel you are getting on, and join up phrase with phrase only to discover new gaps, until finally, in despair, you wish all good music (for that is the only kind that torments you) at Jericho, and fall back on counting up to a hundred to make you sleepy. But sleep sees through you, and eludes you in good earnest, until at last—at last the blessed moment comes when you lose consciousness. Sad that we are never able to appreciate that moment when it comes!

But at sight of the two much-admired pieces I forgot all my grief and pain, and greeted them like old friends. It is hard to believe that there ever was a time when I did not know them, so quickly does the barely acquired treasure become incorporated with the accumulation of long standing. Once known and loved, it is a possession for all time. And, indeed, these pieces seem to me beautiful beyond measure—more and more beautiful as I come to know their bends and turnings, their exquisite ebb and flow, which affects me so extraordinarily, especially in the G minor. Then, too, I

* Joachim played the Brahms violin concerto again in Vienna on February 3, after which the two started on a tour through Poland and Galicia.

† A night spent in recalling the second of the two Rhapsodies, in G minor.

have the comfort which can only come of knowing that
I can feast my eyes and ears on it all as often as I like.
I still think the pathetic bit at the close of the development* unique in its way, and am tempted to join the
worthy Leipzigers in their delighted outbursts over
'these *crescendi*' and 'these *decrescendi*,' and this
working-up on the dominant E until it relaxes peacefully to take a fresh breath on the *lunga* (⌒).†

But the fact that the G minor is my favourite does
not make me insusceptible to the rugged beauty of the
B minor with its very sweet trio. The way the trio
theme is indicated beforehand‡ is quite wonderful.
Indeed, the whole of this episode, with the right-hand
triplets and the expressive basses, is another case where
words are inadequate. One is so glad that the piece
closes with that too, leaving the most impressive part
uppermost in the mind.

Ah yes! you have indeed made us very happy
again—not less by your visit,§ whose only fault was
that of being too brief, like much else connected with
your doings. Have we not been remonstrating with
you this age for letting us wait so long for a real big,
*long-winded* composition ? Just a G major sonata is
really too insignificant an output for one year, and your
Polish tour, which is to steal so much time, we contem-
plate sadly and grudgingly, insatiable and greedy that
we are ! It has been my luck to miss everything that
has been performed of yours this winter‖: the violin

* P. 15, bar 15 *et seq.*   † P. 17, bars 1-7.   ‡ P. 5, bars 19-23.
§ Brahms had called at Leipzig on his way home from a concert-
tour on the Rhine, and it was on this occasion that Frau von Herzogenberg became acquainted with the rhapsodies.
‖ The performance of Brahms's violin concerto on December 28
by Joachim ; of the 8 *Klavierstücke* on January 4 by Bülow ; the
Haydn Variations and *Song of Destiny* at the Gewandhaus under

concerto, the *Song of Destiny*, the sextet, and the unfortunate *Rinaldo*, which was so disgracefully badly done that my poor Heinz came home quite miserable. So you see we have double reason to hope to see you in April, with something good in your pocket, even if it be no G minor. 'One can't always write in G minor.'

My cough has been lively again, and I have had to lie up, bandaged in Priessnitz. My doctor thinks there is a strong tendency to permanent catarrh, which must not be allowed on account of my heart trouble. He is therefore most anxious that we should accept my sister's long-standing invitation to Florence, and convey ourselves thither in the spring. The project seems to me too magnificent, for various reasons. True, the few weeks' complete rest we should have at my sister's makes it practicable, but it still seems too good to come true. I feel I don't deserve it. In any case, the Berchtesgaden visit will not fall through.

Good-bye now, and let your two loyal friends thank you once more for the refreshing message. I suppose we may copy out the pieces, and, if the copy proves irreproachable, even barter it for something else ?

Don't be afraid to scold if you think me too brazen ! —Your old friend,

ELISABET HERZOGENBERG.

### 69. *Brahms to Herzogenberg.*

[VIENNA, *February* 14, 1880.]

Please do not have the pieces written out, as I have a fair copy. I can only send my best thanks, in haste,

---

Reinecke ; the G major sextet at the Gewandhaus Kammermusik and at the Riedel Verein ; and the cantata *Rinaldo* at the Paulus Verein.

for the kind letter which I was delighted to find yesterday on my arrival.—Yours very sincerely,

J. BR.

### 70. *Brahms to Elisabet von Herzogenberg.*

[VIENNA, 1880.]

MY VERY DEAR FRIEND,—It really is not nice of you to go so far away without even leaving an address. It might bring the most important business to a standstill, and I am writing on business to-day!

If Herr Astor* does not know where to forward the letter, it is not my fault. Herr Simrock will assuredly not trouble about my woes, but will simply send a blank title-page into the world.

You see, I want to publish certain two pieces you know of.

Can you suggest a better title than *Zwei Rhapsodien für das Pianoforte?*† You cannot suggest a better dedication—that is, if you will allow me to put your dear and honoured name on this trash.

But how to write it?—Elsa or Elisabet? *Freifrau* or *Baronin? Née* or not?

Forgive all these frivolous remarks, but write a line at once to Ischl, Salzburgerstrasse 51, where I expect to go to-morrow. I hope you will find more to say at the same time, especially that you are in excellent health and are having a splendid time in that glorious city.

In great haste, and with kindest regards to you and Herr Heinz.—Yours most sincerely,

J. BR.

* Edmund Astor, Herzogenberg's friend and publisher.
† The inscriptions over the two pieces in the manuscript are respectively : *Capriccio (presto agitato)* and *Molto passionato.*

*71. Elisabet von Herzogenberg to Brahms.*

FLORENCE, VIA DEI BARDI, 22,
c/o FRAU BREWSTER (*my sister*),
*May* 3, 1880.

MY DEAR FRIEND,—What a charming surprise ! For, in spite of your breathing from time to time of a kind intention to dedicate something to me, I never quite believed in it, especially since Herr Allgeyer's ignominious robbery of the other ; and now you put me to shame by giving me just these two glorious pieces for my own. I need not dwell upon my great delight over the dedication. You know whether I love these pieces or not, and you know whether I am bound to be delighted or not at seeing my name flaunt itself on a production of your brain. So let me say simply thank you, though with all my heart. As to your inquiry, you know I am always most partial to the non-committal word, *Klavierstücke*, just because it is non-committal ; but probably that won't do, in which case the name *Rhapsodien* is the best, I expect, although the clearly-defined form of both pieces seems somewhat at variance with one's conception of a rhapsody. But it is practically a characteristic of these various designations that they have lost their true characteristics through application, so that they can be used for this or that at will, without many qualms—'*und Nam ist Schall und Rauch, umnebelnd Himmelsklarheit.*'* Welcome, then, ye (to me) nameless ones, in your nebulous garb of rhapsodies !

How glad I am that you have been in Italy, so that I do not need to tell you anything. If I say I am sitting

---

* From Goethe's *Faust*. '*Himmelsklarheit*' should be '*Himmels-glut.*'

in the open door of the balcony looking out over the
Arno, almost exactly between Ponte delle Grazie and
Ponte Vecchio, you know what that means, and just
how blue the sky is overhead; how sweet and soothing
the mountains are in the background, and what my
frame of mind is as I gaze on this splendour.  I know
it all under a hundred different aspects, thanks to the
revelations I have had during the past weeks.  I have
involuntarily so woven the detail into the whole, and
again unravelled the whole into detail, that my affection
for this heavenly place is ever on the increase, and I
am sad to think how soon we must leave it, and tear
our eyes from what has become indispensable to them.
I am so glad you have been here too, and have had the
joy of discovering that your eyes can see the inspiring
beauty which surrounds you, even though you grew
up in such distant surroundings.  The wonder is that
we could be content with so little all this time—with a
Katharinenstrasse, an ancient *Rathaus !*  This people,
one humbly confesses, was impelled to produce fine
things, masterpieces, in lavish abundance, to satisfy its
own cravings.  Yet it retained its gay, martial spirit,
and, never content to rest beside its own work, made
such haste to destroy its neighbours' that it is amazing
to find how much escaped destruction.  And to-day
this same wonderful nation is worse than dead!  The
modern Italian who dashes from Bargello to the Palazzo
Vecchio has almost less connection with the history
and art of his country, is almost less worthy to possess
such treasures, than we gaping barbarians; for we, at
least, come imbued with a certain childlike awe.
    But here I am, chattering away when I ought to
be telling you more important things, as, for instance,
that we hope to be at Berchtesgaden early in July;

that the Engelmanns follow with four infants at the end of July, and that we think it would be so very nice and sensible if you joined us there. As Herr Müller* you seemed half inclined for Berchtesgaden, so I hope Herr Brahms will be of the same mind. We will take rooms for you and arrange everything beautifully, and, once you are there, treat you nicely or leave you in peace, just as you wish; in short, you shall have everything you want. It is so particularly nice to meet in the summer. We want it so much. Please, please, tell us soon whether we may count on it.

What can take you to Ischl? Is it so comfortable? I thought half Vienna disported itself there.

You must tell us a great deal about Düsseldorf.† I cannot console myself for not having been able to go for the festival. When the day came, I thought to myself: 'Confound Italy!' In reply to another of your questions, we are very well. Heinrich suns himself like a salamander, and purrs for happiness like a cat. When we are not feeding at Bargello's or elsewhere, he writes coffee-fugues‡ to make up his dozen. We went to two very funny concerts here, and came to the conclusion that it would not do to *live* here, in spite of all the attractions. We should go off our heads in a country which boasts only one copy of the *Bach Ausgabe*, and where all that we value most has literally no shadow of a foothold.

* Brahms had apparently said he would not mind going to Berchtesgaden as Herr Müller—that is, as a private person, without responsibilities.

† A slip of the pen for Bonn, where a festival was held, from May 2 to May 4, to celebrate the unveiling of the Schumann monument. Joachim played Brahms's violin concerto, and was joint-director of the festival with Brahms.

‡ On the notes C, A, F, F, E, E.

But good-bye now, and may we soon meet at Berchtesgaden. How I am looking forward to it, and to the *Rhapsodies* beforehand! I feel like a small capitalist in prospect of this dear, beautiful possession. For the rest, I will answer your last question by signing my own name, such as it is, and such as you know it.— Yours sincerely,

ELISABET VON HERZOGENBERG.

You have always written it in this way. What brings you to this idiotic question?

### 72. *Elisabet von Herzogenberg to Brahms.*

BERCHTESGADEN,<br>
c/o 'ZIMMERMEISTER' BRANDNER,<br>
*July* 11, 1880.

MY VERY DEAR FRIEND,—Is it true, as we hear through the paper (indirectly, for we never open one ourselves), that you are not well?* We can hardly believe it, for it is not at all like you; but I must ask, so as to be ready to let loose all the flood of sympathy I hold ready at your disposal. I should grieve more for you when not very well than for others downright ill, for you are such a complete stranger to illness—lucky man!—and would certainly be a bad patient.

Write a line soon to reassure us, and tell us at the same time what chance we have of seeing you here. We want you badly; the mere prospect makes us happy. I am flattering myself that you will bring a quantity of things this time, either in your trunk or in your head—both for choice—so that we can have a good look at what you have to show, and take it with us on our walks. Ever since the Pörtschach

---

* Brahms was suffering from aural catarrh.

motet* I have been longing for you to write more
choral things; and when I think of you with your
pockets full of good things, like a child's St. Nicholas,
it is always a vision of motets, or the like, which dazzles
my greedy eyes.

Did Ehlert's article in the *Rundschau* infuriate you
too, I wonder?† Why does no one ever say the right
thing? Even praise is offensive from such a source.
I call it low to discuss anyone's work in that cheap,
shallow way. The man puts the things that matter
on one side, and gets off easily with would-be witty
comments and comparisons. Beethoven shows his
profile, you your full face, indeed!‡ Your variations
are different from Beethoven's and Schumann's (as if
they pretended to any resemblance!), yet you 'make
your bow and go out at the door in the same way.'
What is the use of such twaddle? Even at the
mention of the G major sonata, for instance, where
one yearns for a little warmth and sincerity, there
is only incomprehensive stuff about the 'May rain
brushing the heads of the flowers.' Tell me, please,
is it the womenfolk who brought all this mischief into
the world, or do the men say these insipidities of their
own accord? It was news to me that the *Rhapsody*

---

* Op. 74, No. 1. *Cf.* Letters 40 and 41.

† Louis Ehlert (1825-1884), composer and writer on music, had
published an essay on Brahms in the June number of Rodenberg's
*Deutsche Rundschau.*

‡ Ehlert had said : ' Brahms's music has no profile, only a full
face. It lacks the strongly-marked features which stamp the expression absolutely. . . . My observations have led me to conclude
that nothing is so persistently transmitted through many generations
as gestures. . . . His variations have practically no resemblance left
in their faces to those of Beethoven and Schumann, yet they occasionally make their bow and go out at the door in the same way.'

sprang from a 'worldly impulse.' The man cannot even feel the pulse-beat of a piece that stirs one to the very marrow, and yet has the presumption to take stock of an artist's personality and sit in judgment on him!

One should be used to this sort of thing, but somehow rage gets the upper hand every time. If only someone would find the right message to send out into the world! Better leave the beautiful to find its own way into the hearts of men, and let no one write on art at all, than endure this nonsense.

But enough of these sad evils, which we cannot remedy. You must write, write any amount, so that we may forget all the deplorable, futile twaddle we hear in our joy over what you give us.

When may we expect you? Shall I be able to greet the Engelmanns, who are to turn up here soon, with a joyful piece of information? I am not at all sorry the *Rhapsodies* are not yet out (as announced), for I shall now have the pleasure of playing them to Emma as an entire novelty, putting on considerable airs for the occasion.

    \*      \*      \*      \*      \*

We have a cottage piano from Munich, gorgeously black and shiny outside, though it is a wretched little instrument. Still, it is not to be despised, as summer pianos go, and you have a way of making the notes sing on all sorts of pianos, as witness the B flat in the middle part of the B minor capriccio.\* Good-bye now, my dear Friend. Heinz sends kindest regards, and we both look forward to seeing you.—Your faithful

HERZOGENBERGS.

---

\* P. 10, bars 3 *et seq.*

*73. Brahms to Elisabet von Herzogenberg.*

[ISCHL, *July* 14, 1880.]

MY DEAR FRIEND,—You are really too kind and good to bestow another quite undeserved letter on me— undeserved in every sense, for I cannot even claim indulgence on account of my distinguished complaint, which proved to be none at all. My ear elected to take cold, and, as I prefer to keep it in good condition, I consulted an ear specialist. He had it under his inspection three days, waiting for something to develop, but nothing came.*

Had I known in time that you and the Engelmanns were going to Berchtesgaden, I might have been tempted to leave Austria—at least, I think I might. How much more sensible if you came here another time, though! It is really beautiful, and you are free from social duties, and can live considerably cheaper than elsewhere. The fact that half Vienna comes here does not trouble me at present—in fact, I have positively no objection to all Vienna! I should probably fly before half Berlin or half Leipzig, I admit; but half Vienna is quite pretty, and will bear looking at. But I must and will pay you a visit.

The *Rhapsodies* and the new 'Hungarians'† arrived

---

* Brahms was, however, thoroughly alarmed by his sudden deafness, fearing that he was doomed to the same fate as Beethoven. He left for Vienna immediately, having wired his friend Billroth to meet him at the station. Billroth was able to reassure him, and direct him to a specialist. To Brahms's great annoyance, a report of his illness got into the papers through an indiscretion, and he found it a serious matter to reply to all his letters of sympathy.

† A second series of *Hungarian Dances* for pianoforte duet (books iii., iv.) had been published simultaneously with the *Rhapsodies* by Simrock.

with your letter. I wonder if you will simply jeer at them and let them go? They rather amuse me. If they should amuse you likewise, be sure you tell me so. You have no idea how kindly I take to that sort of thing! You will receive them one of these days, as I sent off your address immediately. That reminds me I did not—òr do not—know the Engelmanns' address either, and cannot remember* whether I forwarded the things to them at Utrecht. Please remember me very kindly to them. Anything that has not reached them shall be sent on after.

I am quite willing to write motets, or anything for chorus (I am heartily sick of everything else!); but won't you try and find me some words? One can't have them made to order unless one begins before good reading has spoilt one. They are not heathenish enough for me in the Bible. I have bought the Koran but can find nothing there either.

But daylight has departed, and a man wants his supper. Excuse the answer to your last (which never came), and let me have a real long letter real soon.

Kindest regards to you two and the other two.—
Yours most sincerely,

J. Br.

### 74. *Elisabet von Herzogenberg to Brahms.*

BERCHTESGADEN, *July* 23, 1880.

MY VERY DEAR FRIEND,—It would be easy just to say 'Thank you,' but the rest is the difficulty, and it is just the rest that matters. I have already given you my opinion of the *Rhapsodies* at great length, but am quite

---

* Brahms betrays himself as a native of Hamburg in his use of *erinnern* for *sich erinnern*.

ready to begin from the beginning and tell you all over again what you know without being told. I can see so well now that it is not everything to know a piece by heart, for, with the two pieces before me in all their splendour, I seem to be always discovering new features ; what is more, I am better able to grasp the unity pervading this multiform structure. It is just the finest works of art which, because of this unity, seem to us rather the work of Nature in their inevitableness, their air of having been there from all eternity.

It was a strange surprise to me to find that glorious triplet part, which originally formed the introduction to the trio as well, exalted to a solitary appearance in the coda.\* If you will believe me, I felt so strongly that that bit ought to be saved up to make its powerful effect at the close, that I conceived the audacious plan of writing to supplicate you, but was restrained by my native modesty. Now I find, to my joy, that my instinct did not deceive me. The five fateful bars before the trio suffice so perfectly, and one revels all the more in the close, which must have come to you at a particularly inspired moment.

But I miss that bar at the end of the trio badly. I like the G sharp and G in the more extended original form much better, and shall go by my manuscript—not by Simrock ! There is one note I cannot, cannot understand. It is in the trio, page 6, first bar of the last line : the sustained E. The voices go in such nice contrary motion without it [*sic*].

\* Page 11, bar 7.

I simply can't understand why that third voice should push itself in. But forgive this possibly very impertinent criticism.

Finally, let me thank you once more for giving me—*me*—these particular pieces. I cannot tell you how great a joy they are to me.

And now the 'Hungarians'! I can well believe that they amuse you. Delicious as the earlier ones were, I hardly think you hit off the indescribable and unique character of a Hungarian band so miraculously then as now. This medley of twirls and grace-notes, this jingling, whistling, gurgling clatter, is all reproduced in such a way that the piano ceases to be a piano, and one is carried right away into the midst of the fiddlers. What a splendid selection you borrowed from them this time, and how much more you give back than you take! For instance, it is impossible to imagine—though I may be mistaken—that a melody like that E minor, Number 20, could ever have taken on such a perfect form, particularly in the second part, but for you. Your touch was the magic which gave life and freedom to so many of these melodies. What impresses me most of all in your performance, though, is that you are able out of these more or less hidden elements of beauty to make an artistic whole, and raise it to the highest level, without diminishing its primitive wildness and vigour. What was originally just noise is refined into a beautiful *fortissimo*, without ever degenerating into a civilized *fortissimo* either. The various rhythmical combinations at the end, which seem to have come to you so apropos, would only fit just there, and are amazingly effective—as, for example, the delightful basses in tumultuous Number 15. That one would be my favourite, anyway, if it were not

for Numbers 20, 19, 18—oh, and the short, sweet
Number 14!* If I were to try and tell you all we have
to say about these dances, I should have to quote
passage after passage, until I had copied out nearly the
whole of the 'Hungarians.' I am longing to hear you
play them. Are you really coming soon? We and
the Engelmanns hope so much you will not put it off
too long. One never knows what may come between
to spoil the expected pleasure.

I refuse to believe there is nothing else to be found
for you in the Bible. There is still plenty of material
in Job, which you read with such happy results before,†
and in the Psalms. It can't really hurt you if a thing
has been composed before! For instance, would you
not make your hart pant quite differently after the
water-brooks to Mendelssohn's?‡ Surely such words
have more depth and immortality than many a Heine
poem which has been done a hundred times over.
But perhaps you are only teasing us all this time, and
are bringing the loveliest motets with you.

Kindest remembrances from the Engelmanns, whom
we saw yesterday. It is such a pleasure to meet them
again, and have some real good talks and some music.
They received the *Rhapsodies* and the 'Hungarians'
long ago. Good-bye now, dear friend, and let us see
you here soon. It is true half Leipzig is swarming
here—crowds of parsons!—but, O joy, we know them
not! And the natives—man and beast—are too

---

* No. 14 is Brahms's original work, like several more of the dances
(see Kalbeck, *Johannes Brahms*, i. 66).

† Brahms wrote his motet, Op. 74, No. 1, on words taken from
Job. In writing the *Vier ernste Gesänge*, composed in 1895, Brahms
may have recalled her words.

‡ '*As the Hart pants*,' Mendelssohn, Op. 42, No. 1.

charming.   And you will find excellent coffee at
*Zimmermeister* Brandner's.   And a few people who
like you.—Kindest regards from us both.

                              ELISABET HERZOGENBERG.


### 75. *Herzogenberg to Brahms.*

LEIPZIG, *November* 25, 1880.

Well, here they are, the *Sacred Volkslieder*,* with
a request for a kind reception.   The bad ones and the
most tricky I have kept at home—left them in my
desk—while there are a few quite harmless ones put
in to fill their place; and if the whole collection
hardly comes in the category of easy choral music, it
at least contains nothing that I have not proved to be
practicable.   Embellishment in itself does no harm,
but over-embellishment is more serious, and soon takes
its own revenge.

You know how much a word or two of recognition
from you, however relative, means to me; even a well-
intentioned refusal or condemnation I can, and have
always been able to, appreciate as a kindness.   But
I know, too, how keen an interest this presupposes on
your part, an interest which must necessarily be
spontaneous, and is not to be had for the asking.   If
you realized how I turn over in my mind any casual
remark of yours, you would understand why I am
always coming to you in spite of your anything but
encouraging attitude.

You, as a great master, would be hard put to it
indeed to respond to, or even grasp, all the affection
you inspire by your mere existence, by your presence.
You have become intimate with yourself from the

* Op. 28.   *Cf.* Letters 58, 62, 65.

habit of years, and those with whom you stood on an equal footing are all dead.

When you began to know Schumann you were, I believe, seventeen.* I feel as if I should never be older than eighteen at most with respect to you, so you must put up with something like a love-letter once in a way from such a hobbledehoy—all the more now that we are really starving after a long fast and the bitter disappointment of the summer! Shall we have the joy of seeing you here this winter with something or other? We could meet in Berlin very soon, if you should think it worth while to come over for the Brahms Requiem.†

When I think of little girls like Fillu and Eugenie enjoying the privilege, denied to ourselves, of hearing two new trio movements and two new overtures, I feel very sore!‡ You might at least reassure us. With kindest regards from my wife,—Yours most sincerely,

HERZOGENBERG.

### 76. *Brahms to Herzogenberg.*

[VIENNA, *November* 26, 1880.]

MY DEAR FRIEND,—Your letter has this moment arrived, and I must send a line in haste. Are you

---

* Brahms was twenty when he came to Schumann in 1853.

† A performance at the Hochschule on December 4, conducted by Joachim.

‡ Brahms was not able to go to Berchtesgaden from Ischl until September 13, after the Herzogenbergs had left. Frau Schumann was staying at Vordereck, near Berchtesgaden, her summer house for some years, and Brahms had played to her and her family the *Academic* and *Tragic* overtures, and two movements from the C major trio, Op. 87, which he had written at Ischl. The 'little girls' were, of course, Marie Fillunger and Eugenie Schumann.

really going to Berlin for the 4th? I have promised
to go, and thought of proposing a visit to you on the
7th.  On the morning of the 6th we expect to try my
two overtures in Berlin, so perhaps you will come
and listen, too.  I have promised to do them at Leipzig
on the 11th of January.

\*     \*     \*     \*     \*

Your dear lady kept me so well posted up all the
summer, but unfortunately she failed to tell me you
were leaving so early.  I only learned this disappoint-
ing fact on seeing Frau Schumann, and through her,
when it was too late.  It was so beautiful, too, at
Berchtesgaden, so gay and sociable.

I broke off in the middle of other correspondence,
and must go back to it now.  I hope to thank you
in reasonable fashion for the songs;* my first free
hour is assigned to them.  Please tell me plainly, in two
words, whether you are going to Berlin for the Requiem,
and can stay over the Sunday.  I hope to do the overture by seven o'clock at latest on the 6th.—Yours
most sincerely,

J. Br.


### 77. *Elisabet von Herzogenberg to Brahms.*

LEIPZIG, *December* 14, 1880.

MY DEAR FRIEND,—You would have had a sign
of life from Humboldtstrasse before this if I had not
been such a poor creature, sleeping by day, waking by
night, and as unhappy as a naturally happy person can
be.  To-day I have picked up somewhat, and hasten to
thank you for the delightful hours you gave us here.
It meant so much to us in every way that you

* Herzogenberg's *Sacred Volkslieder.*

came back with us, even though it was only on the excellent A——'s account. . . . Joachim played your concerto splendidly.* We had not heard it, you know (except at Salzburg), since the first time, and were completely enchanted with and carried away by it. It made us feel we had you actually with us after you had left. Now, as each day brings us nearer the 11th, we look forward more and more to your return. The Engelmanns, who had been insisting they must leave on the 10th, have of course decided to stay, and are as delighted as we are; so I hope you will not regret giving the Leipzigers a hearing of your dear, beautiful music. The overtures torment me in my bad nights. I can't quite get hold of the F major theme in the ' Festal,'† and am simply longing for the promised pianoforte scores. And don't forget the *melodische Übungsstücke !*

Our concert‡ on Sunday went off so well that we can hardly console ourselves for not having had you there. You would so have enjoyed *Schauet doch und sehet.*§ It was one of our good days, when every singer is carried outside himself in response to something which cannot be dismissed with the mere word ' inspiration.' Each one has strength for three at such moments, and we really produce something very creditable, feeble little handful as we are! I am always so glad for Heinz, dear fellow ! He so often has a wretched time drumming every difficult interval into their heads.

Good-bye now. Don't stop liking us, and let me

* Joachim had played the violin concerto at the Gewandhaus, this being the third performance at Leipzig within the year.

† *Academische Festouvertüre*, p. 9 of full score, beginning at the ninth bar.

‡ One of the Bach-Verein concerts.

§ Cantata by Bach.

8

assure you of what you know already, that we like you more than a little.—Your

HERZOGENBERGE.

Joachim's variations* are so pleasing and nice ; they were very well received.

### 78. *Brahms to Herzogenberg.*

[VIENNA, *December* 24, 1880.]

I am sending you some Händel duets,† and shall be glad if you will look over the piano embellishments‡ carefully, and still more the German words. There are also some melodious finger exercises which are only too obviously influenced by my tender admiration of the smiling Professorin's§ delicate hands and fingers. I shall want to have a chat about everything when I come. Meanwhile keep it all under lock and key. With best wishes for Christmas, yours,

J. BR.

### 79. *Elisabet von Herzogenberg to Brahms.*

LEIPZIG, *December* 28, 1880.

MY VERY DEAR FRIEND,—What a very great pleasure to have your overture‖ drop from the skies half an hour before we lit our Christmas-tree. My maid brought it in, all unsuspecting, and I, spying the Röder stamp, at once surmised the whole truth. I carried

---

* Joachim had played his own variations for violin and orchestra from manuscript at the same concert as the Brahms violin concerto.

† Brahms was adapting some of Händel's chamber duos for the Peters edition.

‡ The elaborate contrapuntal movement which Brahms had evolved from the figured *Basso continuo.*

§ Frau Emma Engelmann.

‖ The *Academische Festouvertüre,* Op. 80.

the roll to Heinz so as not to spoil my own fun, and he propped it up with due solemnity,* where it outshone all the other nice things, and rejoiced my heart more than I can say. Next day we went to the Engelmanns', first thing, with our treasured roll, and there we played and played the dear overture, and four happy people put their heads together and said what they never can say to your face. If you had seen our expressive smiles, you would really have been a wee bit pleased; for although it may have a noisier reception at Breslau† shortly, no one there will hear and drink in every fine touch, every glorious change in the harmony, more gratefully than the said four people. Only now have I really made friends with the overture. I am the dullest of mortals, and the form bothered me at first with its long Introduction ;‡ also I found it difficult, with all those different themes, to sort out everything in due order. Now that I have grasped it, I quite love it; and when we hear it in January, hear you conduct it for us after having had it in our heads so long that we nearly forget how recent an acquisition it is, then it will be a real Festal Overture for us, too. It was too good of you to remember the

---

* Christmas presents in Germany are spread out in separate piles, usually on separate tables, one for each member of the family. The time of presentation is the afternoon or evening of Christmas Eve ; it takes place in a room set apart for the occasion, of which the chief adornment is a lighted Christmas-tree. A hymn is often sung by way of preliminary, and the whole ceremony of entering the room and examining the presents is attended with much solemnity.—Tr.

† The *Academische Festouvertüre* had been written in recognition of the honorary doctor's degree conferred on Brahms by the philosophical faculty of Breslau University. He conducted the first performance of this overture and its twin, the *Tragische*, on January 4, at the Breslau Orchestral Society.

‡ Pp. 5-17 of full score.

melodious finger exercises, and the duets too, you dear man! Now there is only the ' Tragic ' one left to sigh for.*

And now I am requested to entreat you to fix the date of your coming, if possible. The Engelmanns are in correspondence with various friends in Amsterdam, who are coming for the overture, and are therefore entitled to an interest in the day. So do please make a valiant effort to fix it. The poor young Röntgens, who are here now, will, unfortunately, have to leave before it. We practise together most vigorously. There is a grand Brahms evening the day after to-morrow, when Emma will play the A major quartet, Julius Röntgen the quintet, with a few other trifles thrown in. Amanda, Julius's wife, is to play the violin concerto by heart, just by way of an encore, when the family has already been playing three hours! Oh yes, we all have tough digestions! Engelmann suffers worse than ever from his head. Half his life is spent in dull pain, yet he never breathes a complaint, and has only to look at his little wife to break out in smiles. It really does me good to see him so cheerful and resigned. There is something to be said for my own dear, too, however. The way he distinguished himself at Christmas! I only wish you would get married, just to have an idea how good a husband can be!

Excuse this disjointed epistle. The overture has gone to our heads, and also Ferdinand Raimund's works, one of my Christmas presents. Now I read *Diamant des Geisterkönigs* when I can't sleep at night, and am quite happy. . . .

But it is very consoling that, although there is little

* *Tragische Ouvertüre*, Op. 81.

enough of the true and the beautiful in this world, that little is so abundantly satisfying as to compensate for everything.

Last of all, let me thank you once more. When it is done in writing, at least I don't see you wriggle! Let us know soon when we may have the pleasure of preparing for your visit.—Your

HERZOGENBERGS.

### 80. *Elisabet von Herzogenberg to Brahms.*

[LEIPZIG, *January*, 1881.]

MY DEAR FRIEND,—It is my fate, the moment you are gone, to plague you again to the tune of *Wann hört der Himmel auf zu strafen.** Fräulein Zimmermann,† who asked you, through me, for an autograph to give to Miss Mackenzie, your English interpreter, has just alarmed me by asking if you left it, after all. I certainly told you about it, but did not remind you again, and what good is the one without the other? So, as it is my fault, let me pay the penalty of boring you. Please don't forget. Fräulein Mackenzie appears to have begged hard for it, and Fräulein Zimmermann, who first learnt to love your music through Miss Mackenzie, is anxious to show her gratitude by fulfilling this wish of hers.

Dear Herr Brahms, it is very quiet at the Herzogenbergs' now. We miss you very much, though it is something to have the memory of that good time.

---

* Brahms had written a canon on Uhland's lines

'Wann hört der Himmel auf zu strafen
Mit Albums und mit Autographen?'

(When will this rain of albums cease,
And autograph-hunters give us peace?)

and had given it to Naumann for his 'Illustrated History of Music.'

† Agnes Zimmermann (b. 1845), pianist and composer.

You must come again often! You brought a glow into our hearts again with your music and your friendship; and although this kind of joy is enduring and helps us through the hard times, repetition is as necessary to the ordinary mortal as to the musician, so give us this good old-fashioned sign before long:

Rubinstein and his symphony have fallen through, and 'I canna tell what has come ower me that I am *not* weary and wae!'* . . .

. . . I have one more message to give you. My two maids came rushing up in great excitement after you left, gasping out inarticulate gratitude mixed with all sorts of other feelings towards Herr Brahms, and begging me to render you an intelligible account of their unintelligible thanks. Johannes Brahms, you have obviously been guilty of something which must not occur again, unless you wish to be counted among the musicians who spend their thousand *gulden* on china, and still more on satin knickerbockers!† Seriously, I was rather furious when my two maidens confided in me, and must presume on our old friendship to scold you a little!

Good-bye now. Herr Chrysander's New Year's wish was that you might experience 'that continuity in production without which there is no true satisfaction'; my wish is that we may experience the continuity of your friendship, without which there is no longer any real happiness for your most faithful

HEINRICH AND L. HERZOGENBERG.

* First two lines of Heine's *Loreley.*
† An allusion to Wagner's weakness for satin.

81. *Brahms to Elisabet von Herzogenberg.*

[VIENNA, *February*, 1881.]

DEAR FRIEND,—Forgive the delay in sending the enclosed,* and its shabbiness now that it comes, but I really had, and have, no time. Otherwise I should like to tell you of my travels† and a few other pleasing matters. But I must content myself with saying that the days in Leipzig were delightful, and that I shall come and put up with everything there gladly and often —as long as you are there!

About the enclosed canon :‡ you know that soprano, *tenor*, alto, and bass, come in each four bars behind the other. It finishes when the soprano comes to ⌒ in the repetition, two notes lower of course.

Please send it to Miss Mac—Farren or Ziegen.§ Should you be tempted to give it to Fritzsch (?), I wish it signed J. B., with the further inscription 'From a Leipzig album'!!! But I must write the solution over it, or it would look too mad for anything.

Be pleased to read between the lines at this point my kindest remembrances and thanks.—Yours,

J. BRAHMS.

* The desired autograph for Miss Mackenzie.

† Brahms had been at Breslau from January 1st to 7th, at Leipzig on the 13th, at Münster on the 22nd, at Krefeld on the 25th, at Amsterdam on the 31st, and in February at The Hague and at Haarlem.

‡ The autograph took the form of a four-part canonic puzzle, which was published, according to Brahms's suggestion, in No. 18 of the *Musikalisches Wochenblatt*, April 28, 1881. The riddle was solved the very next day by F. Böhme, and his solution was printed by Fritzsch on August 4, 1881. It is not commonly known to this day that Brahms was the composer.

§ A joke on the name, Farren and Ziegen standing for bulls and goats respectively.—TR,

82. *Elisabet von Herzogenberg to Brahms.*

[LEIPZIG, *February* 24, 1881.]

MY DEAR FRIEND,—I have profited considerably by
Mrs. Macfarren. The canon, which I have copied out
neatly in full score, is most piquant with its en-
harmonics. I am looking forward to hearing it
properly sung, but that has not been possible up to
now, as our friend has first to solve it. Why did you
tell me the tenor had to begin ? That made it so much
easier.

Fritzsch, honest fellow! was quite gleeful at the
prospect of printing something 'from a Leipzig album,'
so please let him have the key.

Thank you for your nice letter, short though it was.
We are much affected to hear that you will come and
put up with everything here gladly and often; it says
more to us than we could trust ourselves to put into
words. Every time we hear how you fare elsewhere,
we feel sad and ashamed and envious.

By way of rewarding you for past favours, may I
now entreat a few more, already promised? You know
the N——s have very little music, and you said you
would go to your store-room and produce something for these good people, who are devoted to
you. You said I was to remind you, which I now do.
You could stow away with them anything you have to
spare, for *everything* is welcome, and everything coveted,
even duet editions of the Requiem and such. Most of
all do they hanker after the F minor quintet, arranged
for two pianos. If you should have that to spare,
great would be the rejoicing. You also mentioned a
few more canons, which we should be delighted to

have. (If you think me too fond of 'jogging' your
memory, please consider that you solemnly authorized
me to make all these reminders!) We had our second
Bach concert on the 19th, and heard so much praise
that we began to have qualms as to whether it really
had been decent. It is certain that no one here understands what we do, and that almost frightens us. The
chorus and orchestra were most enthusiastic, however;
Hinke, our oboist, played *Wir zittern und beben*
bewitchingly, and the trumpet's high C went ringing
through the church in '*Es erhub sich ein Streit*.' Even
the D——s and their set were quiet, so much did they
enjoy it, and said afterwards they would like to hear it
all over again. That was our thirty-fifth cantata, and
we are still young! We have passed the nobility-test*
by three already! But the soloists are always a
trouble. They are so imbued with their soloism that
they can't be quiet and impersonal. Then the musical
side is often so undeveloped. . . . There is so much
vanity and vexation of spirit here below, and so little
pure happiness, that when I think of myself, and the
full measure meted out to me, I am full of shame. For
what has one done to deserve it?

Dear Friend, I know you have no time, and are wish-
ing I would stop. I really will, but not without telling
you that, whenever we two sum up all the love and
beauty in our lives, we never forget to remind ourselves that we have you, and can rejoice both in your
music and in your affection for us.

ELISABET HERZOGENBERG.

* *I.e.,* thirty-two quarterings.—TR.

### 83. *Brahms to Elisabet von Herzogenberg.*

[VIENNA, *March* 2, 1881.]

MY DEAR FRIEND,—I am sending off a fair-sized bundle, but feel, all the same, that I boasted too much. There are no duets or two-piano arrangements, unfortunately. I am really flattering myself that the greater part will remain with you! At least, the two better copies of the Requiems. The bad English edition is for Miss ——. You would have no use for the scores of my Requiem and *Triumphlied?* Or for songs transposed for alto?

The bound volumes belonged to a friend who used to take a great interest in my music. She no longer does so; hears a better sort—in higher spheres.

The canons would only have been lost in all that pack. How can anyone who has done thirty-five cantatas take an interest in such things?

I don't think I even know so many.... Why did you stop when you had only reached the eighth page? No flattery, but when you have such beautiful note-paper it must be as entrancing to write on as it is to read!

But my maestro* is coming, and instead of writing I have been hunting up this music, which please put down to my credit.—With kindest regards, yours,

J. BR.

### 84. *Elisabet von Herzogenberg to Brahms.*

[LEIPZIG] *March* 6, 1881.

You kind person! That was a regular Christmas hamper! My dear N——s, whom I dashed round to

---

* Brahms was studying Italian with a view to travelling in Italy.

see yesterday through a blinding snowstorm, a nice
big parcel under my arm, did not know what to think
at first, and were as delighted as children. Up to now
they have practically lived on attacks made on our
music cupboards, and certain things—as, for instance,
your G minor quartet—would disappear for six months
at a time. And now—they have come into their fortune,
and we shall no longer miss our music. So you see
we profit, too, by what we surrendered to them, and
have kept back various things, since you permitted it :
the sextets in duet form, *Rinaldo* and the serenades,
in return for which we made over the D major, which
we had, to our friends. We rang in Sunday after our
own fashion to-day by playing over the A major with
the deepest delight. We had not looked at it for some
time, and were quite sentimental over meeting the
dear familiar thing again.

The friend who now enjoys the concerts of the
higher spheres was evidently full of love for these
treasures, and I am therefore not sorry that they
should pass from your indifferent hands into our not
unloving care.

Is it really no oversight that the Mozart and Cherubini Requiems were included? Glad as we should be
to have the scores, we have not quite the courage to
appropriate them until you write and say :

> ' Sei guten Muts, O Heinrich mein,
> Nimm diese Bretzen, sie sei Dein.'

And now let me thank you once more, you dear
Friend, in the N——s' name (they will be writing on
their own account), and in our own. It was really
particularly nice of you to take all this trouble and
display such generosity.

To-morrow we have an amusement in prospect. We
are going to Halle to hear Bülow conduct one of his
Beethoven concerts. Heinz is bent on having a look
at the show just once, and I am curious too, though it
can hardly be less impossible than his piano-playing.

Good-bye, dear Friend, and do send us the canons
all the same. We can still condescend to make room
for such trifles. Our 'Miss' thanks you for the
Requiem. She received the German edition after all,
as the N——s had it. She scorns the English one!—
As ever,                                    E. HERZOGENBERG.

### 85. *Elisabet von Herzogenberg to Brahms.*

[LEIPZIG] *March 27,* 1881.

MY DEAR FRIEND,—You delighted us very much with
your portrait, in which we recognize the real you, and
appreciate the good, happy expression which photo-
graphers so seldom catch. It is almost tragic to be
writing to Siena.* Every attempt at communication
seems paralyzed when one realizes so vividly how
safely out of reach you are. How can it interest you
to know what we are doing here under our heavy
leaden skies? I am really touched that you should
desire a letter at Siena. Indeed, I am only writing
to thank you for the good Brahms on the little easel
(which is always falling over), next to the big divan on
which you were sometimes pleased to rest after the

* Brahms went to Italy on March 15. His second Italian tour was
longer and more extended than the first. Theodor Billroth and
Professor Adolf Exner travelled with him, but left him behind in
Rome, where he wished to spend more time. The route lay through
Venice, Florence, Siena, Orvieto, Rome, and Naples, to Sicily, returning by Florence and Pisa. Brahms returned to Vienna on May 7, his
forty-eighth birthday.

enormous fatigues of Leipzig's festivities in your
honour! Heavens! what a sorry figure Leipzig must
cut, when you take your retrospective bird's-eye view
of the winter tours, beside the gay Rhenish towns, and
warm-hearted Holland, where you passed like a hero
from triumph to triumph! It always makes me envious
to read Frau Emma's reports from Amsterdam and
Utrecht.

We are always having fresh trouble and disappoint-
ments here. For one thing, Rust* is having the
G minor fugue, arranged for *orchestra*, played at St.
Thomas's on Palm Sunday. He has also set some *Choral
Vorspiele* for four voices, with an appropriate text, and
he is *your* nominee! We have further endured a
thoroughly bad performance of the second part of
*Faust*.† Heinrich sang in the chorus! He wanted
to look into it closely; and I went too, but only for one
rehearsal. I could not stand their slovenly ways, and
promptly excused myself. It was tragic to hear them
scramble through the ninth symphony, too. Such
occasions always make us wish we could see and hear
you conduct these things—with your swinging beat,
which means so much; your expressive arm-move-
ments, which always respond to an impulse from
within, and are not merely designed to extract certain
results from others; your natural oneness with the
music, which excludes any paltry nervousness, as it
does deliberately planned effects.

Oh, that Halle concert‡ was really charming! But

* Wilhelm Rust (1822-1892), organist and cantor at St. Thomas's.
† Schumann's setting.
‡ Bülow's Beethoven performance (*cf.* Letter 84). The writer saw
fit to correct her harsh judgment of Bülow later. Bülow only posed
as a witty interpreter aiming at special effects—in his piano-playing
as in his conducting—until he was sure of himself, his orchestra, and

one dared say nothing.  Everybody lay prostrate before
this anointed one, who bore himself like a priest ele-
vating the Host in the glittering monstrance for the
first time.  At times he seemed to be giving a repulsive
anatomy lecture.  It was as if he were making the
experiment of stripping an antique statue of its lovely
flesh, and forcing one to worship the workings of bone
and muscle.  It is pleasant enough to realize the spring
that works the machinery, but it ceases to be pleasant
when it is laid bare and pointed out in the coarsest
fashion.  Bülow's affected little pauses before every
new phrase, every notable change in harmony, are
quite unpardonable.  In the last movement of the
A major he even introduced full stops here, there, and
wherever he saw fit ; every bar had its own particular
shading.  The *Coriolan* overture was played with a
slowness without precedent, even where the climax
comes; the exciting 'cello part sounded strange enough
in such tempo.  In short, the whole performance was
designed to show *himself* in Beethoven's mantle.  When
he turned round in his inimitable way to take stock of
the audience—needless to say he conducted everything
without a score—I couldn't help thinking of someone
else, who once said to us before a Gewandhaus concert : ' If only I don't forget I am at a concert this
evening, and stop the orchestra, as I easily might,
without thinking !'

By the way, we had your friend Th. here.  He is a
quiet Hamburger, but no ' stick '; for when Kirchner
began to abuse—(much to my alarm), Th. laughed

---

his audience.  His extravagances were to him a necessary coercive
measure.  Once he felt himself master of the situation and at home
with his audience, his interpretation lost its personal character, and
became a simple expression of the music, which he had really at heart.

quite gaily, and said it was delightful to hear anyone speak his mind in that way. Kirchner has written some graceful and pretty—that is, really appropriate—duets : a perfect shoal of them, of course! He is as prolific as a rabbit, and really produces nothing but these tricky little wrigglers. Yet all his things are so graceful, and so exquisitely musical, compared with all the amateurish trash one sees, that one cannot but welcome them.

But I have let off steam enough for one day. Let me just congratulate you on having really set foot in Italy. I am so glad I know Siena, and can picture your delight when you come upon the amphitheatre-like market-place. If you should come in for the races there, they are said to be most exciting. The people wear their oldest clothes, and the decked-out horses tear down the enclosure at such a pace that there is invariably some small mishap. The winner has a seat at table when they hold their feast, and has its nose kissed by the women who backed it. If you have a chance, you should drive through San Gimignano to Volterra. The scenery is gloriously wild and impressive, and Volterra is quite unique. It was there I heard a small boy sing something which reminded me of the second movement of the concerto.* It had fascinating words

about a chamber in which a thousand memories lay buried. The marble workers spend half the night,

\* Brahms, violin concerto :

OBOE.

etc.

or the whole of it, singing, and one of them said : ' He is *unwise* who sleeps at night ; for if we work by day, when are we to sing ? ' Ah, how beautiful everything is there; how wasteful, how natural and inevitable ! There is such reckless profusion of light and warmth and unconscious beauty that one ends by accepting it all as a matter of course.

I can think of you in the midst of it all without envy, for you deserve it ; but I do begrudge it hideously to some who go. Take care of yourself in Sicily, for everyone catches cold there. Keep it well aired, our old friend—the dear, brown, no longer muddy overcoat.*

Well, good-bye. I shall not write again for a long time, which accounts for the disgraceful length of this. You are travelling with Professor Billroth, are you not ? How nice if we could meet him some day ! Why does he never come to a *première* at the Gewandhaus ? One more, thank you for the Requiems which we have now really appropriated. Kindest regards from the Röntgens and ' Miss.'—Ever your devoted

HERZOGENBERGS.

### 86. *Brahms to Herzogenberg.*

ROME, *April*, 1881.

DEAR FRIEND,—I am just back from Sicily, and must really send you at least a line or two. My steel pen† will not inspire me to more, and it is impossible on other grounds. Will you give the enclosed to Fritzsch ?

---

* Brahms was always reluctant to order a new suit of clothes on account of the trouble it involved. He would wear the same things year after year, and much resented being reminded by his friends that his wardrobe needed replenishing.

† Brahms used quill pens which he trimmed for himself.

The solution will be printed later, so I can send it any time.* No need to say how much I am enjoying myself here. I hope my letters are being published, either by Fritzsch or in the *Tagblatt?*—and I should be sorry to repeat myself!†

Many thanks for writing to me at Siena; I shall go there again on the way back. But everything is so undecided—indeed, I prefer it so—that I cannot ask you to write. My movements depend on my whim, the weather, and various attractions that may offer.

So for to-day I will content myself with settling Fritzsch's affair, while asking you to be content with the assurance that I often think of you, and should be only too glad of a long chat. But that is out of the question.—Yours ever,

J. BR.

### 87. *Elisabet von Herzogenberg to Brahms.*

JENA BEIM PARADIES,‡ July 3, 1881.

DEAR FRIEND,—I once had a terrible aunt, who, as she came out of a splendid picture-gallery, exclaimed with feeling: 'All very fine and nice; but it is of far greater importance that we should love our Saviour!' I should like to say something of the kind to you in your voluntary hiding. To go to Italy and feast your eyes and take your fill of enjoyment is all very fine and nice; but to remember your friends just occasionally is of importance also. Do let us hear something about you, particularly your present whereabouts, and

---

\* A fresh copy of the canon (*cf.* Letters 81 and 82) for the editor of the *Musikalisches Wochenblatt*. Brahms's solution was never published.

† This is not to be taken literally. He not only sent no descriptions of his travels, but declined to have letters forwarded.

‡ An old-fashioned pleasure resort on the bank of the Saale.

whether there is any chance of seeing you at the end of the summer, for that is the only time left at our disposal. We have had such strange bad luck this year. The first calamity is that we are still tied here (I literally, on my back*), where I had the indiscretion to entrust myself to a doctor. He has restored my good health and spirits, I admit, but only after two months. The second is, that instead of going to a dear little cool Alpine place to convalesce, as one would like, or to a nice little wood near by, we are going to— Venice, musty and unattractive as it is just now. My poor broken-down mother hopes to find it bearable there for the summer. She has no courage to try any place farther north again, with her bronchitis and lung trouble.

It is hard on us, but we remind ourselves that one only has one mother, and ought to be willing to sacrifice something for her. I am hoping the sea-bathing will set me up. I don't know how long we shall be able to stay there—possibly only a fortnight. After that we go on to the Ritten above Bozens, to Heinrich's relatives. The air is splendid, and will, we hope, compensate us for the canal odours our devotion has led us to absorb. We shall then be free for a short space in September, and who knows if we may not meet you somehow, by hook or by crook? If you were at Pörtschach, as of old, we should like to visit you there; but I fear Ischl will claim you again, and that is too far out of our way. Or will your September movements be more favour-able to us? That would be delightful. . . . But do send a sign of life first of all, for I am so shut up here. I was quite alone the first month,

* The letter is written in pencil.

without Heinz even, for he could not leave Leipzig
any affection from outside is therefore doubly welcome. Music means more than it ever did, after two
months' deprivation, and nothing in the world could
give me more pleasure than to have any odd scrap of
manuscript paper, that somebody had no particular
use for, sent me in a letter. I really think anything
new of yours, if it were only a few bars, would set
me up so that I should be given my liberty some days
sooner, and pronounced cured. You are sometimes
moved to do things from 'sheer kindness of heart,' as
Herr Chrysander* once discovered; there were one or
two things in his clever little article which delighted
us by their genuine enthusiasm. But I was amused
at the way he dragged in his Händel, and the Bach-
worship, which seems to him one-sided, even in you.
Händel is to Chrysander much what Wagner is to
Fritzsch—a Jack-in-the-box, always popping up un-
expectedly. But the most amusing thing of all was
to have (in a recent number of Fritzsch's paper)
Wagner pop up, pressed by some invisible spring,
in a discussion on the Gregorian chants, if you please!
The point was that his reforms were founded on the
*choral!* Heavens! what idiocy one does read (or as
a rule does not read, but Jena is so demoralizing!),
and how brightly an article like Chrysander's shines
by contrast! It says so much for it that, dear as is the
friend under discussion, one does not take offence at
any point.

Do you know anything about Frau Schumann?
I only know she is going to Gastein. My last com-

---

* Friedrich Chrysander (1826-1901) edited Händel, and wrote his
biography in the *Allgemeine Musikalische Zeitung*, of which he was
editor. The article referred to is in No. 22 of vol. xvi.

munication with her had to do with some of Schumann's proof-sheets, which worried me considerably, as I knew nothing of the *deliberately* differing versions of the *Davidsbündler.* How do *you* play the passage in the last number, or last but one (*Wie aus der Ferne,* B major)?

Like this, or with E natural straight away? We are told to play it with E now, but E sharp seems to me incomparably better. How effectively the E comes in after it! In Kirchner's manuscript it is different again. There is no E sharp, but a depressing double sharp before the F. What an overwhelming task this editing must be! Who would be responsible for deciding on a particular E or E sharp for all eternity?

My devoted Heinz sends very kindest regards. His room is over mine—a student's den like this one. Jena is a friendly little place. One would like to be here with an opportunity of seeing more than one's own four walls. Heinrich has explored all the mountains, and is in ecstasies over the positively Alpine flora here and the peaceful German landscape.

Give you greeting! Send us a line before we leave, please. I shall only be here one week more precisely. The whole Röntgen family is in Amsterdam for the christening. That dear, happy couple! Jena in Paradise is, as you see, the abode of yours sincerely,

ELISABET HERZOGENBERG.

## 88. *Brahms to Herzogenberg.*

[PRESSBAUM, *July* 5, 1881.]

Are you not going to send me a line one of these days ?\* Where are you now, and where do you go next ?

You really are too careful to avoid Austria now that I am there.

I am spending the summer at Pressbaum, near Vienna. How nice it would be if you came to visit your friends in Vienna, and me thrown in ! Your wife has, I believe, been undergoing treatment from Franz or Voretzsch†—or possibly a regular *Kur?* Meanwhile do please let me have a line.—Yours very sincerely,

J. BR.

## 89. *Brahms to Elisabet von Herzogenberg.*

[PRESSBAUM, *July* 7, 1881.]

MY DEAR FRIEND,—Just a hurried note to thank you for your most kind letter. I had just sent off a shabby card, being lazier than you.

I can understand doing anything for one's mother, but I presume you asked a doctor's permission before arranging to go to Venice at this time of year !

I am spending the summer at Pressbaum, near Vienna. My little villa is quite charming, and I often think how nicely it would suit you two. I confused Halle and Jena with respect to you. Don't spoil the effect of your *Kur* by the journey to Venice ! . . . I should like to send you something worthier than these hurried lines, but it is impossible just at

* The letters had crossed.          † Two Halle doctors.

this moment. I don't mind telling you that I have written a tiny, tiny piano concerto* with a tiny, tiny wisp of a scherzo. It is in B flat, and I have reason to fear I have worked this udder, which has always yielded good milk before, too often and too vigorously.

Frau Schumann is just leaving for Gastein. She *expects* to go to Italy in the autumn.

But I am just off to Vienna, and your stay 'near' Paradise is also at an end. I only ask to be kept more or less posted up, and should like to be able to look forward to Berchtesgaden.—With kindest regards, yours most sincerely,

J. Br.

### 90. *Elisabet von Herzogenberg to Brahms.*

Jena, July 10, 1881.

How very nice of you, my dear good Friend, to take up your pen again immediately! I have to thank you doubly, since you had such good news to send of a tiny, tiny piano *Konzerterl* with a tiny, tiny *Scherzerl*,† and in B flat—the true and tried B flat! That is something to look forward to until the autumn, 'something to keep jolly'‡ when other things go wrong—as, for instance, our meeting, which seems to me very problematical. Think a minute! *Last* year we did go to Berchtesgaden, but this year it is really too far out of the way. Last year no Brahms came to see us,

---

* The great B flat concerto, Op. 83, in four movements. Brahms sent it when completed to his friend Billroth on July 11, with the note : 'I am sending you some small piano pieces.' It was actually finished on July 7.

† *Scherzerl* is the name given to the crusty ends of a long roll of bread in Vienna.

‡ Frau Herzogenberg's own words in the original.—Tr.

much as we desired it, while this year he is quite
ready to go! It is always the way: *Da wo du nicht
bist, ist das Glück.** You know, by my card, that I
realized the impossibility of completing my *Kur* in
Venice with my mother, and that, having discovered
the possibility of sea-bathing until September, we
decided to put off the Venetian journey until then.
It was a load off my mind, for I had no peace for
thinking of the average temperature there (22 degrees
Réamur), especially as I always have to lie down (in
a darkened room) when it is 23 degrees. It has turned
cooler now, and the very thought of the Tyrol is cool
and refreshing.

Why are you so far away in your fine villa, you
spoilt person? If you have your seven beds as usual,
you might really invite us, you know.

\*        \*        \*        \*        \*

And now good-bye. You shall hear from us, and
I hope some kind fate may bring us together. Meanwhile you have given us something—a great deal—in
announcing your concerto.

We shall certainly be another six days here. I am
still a prisoner, and can only detect the spring (now
past!) through casual signs, the particular one being
a blackbird, who sings every day:

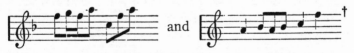

I am in such good spirits over my approaching
release that it makes me babble.—Yours, as ever,

E. H.

* From Schubert's song, ' The Wanderer.'—TR.
† The melody of *Freut Euch des Lebens*.

91. *Elisabet von Herzogenberg to Brahms.*

GRAZ, *October* 1, 1881.

MY VERY DEAR FRIEND,—Late as we are in knocking
at your door, we hope very much to find you at home.
We were delayed in leaving Venice, after a month
spent there, by my not being well, and have had to
make a further halt here for the same reason. We
shall arrive in our old Leipzig a whole week late, like
real tramps; yet we cannot resist stopping in Vienna
to shake hands with a few dear friends. It is difficult
to fit in everything, as we can only stay two nights;
so we must arrange our meetings with great care, if
we don't want to miss the best. If you are still at
Pressbaum, we should prefer to look you up there, as
we particularly wish to see you in your beloved
' *Waldeinsamkeit.*' We hope, too, that our thirsty ears
may drink in a tiny something which we can take
away with us, and feast upon, until the good time later
on when you come with it yourself. But who knows
whether you are still there in this wintry weather?
I am writing to Karlsstrasse for safety. Please let us
have a friendly word in reply immediately, and should
this reach you later than to-morrow, please send a
telegram telling us where to find you. We shall not
stir out until four in the afternoon, so we shall probably
be here to receive your answer. Anyway, we must
see our dear friend, if he is in or near Vienna. We
should like best to come early on the 6th and steal one
of your beautiful mornings. We are tied until eleven
o'clock on the 5th by a sister who is passing through,
and I am expected to lunch at my friends the
Obersteiners', in Oberdöbling. We have placed our-

selves at Epstein's* disposal for the evening. I have
not seen him for years, and owe him some consideration. But, as I said, I should like to begin the day
well, and with you, on the 6th, if you can do with us.
How I hope you are still there! Otherwise the
measure of our ill-luck for this year is really full. The
6th is called Thursday, and we are called Herzogenberg, and are staying at a certain Ruhberg, to
which address may it please you to write. We are
longing to see you, dear Friend, to rifle your drawers
and to revel in your music and your kindness.

If you like us half as much as we like you, you too
will look forward just a little to seeing your sincerely
devoted                              HERZOGENBERGS.

## 92. *Brahms to Elisabet von Herzogenberg.*

[VIENNA, *October*, 1881.]

Welcome most heartily to Vienna! I shall certainly
be at home at eleven o'clock, though all on heaps. But
you travel like royalties positively, only more so, for
one cannot even stand and watch your arrival.—Your
supremely delighted                        J. BR.

## 93. *Elisabet von Herzogenberg to Brahms.*

[LEIPZIG] HUMBOLDTSTRASSE,
*October* 28-29, 1881.

I have been so smothered in household rubbish and
Leipzig smuts that I have been an incredible age
thanking you for all your kindness in Vienna. The
treasures we carried away with us, the gratitude which
stirred us without ceasing, my feelings henceforward
when I write Karlsstrasse 4, now that I can take a

* Her old master (*cf.* Letter 17, note).

personal interest in that excellent dwelling-place—all this I hope you are better able to imagine than I to describe. Above all, remember that we (much like you) never mean more than when we jest or even say nothing at all—as, for instance, after *Nänie.** I envy people who vibrate eloquently on receiving great impressions. I vibrate myself, Heaven knows; but even a dog is more eloquent, for he at least howls at the moon—which I choose to consider a sign of enthusiasm in this case, to bear out my statement. But the mortifying reflection inevitably follows : how eloquent one becomes as soon as there is anything to criticize! There is such a fine choice of words for deliberate fault-finding, yet one seeks in vain for the right, the comprehensive word to relieve one's feelings after moments of real enjoyment. But what a poor thing speech is, even for the born speaker! Are not the few expressions we have to describe all that is best and finest done to death? Yet one would so like to reserve a distinctive word for every individual genius, just as one would like to have a *du* for one's husband as distinct from the *du* of one's good friends. But we must make the best of what we have, and be thankful when the very one to whom we would fain say something—you, for instance—are as good at divining as we are tongue-tied.

We have had an eventful week, which is not over yet. The last Gewandhaus concert provided a remarkable programme: Hiller's *Demetrius,*† Liszt's

---

* Brahms's *Nänie* for chorus and orchestra, Op. 82, dedicated to the memory of Feuerbach, the artist, was begun in 1880, the year of his death. Brahms had completed it during the summer, and played it to the Herzogenbergs in Vienna.

† Overture by Ferdinand Hiller (1811-1885), pianist, composer, and writer on music.

*Tasso,** and our dear good Julius,† a worldling between two entirely discredited prophets. If Hiller pays any more visits to the invisible world (you heard of his latest delicious production, in which Schumann and Mendelssohn tell him such charming home-truths?‡), he will have to listen to some nice things from the blessed Demetrius. It is hard to say which is worse : the decent dulness of a Hiller or the indecent dulness of a Liszt! Both are intensely exhausting. Julius Röntgen, with his piano concerto, proved a graceful and agreeable contrast, refreshingly musical. You were very unmistakably sponsor to the composition— he can hardly pretend to have invented it all himself— but, dear me, we can't all live on our income! Most people borrow somewhere, and when it is from the right person it is pretty enough to listen to, particularly when, as in this case, one feels the young pulse of a genuine musician and a thoroughly nice fellow beating through it all. It is good to find such a warm, unfailing flow of sentiment, even though it be borrowed sentiment, and the audience were of that opinion. But the critics put on their wisest, most annihilating expression, and harped in a superior way on the lack of originality. 'Under the ban of Brahms' is to them conclusive. . . . Mothers are to be envied indeed, even the one, mourner though she be, to whom you dedicate the dirge.§

To us this piece is as the dearest and most splendid

* Symphonic poem for orchestra.

† Julius Röntgen.

‡ Hiller had published a series of articles in the *Deutsche Rundschau*, called *Besuche im Jenseits*, which he afterwards incorporated in his *Erinnerungsblätter* (1884).

§ Brahms had dedicated *Nänie* to Frau Henriette Feuerbach, the artist's mother.

of our possessions—for we do possess it in part—
though we wish Abraham* would hurry up, or, better
still, that you would, so that we can soon hear it again,
and many times over.  The Röntgens are always
asking us to 'describe' it, and the concerto too†; but
I am not Ehlert,‡ and could find nothing to say about
them that did not sound insipid.  Nothing but hearing
them can be of any use.  And now for my great
request!  Please, please, please send me the piano
score of the orchestral part to practise, so that you will
not have to suffer so much when you play it with me.
I am sure you will; you are so pious and good.  I
know Brüll § has played it with you (lucky those who
were present!) and it may be lying there idle at this
moment.  In that case it would be much safer here,
where its only danger lies in being torn to pieces
through excess of zeal.  When, when are you really
coming?  Has your vacillation come to an end?  How
long shall you stay, and will there be a performance
of *Nänie?*  The *Thomaner* are not equal to it by themselves; you must have the Gewandhaus chorus.  We
were thinking it would be suitable for the New Year's
concert, when the *Thomaner* are always pressed into
service, and would prove a useful reinforcement.
People are saying you will be here in a week or ten
days.  We alone have no information.

* Dr. Max Abraham, head of the firm of Peters at the time. *Nänie*
was published by him in 1881.
† The two new compositions which Brahms had played to the
Herzogenbergs in Vienna.
‡ *Cf.* Letter 72.
§ Ignaz Brüll (b. 1846), composer and pianist.  Brahms much
appreciated his quick comprehension and clever, musicianly playing,
and often asked his assistance when he wished to introduce any of
his larger compositions to his intimate friends in Vienna.

Most of us here grudge your generosity to Bülow.*
He made himself very, very unpopular last year by
seizing the first opportunity of abusing the Gewandhaus, upon which the orchestra refused to play the
ninth symphony under him again.

Heinrich sends messages. If you only knew how we
two look forward to seeing that good old brown overcoat! Only yesterday (I must explain that a whole
section of Liszt's *Christus*† comes between the beginning
and the end of this scrawl) we were saying: Really, how
*can* such contrasts exist side by side? and how can one
person conduct—to-day a certain *Requiem*, to-morrow
this *Christus?* How is such an organism to be classified?
This music is detestable, and will 'sink into oblivion
without a ripple.'‡

Good-bye, good-bye, giver of much good! We look
forward to seeing you.—Your devoted

HERZOGENBERGE.

## 94. *Brahms to Elisabet von Herzogenberg.*

[VIENNA, *November* 2, 1881.]

DEAR FRIEND,—I am taking up a scrap of paper
to write, not a letter, but a slight acknowledgment
of yours. I cannot send the concerto, as it is already
in Simrock's hands (arranged for two pianos, by the
way). I am coming for the first of January, but there
will be no *Nänie*. The *Thomaner* are not available, as
Rust very lucidly explains in a lengthy epistle. It
really is terrible, the things they expect of these
youths!

\* \* \* \* \*

* See note to Letter 95.　　　　† Oratorio.
‡ The words are a quotation from *Nänie.*

It was charming at Meiningen,* you know.  We did some very fine and very enjoyable music.

But a poor touring concert-giver like myself has a lot of correspondence, and we can have a good talk on New Year's Eve.  If you think *Nänie* could be done without the *Thomaner*, please speak to Limburger or somebody about it  I can't write myself—but wait! I have to write to Limburger, anyway, so I will just mention it, and you can proceed or not as you like.

*Addio*, and forgive this slovenly writing.—Yours,

J. Br.

### 95. *Elisabet von Herzogenberg to Brahms.*

[Leipzig, *November* 14, 1881.]

I must just tell you, dear Friend, that we have had *Nänie* here for one day.  We gave up a stupid Sunday to her, as far as we could for interruptions. *Nänie* is now my best friend.  I am always playing it in imagination as well as I can remember it, and revel in the syllables which scan so perfectly.  I sing hymns of praise to the hexameter which has served you so well, and am so happy in the added wealth with which you have again enriched us.  *Nänie* is one of

* Bülow had surprised Brahms in July, 1881, with a very cordial invitation to come and use the perfectly drilled Ducal Orchestra (he had been *Hofmusikintendant* at Meiningen since October, 1880) to rehearse any novelties he might have.  Brahms replied that he had only the piano concerto, which, much as it needed rehearsing, was hardly suitable for Meiningen.  Bülow insisted to the contrary, and Brahms was easily persuaded.  He went to Meiningen in the middle of October, was received with much consideration, and returned to play his concerto on November 27.  Bülow conducted on this occasion, and the result was an ideal rendering.  In the meantime Brahms had played it at Buda-Pesth on the 9th, and Hungary enjoys the honour of having secured the first public performance.

those things of which you cannot merely say you have
heard or played them, but rather that they have been
an experience. But I am so glad I heard you play
it first of all in your cosy Karlsstrasse! That exquisite
earliest impression will always remain, side by side
with all subsequent hearings. Even if they do not
give it at the Gewandhaus,* we two feel that we have
heard it and know something about it. It was a very
great help, too, to have a copy by us, and play it
through a time or two. How vividly it stands out
in my memory, each part for itself and the whole
in its wonderful unity! One is loth to pick and
choose,—but oh, the sweet Aphrodite part in F,
the bewitching passage at the splitting of the Eber,
the splendid seething of the wave-triplets in F sharp
when the goddess rises from the sea, the syncopated
weeping of the gods, and the breathless suspense at the
words, ' *Dass das Schöne vergeht,*' where it dies away!
One would like to mention everything, but above all the
blissful ending, for which you deserve every blessing!
How thrilling are the different voice entries, and how
splendidly it works up and lingers on the dominant—

passing with the more refreshing effect into D major
at the words, '*im Mund der Geliebten*' (I have written
it all wrong, of course. I don't know this particular

---

\* The Committee decided on the piano concerto, which Brahms
accordingly played on January 1st.

place well, but you know what I mean, and agree,
I hope, in thinking it splendid). That F in the basses
is a triumph.

Good-bye, you dear man! We are as proud of you
as if it were our fault that you did such beautiful
things!

It ought to rejoice your soul that you are able to
bring happiness to so many in this weary world, though
to few in such full measure as to your devoted and
grateful

HERZOGENBERGE.

### 96. Brahms to Elisabet von Herzogenberg.

[VIENNA, November 14, 1881.]

MY VERY DEAR FRIEND,—It is *only* because you spoke
of coming to Meiningen for one or other of the concerts
that I am writing to say that the works of yours most
humbly, the undersigned master, are put down for the
27th of November (*a.m.!*).

There is a public rehearsal at seven o'clock on the
evening of the 26th, and you might listen privately to the
Haydn *Variations*, etc., in the morning. In short, you
will be able to enjoy a regular surfeit of the works of
yours etc., and you will never hear the things so well
done at Leipzig.

I shall be at the Sächsischer Hof. If you really are
coming, please write and engage your rooms there in
good time.

N.B.—The 'Tragic,' the piano concerto, the 'Academic,' and the C minor symphony, are put down
for the concert.

N.B.—*Rooms only*, mind! Your most humble servant
will see to the tickets.

It really is worth while, particularly if you take a few days and hear some of the rehearsals. These fellows play quite excellently, and they have no conception of such rehearsing, such practising, at Leipzig. You have no idea what pleasure it would give yours etc., to see you there.

Kindest regards to your trio-composer,* and perhaps you may find a word to say to yours etc.,

J. Br.

From November 20th to 22nd: Stuttgart, Hotel Marquardt.


### 97. *Elisabet von Herzogenberg to Brahms.*

[LEIPZIG] *November*, 1881.

The practice of self-denial is supposed to be salutary, and I must seek comfort in that; for I cannot go to Meiningen, and I am going to tell you frankly why! We have to be particularly careful over what we spend just now at the end of the year, for what with my 'battle of Jena' and the dreadful long journey to my mother in Venice, we have spent such a lot already.

I am skimping my poor people and must skimp myself, and deny myself the greatest, the best, most beautiful treat I could ever have. I need not assure you at great length how hard it hits me. You know me, and you know how I should appreciate hearing my most-beloved music so delicately treated, when I usually hear it done in a rough, slovenly fashion. But, as I said, one must be firm with oneself on occasion, when reason demands it. Heinrich can't resist it, however; he can do a short stay cheaply, as

---

* Herzogenberg.

he is only one, and it will be almost half as good as going, to hear all about it from him, and to think of him there. But I do claim a little sympathy, for mine is assuredly no small sacrifice.

But let me thank you for writing, and for really caring, as it seemed, for us to come. That is dear of you, and my only request is that you will think of me a wee bit in the particularly beautiful parts—for instance, at the end of the first movement of the C minor,* where those yearning chords come on the B flat minor beats.

Just so will your only half-resigned E. H. yearn on the 27th.

### 98. *Brahms to Elisabet von Herzogenberg.*

[VIENNA, *November* 18, 1881.]

Many thanks for your kind letters. What must be will be! But I should think twice before letting my husband go off alone. You could make up for it by economy somewhere—about New Year, for instance !†

Kindest regards in any case from a poor

TRAVELLER.

### 99. *Brahms to Elisabet von Herzogenberg.*

[VIENNA, *December* 26, 1881.]

I wish I could have announced my arrival at the Palmbaum or at your house, but it would not come in

---

* The C minor symphony. See full score, p. 25, bars 13-15.

† The economy to be practised on the occasion of his own proposed visit to them.

time. I may turn up before this post-card, in the small-hours, when even a poet has turned in—or is not yet up. Take the precaution to read the police news these days anyway. . . . I may have been charitably run in!—Your poor

J. BR.

### 100. Elisabet von Herzogenberg to Brahms.

[LEIPZIG] *January* 3, 1882.

MY DEAR HERR DOKTOR,—Here are the desired bird-notes.* If you had not left definite orders, I should really be ashamed to send you such discreditable stuff, although, looked at in a humorous light, it has its charm. Hanslick's cordial words were so refreshing after it. My dear father sent me his critique this morning as the 'best New Year's greeting,' and I have just read it properly. I could almost envy the man his power of expressing himself, if not exhaustively, yet with an intuitive sympathy, which not only provides an outlet for his own feelings but helps others who have no command of words to express theirs. I am one of the most helpless, and my Heinz another. How often do we stand dumb and miserable before you, seeking comfort in the thought that you must know whether we have the right sounding-board for

* The Leipzig press notices. One of the critics was named Bernhard Vogel (=Bird), hence perhaps the expression. He wrote for the *Leipziger Neuesten Nachrichten*, and is the author of a monograph on Brahms. The *Musikalisches Wochenblatt*, edited by Fritzsch, which had championed Brahms warmly from the first, was obliged to admit that the attitude of the public towards Brahms's new compositions (he had played his concerto and the two rhapsodies, Op. 79, on New Year's Day) was rather apathetic than encouraging. 'One can hardly say,' ran the notice, 'that the *Gewandhäusler* showed any particular appreciation of their guest's importance in general, or of his new work in particular.'

your music in our hearts, and the right reverence for its author.  But it does seem sometimes as if you were hardly conscious of it, as if it wanted putting into words. . . . Your clumsy friends have their worst moments then.

You were rather harsh with Madame de Herzogenberg recently, and she had neither sufficient wit nor nerve to hide the fact that she was hurt.  I ought to be sorry, but it is my weakness to imagine that you may remember the incident with the same kind leniency as that of the Ischl dog, who—more sensitive than myself—could never forget that blow, while I am already comforted by the attitude with which my imagination credits you.

Besides, we should be quite too badly in your debt if you did not occasionally need forgiveness yourself!

God bless you for your good deeds, and may you be very, very happy now that you are entirely with people who, Hanseatic* as they are, know how to appreciate you, though few can do it so thoroughly as your ever-grateful old                    HERZOGENBERGS.

101. *Elisabet von Herzogenberg to Brahms.*

[LEIPZIG] *March* 11, 1882.

MY DEAR FRIEND,—I happened to take up your letter†
again, and find, to my horror, that you propose to come
on the 17th.  But the Brahms-concert‡ is next Tuesday,

---

* Brahms had gone to Hamburg from Leipzig to play his new concerto there on January 6.

† The letter is missing.

‡ The 'Brahms-concert' was the second of three concerts given at Leipzig by Bülow with the *Meininger Kapelle*.  On this occasion he conducted the C minor symphony and the orchestral variations on a Haydn theme, and played the pianoforte concerto in D minor.

the 14th, so do, for Heaven's sake, be here! Bülow will surely have set you right in the meantime, but I will send off these lines for greater safety.

How we are looking forward to seeing you!—Your faithful

HERZOGENBERGS.

In Bülow's Mendelssohn-Schumann concert, Schumann was represented by the *Hermann und Dorothea* and *Messina* overtures, and the *Phantasie* for violin—to us an inexplicable selection.*

### 102. *Brahms to Elisabet von Herzogenberg.*

[VIENNA, *March* 13, 1882.]

Your letter is a welcome intimation that B.† is not counting on me, or he would certainly have notified me of the change.

If he had, I think I should have come to listen to all three concerts, taking trips to Weimar and Jena in between. I had all sorts of plans!—In haste, yours,

J. BR.

### 103. *Elisabet von Herzogenberg to Brahms.*

[LEIPZIG] *March* 15, 1882.

MY VERY DEAR FRIEND,—I must lose no time in telling you how splendid it was yesterday. I have never heard your things done like that before. The only time we have a glimpse of their real effect is when you conduct a first performance; any subsequent performances are listless, mechanical readings. But even

---

* Bülow's object was to overcome what he considered to be an unwarranted prejudice against the works of Schumann's latest period.

† Bülow.

when you are there, what can you get out of such
short rehearsals? This time there was beauty of
sound to satisfy the senses, while every feature was
brought out with due effect. Above all, there was a
glow of genuine enthusiasm over the whole, sufficiently
infectious to cause even a Gewandhaus audience to
relax. Do you know, they quite lost their heads at the
end of the C minor! The din was so great that we
had to ask ourselves if that were really the Gewandhaus with the same people sitting there. The fact is,
there was *not* the usual preponderance of prim, tiresome
femininity, barely out of its teens; but fresh, young,
listening faces and older ones who cannot get into the
Gewandhaus ordinarily were there, all under a spell
that deepened with every number, all attention from
head to foot, smiling happily at this or that point—in
a word, so charming and sympathetic that one felt like
kissing some of them. As the Allegretto* in A flat
received comparatively little applause, Bülow promptly
repeated it. Then came the deluge! Oh, how happy
we were in our corner: Ethel,† we three, the enthusiastic Reuss,‡ Bezold and the Engelmanns, the Wachs,§
and old Frau Holstein!‖ We made a heathenish noise,
my brother¶ shouting *encore* at the finish like one
possessed, though whether he wanted the whole
symphony or only the last movement repeated he
refuses to say. We were just like children, and all
felt we had come into our own at last. Bülow has

---

* The third movement of the symphony.

† Miss Ethel Smyth.

‡ Heinrich XXVI., Prince of Reuss-Köstritz (b. 1855), a well-known
composer, pupil of Herzogenberg.

§ Adolf Wach (b. 1843), a famous jurist, Mendelssohn's son-in-law,
had been Professor at Leipzig University since 1875.

‖ Hedwig von Holstein.              ¶ Ernst von Stockhausen.

never impressed me as he did last night. The accompaniment to the D minor concerto was literally perfect, and I heard many of my favourite bits properly brought out for the first time. On the other hand, I remembered how differently a certain person played the piano part. I thought Bülow's interpretation of the F major subject in the first movement lacked simplicity, breadth, and fervour. I always felt those crescendos and diminuendos miles ahead, whereas the orchestra, to a man, gave a complete impression of spontaneity. His technique was colourless, too ; he does not play the chain of octave-trills half as loudly or as well as you. I thought him best in the Adagio. On the whole, he certainly appealed to us yesterday; we thoroughly enjoyed it. His genuine, unreserved devotion to your music was so evident, and, alas ! so unusual a thing here, that we felt as if we were among friends again after living with strangers. For you know (though I can't resist repeating it) that your music is as indispensable to our existence as air, light, and heat. You can't think how glad we are not to have to give the dead masters all our affection and enthusiasm, and how glad that the one to whom we already owe so much still lives and labours, and is, we hope, neither inaccessible nor quite indifferent to us. Yesterday, when the horn first rang out in the last movement, it seemed as if you were sending us a glorious greeting from afar. You, poor thing, can never be a mere listener to music. You are really to be pitied.

Bülow enjoyed himself greatly yesterday, one could see, but was much taken aback by your absence. We did not tell him before the concert that it was his own fault, for fear of exciting him, and afterwards had no opportunity We had just time to thank him, and saw him no more that evening, as he had visitors.  So we drank your health instead with the Kirchners, the Wachs, the fat one and Ethel, in our little room, and you would have realized from some of the remarks that went flying about that your music takes deeper and deeper root in all our hearts.  The Wachs are real devotees, too.  The fat one—that is, my brother —sends word that it was only the fear of intruding, when you were so surrounded, that kept him from saying good-bye to you at the *Tonkünstlerverein.*  In spite of his size, he is always making himself small figuratively, dear, modest fellow.  But now good-bye. Heinz would like to embrace you if you will allow him. He was so happy yesterday.—Ever yours,

E. H.

The staccato passage which comes before the lovely B flat minor in the coda of the first movement* was amazingly effective, sharp and clean-cut as we never heard it here.  The pizzicato ♩♩♩ immediately after the second subject was capital, too.†  The energetic passages were indeed wonderfully worked out all through, if I except the fabulous roaring-lion basses after the *stringendo* in the introduction of the last movement.  You forced them out so magnificently, while he did not exert half enough pressure.  The *stringendo*

---

* In the C minor symphony.

† This is a mistake.  The particular passage (p. 11, bar 2 of the full score) has this figure—

brought first by the violas, marked *col arco,* while the other strings give a *pizzicato* chord.

itself was superb. I longed for our own oboist in the Adagio, for his sustained G sharp* is quite another thing, and he plays more artistically altogether. But the Meininger clarinettist is great !†

### 104. *Brahms to Elisabet von Herzogenberg.*

[VIENNA, *March* 18, 1882.]

Just a word of thanks to you and the dear ' Miss.'‡ I shall try and revenge myself as well as I can on you both for your kind letters before long.—Kindest regards,

J. BR.

### 105. *Brahms to Herzogenberg.*

[VIENNA, *March* 21, 1882.]

DEAR FRIEND,—May I make a small *(mf)*§ demand on your kindness? Härtels have asked for my subscription for the twenty-seventh annual set of the *Bach Ausgabe* (1877),‖ before sending me cantatas 131 to 140. I have the cantatas 121 to 130, but not the thematic index or the last volume (iv. ?) of chamber-music (violin and violoncello).

Are the two volumes in the twenty-seventh set (1877)? I have no record of them in the bound volumes. The *Art of Fugue* and the *Choral Vorspiele* are there ; I hope there is nothing else missing. . . .

Would you mind paying five *thaler* for the current

---

* P. 29 of the full score.

† Richard Mühlfeld, the famous clarinettist, for whom Brahms afterwards composed his various chamber pieces with clarinet.

‡ Miss Ethel Smyth.

§ Brahms had a particular affection for *mezzo-forte* effects.

‖ The standard critical edition of Bach, published by Breitkopf and Härtel.

year, and if required another five for the last but one,
and having the volumes forwarded to me immediately?

Please don't be angry, and don't let your wife and
the dear 'Miss' be angry at my answering their nice
letters in such a way.

But I am probably coming myself soon. I have to
conduct my Requiem at Hamburg on Good Friday, and
expect to look in on you on the way home.

How about a little journey at Easter? I should like
a few days at Weimar and Jena. If you would come,
too, and prowl round with me a few days, it would be
quite delightful, by Jove! and much better than Humboldtstrasse, which could still be taken on the way.
Send me just a line.—Yours,               J. Brahms.

### 106. *Herzogenberg to Brahms.*

DRESDEN, *March* 25, 1882.

MY VERY DEAR FRIEND,—The enclosed receipt will
convey the sad assurance that you really owed for the
twenty-seventh series. I probed as far as the company's
ledger, and established the fact beyond a doubt. I
suggested to the treasurer that they might send you
the publications annually, to be paid through the post
at your end without waiting for your member's subscription. He is quite willing, and is only waiting for
your authorization. You might entrust me with that
too; then I shall perhaps be the gainer by another nice
little note like the last.

We are here for a few days (until Tuesday) with our
brother Ernst.* We might even hear Reinthaler's
*Kätchen†* if we went to the theatre, which is very

* Ernst von Stockhausen.

† *Kätchen von Heilbronn*, prize opera of the year (1881), by Karl
Reinthaler.

doubtful! We travelled in the same carriage with Reinthaler without knowing it, until he introduced himself at Riesa by turning to my wife and announcing with great firmness : 'You are Frau von Herzogenberg; I am Reinthaler. You got in at Leipzig, and mentioned the name Brahms in the course of conversation, which is quite enough for me.' So much notice did we attract!

As to the Easter prowl, neither could we imagine anything more delightful, though the how and where and whether would have to be discussed of course. For the present we shall count on your visit to Humboldtstrasse, all of us down to Fanny, Ponto, and our 'Miss.' Liesel is just writing to Epstein, who proposed a visit to us at Easter last autumn in Vienna. As soon as we hear anything definite from him we will write again. Perhaps you could come to us *before* going to Hamburg in any case ? How's that? Or do you feel like playing duets with Epstein at our house?

Kindest regards from us both and a request for a post-card, if possible before we leave (Kurfürstenstrasse, 27).—Always yours sincerely,

HERZOGENBERG.

## 107. *Elisabet von Herzogenberg to Brahms.*

[LEIPZIG] *April* 6, 1882.

DEAR FRIEND,—It is very sad—Epstein is coming! I don't mean, of course, the fact that he is coming, for I am very glad, but that it could not be a little later, so that we could have our nice little spring outing. Our lament is a three-part canon! I enclose a miserable photograph of the head of Feuerbach's charming Madonna, just to show my good-will. I wanted to give you some idea of this beautiful picture which you never saw, but the stupid Dresdeners could produce nothing better.   But I am very backward in thanking you for the happy twenty-four hours you gave us. How can I tell you what such an evening with your songs means to us!*   You can't imagine what it is to sit, and dip, and sip at the fountain-head, indulging oneself to the full in unvarnished delight—or can you, I wonder ?

Excuse this hurried, scrappy note, but I have a visitor in my room in the shape of a snuff-taking old aunt, a Holsteiner all over, who discourses so worthily between the pinches that it is impossible to write.

I know someone who would be happier listening to-morrow† than you conducting, for it is all 'stuff' to you!   Think of me when you come to *ewige Freude*. . . .‡

Epstein has not *quite, quite* definitely said he is coming.   If in the end he telegraphs 'Not coming,' we may after all telegraph 'Coming'. . . but on the whole you may be glad to be at the end of your pilgrimages.§

Heinz is at a charity board meeting, but instructed me to send every imaginable kind message.—With kindest regards, yours gratefully and sincerely,

E. HERZOGENBERG.

* Brahms had responded to the 'nice' letters by sending a parcel of songs to form a supplement to those sent before, and now published as Op. 84-86.

† At the performance of the Requiem in Hamburg.

‡ The close of the second part : '*Ewige Freude wird über ihrem Haupte sein.*'

§ In the original the writer rings the changes on the four different meanings of the expression *am Ende*, using it to express 'in the end,' 'after all,' 'on the whole,' and 'at the end,' respectively.—TR.

108. *Brahms to Elisabet von Herzogenberg.*

[VIENNA, *April*, 1882.]

MY DEAR FRIEND,—I hope you still have my song, *Therese?*\* I should be particularly pleased if you could honestly give your approval to the following version:

Du milch-jun-ger Kna-be, wie schaust du mich an,

and

al-le Rats-herr'n in der Stadt und al-le Wei-sen der Welt.

One version is as old as the other, though not, perhaps, so simple to sing. But although this one has been more generally copied and sung, I cannot get used to it, and am puzzled to know what to do.

Sing the song through again, both of you, and let the poor youth languish at the piano meanwhile; then send me a line.—Yours most sincerely,

J. BR.

109. *Elisabet von Herzogenberg to Brahms.*

[LEIPZIG] *April* 26, 1882.

MY VERY DEAR FRIEND,—With the best will in the world, I cannot take to the old-new version, and Heinrich feels the same about it. I should feel quite sad if you insisted on it. The simpler form

\* Op. 86, No. 1.

seems to me to go much better with the counterpoint
on the piano than the other jagged version, and to be
much more in keeping with the song, where clear
diction matters far more than voice display. Just try
singing to yourself, in the light manner that suits the
piece, that jump to the octave below! Is it not clumsy
compared with the simple repetition of the three
notes?

I do beg you won't meddle with the dear little song
any more, but rest satisfied with the simpler version.

When can we have another look at all the beloved
songs? We are probably going to Frankfurt in May
to dear Frau Schumann (I have begged off Jena!),* and
it would be glorious if we could try your new ones
with Stockhausen.† I am always thinking of the
F major,‡ and preferably in connection with Stockhausen, who is, after all, the only one to sing it. This
part—vaguely as it is outlined in my memory—

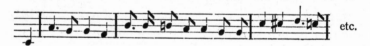 etc.

tugs at my very heart-strings.

. . . But I must stop. Remember us to the dear
kind professor,§ whose visit we enjoyed so much.
What a splendid creature he is! You must tell him he
made several conquests here. Good-bye, dear friend
and Doktor. Where shall you go this summer?—
Ever your devoted friends,

ELISABET AND H. H.

* She was to have gone there for another course of treatment for
her heart trouble (cf. Letter 87).

† Julius Stockhausen had settled at Frankfurt to teach singing
in 1878.

‡ *Feldeinsamkeit*, Op. 86, No. 2.            § Epstein.

110. *Brahms to Elisabet von Herzogenberg.*

[ISCHL, *May* 15, 1882.]

Here it is, then, with my kindest regards,* but I must really see the name printed on a title-page, or how am I to know it?

I am at Ischl, and the weather is horrible—appalling! It rains (or snows) incessantly: *schwarz ist das Kraut und der Himmel nur erst!*† There is a stove in this room (lighted, too!) and I must have one put in the other.

And this is Ischl—on the 15th of May!

All is well with the 'milk-white youth'‡—that is, according to your wishes. I could let you have the songs now, but you are not going to Frankfurt after all, but to Halle. And where next? not to Berchtesgaden, of course? That would be too near to me, eh? What about Bayreuth? I am meditating it, though I am convinced that we shall have *Parsifal,*§ at any rate, in various places next winter.

---

* The letter accompanied an autograph promised to Miss Ethel Smyth. Frau Herzogenberg's letter containing the request is missing.

† Quotation from the song *Über die Heide,* Op. 86, No. 4, in which the last words actually read: *und der Himmel so leer.*

‡ *Cf.* Letter 109, 110, the song quoted.

§ Wagner's *Parsifal* received its first performance at Bayreuth in July, 1882. The work was to be Bayreuth's monopoly, as is well known. Brahms often regretted never having been there. In the summer of 1882 he writes to Bülow: 'The fact that I cannot come to a decision about Bayreuth probably means that I am unable to produce that "yes." I need hardly say that I go in dread of the Wagnerians, who would spoil my pleasure in the best of Wagners. I don't know yet what I shall do. I may take advantage of my beard, which still allows me to trot about so nice and anonymously.'

51 Salzburgerstrasse.\* Write that down now on
a few envelopes, and send one occasionally to yours
very sincerely,
                                                J. BRAHMS.

### 111. *Elisabet von Herzogenberg to Brahms.*

[LEIPZIG] *May* 18, 1882.

MY VERY DEAR FRIEND,—Many thanks for your kind
promptitude. I, the petitioner, and Ethel *Smyth*, the
favoured one, are both greatly touched by your kindness. But where did you gain this fabulous experience
in writing letters of introduction? Such elegance and
finish—you might be a Frenchman! . . . a far cry
from your usual self.†

But please don't get it into your head that I am going
to Halle (by which you again mean Jena). I told you
I was let off, and that we were going to Frankfurt.
After that we have one duty after another to pay off—
a visit to Heinrich's family in Bohemia, and another to
the poor invalid W. at Graz. Then we may relax for
a brief space in some little corner of the mountains,
probably in Carinthia or the Tyrol as being the nearest.
If you still had your abode at Pörtschach, we should of
course make you a visitation; but Ischl!—really providence seems bent on upsetting our nice summer
plans.

Until Whitsuntide any communication here will find
us. I hope you were not teasing me about the songs?

---

\* Brahms's summer home at Ischl in 1880 and 1882, and from
1889 to 1896 (*cf.* Victor von Miller's *Brahmsbilderbuch*, pp. 98, 101.

† As Brahms had said in his letter that he must see the name
Ethel Smyth printed on a title-page before he could be supposed to
remember it, Frau von Herzogenberg jestingly assumed that he
intended an indirect recommendation of the coming composer to
publishers.

If you were, I only hope your 'blackened vegetation' and 'blacker skies' will persist.

Ethel sends kind remembrances. Do you know she is going to begin and work on her own next winter, in Florence, where you may perhaps meet. She imagines she can finish all her fugues on the dominant there un-rebuked. I am very curious to know how she will get on. One good thing is that she will not hear too much Brahms.

But good-bye, and let something penetrate to us from your winter-quarters, which are doubtless very cosy, and will be productive of many beautiful things.

ELISABET HERZOGENBERG.

112. *Elisabet von Herzogenberg to Brahms.*

WERNSDORF BEI KAADEN,*
*July* 13, 1882.

MY VERY DEAR FRIEND,—You know from experience that, try as one will, it is sometimes impossible to get any letters written. . . . It was so nice and comfortable at Frankfurt in Frau Schumann's grand new house. We much enjoyed our week there. It was too charming to see her in her professional capacity, as, with flushed cheeks, she brought forward her best pupils to play to us—severe and lenient, teacher and mother by turns, as she listened. I could not help thinking to myself: 'How nice to be born again and become her pupil!'

I shall never forget an evening at Stockhausen's, when he sang *Dichterliebe*† to Frau Schumann's accom-paniment. It was all so fresh and spontaneous. I

* A town in North-Western Bohemia.
† Schumann's song-cycle.

11

had never heard him do that particular cycle, and was quite carried away at times by his profound sincerity and vigour. . . . There was a princess, about whom I had grave qualms; but I believe I am easily pre-judiced by a powdered nose in conjunction with a pince-nez. When she went up quite close to Frau Schumann in a confidential way, I thought of Eglantine and Euryanthe, and really suffered tortures; while to see Euryanthe rub her hands, and ward off the other in her touching manner, was as good as a theatre.

Of course we called on the Dessoffs,* and I can only say: How can a Saxon become such a northerner? What an age it takes, invariably, for any two people to come out of their shells! They meet as *Kapellmeister* and Mr. So-and-so, or as anything their particular place in the world causes them to represent, and the commonplaces and deliberately impersonal remarks that pass between them are heart-breaking. Only children are genuine. I was enchanted with your little godchild Johannes,† who, when I beckoned him to sit beside me on the sofa, said firmly but prettily: 'No, I am not tired.'

But you must be by now, and I will say good-bye. Perhaps you will favour us with a few lines at Bestwie, Schloss Bestwie, Post Bestwie, Bohemia, where we shall be the coming week. We hope to be at Graz on July the 1st, Körblergasse 32.

Why have your songs not come? Do please send them *as soon as possible*.—Kindest regards from your faithful                              HERZOGENBERGS.

* Otto Dessoff (1835-1892), formerly conductor of the Vienna Philharmonic, was appointed first conductor of the *Stadttheater* at Frankfurt in 1881.

† Dessoff's little boy.

113. *Elisabet von Herzogenberg to Brahms.*

GRAZ, KÖRBLERGASSE 32,
*July* 24, 1832.

MY VERY DEAR EIGHTY-SIXTH!*—It is not often that
I have three books of new Brahms songs in the house
for five days without sitting down to thank the kind
donor.  I value the collection all the more for the fact
that it gives me a chance of meeting all my old friends
again.  For I am just like the mother of 'Naz' in the
dear Lower-Austrian poem, who looks forward to
heaven because she will meet all the people who have
gone before.  'They will all know us at first sight, and
Naz will be the most beautiful of them all.'  Well, I
know all these at sight, and know them thoroughly;
for I have refreshed my knowledge of those I knew
superficially, while the half-understood ones now speak
with greater conviction, as for instance the *Nachtwandlerlied,*† which has only just dawned on me.  I am
particularly fond of the ending, '*Wie vom Licht des
Vollmonds trunken,*' with its beautiful creeping accompaniment on the G, and the crescendo in the voice ; then
the rise in the music at '*Weh den Lippen, die ihn riefen,*'
and the way it sinks back into the $\frac{6}{4}$ figure of the first
part, which, in its dissatisfaction, seems made for this
haunting song.  The richness of it all, in combination
with its perfect simplicity, is what delights me.

But I am insatiable in my affection for *Feldeinsamkeit.*‡  How your soul must have rejoiced when
that first line came to you, which captivates us so
promptly and charms our ear by its perfect pitch,
bathing us in its warm, soft flow !  How you must

---

* The last of the three books of songs is numbered Op. 86.
† *Nachtwandler,* Op. 86, No. 3.  ‡ Op. 86, No. 2.

have revelled in the lovely modulation into D flat
major, too, at ' *tiefe Träumen* '—for I hope you do enjoy
these little master-touches — and in the return to
C major, which is achieved so quickly, and yet so
gently, with time even for a lingering caress! I am
fonder of *Todessehnen* than ever, but I am less willing
to submerge myself in *Versunken** on account of the
forked lightning character of the voice part. The
eighty-fifth book brings all the good old times back
again, and I think of the secret rummaging in drawers
at Pörtschach (what a pity you are no longer there!
we could have come over so easily from here) as I
look on the old songs in their new garb. *Waldein-
samkeit†* is another inspiration such as you don't have
every day—I question whether it is not the finest in
all three books—the sort that makes one unconsciously
hold one's breath to listen ; a glorious thing, full of
lofty emotion, and yet so human in its appeal, born as
it is of deep personal experience. The man who can
listen to it dry-eyed is surely past saving! The little
ones for one or two voices, *ad libitum*, are the
winningest little rogues.‡ How innocent they are!
It is like looking into the faces of children—well-
brought-up children, such as, say, Schubert's or
Beethoven's might be. I can hardly imagine anything
prettier or daintier than the lines of the mother's
melody in *Sommerabend*,§ and the repetition of that
one line of the words. How ingeniously that part
finishes, too! I delight in every little stroke, as if
it were a fine old engraving—by Dietrich,‖ say, in
whose work art and strong natural emotion are as

* Op. 86, No. 5.           † Op. 85, No. 6.
‡ *Romanzen und Lieder*, Op. 84.     § Op. 84, No. 1.
‖ C. W. Dietrich, painter and etcher of the eighteenth century.

indistinguishably blended. Perhaps the *Beerenlied** is
even more lovable, in the gay insouciance of its modulation to E flat minor (that chameleon-like key with
its D♯, so perplexing at the first reading!), and the
calm way in which it sidles into B major. I also take
some pleasure in the delicate quaver accompaniment
at the first mention of the 'beloved,' which is so
charmingly extended, the second time, to suit the
'ripe red kisses,' and the sudden and very convincing
return to luminous E flat major. Ah yes, the privileged master-hand can carry us at full speed, as
unconscious of our actual movements as a beautiful
deer in flight; whereas the less supple runner makes
us pant and puff in a piteous way. *Spannung†* I find
strangely touching. '*Du sollst mir Antwort geben, mein
Engel,*' is so urgent, so sweetly persuasive. The words
are so beautiful there, and the A major at the close—
and the fond union of the voices—is so exactly after
my own heart; indeed, it goes straight to my heart.
And so as usual I may close by thanking you sincerely,
dear Friend, for is it not the things which appeal to the
heart that make life worth living?

I wonder if you will favour me with a few lines,
averse as you seem to writing this summer! I should
so like to have some idea what you are doing, and
whether you are thoroughly enjoying your two
stoves. What a succession of lovely days! We are
quite languid from this perpetual 22 degrees in the
shade. I can only exist by bravely ignoring the heat,
in which I scribble my six hours a day at Italian. I
have at last followed your wise example,‡ and am

* *In den Beeren*, Op. 84, No. 2.        † Op. 84, No. 5.
‡ Brahms was learning Italian to arm himself for further travels in
Italy.

labouring at this cruelly beautiful language, which makes one long to be at the summit while still fumbling at the foot of the ladder. However, I already know a few Tuscan proverbs, one of which I will quote, because it will both bring grist to your wicked mill and serve to excuse me for sending nothing better than a gossiping epistle by way of thanks for your songs: *Le parole sono feminine e i fatti sono maschi!* \*

Now I will say good-bye—with just one request. When you write, please tell me about poor Faber.†  I saw him at the end of July in Vienna, and was horrified; he looked so much worse than I expected. I should like to know your opinion of him and Billroth's report, for doctors hardly ever tell us women the truth.

Poor dear fellow! It went to my heart to see him such a wreck. I only hope he does not see the secret dread with which we examine him. No news from St. Moritz, unfortunately.‡

And now farewell. We are here until August the first, after which we shall potter about in the Tyrol and wind our way gradually to Venice, where I hope the Lido may be merciful. My mother writes, by the way, that it is not at all hot there. Heinz sends messages and messages, and is sending the psalm§ in print. We have both enjoyed it so much.—As ever, your grateful and devoted

E. Herzogenberg.

---

\* From Giuseppe Giusti's *Raccolta di proverbi Toscani*, p. 126 ('Words are [in Italian] of the feminine, deeds of the masculine gender'), or, more accurately, *Le parole son femmine e i fatti son maschi* ('Words are women, deeds are men').

† Arthur Faber, their mutual friend, was dangerously ill.

‡ From Frau Schumann.

§ Psalm cxvi. for mixed chorus *a capella*, Op. 34.

114. *Brahms to Elisabet von Herzogenberg.*

[ISCHL, *July 27*, 1882.]

I am sending you a little ditty* which will be a more satisfactory immediate expression of thanks than a letter. It rather hopes to earn another letter! You will be sure to send it back when you leave, on the first?

Meanwhile kindest regards and thanks. More next time.—Yours,                                    J. BR.

115. *Elisabet von Herzogenberg to Brahms.*

INNICHEN, GASTHOF ZUR SONNE,
*August 6*, 1882.

MY VERY DEAR FRIEND,—I am at last able to thank you properly both for the loan of the quintet and for the dear, lovely thing itself, which has already given me such pleasure, and will give me still more this winter if we hear it at Leipzig. I feel sure we shall, for since Father Röntgen† made such a sensation with the G major sextet at the *Kammermusik* that time, there is no holding him. True, the poor fellow will be in very low spirits after his trials this summer (his wife has been ill seven weeks with acute muscular rheumatism, and is only allowed up an hour at a time, smothered in cotton-wool); but I expect I shall be able to rouse him by playing him the first movement in October (what a blessing I got an accurate idea of it!), and the first *largo* in the second movement, which is one of the most overwhelming things I know. He may well envy the favoured 'cello and viola there,

* The quintet in F, Op. 88 (MS.).

† Engelbert Röntgen, leader of the Gewandhaus orchestra and of the quartet.

but his own turn comes in the A major movement, particularly in the variation.   How amazingly clever these
trios are—lively and gay, yet full of meaning!  This
part, too:

which dies away so charmingly !

But the short Adagio remains my first favourite.
It is so lovely that you are almost angry at being torn
away from it by the Allegretto just as you had lost
yourself in the solemnity of C sharp minor, and just
after that incomparable cadence:

$$\text{C}\sharp, \text{ A, D, G}\sharp, \text{ C}\sharp$$
$$\begin{array}{cc} 3 & 5\sharp! \\ & 3 \end{array}$$

And how beautiful this is !—

* The passage reads as follows in the score, p. 22, bar 6 :

particularly where the second violin takes up the
dying plaint of the 'cello:

What delighted me so particularly in the first movement was its transparency.  How grateful one is for
this lucidity of form, this unaffected loveliness, which
you treat strictly according to rule, and yet as if you
had yourself invented this particular form to suit it!
It is refreshing to see the framework exposed in such
bald, prosaic fashion.  The bridge-passage, especially
the motif you turn to such good account in the
development,

is so obviously leading up to something, and the
cleverly deferred cadence on the dominant

with the engaging false relation (F—F sharp) between
the second fiddle and viola in the second bar† gives
unmistakable warning of the new idea that is coming.

* Neither this passage nor the previous one is accurately quoted
(*cf.* p. 20 of the score, last four bars).

† See p. 11 of score.  All the musical quotations scattered about
the letters are from memory, the manuscript having been returned
before these notes were made.

And how beautifully it does come, on the viola! (Won't
Julius Röntgen have a good time!) I love the change
to F sharp minor, with the passionate rise to G sharp
and A on the viola.* Then the place where the fiddle
takes up the theme, and F sharp minor blossoms into
A major, while the second fiddle chimes in a third
below, is simply bewitching; nor is that luminous
touch of D major to be despised!

The development, which promises to be almost too
severe, has such charming surprises in the two interrupted cadences on E,†

and afterwards on G; and the triplets, which come
billing and cooing close on their heels, work up so
beautifully the second time to the pedal-note C on
their way home to the almost-forgotten F major.‡ The
old gay rhythm,

which breaks in upon the peaceful return of the principal
subject, is soon subdued to form a fitting accompaniment to the sober modulation to D flat.§ (You seem
particularly strong on modulations into D flat, Herr

Brahms!)  Then, after whirling through the keys to
the dominant on E flat,* it swoops down to the minor
ninth on C,† which ushers in the exciting final stage
of the working-out with its decisive and powerful
close.  (The final cadence—B flat minor, G flat major,
C major‡—is magnificent!)  There is just one note—
C flat—which puzzled me sadly in this bar:

It seems to clash so painfully with the F, which
marks the passage as distinctively major.  Please do
not be horrified at this audacious airing of my opinions.
You did ask me to write, you know, and the only way
is to do it as if—well, as if I were writing to anyone
but you, who must be unspeakably bored by a
description of what you know better than anyone.
But I shall not let you off the *coda* in the first movement, so please submit to being told how bewitching
it is.  It positively lulled me to sleep on the journey
from Graz with its charming swing.

But I have one great objection to raise (Heinrich and

1 breathed it simultaneously) : the two last 'time's up !'
*tempo primo* bars are very disturbing after that splendid dying elegy. It really is as if your pen, not you,
were responsible, as if you had done the conventional
thing without troubling yourself further. Why cannot the movement close in a subdued key? Why
this conventional 'rouser' to cut short a blissful
dream ? '*Weh den Lippen, die ihn riefen !*'* say I.

But take heart. Not a word of the last movement,
as I hardly know it at all. I could not master all
three in those few days (the greater part of the time
was devoted to my poor relatives and my neglected
Italian studies), so I had to make a selection. And
just this last movement wants hearing, I should say,
before one can take it all in. Also it is less lyrical in
character, and we women folk, if given the choice of
three movements, are sure to seize the lyrical ones.
Also it is the most difficult to play, and I must needs
choose that particular time to fall on my left thumb
with my full weight, and sprain the wretch badly.
Heinz derived some amusement from discovering a
certain similarity of structure and treatment between
this movement and the last of his trio in F. He was so
proud and pleased, for not only in the first subject,

but in the second, and in the way they blend, are there
traces of it.† He is to-day doing his first climb this
year, dear fellow. He got up at five, quite radiant, as

---

* Quotation from the *Nachwandler*, Op. 86.

† The resemblance was purely accidental, but Brahms was, as
a matter of fact, fond of appropriating other people's themes, partly
as a challenge to the critics, whose comments on their discoveries
always amused him.

my sleepy eyes could see, and left me in solitude with my correspondence and a sore throat which demands my attention every now and then. The harsh wind, combined with the dust I swallowed yesterday, may have given it me. My song is, not *Das Grab ist meine Freude*,\* but 'permanganate of potash is my delight.' It is very nice here. The air tastes good, and is scented with wild-thyme—I never sniffed anything so sweet—and the Dolomites light up gorgeously, while the rest and quiet are most refreshing. Our little inn, too, is excellent. The fare is good—I might almost say delicate—and everything is so cheap, one forgets to pay! I heard from Bertha Faber to-day. They break up on the 12th, and expect to be at Letto-witz on the 20th.† I do hope it is safe for him to go there; he will not be put off. Your message will find me here until the 12th. I am determined not to lose it, for you promised! You really must not mind my saucy chatter. You will at least glean that a beautiful thing like your quintet is not wasted on me when you send it. I did wrap up the manuscript on the 2nd, but there was none to take it into town (Körblergasse is country), so it wouldn't reach you until the 4th. If you sent me things oftener, I might learn to read your manuscript as fluently as a printed page.

A fond farewell, and thank you once more.—Yours,

ELISABET HERZOGENBERG.

### 116. *Brahms to Elisabet von Herzogenberg.*

[ISCHL, *August* 8, 1882.]

MY DEAR FRIEND,—It is really unfortunate that I am obliged to write at once, as it really cannot be done.

---

\* *Cf.* Letter 65.—TR.

† The estate of the Faber family.

I should have liked to thank you at leisure for your kind letters. As it is, I will only assure you that it is extremely pleasant and *necessary* to hear a genuine word of approval about a new piece. My best thanks are therefore due to you, and to your Heinz for looking through the third part. So it seems I copy him not only consciously, but unconsciously.* But shall I never shake off the theologian?† Here are all these new things going—and what comes my way? This Psalm, of course! I may add that I enjoyed it thoroughly, and heard in imagination a chorus singing it and rejoicing in its flow of melody. But—it always costs me a pang to take up a psalm so 'unheathenish.' I have just finished one which is actually heathenish enough to please me and to have made my music better than usual, I hope.

\*     \*     \*     \*     \*

But as this was not to be a letter, I have written enough. Turn over, and you will have the pleasure of seeing the very latest bridegroom.‡—Yours most sincerely,

J. BR.

I am not at all clear about Innichen (Innigen?). Does it lie at the entrance to the Ampezzo Valley, the village on the other side of the line?

* Brahms alludes to the liberty he had taken in *O schöne Nacht* (*cf.* Letters 15 and 19).

† Brahms really prided himself on his Biblical knowledge, in which he was a match for any theologian. He had always taken pleasure in hunting up 'godless' texts in the Bible. Nothing made him angrier than to be taken for an orthodox Church composer on account of his sacred compositions. His *Vier ernste Gesänge* (see Letters 275 and 277) are not the only protests he made.

‡ The note-paper bore a vignette of Bülow, who had been married to Marie Schanzer in July.

### 117. *Brahms to Elisabet von Herzogenberg.*

DEAR LADY,—Will you kindly make my excuses to 'Papa' Röntgen? I have only one copy of the score and parts,* and cannot spare them just now. My copyist is busy, too, or I would have them written out. In fact, it can't be done, much as I should like to think I had earned a smile from 'Mama'!

Having made the first plunge, I may now begin to swim! I found an alarming pile of letters here, and can write variations on the theme: 'I don't like giving concerts.' From Moscow and St. Petersburg to ——, they will all receive the same answer.

A parting smile for this friendly sheet; then I turn to the next.

I suppose Kirchner is still there, and will be?—Very kindest regards from

J. BR.

### 118. *Brahms to Herzogenberg.*

[FRANKFURT A/M., *December* 29, 1882.]

DEAR FRIEND,—I am just off to the concert. To-morrow I go straight to Vienna, where I am playing on the 4th, and I leave Amsterdam on the 13th! So I can only sigh a refusal to your engagement. I feel quite melancholy when I think of the fat fee! However, it's impossible this time. — Kindest regards. Yours,

J. BR.

* Of the Quintet in F.

119. *Brahms to Elisabet von Herzogenberg.*

[VIENNA, *April* 15, 1883.]

You will now be able to play the concerto on two pianos.* . . . I hope you won't mind my inflicting two copies on you to that end!

Many thanks for your very kind messages. The professor† did actually come!—Sincerely yours,

J. BR.

120. *Elisabet von Herzogenberg to Brahms.*

[LEIPZIG] *May* 5, 1883.

MY DEAR FRIEND,—In these new-German *Musik-verein* days,‡ it was comforting and refreshing to think of you and your coming birthday, and remind ourselves that we belong rather more to you than to the *Musik-verein*, stamped though we are with Riedel's order (V.M.), initials which are held to add distinction to even Wagner's list of honours. You may be glad to have escaped all that we have been through since the 3rd, from Dräseke's *Dies Iræ* by way of M. Vogel's and H. Zopf's songs, Russian symphonies and quartets§ to the introduction and the transformation business from *Parsifal*. Oh, I know there is occasional evidence of real talent and vigour (as in the Borodine symphony),

---

* The Concerto in B flat, in Brahms's own arrangement for two pianos, was published by Simrock at the end of the year 1882.

† Probably Professor Engelmann from Utrecht.

‡ A *Tonkünstlerversammlung* of the *Allgemeinen deutschen Musik-verein* was held at Leipzig from May 3 to May 6. Karl Riedel, one of the founders, had been president of the *Verein* since Brendel's death in 1868.

§ A string quartet by Rimsky-Korsakoff, and Borodine's Symphony in E flat.

but side by side with such atrocities, such amateurish-
ness, that it seems as if the new German *Musikverein*
had taken pattern by Busch's little remark at the
end of his St. Antony:

> ' Lots of great sheep are admitted, and so
> To one nice little pig they can hardly say no!'

One can't help getting angry, and feeling it a dubious
pleasure to hear your *Parzenlied*\* at such a concert.
Equal rights for all is an unfortunate principle applied
to art, for art is and always will be aristocratic. As we
listend to your *Parzenlied* in the rehearsal at the Crystal
Palace to-day, we felt much as if a Spanish grandee had
strayed into a tavern.

Wüllner sat next to us, and was some consolation, for,
naturally, we could not discuss your *Parzen* with the
*Meister.*† And so there were three noses glued to the
dear score, and three hearts thanking you, each in his
own way, but in good faith.

Nikisch‡ took a lot of trouble, and did all that anyone
could do at Leipzig, where the ladies of the chorus are
not much concerned as to whether they sing flat
or sharp, although they can look languishing, and sing
from memory with their arms folded. Certain passages
always sound out of tune, and just that heavenly
passage, 'And wait in vain,' did certainly wait in vain
for purity of intonation. But in spite of it, the actual
sound effect, which was the one thing we could not
imagine beforehand, gave it all the fascination of an
absolutely unknown work. Some places, which we had
had hard work to understand and like, from reading the

---

\* *Song of the Fates* for chorus and orchestra, Op. 89.

† Franz Liszt, who had been specially invited to the Festival.

‡ Arthur Nikisch (b. 1855), the famous conductor, at that time
first conductor of the Leipzig Opera.

12

score—for instance, the violent changes at *So stürzen die Gäste geschmäht und geschändet* (I was guilty of much heresy over that C minor and A minor, and the cruel place farther on at the word *tiefen !*)—seemed quite powerful and convincing when we actually heard them, and we gave in to the beautiful inevitable with a good grace.

But you are sure to have heard plenty about it, not to speak of your own consciousness of its value, and I will not dissect our enjoyment for your benefit, but merely thank you for the gift, and tell you how we felt in that pure air, that lofty region, after the very mixed odours of the new-German *Musikverein*.

We are at last sending the belated copy of Chodowiecki,* which I ferreted out after much trouble, the edition being completely sold out, as I told you. The little volume should have been your Christmas present, but you must please accept it as a small birthday remembrance now. Heinz sends greetings from the depths of his good, honest Middle - High - German heart. He has had quite enough of the new-Germans, and said the other day, after hearing the violin concerto (very sympathetically played by Brodsky):† 'His old brown overcoat is worth three hundred of that other crowd!' We are very tired, and long for *Waldeinsamkeit* and the B major mood (*Ich sass zu deinen Füssen*),‡ which the nightingales in the Rosenthal§ fail to conjure up.

* Probably Chodowiecki's *Travels, Berlin to Danzig, in* 1873, a facsimile reproduction.

† Dr. Adolf Brodsky, violinist, at that time Professor at Leipzig Conservatorium, now Principal of the Royal College of Music, Manchester.

‡ Op. 85, No. 6.

§ A wooded park just outside the town.—TR.

Good-bye. Bestow a little affection on us, and I should not mind having another sheet of music-paper covered with scribble, with eight pages of Strauss waltzes by way of wrapper!*

D'Albert† is in hospital with measles. That is what comes of

or ♭♩ ?

'It is all the same to us—
For what does it matter to us?
It matters nothing to us!'§

But all my feathers are stroked the wrong way this morning, and this festival is not favourable to letter-writing, so make a few excuses for

E. HERZOGENBERG.

## 121. *Brahms to Elisabet von Herzogenberg.*

[VIENNA, *May* 9, 1883.]

Many thanks for everything—except for the beautiful book, which you must allow me to consider as a loan. I propose to enjoy it thoroughly, and return it as your property when I come myself.

If I were not off to Cologne‖ in a couple of hours, I would write—and thank you—at greater length, and that *not* by crossing this card, but by taking another!— Yours,

J. BR.

* Brahms's way of sending an autograph.
† Eugen d'Albert (b. 1864), famous pianist and composer.
‡ The opening of Liszt's Concerto in E flat, which D'Albert played on the second day of the Festival.
§ A Viennese street-song.
‖ Brahms played his B flat concerto and conducted his second symphony there at the Sixtieth Lower Rhine Festival (May 11-15).

### 122. *Brahms to Herzogenberg.*

[WIESBADEN, *May* 20, 1883.]

I have lighted on incredibly nice quarters at *Wiesbaden, Geisbergstrasse* 19.\* It is really worth while, and in every way desirable, that you should come and inspect them. You will be filled with envy, but come all the same.

When are you taking your holiday, and where ?—Kindest regards from yours,

J. BR.

### 123. *Herzogenberg to Brahms.*

[LEIPZIG, *October* 1, 1883.]

MY DEAR FRIEND,—I have just addressed a letter of Limburger's to you, as well as I could, and cannot suppress the desire it has given me to write myself, especially as I know what is on the cards. Do please do it—come to Leipzig with your symphony. Limburger has probably sent you the programmes for this winter. You can choose any date that suits you. It would be nice, of course, if you conducted the *Parzenlied*, which is due on December the 6th, at the same time. We heard it at the festival in the spring in such remarkably slow tempo; very convenient for making its acquaintance, but hardly as it should be !

Or, if you would rather avoid Raff's *Tageszeiten*,† which is to be sung immediately after yours, you might come to us from Berlin, a geographical combination not to be despised in view of the exciting

---

\* Brahms finished his third symphony here in the course of the summer.

† Joachim Raff (1822-1882), composer. The *Tageszeiten* (Op. 209) is a cantata in four movements for chorus, piano, and orchestra.

season before us. Anyway, don't leave us poor hungry wretches here out of the reckoning, or say: *Du siehst, mein Sohn, die Zeit wird hier zum Raum,** which must mean something very bad, as I no more understand it than I do the witch's multiplication table.

If you do come, our spare room is at your disposal, not only here at Leipzig, as a matter of course, but also in the year '85 in our own little house at Berchtesgaden, parish of Königssee, land-register No. 110.

I can't believe—until I hear it from your own lips—that your enthusiasm for the Niederwald monument is leading you to settle in Wiesbaden for good,† in spite of the fact that you are not the composer of *Die Wacht am Rhein.* Is the great Croatian monarchy too much for you, with its leanings to Dvořák rather than to yourself, or—your ambition makes me giddy !— do you aspire to the directorship of the Wiesbaden Court Orchestra ? Please enlighten us. People here look upon us as a sort of Brahms-Wolff,‡ and we must be primed to answer their many inquiries promptly, or they will begin to think us pretenders— which we should not like !

So please send one of your model letters to Limburger to say you accept, and one of your short friendly notes to us to say you are coming and like the idea.—Your devoted

HERR—UND FRAU—ZOGENBERG.

* Quotation from *Parsifal* (*Zum Raum wird hier die Zeit*).

† Brahms's opponents had diligently spread the rumour of his leaving Vienna, which had arisen from a casual remark of his to the effect that it was becoming practically impossible for a German to live in Vienna. Count Taaffe's Czech policy was abhorrent to him.

‡ Hermann Wolff (1845-1902), the first concert agent, known as ' Concert Wolff.'

By the way, why have you written nothing for
Luther? You have only yourself to blame now if
you should have to listen to the Meinardus\* oratorio.
Meinardus acted prudently, and finished it in good
time, thirty years ago, while his colleague Beckmesser
did the printing and advertising in three weeks.
Bach's *feste Burg*† is also to be murdered in various
places. I had to employ a troop of copyists to meet
all the commissions I received. But I would rather
have that; for a noble joint, badly cooked, is not half
so unwholesome as very stale or very new rolls.

### 124. *Brahms to Herzogenberg.*

[WIESBADEN, *October* 3, 1883.]

Do you mind telling Herr Limburger that I have
just received both your letters, but am off to Vienna
in two hours, and shall not be able to collect my
calendar and my thoughts until I get there? Thanks
for your kind letter, and good luck to your house
(or castle) building enterprise and the happier time to
follow. And may the happy time last long enough to
bring illumination as to that profound (?) saying !‡—
Kindest regards to you and a few others, from yours,

J. BR.

### 125. *Elisabet von Herzogenberg to Brahms.*

LEIPZIG, *November* 24, 1883.

DEAR, DEAR FRIEND,—We should so like your cor-
roboration of the good news that you are coming in

---

\* Ludwig Meinardus (1827 - 1896), writer and composer. His
oratorio *Luther at Worms* had a considerable vogue on the occasion
of Luther's Fourth Centenary, celebrated throughout Protestant
Germany on November 10, 1883.

† Bach's Reformation cantata.

‡ The Wagner quotation in Letter 123.

February with the new symphony. You know who the chief rejoicers will be, so please send us a line to set our doubts at rest.

How about the *possibility* of studying the score a little beforehand ? I should enjoy it ten times as much, being unfortunately as slow as I am a fond listener. As Wüllner and Joachim are doing the symphony, one after the other,* I venture to think that an ordinary mortal might be able to lay hands on the score, even without the design of conducting it. But you would first have to allow it, then to put in a good word for me, with yourself or with someone else. Do be very nice and try to secure me this immense pleasure. I put it urgently at the risk of your thinking me too bold, for I always think modesty an unpractical thing in itself, and everyone is justified in expressing a vigorous wish occasionally. Besides, I feel I need some compensation for the long silence to which I was condemned last summer.

I hope you will bring a few songs or other trifles in your old brown overcoat pocket. That would be too delightful. I am longing for some new songs, because I like the old ones so very much, that is, more and more, and feel more courageous than usual about singing—which is so different from just reading— them. I made a feeble attempt at the *Regenlied* yesterday, but had to give it up, for it reduced me to tears.

We get a terrific amount of music here. If we went to hear everything, we should soon be in our graves, but we are very diplomatic. We had to go to the last Joachim quartet concert, though. They really play

* In Berlin. Joachim conducted it on January 4, 1884, while Brahms conducted it himself at Wüllner's concert shortly after.

like Bellini cherubs, their tone is so deliciously pure.
I only wish you could hear your A minor* played as
we heard it the other day.    You don't get that in
Vienna!  It sometimes seems impossible to imagine
you among all those sugary people until I remind
myself how little you care about hearing yourself at
all.  We could really do with a little more froth and
flavour in our orchestra here; it is so often too sober
and reserved for anything.   Yet your C minor† was
amazingly good, and will go splendidly in a year or
two, for the Leipzigers are even slower than I am.
The Scherzo—I mean the A flat movement—and the
finale were quite beautifully played the other day.
You could feel they were putting their heart into it,
not merely playing what was set before them.   We
were delighted with your Dutchmen,‡ who happened
to be there.   They were so rational in their opinions
that we found them quite refreshing, and were soon
on good terms.   We have had Grieg here for some
time.   What a charming, sensitive nature he has!
He has determination of character, too, which is so
rare that one can condone this sort of thing

more easily than in some others. . . .

* Quartet in A minor, Op. 51, No. 2.        † Symphony No. 1.
‡ Sillem and Koopmann by name, friends of Brahms from
Amsterdam, who were at Leipzig on a visit.
§ From the 'cello sonata, Op. 36.

But I must stop. Once more I beg you will not throw the first part of my letter into the waste-paper basket—I mean the gigantic inside one which we all carry for the things we want to forget. It means so much to me—and we ought all to help each other!

Let us hear something of you to make sure you still care about us a little.—With kindest regards, your devoted

HEINRICH AND ELISABET HERZOGENBERG.

Please remember us to Epstein and Faber. My husband will soon be sending a parcel of new things —'when'* you allow it. Abraham† is publishing a string quintet of Ethel's.‡ Please say whether you cannot stay a little longer this time. It would be such a fine chance for having some music. We have two such good new players, Petri§ and Brodsky, who are very anxious to play with you.

## 126. *Brahms to Elisabet von Herzogenberg.*

[VIENNA, *November* 29, 1883.]

DEAR LADY,—Accept my best thanks. I am only waiting until the promised parcel arrives to repeat them on the largest-sized note-paper. *If* I can, and *when* I can,‖ I shall be happy to send you my modest

---

* A deliberate use of 'when' for 'if' as a specimen of South German dialect.

† Of the firm Peters.

‡ Miss Ethel Smyth.

§ Henri Petri (b. 1856), pupil of Joachim and of Brussels Conservatoire, had been appointed leader of the Gewandhaus orchestra in 1882.

‖ The 'if' and 'when' are a protest against the 'when' in the preceding letter.

symphony.\* Not that your reasons have any weight with me—quite the reverse! You will master it in no time.—Always yours,

J. Br.

### 127. *Brahms to Elisabet von Herzogenberg.*

[Vienna, *December* 21, 1883.]

My very dear Friend,—Keeping a promise implies having made one. This I shall do as soon as I can, but to-day I will just write two lines of thanks for your parcel full of interesting things.

If I take them to the piano, I am transported to your nice comfortable rooms, and can distinctly hear your very sweet singing. But if, like a true German, I begin to grumble, a sudden alarm seizes me, and I think: 'Better be quiet; all that applies equally to yourself, and your music has such a dreadful bachelor ring into the bargain!' Some of the grumbling I shall be able to let off on Heinz without exposing myself too much. I feel most at home in your study, with the first two and last two of the duets. They must surely be your favourites, too?†

His music, or his way of writing, often reminds me of his charming rhymes, and, now that I remember, I particularly want you to save up all his Christmas verses this year for me to read.

I have suddenly decided to send you a few songs.

* 'Modest'—in reference to a quibble he had once had over the word with Frau von Herzogenberg, and also with a view to damping her expectations.

† Duets for soprano and tenor, with pianoforte accompaniment, Op. 38. Brahms specifies No. 1, *Die Waise;* No. 2, *Begegnung;* No. 8, *Äolsharfen;* No. 9, *Im Abendrot.* Herzogenberg named the new house he built for his wife at Heiden, on Lake Constance, after the last of these. She died before it was finished.

I hardly know whether to ask you to forward them to Simrock?*

Perhaps you will favour me with your candid opinion of them? I am also sending a very beautiful thing of Muffat's,† which you may not know. I now have the original edition, so do not need the copy.

Besides which I am asking Simrock to send you one of my very special favourites.‡ I can't get it here in its original garb (that is, language), and have never seen it at your house. If you should fail to share my enthusiasm, I shall be happy to tuck it under my arm and carry it off again in February.—With kindest regards, yours,
J. BRAHMS.

128. *Elisabet von Herzogenberg to Brahms.*

LEIPZIG, *January* 6, 1884.

DEAR FRIEND,—I am at last writing to thank you in due form for sending the songs, which we were so delighted to have. It is really too nice of you to think of such a thing in the thick of your winter campaign, even going to the trouble of tying up and addressing

* For the purpose of publication. They were the six *Lieder und Romanzen für vierstimmigen gemischten Chor, a capella,* Op. 93a.

† Georg Muffat (1645-1704), famous in his day as an organ composer. The *Passacaglia* in G was from his *Apparatus Musico-organisticus.* Brahms admired it very much, and had copied it out for his own use.

‡ Bizet's *Carmen,* for which Brahms had at first conceived a violent dislike, on account of its unconcerned mingling of tragedy and light comedy. But the French composer's wealth of melody, and his broad treatment of his subject, soon triumphed over Brahms's æsthetic scruples, and the consciousness of having been unjust (if only in thought) to an inspired musician helped to drive him to the other extreme. He never wavered afterwards in his love for *Carmen,* which even usurped the place of *Die weisse Dame* in his affections at ti mes.

the parcel yourself. But it is the fact of your remembering Humboldtstrasse (appreciative it undoubtedly is!) that most touched us. I will confess, in compliance with your request for a 'candid opinion,' that we do not like all the songs equally well. There are certain passages to which I cannot reconcile myself at all. Indeed, I aired my opinions as brazenly as any old carping critic, though I tore up all I had written in the end, for 'what does it matter to *you?* It matters nothing to you,' as, fortunately, I was able to see.

*Fahr wohl* is very graceful and pleasing, so are *Süsser Mai* and *Mädchen,** particularly the entries of the solo *Mädchen.* Taken all together, the gentler songs appeal most to me. Even in *Fahr wohl* there is one place which does not seem at all like you, but you will probably laugh, and bring me to reason. How I am looking forward to the good month February!

The symphony has practically robbed us of sleep. Everyone sends us cruelly gushing letters, describing it as grander and more perfectly lovely than its two predecessors, while we sit here holding our empty cup, and with no immediate prospect of seeing it filled. Joachim had it with him when he was playing quartets here, but was too conscientious to show it us! Fortunately, we only heard of it later, or we should have given him no peace. You can imagine how pleased we were that Joachim did a new quartet of Heinrich's, in Berlin and here. I wish you had heard it too, for, as one can always say with the old peasant woman : *Mettez-y votre main, il n'y manquera plus rien.†* It is

---

* *Lieder und Romanzen,* Op. 93*a*, Nos. 4, 3, 2.

† Herzogenberg's string quartet was published, together with the two earlier ones, by Rieter-Biedermann as Op. 42. The three are dedicated to *seinem hochverehrten Freunde* Johannes Brahms.

only when *you* approve of anything he does that Heinrich feels like my uncle, the *Geheimrat*, who woke in the night, and said to his wife: 'Rosa, I am "Your Excellency"'! (His new dignity dated from the day before.) Joachim was unusually simple and charming this time, and his two fine boys are so becoming to him! But a man's sons are indeed his best adornment! . . .

Once more many thanks for the songs (I may keep them until you come ?), also for the delightful Muffat and your very special favourite, who is in good hands with me. I have no quarrel with the music, but only with the horrible shock one receives on first seeing *Carmen*, and the tactlessness of springing that tragic ending on an unsuspecting audience tuned to comedy.*

Prince Reuss† passed through yesterday, and, although he is going to be married, took a keen interest in your exclusively 'bachelor' music,‡ to Heinrich's delight. I, meantime, was condemned to make an unfortunate pupil's life a burden to her.

I shall waste no New Year wishes on you, for you want nothing—or at worst a copyist who is a model of neatness; but our New Year wish for ourselves is that you may still spare us a little affection, and add much that is new to the old store.—Ever your faithful

HERZOGENBERGS.

---

* Her æsthetic instinct was not at fault, but she was too open-minded to reject the good with the bad.

† See Letter 103, note.

‡ See Letter 127.

129. *Brahms to Herzogenberg.*

[VIENNA, *January* 11, 1884.]

DEAR FRIEND,—So far as I know, you neither possess this book * nor know of it. I imagine it should interest you considerably, and enable you to forget the voluminous Böhme† with great speed. I shall enjoy going through it with you at Leipzig; it will be as good as a country ramble.

In about a week I hope to send you the too, too famous F major, in a two-piano arrangement, from Wiesbaden. The reputation it has acquired makes me want to cancel all my engagements.‡—Very sincerely yours,

J. BR.

130. *Herzogenberg to Brahms.*

MY VERY DEAR FRIEND,—Many thanks for the pleasant surprise. The book is delicious, and it is so good of you to think of me and take me in hand at all this distance. My conversion was an easier matter than you thought, for, compared with this sweet outpouring of melodies, Böhme's collection already seems to me more like a frozen ditch, which has first to be hacked

---

* An old collection of German volkslieder.

† Böhme's *Altdeutsches Liederbuch* (*cf.* Letter 62, note, and Kalbeck, *Life of Brahms*, i. 390).

‡ After the first performance of this symphony (No. 3 in F) in Vienna on December 2, 1883, a veritable triumph for the composer, various daily papers and periodicals had asserted that not only did it far outshine its predecessors, but also that it was the best thing Brahms had ever produced. Brahms was exceedingly annoyed by this extravagant and unjust praise, especially as it raised expectations which he thought could not be fulfilled. He conducted the symphony at Wiesbaden, where it had been written, on January 18, 1884.

before the poor little blossoms can be dug out of the mud.  Or shall I compare it to a naturalist's cabinet, in which the wretched little birds, preserved in arsenic, look at one so stupidly with their glass eyes ?  But we can decide this when we meet—that is, if we Herzogenbergs have room for a thought of anything but the all-famous F major!

By the way, should you have any objection to conducting the B flat concerto for little Julius Röntgen on that occasion ?  We should think it very graceful of you, as we can easily imagine the dear boy's delight. We are also endeavonring to include the Rhapsody, an overture, and a few songs and piano pieces by Brahms.  You need only give your blessing, and be very nice in making allowances for us all.  Then it will be a real festival for us and for the greater part of the audience, who are only waiting for a sign from above (Limburger, etc.) to render unto Cæsar that which is Cæsar's.

We cannot watch Engelmann's departure to Wiesbaden without a pang;* not that we grudge it him, Heaven knows; but we wish we could go too.

Oh, and please remember to send the two-piano symphony.  Prince Reuss made us crazy with a few fragments of it.  You yourself might come with it, or at least as soon as you possibly can.—With kindest regards from the impatient wife, your grateful

HERZOGENBERGS.

* Professor Engelmann had obtained a long leave on account of his health.

131. *Elisabet von Herzogenberg to Brahms.*

[LEIPZIG] *February* 11, 1884.

Ah, the bitter, bitter parting! We are in the act of
sending away our dear, dear symphony.* Yesterday
was Sunday, when the parcel should have been taken
to post before eleven o'clock, but I couldn't bear it!
It is really good of me to send it to-day, don't you
think, dear friend? Heaven has rewarded me for
keeping my promise, too, for I have managed to
commit the two middle movements to memory most
beautifully, and the first one very nearly. So I can
amuse myself endlessly with the treasure I have
stored, though the remainder bothers me sadly. It is
now my very best friend—the symphony—and the
giver of it a real benefactor.

Enjoy yourself thoroughly at Cologne† among these
enthusiastic folk, whose hearts go out to you; but without quite forgetting the handful of people in this cold-
blooded city who would willingly challenge all the
rest of your admirers put together.

And think of us to-morrow when the famous E flat
comes in in the first movement.‡ That passage will
live!

But there—one might run on for ever!—Your devoted

HERZOGENBERGS.

* Brahms had conducted the symphony on February 7 at the
Gewandhaus, after which Hermine Spiess sang Schubert's *Memnon*
and *Geheimes* to the orchestral accompaniment arranged by Brahms,
and several Brahms songs. On the day before, Brahms played his
violin sonata at the first concert of the new Brodsky quartet.

† Brahms conducted the symphony and the *Song of the Fates* at the
eighth Gürzenich concert on February 12.

‡ The romantic horn part, p. 24 of the score, bar 5.

132. *Herzogenberg to Brahms.*

LEIPZIG, *March* 24, 1884.

MY VERY DEAR FRIEND,—I feel very young and foolish to-day, in spite of my forty years, as I produce my *pensum* for your inspection. I am only thankful I need not attempt any justification, either for my pieces — which do not come into account — or for the dedication. That part of it is over.*

I should, however, like to take this opportunity of asking you to believe in my devotion to you, in my joyful appropriation of every one of your productions as a favour personal to myself. Indeed, I am no hypocrite; the light and warmth which you spread over the whole world would leave me cold did I not feel that you had reached this elevation for my sake, for my own insignificant personal happiness! And that makes you my *friend*, whether you will or no. You are so full of kindness to me.

Incidentally you light my own little path so lovingly that I hardly notice the twilight in which I ought to be blundering, but brave the light of day with a whole heap of things, such as these quartets. As they had the unusual good fortune to bear your name as a banner, I have conceived a positive respect for these my own children.

Do not resent my little speech, dear master. It is a loyal heart which interposes all this parable and hyperbole to screen its nakedness from you.

My wife, whose illness put an end to our Dresden

* The reference is to the three string quartets mentioned in Letter 128.

pilgrimage,* and—almost—to all the joy of my life, has at last taken a turn. We are even making plans for the future, though she will hardly be able to put her nose out of doors before the middle of April.

She sends the gayest messages, as convalescents are apt to do.—In unwavering devotion, yours,

HERZOGENBERG.

### 133. *Brahms to Herzogenberg.*

[VIENNA, *March* 28, 1884.]

DEAR FRIEND,—What a lot of good things at once— the good news of your wife and the dedication! I hardly know which pleases me more, the pieces dedi-cated or the dedication itself. Both have exceeded my anticipations, for I had looked forward to seeing my name on one quartet — and behold it is on all three!

I knew I could count on enjoying the music, and my enjoyment is so great that I really hesitate to say any-thing just at once. I am so ready to praise, and you to turn suspicious, I fear! One thing is certain; this great opus is your best, and whenever your wife's enthusiasm finds vent in playing it through, be sure that I am happy to follow her from beginning to end.

Ah yes, the dear wife! What were the whole dedication, had she not, with her usual kindness, consented to get well?

---

* A succession of concerts devoted to Brahms's music was given in Dresden, March 5-10. On the 5th Brahms conducted his *Rhapsodie* (Hermine Spiess being the soloist), and the final chorus from *Rinaldo ;* on the 7th his new symphony (No. 3); while Bülow played the Pianoforte Sonata in F minor on the 10th. Frau Herzogenberg's serious illness prevented their going.

To you it would have meant the loss of everything, and even to others, her friends, something of the best in life.

If your spirits go on rising, and you care to write, let me know. Have they recommended a *Bad*, or can you look forward to your new house ? I think of going to Ischl ; we must meet there in the summer.

I have here on my table two of Beethoven's cantatas which no one can have seen for at least fifty years— hardly, indeed, since they were written in 1790—one on the death of Joseph II., the other on the enthronement of Leopold II. And you might have had them from a Leipzig antiquarian the other day! The F major part from the finale to *Leonore* is introduced in the former !*

Once more my very hearty thanks. I am just going to play it, much better, on the piano, and shall think of you both affectionately.—Ever yours,

J. BRAHMS.

134. *Elisabet von Herzogenberg to Brahms.*

LEIPZIG, *April* 10, 1884.

DEAR FRIEND,—I have to break to you the sad news that Chrysander's eldest son, who was serving his

---

* The cantatas, written out by a contemporary copyist, had been presented to Brahms by Eduard Hanslick, who had received them from an admirer, Armin Friedmann, who in his turn had them from an antiquarian in Leipzig. Hanslick was just going to Karlsbad for his health, and left them with Brahms. Brahms's letter in reply was of extraordinary length for him, and was obviously intended to be made public. It is typical of his attitude towards the fashion of printing everything bearing a distinguished name, and has been included in Hanslick's musical essays, published in 1899 under the title *Am Ende des Jahrhunderts* (see pp. 379-383).

13—2

year* here, died the night before last in the military hospital.  He had outgrown his strength, and suc- cumbed to a violent inflammation of the lungs in a few days.  His poor father came too late to see him alive.  He was all alone; his brother, who had been here, was home for the Easter holidays.

Heinrich has just gone with Spitta, who has been here some days, to Chrysander, to accompany him to the station, where he is to meet the coffin and take it home by a night train.

We are all quite heart-broken, and can think of nothing else.  He was such a dear, promising fellow, the joy and pride of his father, who saw in him not only a son, but a spiritual heir.  He had so often said to Spitta, in speaking of him, that he would know just what to do when his father died, and could carry on his work to completion.†

The old problem presents itself: 'Wherefore is light given to him that is in misery?'‡ while this youth is cut down on the threshold of life!

The sight of such grief makes one almost—almost!— wonder whether the superficial people are right who say it is better to have no children to lose.

I know you will sympathize deeply, and your sympathy will mean much to the poor father.  I thought I would let you know at once.

Your very, very kind letter was a great joy both to Heinrich and myself.

You would not believe how many times we read it.

Recovery is delightful in any case, but doubly so

* Educated men are usually able to avoid the compulsory three years' service by serving one year at their own expense.—TR.

† Chrysander's Händel biography, of which the first half of the third volume had appeared in 1867, remained unfinished.

‡ Motet by Brahms, Op. 74, No. 1 (Job iii. 20).

when our best friends hold out their hands to welcome us back.

But we realize, too, how bitter death must be. Poor Chrysander!

No more to-day, except a warm message of thanks from

E. HERZOGENBERG.

135. *Brahms to Elisabet von Herzogenberg.*

[VIENNA, *April* 24, 1884.]

MY DEAR FRIEND,—Many thanks for your letter, though it was indeed a bitter disappointment. I put it by so confidently to enjoy it undisturbed after looking through the rest of my correspondence. And then—what a tragedy! Don't you see now that it is a trifle to the Deity to inflict worse punishment than childlessness! This poor man had no pleasure in life outside his work and his home.

But I am writing with a purpose, and must ask to be excused the indelicacy—or whatever it may be—of coming straight to the point.

I sometimes wonder if it might not be good for your health to leave Leipzig, and settle—say, in Graz ?

In this case, I should suggest Wiesbaden, with the added information that their *Gesangverein* is conductor-less. I strongly recommend the post to Heinrich.

Wiesbaden is undeniably a watering-place, but there are some excellent and charming people there, whom I could name and recommend to you.*

The *Gesangverein* there has possibilities which Leipzig does not offer. The former conductor was

* Brahms had in mind principally the house of Rudolf and Laura Beckerath, where he was quite at home.

not much good so far as I could judge. There are two good orchestras in the town, at the *Kurhaus* and the opera. Then consider the favourable position— with Frankfurt so near, for instance. I will make inquiries at Wiesbaden, in any case, to know whether anyone has been appointed. And now I will stop— one minute though! We much enjoyed hearing a trio of Heinz's for piano and strings at Door's* the other day. I hope Epstein's letters are better to read than mine. He has no such tiresome and difficult ones to write as the one I have to send to Cologne at this moment!†—Ever yours sincerely,

J. Br.

I have here, by the way, two Beethoven cantatas that not another soul knows. They were written in 1792 on the death of Joseph II. and the enthronement of Leopold respectively. We Viennese do get hold of these titbits occasionally!‡

### 136. *Herzogenberg to Brahms.*

[Leipzig, April 25, 1884.]

Dear Friend,—How much could I say in reply to your most kind letter, had I but a tithe of the fluency you impute to Epstein! But how can I write with hampers and packing-cases everywhere, the furniture

---

* Anton Door (b. 1833), Viennese pianist, whose trio-evenings were very popular.

† The post of Director of the Gürzenich concerts and the Conservatorium was to become vacant in October through the retirement of Ferdinand Hiller (1811-1884), and there were negotiations on foot to appoint Brahms successor.

‡ Brahms had evidently forgotten his letter on the subject, written on March 28.

upside down, and the somewhat complicated arrangements for our final concert on my hands?

The name Wiesbaden is indeed music in the ears
of a Leipziger.  It really makes one's brain swim to
think of those healthy, joyous, musical women's voices,
and the tenors with their high B flat.  It would be
charming if you could find out casually whether the
Wiesbadeners have waited for me.  The very climate
for my precious wife, too!  I really think I could
let everything slide: my new house into which I
move to-morrow on a five years' lease, the good old
*Bachverein*, and all the delicate threads that bind me
to Leipzig, taking my last little fling at the eleventh
hour, if—there are, of course, many 'ifs,' but I could
consider them later.  You might, however, tell me
just one thing, as you have spent a summer there.
Does the *Verein* get any rest in summer?  It seems
doubtful, as Wiesbaden is a watering-place.  I should
not much like selling my house at Berchtesgaden just
now, when I am looking forward to working there.
But instead of trespassing on your kindness with a
string of questions, I will write by this post to our
discreet Engelmann.  He often goes to Wiesbaden—
has been there just now indeed, and must know the
ropes more or less.

Cologne is off, then?* It is a pity, as we might
have been your neighbours!

You cannot conceive of poor Chrysander's misery.
We were all too late to see the dear, good, tall young
fellow, as we only heard of his illness the evening before.
And so it happened that he died alone in hospital.
They had not even a bed long enough for him.  But
old Chrysander has, all the same, an iron constitution,

* Brahms had refused the post.

as Spitta and I discovered when we spent the following day with him. Although in bed to recruit his strength, he entertained us with the most wonderful auctioneer's tales, and was full of all sorts of plans for the future. We both felt that the terrible blow had failed to crush him. He went off in the evening with his sad burden, and was worked up into a state of misery that would melt a stone, spending much more than he could afford on taking his son home to the old village cemetery. What a mixture the man is—iron and gold!

I write your address, Karlsstrasse, with a certain awe, for have you not been writing hard there these two months (composing a couple of symphonies, I dare swear!) in enviable possession of the Beethoven cantatas! We, too, have our treasures, though without being able to enjoy them fully, for we have no piano, being in a state of gradual dissolution. Fortunately, however, the F major* is still fresh in our memories. Simrock kept his promise nobly, and we thank you heartily.

My wife still coughs a good bit, but is behaving well on the whole and sends kindest regards.

Address—here still.—Yours most sincerely,

HERZOGENBERG.


137. *Elisabet von Herzogenberg to Brahms.*

[LEIPZIG, *May* 5, 1884]
GOETHESTRASSE, 9.†

DEAR FRIEND,—We are sending you the little portrait of Felix Mendelssohn as a child.‡ Dear Frau Wach

---

\* Symphony in F.          † Written at the Wachs' house.

‡ A reproduction of Wilhelm Hensel's pencil drawing. Brahms liked the serious, expressive face of the child, and hung up the portrait in his music-room.

got it for us—one of the few copies strongly guarded by the family 'Fafners.' She was pleased to hear how much you liked it.

Enjoy yourself thoroughly the day after to-morrow,* and remember how many people are made happy by your existence and by a share in your affections. If you will let your kindness and friendship celebrate as many happy returns as those we wish you, Herr Doktor, we may yet live to sun our grey hairs in the light of your good-will. Has anything come of the inquiries you promised to make at Wiesbaden? Your letter roused many expectations, and gave us much to think of. It seems incongruous just when we are settling into a new house, and hammering in nails as if for all eternity. Zeitzerstrasse 24*d* is the new address. I am not there yet, but am being spoilt by these kind Wachs, who wanted to spare me the fatigue of moving.

Good-bye, and may this be a good year for you—rich in treasure for us!—Ever your old friend,

E. Herzogenberg.

Frau Röntgen, who has just come in, wishes to be warmly remembered to you.

## 138. *Brahms to Elisabet von Herzogenberg.*

[Vienna, *May* 8, 1884.]

Dear Friend,—I start for Italy to-day,† so shall find the sweet child-portrait on my way through again at

---

* His birthday.

† Brahms's fourth tour in Italy was made in company with Rudol v. d. Leyen, a friend from Krefeld. They went by way of Trient and Lake Garda to Upper Italy, where they were the guests of the Duke of Meiningen at Villa Carlotta on Lake Como (see R. v. d. Leyen's *Johannes Brahms als Mensch und Freund*, p. 40).

the end of the month—I have to go to Düsseldorf*—
ugh! Very many thanks for your kind thought of me.

Would your husband care to make inquiries of
Madame Leonhard Wolff at Wiesbaden, mentioning
my name? Wolff is a very nice fellow. He would
have liked to secure the post for Richard Barth,† who
has, I hear, declined it.

Please remember me to your kind hosts.—In haste,

J. Br.

Zeitzerstrasse? Zeigerstrasse? Zietenstrasse?‡

139. *Elisabet von Herzogenberg to Brahms.*

[LEIPZIG] ZEITZERSTRASSE, 24d II.,
*September* 13, 1884.

DEAR FRIEND,—I think I have been too backward
this time. I ought to have wormed some crumbs of
news out of you, for my present famished condition
might have been avoided, even without transgressing
the self-imposed limits of my modesty as a correspondent. So I hope you will be generous, and write me
a friendly line or two at once. Our failure to meet
this summer is an error which can only be rectified
next year, for our meeting during the winter is an
assured thing apart, and I only hope we may have full
measure this time.

As you see, we are still here, and have various
beautiful cantatas coming on; the 44th will be the
next. I am so well that I can look forward to the

* Brahms conducted his third symphony and the *Song of the Fates*
at the Lower Rhine Festival.

† Richard Barth (b. 1850), violinist and conductor; author of a
valuable monograph, *Johannes Brahms und seine Musik.*

‡ The Herzogenbergs' new address.

winter without alarm, though I shall be forced to keep strictly to a certain diet, designed to make me more podgy than I already am.

Nothing came of the Wiesbaden scheme, as of course you realized long ago, dear Uncle Brahms! Their affectionate concern for our welfare was evidently not equal to yours. Afterwards we were glad, for it transpired that the climate was much too relaxing for me, and *most unsuitable* for anyone with a weak heart. Since then we have had various other offers, of which the most attractive was a call to Berlin. Heinrich has, in fact, found it irresistible, and has practically promised to present himself, in due time, and see how school-mastering suits him.* But an unfortunate misunderstanding (either poor Joachim was absent-minded, or Heinrich too greedy for the honour which, like Julius Cæsar, he had refused three times!) led us to assume that it was a question of taking it on in January, and a report to that effect was spread far too rapidly. All our endeavours to stop it are ineffectual, and, for the first time in our lives, we have incurred the imputation of being indiscreet and neither able to wait nor to hold our tongues. I hope it will not come to the ears of the worthy Kiel,† who is to remain at his post this winter, although resigned to being pensioned off soon. If you should be asked, please say that you know us to be more taken up with our Bach performances here than ever—' Abide with us '‡ being one on the list.

---

* Herzogenberg had been offered the post of Principal of the *Academische Meisterschule* for composition, and director of the theoretical side at the *Hochschule*, together with the title of Professor.

† Friedrich Kiel (1821-1885), composer and theorist, Herzogenberg's predecessor at the *Hochschule*.

‡ Bach's cantata.

And, really, Leipzig does not seem so bad, viewed in the treacherous light of a vague melancholy at parting, and enhanced by the great comfort of our new house. I hope you will soon come and give our spare room a look of having been used. You promised us so many Christmas treats at Wiesbaden, and little as I grudge our dear Engelmann all these good things in his year of holiday (of which we were all so glad to hear), you must spare us something too, and not deprive us of the oft-repeated favour of looking at some beloved new work *avant la lettre*. Two years ago you were particularly good about the F major quintet, and it seems to me you might rejoice my heart with something new again. I consider I am not undeserving, for do I not acknowledge it to be my greatest pleasure, and have I not left you in peace ever so long, piously contenting myself with silent raptures over *Magelone* and the *Serenades !** And when have you promised to come in response to Herr Limburger's entreaties ? . . .

Good-bye for to-day, and please let fly a leaflet which will bring you vividly before us. You may leave the famous post-card addressed to us, which is supposed to be lying in your writing-case, for another time

Lina Röntgen played your D minor concerto, at the first Gewandhaus yesterday, with such delight and enthusiasm that it was a pleasure to hear her. Farewell, remember us, and let us hear from you.

E. HERZOGENBERG.

* Brahms's songs from Tieck's *Magelone*, Op. 33, and the *Serenaden*, Op. 11 and 16.

### 140. *Brahms to Elisabet von Herzogenberg.*

[MÜRZZUSCHLAG, *October*, 1884.]

DEAREST FRIEND,—I have to go back to Vienna
to-morrow morning, and have no time to answer your
kind letter properly. I just wish to say that I will
subscribe £25 for our friend.* I understand nothing
about money matters, but if they keep to their decision
of only giving him the interest, and should the sum
collected be very moderate, I would send another
£25 on condition that this second half went to him
direct.

Besides my thanks I have really nothing worth
sending in reply, for even this,† which I enclose by
way of a greeting, is in the publisher's hands. But I
will see that he does not inflict a copy on you as well!
—With kindest regards, yours,

J. BR.

### 141. *Brahms to Herzogenberg.*

[VIENNA, *October* 21, 1884.]

Some precocious person wrote protesting against
the use of *mp, mezzo-piano*,‡ in the course of the summer.
Do me the favour—seriously!—and get the notice for
me. Who wrote it, and where did it appear? Probably in Fritzsch's paper;§ you might ask him first.
Too much of this foolishness goes unnoticed. My name

* The paragraph suppressed in the preceding letter contained an
eloquent description of a poor musician in great straits through no
fault of his own.

† The manuscript of *Gestillte Sehnsucht*, Op. 91, No. 1.

‡ In Emil Breslaur's music-teachers' periodical *Der Klavierlehrer*.
Brahms was fond of using *mp* to denote a fine shade between
'mezzo-forte' and 'piano.'

§ *Musikalisches Wochenblatt.*

is not mentioned, but my weakness for *mp* is well known.  I may count on the notice?  I hope to hear about that business matter as well.*  Thanks for the last letter—soon to be last but one, I hope.—Sincerely yours,

J. BR.

### 142. *Brahms to Herzogenberg.*

My name is of course at your service.  I discussed the matter with Hanslick; he may not make it public, I suppose?†  Not that it would be any use here, as I know, for our friend is too little known.

Don't forget to hunt up the article with the attack on *mp* !—Sincerely yours,

J. BR.

### 143. *Elisabet von Herzogenberg to Brahms.*

[LEIPZIG, *October* 26, 1884.]

DEAR, DEAR FRIEND,—You should have been thanked at once for all your kindness, but your most kind letter, made doubly precious by your prompt, noble sympathy and the welcome manuscript, reached me in Berlin, where I had no free moment; and, like you, I don't care to write post-cards where I feel letters.  But few things have given me more pleasure than your £25.  Truly you are of the 'cheerful' givers whom 'God loveth,' and the general attitude in 'high' and 'highest' circles is, alas! such as to throw yours into special relief.  I am curious to know how much we shall collect altogether.

Heinz promises to make the *mp* article his special

---

* The fund which was being collected for a musician.
† Refers to the same fund.

concern, and if possible to unmask the writer. He has missed finding Fritzsch twice already. I believe he is always with his *Thekla.** That is my name for the Adiophon,† which seems to be a great success, and not only with sentimental women.

I would rather say nothing about the alto song‡ until I have tried it over thoroughly with the viola. At present I am distracted by the two voices, and am most in love with the exquisite cadences, particularly *Wann schlaft Ihr, wann schlaft Ihr ein?* with the beautiful G minor-E major harmonies, and the way in which the viola catches up the theme from the voice. But that *Lispeln der Winde* is difficult for even a clever singer. Why are you sometimes so cruel as to turn poor women into oboes or violins? Is it because you begin with a B, like a certain other relentless person?§ How easily *Sie lispeln die Welt in Schlummer* pours out of our grateful throats immediately after!

I am as happy as a child (indeed, your gifts—yes, gifts!—invariably turn me into a child) as I look at it and try it over, revel in it—you know to what extent! Will it appear in company with '*Joseph, lieber Joseph mein*'?‖

Heinz's kindest regards, and he would like to know if the Fourth Symphony is true?¶ Julius Röntgen declares it is, but Heinz says you would never have kept anything of the sort from us all this time; it would be

---

* Poem by Schiller, composed by Schubert.

† A piano with tuned forks in place of strings, invented by Fritzsch and Fischer.

‡ Op. 91, No. 1.                    § Beethoven.

‖ The second of the two songs, with viola obligato, published in 1884 as Op. 91.

¶ The fourth symphony was commenced in the summer of 1884 at Mürzzuschlag.

too unkind of a generous person like you.* We do not need to have our appetites whetted in this case.

If you ever write that letter that is supposed to be coming, please say how Arthur Faber is, and remember us very kindly to them. Also to Epstein, please. With all the old—and much new—grateful affection, your faithful

HERZOGENBERGE.

### 144. *Brahms to Herzogenberg.*

[VIENNA, *November* 18, 1884.]

I can't compete with you luxurious Leipzigers. Five thousand marks for the manuscripts! No need for an auction! And the stack of *Klavierlehrer*† took my breath away. Must I send the silly stuff back? Of course with many thanks for the trouble taken! But who would keep it? Not even Herr Fritzsch, surely. Just let me know whether it may go into the paper-basket of—yours sincerely,

J. BR.

### 145. *Brahms to Herzogenberg.*

[VIENNA, *November* 21, 1884.]

I am far more grateful for your long letters than you might think. Please consider my purse quite at your disposal. The *mp* in the *Klavierlehrer* has developed into so vast a puddle that one can only beat a hasty retreat. Probably I happened to see just

---

* Brahms was never known to discuss his plans or his compositions while they were in progress, but this did not prevent the wildest guesses and conclusions on the part of others. Röntgen could only have learned the fact by the merest chance.

† Copies of the Bach cantatas, written out in Brahms's own writing, had been offered for sale.

one number that summer. Many thanks to Herr Fritzsch,* whose paper seems very fine and classical by contrast—in spite of St. Kolf!†

Heckmann is doing your—our quartet‡ (No. 1) to-day. His first concert made a most favourable impression. It will be very good.—Sincerely yours,

J. Br.

### 146. *Brahms to* erzogenberg.

[VIENNA, *December* 1, 1884.]

DEAR FRIEND,—Just a hasty line. I have concerts every day, not only in Vienna, and not only those at which I play, but some at which I have only to listen, which is very exhausting!§ I expect to leave here on the 4th for Hamburg, etc. But I have to send you 1,750 marks more for our purpose. ‖

I should like to—and would really—write at length about your quartet : how well the Heckmanns played it, and how much I enjoyed it, but it really is not possible. The other day I was just off to Pesth ; to-day to a concert. I sincerely hope to see you on my way home through Leipzig in due time. My address at Hamburg is Café Moser (Rathausmarkt), or at Simrock's.

Perhaps you will send me a line.—Yours most sincerely,

J. Br.

* Herzogenberg had ordered a whole year of the periodical through Fritzsch (see Letter 141).

† J. van Santen Kolff, a contributor to the *Musikalisches Wochenblatt*, who had written a series of essays on *Erinnerungsmotiv-Leitmotiv.*

‡ In G minor, Op. 42, dedicated to Brahms. Robert Heckmann's quartet evenings soon became a popular institution.

§ Bülow's tour with the Meininger orchestra in November and December included concerts in Vienna, Buda-Pesth, and Graz, at which Brahms played his B flat major concerto.

‖ Towards the fund mentioned in Letter 150.

147. *Elisabet von Herzogenberg to Brahms.*

[LEIPZIG] ZEITZERSTRASSE, 24,
*December* 4, 1884.

DEAR FRIEND,—Many thanks for your last card, and
yesterday's note, from which we gather that you will
have to pass through Leipzig before long, and are
so good as to like the prospect. We should be still
happier if you could tell us the date, if only approximately. For, about the 8th or 10th we are expecting
Hildebrand, the sculptor, to stay, and we prefer to
avoid 'false relations,' as we have the skill neither
of Bach nor of Brahms in dealing with them. The
said sculptor is coming to learn Frau Schumann by
heart, with a view to modelling her (it fell through
once before), and to take his fill of the music he cannot
get at Florence. He might hear plenty on the three
festival days* if he can gain admittance to the concert-
hall, but there is the difficulty! He will have practically to produce a certificate of good behaviour, like
Tamino, and above all an assurance of his discretion ;
for so many of the old season-ticket holders have been
turned away that exception in favour of a new-comer
can only be made secretly. There is great excitement
among the public and the directors. It is to be hoped
that they will finally produce something to justify
it all. The third evening is bound to be good, but
it is a question whether Händel's *Messiah* (Robert
Franz)† and the Choral Symphony will go much better
than usual.

Your 1,750 marks are just to hand. We envy you

---

* To inaugurate the opening of the new Gewandhaus on
December 11, 12, and 13.

† Robert Franz's edition of the *Messiah*.

the fine harvest you have reaped. Ours is so much poorer, in spite of all our efforts and the various appeals in writing which I have perpetrated.

Tell me, wasn't Heinrich's quartet a failure in Vienna? We realized it perfectly from a post-card Heckmann kindly sent. However, it did not trouble Heinrich at all. The '*one person who matters*' said he had enjoyed it, and that being so, one can afford to be indifferent to Viennese opinion in general. It would be tragic enough if it were the other way round.

Is it true that you are writing a 'cello concerto?* And why are you so uncommunicative, so doubly uncommunicative, when you know how much we should enjoy it in expectation? It is very unkind of you. I feel rather like Limburger when I press you for something new, while there is so much one may still learn from the old, not to speak of one's affection for the things. Indeed, one is always being drawn to them afresh by the discovery of new beauties. In the G major sextet the other day, beautifully played by Brodsky and his colleagues, I heard much that had been hidden before. It is like having a flashlight turned on first one place, then another, all the discoveries going to enrich the precious inner store. That was Heinrich's case when he heard the Requiem (lucky man! I could not go) and sat with his nose in the score all the next day. He could not calm down at all, and insisted again and again that it was not sufficiently acknowledged as an *event*, and that people did not realize it as they ought.

But I must stop. Have a good time at Hamburg and everywhere else, and let us know if you are likely

* One of the many false reports spread about Brahms's work.

to touch Leipzig, so that we may 'exalt every valley' as far as possible. Farewell. Be our friend now and always!—Your faithful

HERZOGENBERGS.

148. *Elisabet von Herzogenberg to Brahms.*

[LEIPZIG] ZEITZERSTRASSE,
*December* 29, 1884.

DEAR KIND FATHER CHRISTMAS,—You cannot think how delighted we were by your surprise visit. We are taciturn folk with small skill in demonstrating our feelings by pretty speeches, but we hope you were not blind to the warm reception our hearts gave you. Just at this time too, when one is greedy for good things, your visit was the very best thing that could happen to us. And let me add a word of special thanks for your angelic patience when the whole house was upset, the spare-room crammed so full of Christmas things that there was hardly room for the good Brahms, and you had to make shift with that treacherous sofa the first evening. It all went to show, along with your other good deeds, what a nice person you are, and how kindly disposed towards ourselves. All the beauty of the Christmas days departed with you, and the usual tiring round set in. There was the tiresome Russian soirée, which passed without bloodshed, but left an unpleasant taste behind, as is always the way when one has no real interest in a thing. I called on the Brodskys yesterday, and told them you had been here. 'It is true, then!' they exclaimed. Little Novaček* had seen 'him' in the Zeitzerstrasse, and was lamenting that he happened to be on the opposite

* Ottokar Novaček (b. 1866), violinist and composer.

pavement, whereupon Brodsky had stormed, and wished he had been in Novaček's place. 'Fools have all the luck,' he declared. And when I saw the genuine disappointment of this devoted admirer of yours, I was really sorry I had given him no opportunity of meeting you. I came to the conclusion that you must not be allowed to go off in such haste another time, leaving your many friends to feel they have been done out of seeing you. You are sure to be giving concerts up or down the Rhine during the winter, so do make us happy once more. I promise you a better time than the last, and you shall never have that silly little glass for your marsala* again! Also, there is plenty of Brahms-wine left.

We are at last to have a chance, this week, of trying the alto songs with viola; players are notoriously scarce in this city of music!

There was something I forgot the other day. Little Professor Bischoff† of Graz has been begging for *years* for a scrap of your manuscript, but, as I am too stingy with my own few treasured specimens, I can't be expected to give him any. So do please remember the poor man, who is one of the true music-lovers, not the doubtful connoisseur type. Perhaps you will send something along with my boldly demanded Christmas present (the songs)? Since you are our benefactor, a little more or less makes no difference! We are past modesty, and only ask to remain your

DEBTORS.

* Brahms was very fond of this wine, which reminded him of Sicily.

† Ferdinand Bischof, to whom Herzogenberg dedicated his *Vier Gesänge*, Op. 40.

They are playing a much-praised symphony (in manuscript) of Bruckner's* to-morrow. What do you think of this amazing person ?


### 149. *Brahms to Elisabet von Herzogenberg.*

DEAR FRIEND,—Accept my profound thanks for the half-crown and everything else besides. To save writing too many letters, I will send you a specimen of my Scarlatti† which may interest you — it charms me !

Your orders concerning Professor Bischof shall receive prompt attention.

I promised you the first volume of Schubert‡ (the first four symphonies), but Härtels have only sent me one copy. But don't think of buying it; only tell me if you really want it. You will certainly have an opportunity of looking at them, and it seems to me

---

* Anton Bruckner (1827-1896), a much-fêted Austrian composer, whose works gave rise to considerable controversy. Nikisch was conducting his seventh symphony at a 'special' concert at the opera-house.

† Besides the rare Czerny edition of Scarlatti, Brahms owned several of the sonatas in the original edition, and over 300 old copies of the *Klavierstücke*, amongst them 172 unpublished pieces from the famous collection of Abbate Santini.

‡ Brahms had undertaken the revision of Schubert's symphonies for the complete edition, published by Breitkopf and Härtel, a responsibility he afterwards regretted. His objections to the posthumous publication of inferior compositions, which the composer is no longer able to defend, are expressed with great plainness in a letter to Marie Lipsius (La Mara), written in May, 1885 (see La Mara, *Musikerbriefe aus fünf Jahrhunderten*, ii. 348). But when the ten volumes of Schubert's songs appeared (edited by Mandyczewski), he changed his mind, and regretted the superficial way in which he had fulfilled his share of the work, as much as his declaration that there was no sense in publishing these examples of an early stage of the composer's development.

unnecessary to possess all these things and have so much superfluous stuff lying round. For the same reason I am loth to send you the desired bad songs!

So Wiesbaden is again on the cards. I need not dwell on it, as you will be seeing the Engelmanns,* who can tell you everything.

No more to-day.—With kindest regards, yours,
J. Br.

150. *Elisabet von Herzogenberg to Brahms.*

DEAR FRIEND,—The dear old songs, your Christmas present, reached us yesterday. I could almost thank the unknown person who stole our original copy for the pleasure it gives me to receive them again from you. I feel quite sentimental when I look at my old friends in their new cover—their uniform—which makes it impossible to distinguish them from any of the others by the title-page—a modern invention which, like many others, has its disadvantages.

Our friend Hildebrand will have delivered our messages, and told you of the Bruckner excitement here, and how we rebelled against having him thrust upon us—like compulsory vaccination. We had to endure much stinging criticism—insinuations as to our inability to detect power under an imperfect exterior, or admit a talent which, though not perhaps fully developed, still exists, and has a claim to interest and recognition. We are not to consider artistic results everything, but to admire the hidden driving-power, whether it succeeds in expressing itself satisfactorily or no. That is all very well in theory, but in practice it all depends on the value of this driving-

* See Letter 130, note.

power.  Unless it is very great, one can only hold aloof, and resign oneself to be abused of the philistines, who have eyes for beauty only when it wears their own colours.  We wished we had you to back us up, and could hear your sound views, which are based on super-abundant experience and are therefore worth more than all the theories of the wise, all the mere instincts of the simple.  And, who knows? you may agree with us, the simple; and that is what I particularly want to know.  It would be such a help.  Integrity of judgment is, to one of us, as precious in the domain of art as in human jurisdiction, and it oppresses us to appear as narrow-minded, ungenerous, timid observers, so afraid of overrating that they lose all sense of justice.

You must excuse this letter, which, superfluous as it must appear, could only be written to you; for who else could give us the desired answer?  Thank you again for the songs.  If Bruckner had written *Kränze*, or *Liebesbotschaft*, or *Die Liebende schreibt*, or *Abenddämmerung*,* I would search the symphony through half a dozen times for that hidden gold; but I think the fact is, that whoever could write the one would never be guilty of the other.

Good-bye, and don't be hard on your tormentor, but answer—if only with one word.—In old and renewed friendship, yours,

E. Herzogenberg.

I delighted Gouvy† the other day by telling him you had been praising his French songs to me.  He ordered them forthwith, and I now have the whole

---

* Brahms, Op. 46, No. 1 ; Op. 47, Nos. 1, 5 ; Op. 49, No. 5.
† Ludwig Theodor Gouvy (1822-1898), distinguished composer.

fat book of Ronsard before me. I was surprised to find so much grace and vivacity in many places, being misled, I suppose, by his air of weariness. Yet how amateurish his work is in detail! For instance, he never ventures on this close—

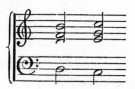

but always has recourse to the horrible chord of six-four on D. Young Wolf* has redeemed his symphony (which you unfortunately did not suppress before it saw the light) by some very charming new songs.

### 151. *Elisabet von Herzogenberg to Brahms.*

LEIPZIG, *January* 11, 1885.

MY DEAR FRIEND,—How happy you have made us again with the gay, dainty Scarlatti piece, which I am always playing, and the dear touching song,† which makes me long to be a tenor, so as to sing it properly. The song has given the poem new words for me; it is so different, so much more beautiful in the light of the music. '*Es dunkelt schon, mich schläfert,*' and the word *Tag*, which comes in so finely on that D, are both there in the poem, and yet they mean more than they did. It is as if they had always waited for that particular dress. How nice of you to smuggle the sheet between the pages of Scarlatti! You know

---

* Johannes Wolf (b. 1869), a pupil of Spitta, subsequently gave up composing for music history, and became tutor at Berlin University.

† '*Der Tod, das ist die kühle Nacht,*' Op. 96, No. 1.

what a joy every new note of yours brings, and what a double joy to see it before all the singers, great and small, have flung themselves upon it.

We played the alto songs the day before yesterday. Klengel* has a splendid viola, and plays well, so we had a delightful time singing and listening to the two pieces. The old *Wiegenlied*† is still my favourite. It sounds so beautiful, and the way the voice soars above the viola is too lovely. The strong legendary flavour which characterizes it seems peculiar to this song, and you might hear it and play it any number of times without breaking the charm. The microscopic alterations did not escape me—an F in the bass (which is probably omitted by mistake in the corresponding passage?), and a lovely D flat in the voice-part in '*Ach wie so müd er ward.*' We and the viola are going to journey to the Engelmanns to-day. Spies‡ is spending the day with them, so I shall play the part for which I am suited, and accompany her. It will be a pleasure to hear the pieces sung for the first time in her lovely voice. It wants a magnificent, full voice to hold the balance against the almost excessive variety and rhythmical complications of the D major piece.

How I envy you your Scarlatti, if there are many such excellent specimens! What an ingenious fellow he is, with his arpeggio figures in the unexpected A major part, and the long modulation, which has no reference to the piece itself, and his sudden recollection

---

* Paul Klengel (1854), a violinist, elder brother of Julius; conductor of the 'Euterpe' at Leipzig from 1881 to 1886.

† Founded on an old sacred melody, '*Josef, lieber Josef mein,*' which Brahms found in Corner's *Gross-Katholisches Gesangbuch* of 1631. Liszt made it a leading theme in his *St. Elisabeth*, and Herzogenberg in his *Geburt Christi*.

‡ Hermine Spies, the singer.

of the subject and prompt return to it! Ah yes, a robust talent may take liberties which become preposterous in weaker hands.

Dear Friend, thank you again for everything, keep us in your affections, and, when you write, breathe one word about Bruckner. You are not afraid of our leading you on, and then proclaiming abroad: Brahms says we are right! We will lie quite low about anything you say, but a word we do crave for our own peace of mind. What do you think of the *Vierteljahrsschrift?* \* Heinrich is so glad, because we shall hear something of Chrysander again. You probably know that he has been taking Spitta's lectures for him (Spitta still has to be careful), and comes over from Hamburg† every fortnight for the purpose.

Good-bye for to-day. Heinrich declares you have not really gone away, so vividly does he see you at every turn, and recall every word you said to him. The Scherzo has been put on a separate footing, and there is a new one for the second subject of the first movement, to my great delight.‡ Yesterday we heard your C minor quartet§ again after a long interval. I can only bear to hear Joachim play the two corner movements; the humbler sort do not know how to handle them. But the two middle movements sounded beautiful, and are really too splendid; or do you know anything much more charming than the third, or more affecting than the second?

* The *Vierteljahrsschrift für Musikwissenschaft* had just been started by Spitta, Chrysander, and Adler. It was published by Breitkopf and Härtel up to 1894.

† Chrysander lived at Bergedorf, near Hamburg.

‡ Probably refers to Herzogenberg's symphony in C minor, Op. 50, then in progress.

§ Op. 51, No. 1.

When, when are you going to announce the birth
of your youngest mysterious opus?*   Were we not
amazingly tactful and discreet when you were here?
Are we not excellent people, anyway?   Good-bye.
I really shall not write again for ages, but am your
devoted

E. H.

### 152. *Brahms to Elisabet von Herzogenberg.*

[VIENNA, *January* 12, 1885.]

DEAR LADY,—I understand!   You have sat through
the roaring of Bruckner's symphony once, and now,
when people talk about it, you are afraid to trust the
recollection of your own impressions.

Well, you may safely do so.   Your delightful letter†
expresses most lucidly all that can be said—all that
one has said oneself or would like to have said so
nicely.   You will not mind when I tell you that
Hanslick shares your opinion, and read your letter
with pious joy!   But one symphony and one quintet
of Bruckner's have been printed.‡   I advise you to
get them to look at, with a view to steeling your mind
and your judgment.   You will not want me!

\*        \*        \*        \*        \*

With supreme ill-humour, deepest respect, and
kindest regards, yours,

J. BR.

* The fourth symphony in E minor.
† Letter 150.
‡ The third symphony in D minor, dedicated to Richard Wagner,
and the quintet in F major.

153. *Elisabet von Herzogenberg to Brahms.*

[LEIPZIG, *January* 14, 1885.]

DEAR FRIEND,—If I write again to-day, it is all your own fault for being so kind. In the first place, you will send us things which I cannot accept quite in silence, and then you wrote me such an embarrassingly charming and consoling letter, for which you must also be thanked. It has done us a world of good, inducing a state of sudden placidity which enables us to listen unmoved to the most extravagant nonsense about poor Bruckner, so strengthened are we by the approval of one on whom we 'invincibly depend,' as Hölderlin (whom I am reading) says of Schiller. But although we can arm ourselves with placidity at a pinch, no one can console us for the fact that, in this world of so-called culture, there are so many, many people ready to be imposed upon by any inflated windbag, if its appearance is made with due pomp. One or two not quite impossible *motifs*, like grease-spots swimming on the top of weak soup, and there we have ' *Meister* ' Bruckner's whole stock-in-trade, while those who do not make immediate obeisance are stamped as unbelieving Thomases, who want signs and wonders to convince them.

I should just like to know who started the Bruckner crusade, how it came about, and whether there is not a sort of freemasonry among the Wagnerians. It certainly is rather like a game of taroc, or rather that form of whist in which, when 'misery' is declared, the lowest card takes the trick.

I am genuinely delighted with the Sophocles.* I

* A new translation of Sophocles by Gustav Wendt (b. 1827), dedicated to Brahms, and presented by him to Frau von Herzogenberg.

little thought you were so seriously concerned with
my education when I answered all your cross-ques-
tioning so unsuspectingly, displaying my appalling
ignorance at the mention of Donner.* How charming
that I should just have invested in a copy of Hölderlin,
the lover of the Greeks, in an edition that was once
Schwab's† own, too, decorated with his marginal notes!
Heinrich sends respectful and most affectionate greetings. He is deep in organ-parts for three cantatas, and
the St. John Passion-music for March the 21st.‡
We heard the *Wasserträger*§ again after a long
interval the other day. How nice it is to feel that
as we grow older we appreciate these things more,
and strengthen our allegiance to the true gods!
 With kindest regards, many thanks, and no further
trace of ill-humour,             E. HERZOGENBERG.


154. *Elisabet von Herzogenberg to Brahms.*

[LEIPZIG] *February* 13, 1885.

DEAR FRIEND,—Now that I know you to be back in
Vienna, I will delay no longer in sending one lady's
thanks for the *Tafellied.*‖ I only wish we had here,
as in the Rhineland, the right voice material as well
as the right temperament for singing this graceful
glee straight away while sitting at table, instead of

* Josef Jakob Christian Donner, the well-known translator of the
classics.
 † Christoph Theodor Schwab, the first editor of Hölderlin's
complete works.
 ‡ The Leipzig *Bachverein* performed the St. John Passion-music in
celebration of Bach's birthday.
 § Cherubini's opera.
 ‖ Brahms had written a *Tafellied* (table-song), '*Dank der Damen,*'
Op. 93*b*, for the fiftieth anniversary of the Krefeld *Singverein* on
January 27 and 28, and conducted it himself.

first practising it like any solemn motet. But the fog
and the soot, timidity and other causes, all combine
against the fulfilment of any such wish here. What a
happy selection you made this time, too! What witch-
craft leads you to open books of poems at just the right
place, where there is still treasure for the composer?
By way of news to-day I may say that we are
really in for Berlin.* The decree, stamped by the
*Ministerium* for 'ecclesiastical, scholastic, and medical
appointments,' lies before us in all its glory, so I
suppose we may consider it settled. They have at
last decided on the charitable fiction that Kiel is to
have indefinite leave of absence, while Heinrich is to
act as supply. This is by far the most satisfactory
way, as it leaves a loophole of escape if the arrangement fails to suit either Heinrich or them. It makes
it much easier for him to accept the post. These
decisions are always difficult, even to happy people
like ourselves, who take their shell—their feeling that
life depends on their being all in all to each other—
with them everywhere. And Berlin never really
attracted us. You know how it came about—how we
felt ourselves superfluous here, and how they insisted
we should be in our right place there, and so we
decided. We realized clearly, though, how much less
a decision depends on ourselves than on fate and
chance. If the Wiesbaden negotiations had not
dragged quite so much, we should have accepted
with eagerness, for the plastic chorus material there
attracted Heinrich far more than the honour of sitting
on those gilt chairs† (with the Berliners), which, as

* Herzogenberg's appointment to the *Hochschule.*
† Herzogenberg had, further, been elected member of the Academy
of Arts. A portrait included in this volume shows him in his
academical robes.

Wilhelm Grimm says, are 'wooden after all, and not
exempt from the worm!'

'They hide everything under a correct manner,' he
goes on to say, 'and think themselves cleverer than
anyone else.' Pray Heaven we may not be infected
with this poison, but keep our low opinion of ourselves (in the best sense). When these great changes
come, we ought to be glad to be past our first youth,
and therefore able to sift the chaff from the wheat
without haste or prejudice.

But wherever we go, you must be the same to us,
and provide us with new joys!

I had the bad luck to miss the D major symphony,
so nicely done at Klengel's concert, and more recently
your 'deeply intellectual' *Song of Destiny** (O shade
of Fritzsch!)

Good-bye, and send a line to your devoted

HERZOGENBERGS.

Was Bruckner's quintet really such a success?†

## 155. *Brahms to Elisabet von Herzogenberg.*

[VIENNA, *April 25*, 1885.]

I should be most happy to send some songs could
I be sure they would bring in a kind word. But my
song-copyist‡ is on tour with the Strauss orchestra.§

For to-day kindest regards.—Yours,

J. BR.

* Op. 54; quotation from the *Musikalisches Wochenblatt.*

† Bruckner's quintet was performed in Vienna for the first time
on January 8, 1885, at the Hellmesberger quartet concert. The
Adagio alone had a *succès d'estime.*

‡ Wilhelm Kupfer, a 'cellist, native of Hamburg, acted for many
years as copyist to Brahms.

§ Eduard Strauss's orchestra.

156. *Brahms to Heinrich and Elisabet von Herzogenberg.*

[VIENNA, *May* 6, 1885.]

MY DEAR FRIENDS,—I have succumbed to the temptation of sending you a few songs. *In case* there should be any question of it, I must ask you not to have the *Nachtigall* or the *Wanderer** copied. On the other hand, I should be very glad if you felt like giving me your opinion of the two little creatures.

I need not say that they are more or less twins—on whom I am now trying all sorts of experiments. I have given the nightingale a new note, for instance ;† but it is not the thing yet, by any means.

It would be charming if you had a little word to say to each little song. No need to apologize if the verdict be a hard one, a curt 'away with them!'

I have to add that I should, of course, send more Scarlatti if there were any others as good. I have over 300 beautiful old manuscript copies, of which 172 are unpublished.‡ Czerny made use of them for a collection, which is as admirably selected as edited. His edition, containing 200 pieces, probably stopped short where it did by chance, or he would hardly have overlooked your specimen. You should really try to get a copy (Czerny's edition, Haslinger, Vienna) through some good antiquarian. It is rare now. I had to wait a long time before I could find a complete copy. Please write very soon.—Yours,

J. BR.

* Op. 97, No. 1, and Op. 106, No. 5.

† Brahms had taken the melody to '*Hier, wo sich die Strassen scheiden*' from the *Wanderer*, and adapted it for the *Nightingale*. Any attempt, therefore, to detect the nightingale's note in the four introductory bars or the song itself is obviously unjustifiable. There could be no better argument against ' programme music.'

‡ *Cf.* Letter 149.

15

### 157. *Brahms to Elisabet von Herzogenberg.*

[VIENNA, *May* 17, 1885.]

I start for Mürzzuschlag (Steiermark)\* in an hour, and, once there, hope you will not keep me waiting many hours for songs and opinions!—Kindest regards,

J. BR.

### 158. *Elisabet von Herzogenberg to Brahms.*

[LEIPZIG] *May* 21 *and* 22, 1885.

DEAR FRIEND,—I suspect your card was designed not only to convey a 'change of address,' but to admonish! I am sorry, for you evidently think I have kept the dear songs too long, and my conscience, which was clear—I considered myself justified in keeping them—becomes burdened. Yet I could not part with them, for the few moments I could devote to the sweet things were snatched with difficulty in the intervals of such pleasant occupations as packing 'moth-boxes,' shaking carpets, preparations for removal, and all sorts of things a bachelor has no idea of. Certainly I enjoyed the songs all the more, and have fallen hopelessly in love with some of them. I may as well say at once that I give my unqualified approval to the beauty in D flat (Daumer's words) with the middle part in E major.† It must be one of the most glorious songs in the world. It is so ideal for the voice, so vigorous in conception ('*ich gäbe viel, um zu erfahren*'), and so happy in the lines of its melody which flatter both singer and listener. Above all, how perfectly words and music are blended in their deep emotion, their lovely animation! Such

---

\* Brahms's summer house.     † '*Wir Wandelten*,' Op. 96, No. 2.

loving care has been lavished on every detail, and
each tiny variant has its calculated effect in rendering
the particular part more impressive, as, for instance,
the quavers introduced at '*In meinem Haupte die
Gedanken*,' and the harmonies, which are changed in
position only. It is a pleasure to see and feel it all,
and one sings with such conviction at the end: '*so
wunderlieblich sei auf der Welt kein anderer Hall!*'
Next in order comes *Meerfahrt*,* with those strangely
affecting horn-blasts, the F sharp over the A minor
harmony, the C sharp over the E minor farther on,
and last of all the B natural.† They come with startling
freshness, and must be classed among the wonders
which, to the end of time, will be evoked in response
to any great force demanding expression, exhausted
as the available store of musical material often seems,
and actually is, to the non-elect. Tell me, have you
not a special weakness for *Meerfahrt* yourself? My
attitude towards it and the D flat song is that of children
who, when asked, 'Do you like me or So-and-so best?'
reply, 'I like you best, but I like So-and-so best too.'
*Meerfahrt* has just that dignified leisure, that true *soste-
nuto* character and fine breadth of outline, which you are
so well able to command. What a reposeful, wholesome effect of tonality there is in spite of the originality
of the harmonies! What an entire absence of uncertainty
as to where one stands, or the direction in which one
is being taken, and how beautifully the subdued
anguish of the diminished 7th melts into the opening
key of a minor,‡ while the voice takes that despairing
F sharp for the first time§—how piercing, how impressive it all is, and yet how restrained!

* Op. 96, No. 2.                † Bars 3, 29, 58.
‡ Bar 48 *et seq*.              § Bar 54.

I am afraid of not saying the right thing about the *Nightingale* and the *Wanderer*, for the fact is, only one of them meets with my entire approval—the *Nightingale*, which I like *very* much. The melody has the bitter-sweet of the real nightingale's song; they seem to revel in augmented and diminished intervals, passionate little creatures that they are!—and the simple tenderness of the F major part is so charming by contrast.* How finely the climax at '*Verklungenen Tönen*' is prepared, and how happy the return to the opening motif at the words, '*In deinem Leid ein leiser Wiederhall*'! Indeed, this song, delicious as the first tender green of the woods, seems to me '*gefunden*,' inspired from first to last—*nichts zu suchen, das war sein Sinn*†—whereas the *Wanderer* has a touch of the chilly North; one misses the pleasing contrast, which the second part fails to supply satisfactorily.‡ In any case, it would not come well *after* the *Nightingale*, and could only detract from its effect by being placed *before* it. Please suppress me if I go too far, but remember, at the same time, that I am but obeying your orders!§ And before you forget that fact, I may as well confess that I cannot reconcile myself to one song, and that is the *Mond*, '*der sich leuchtend dränget.*'‖ Either I am

* '*Nein, trauter Vogel, nein!*'

† Quotation from Goethe's *Gefunden*.

‡ As a matter of fact, the *Wanderer* was the older of the twin songs, and had therefore the greater claim to being '*Gefunden*.' Brahms may have had the *Nightingale* in his mind, but it was not written until later.

§ Brahms eventually recast the *Wanderer*, and included it in Op. 106 much later.

‖ Heine's poem '*Wie der Mond sich leuchtend dränget.*' Brahms suppressed the song, possibly on account of this adverse criticism, and gave up the idea of a series of Heine songs which he was then contemplating.

quite irresponsible and capricious in my tastes, or it really is not on the same musical plane with the others. To put it brutally, I feel as if it had only the contours of a Brahms piece—what is called mannerism as distinct from style. I don't know how to express myself without being guilty of impertinence, but neither can I be silent without feeling myself a traitor to your songs in general. For are they not our lodestar, the standard by which you measure our education, and have we not a right to demand the very highest of our master? How can we *Brahmsianer* sanction a melody like this, with its intricacies and its restless harmonies, after all the treasures of inspiration showered on us! I really feel strongly that this song is not to be mentioned in the same breath with the others. But I revive again when I come to the B minor (Heine's),* with its exquisite fervour, so tender and pleasing in addition to its ingenuity. It is a gem indeed, a marvel of compactness! One never tires of playing it. How unfailing, too, is the appeal of the closing passage ('*Nehmt mit meine Tränen und Seufzer*')!

'*Auf dem Schiffe*'† is charming, with its sail-flapping accompaniment, and the little volkslied in E flat‡ is expressive and unaffected. But I cannot bring myself to like this bar:

*Voice :* A♭—G—F.

---

* '*Es schauen die Blumen,*' Op. 96, No. 3.          † Op. 97, No. 2.
‡ '*Trennung,*' Op. 97, No. 6. The key is F, not E flat. Brahms

That is one of the wicked, false relations which are
hardly in place in this simple little song, so engaging
and well-behaved in other respects.  Halm's ' *Winter-
nacht* '* makes me sad.  Those dry verses never
deserved that you should set them to music.  Singing
them makes one shiver for a fur coat!  But *Lady
Judith*† is something like a poem!  The words are
splendid and the music delicious.  It is too short,
though.  One almost wishes you had treated it in the
only possible way—that is, not strictly in strophes, but
with some alteration or extension of the last verse.  It is
over so quickly, and there is so much concentration in
the poem that one feels it all the more.‡  The variation
of the accompaniment to the *Wanderer* strikes me as less
happy than the original form.  After singing through all
the three several times, I can only say I think the
*Nightingale* so bewitching as to justify a little self-
denial.

In your letter you speak of ' some songs' that you
are sending.  Are there more to come?  What a
splendid haul this was!  What a pleasure you must

transposed the song a semitone, probably to make it more effective.
The unpleasant false relation in bar 14 is avoided as follows :

* This song was never published.  There is no *Winter's Night*
among Halm's poems, but a *Snowstorm*, which corresponds to the
description.

† ' *Entführung*,' Op. 97, No. 3, words by W. Alexis.

‡ Brahms followed this advice, and lengthened the last verse by
one bar to lend the climax additional emphasis.

take in stringing together all these pearls that come to you in such quantities, all the finest and best!

Thank you for sending me the dear pile. I and my Heinz know no greater bliss than to dive into a new hoard such as this. If you could but hear our delighted exclamations, and see our bear-play in the form of vigorous pokes and pushes when we come to anything particularly fine or beautiful, you would have to be pleased with such evidence of your own power to please.

I wish you—and ourselves—a productive and refreshing summer culminating in a grand autumn explosion. I hear rumours of a symphony—as usual! —but this time the Princess of Meiningen* is prepared to swear to it. I myself have visions of a string quartet, suggested by one of your mysterious remarks on a post-card.

And I know what I should like for Christmas: the A minor song, *Meerfahrt*, in your own writing. If you consider the request audacious, I take it back— like the Leipzigers. To-day the A minor is my only love; to-morrow it will probably be the D flat major.

Heinz sends very kindest regards. He would so like to see you in *our* mountains, and have you sitting at our table. It would be lovely in July, when we are by ourselves; we expect to be inundated with relatives in August, and there's an end to my freedom! Good-bye, and thanks once more.—Yours,

ELISABET HERZOGENBERG.

* Princess Marie of Meiningen.

159. *Elisabet von Herzogenberg to Brahms.*

[LEIPZIG, *May* 24, 1885.]

'Nehmt mit unsre Seufzer und Thränen,
Ihr Lieder schwermütig und trüb.'*

It is not my fault that they were not sent off before
to-day. The post-office would not take them in a
wrapper—the way they came—and afterwards it was
too late. Woe is me that I forgot to copy out the
words of the *Nightingale* (I might have been allowed
that much!); I can of course remember the music.
We are all quite intoxicated with the A minor song.
Inspirations of that order are none too common. Do
please send a card to say that my little guests have
arrived safely!

E. H.

160. *Brahms to Elisabet von Herzogenberg.*

[MÜRZZUSCHLAG, *May* 28, 1885.]

Many, many thanks for your letter, which could not
have been kinder or more satisfactory. Moreover, it
coincides remarkably with my own casual ideas and
wishes, although you frequently see blue sky where
mine is overcast. I hardly think, by the way, that
anyone need mind speaking plainly about my things,
given the one condition of genuine, heartfelt interest.
For one thing, I am far from thinking my capacity for
writing good stuff unlimited, and for another I do not
take a provisional opinion too seriously—and, after
all, tastes differ!

But you have no idea of the enjoyment one can

* An adaptation of Heine in '*Es schauen die Blumen*' (Brahms,
Op. 96, No. 3).

extract from a mere handful of songs, by reading them in the light of your descriptions.

But to come to the point—you missed one out. I do really want to hear a word or two about the Rhenish volkslied, '*Dort in den Weiden,*'* if it has not faded from your memory. Or did it escape you altogether? It was on the back of *Lady Judith.* Here it lies, peeping at me, and I don't know what sort of a face to make!

Be sure you let me know when you go to Wiesbaden. (Is any address necessary?)

With my warmest thanks and kindest regards to you both, yours,

J. BR.

161. *Elisabet von Herzogenberg to Brahms.*

LISELEY, *June* 3, 1885.
KÖNIGSSEE.

My DEAR FRIEND,—Your letter was a real joy and consolation. It stands me in good stead that you do not take preliminary judgments too seriously, for that helped to make you indulgent with mine. Yet I confess it seems to me hardly right to speak of *preliminary* judgment in the case of songs, which are on a small enough scale to be taken in at a glance, though it would apply, I admit, to orchestral and chamber music. I am, of course, taking an intimate acquaintance with the composer's method for granted. I know these new songs, for instance, as well as I ever shall, and my opinion of them will be the same a year hence. In the same way I was able, after looking through them several times, to pick out my favourites among the latest arrivals.

Besides, you say yourself that your own estimation

* Op. 97, No. 4.

of them tallies with my remarks. So I forgot to mention
the *Willow Song.** I think I remember it, however.
Doesn't it go like this,

and have a fine ritornelle on the same melody, with
this bass in quavers after the beat?

Yes, I remember—that was it! But the song itself
somehow failed to captivate me. I thought to myself
how much I should like it if I did not know the other
Brahms songs; knowing them, I realized how spoilt
I was! It seemed to me you had given us much the
same message before,† only told more prettily and
weighing heavier in the golden scales; while everything that charms me most in the other songs is, I
feel, being said for the first time. A feeling of this
sort always cripples one's receptive faculties even for
things that are good and beautiful in themselves. For
instance, it prejudices me against *Sappho‡* (which is,
I am sure, really beautiful) among the last-published
songs. To my mind, you had expressed that very
shade of emotion with more grandeur, more simplicity,
once before, using similar material; but I, true to
my former gods, am not to be diverted from it, but

* *Weidenlied*, Op. 97, No. 4. The melody is quoted correctly, but
not the harmonies of the ritornelle. Brahms uses the dominant
seventh on A, not the diminished seventh on A sharp, in the third bar.
† *Cf.* Kalbeck (Johannes Brahms, i. 160 *et seq.*).
‡ 'Sapphic Ode,' Op. 94, No. 4.

turn with the greater fervour to the best you have given me.

Over and above this I consider the little *Willow Song* unvocal, and I never like the accompaniment to follow the notes of the melody—it rarely fails to embarrass the singer.

I have been wondering what could be done with Judith,* and whether you could not add a train to the proud lady's robe. Or do you object to making the last verse different on principle ?† It seems so painfully abrupt and scanty. Do think it over again, please!

The A minor song,‡ with its final '*trostlos*,' still haunts me perpetually. It follows me to bed, and, once I begin, I have to go through with it to the glorious ending.

We are very happy in our dear little house, and thoroughly enjoy hearing the blackbirds

and finches. Some robins have made their nest in our bushes, to our great joy. After a great deal of rain, we have blue skies and sunshine again. If we were more selfish, and did not take life so seriously or forecast trouble, how happy we might be! Good-bye, and thank you once more. You must know what it means to me to be allowed to write to you quite freely all that I feel.

* Op. 97, No. 3 (see Letter 158, note).
† Brahms had no such objection, but frequently handled his poems with great freedom.
‡ *Meerfahrt.*
§ Frau von Herzogenberg rightly traces the motif in the *Nightingale* and the *Wanderer* to the blackbird's note, and not the nightingale's.

Heinrich sends kindest regards, and suggests that, as
you have been so kind once, you might, without fear of
turning our heads, send us the quartet or the symphony
or whatever 'the thing' (see Limburger!) may call
itself before it becomes public property.
And when are you going to pay a visit to Liseley ?*

### 162. Brahms to Elisabet von Herzogenberg.

[MÜRZZUSCHLAG, *June* 6, 1885.]

Please forgive my misplaced lecture. It was absolutely no reflection on your kind letter, and must have
looked black indeed by contrast.

All the same, taken *con discrezione*, strictly for general
application, and in the friendliest possible sense, it may
come in useful another time !

Can you find out, and let me know, when the Duke
of Meiningen is expected ?†

If you should meet a certain Frau Dr. Anna Franz
of Vienna during the summer, I hope you will like the
dear, kind woman. I might give her a card for you ?
She certainly stands to gain by it.—Most sincerely
yours,

J. BR.

* The name given to the house Herzogenberg had built at
Berchtesgaden.

† George II., Duke of Saxe - Meiningen and Hildburghausen
(b. 1826), was an intelligent patron of music and the drama. He
married in 1873 a very musical actress, Ellen Franz, a pupil of Bülow,
who received the title *Freifrau* von Heldburg. From the time of
Bülow's appointment as conductor at Meiningen in 1880, the Duke
took a great interest in Brahms, whose frequent visits to the palace
ended in establishing particularly friendly relations between them.
Meiningen was the first town to erect a monument to Brahms. This
was executed by Hildebrand a year after the composer's death in
1897.

*163. Elisabet von Herzogenberg to Brahms.*

LISELEY, *August* 7, [1885].

SIR,—We do not wish to be importunate, but I should like to remind you, before it is too late, that, in case you still have any idea of coming over, it is particularly desirable for us that it should be soon. Otherwise we should have neither the pleasure of putting you up, nor the leisure to enjoy your visit. For from the 15th onward we are, as I told you, to be besieged by an army of relatives, twelve deep, and shall not have a moment to ourselves, still less for a friend with whom one does not wish to be stingy. It would indeed be a sore trial to have that friend close at hand without being able to enjoy his company. 'Rather will I stab myself to death with a pluperfect fifth!'* than suffer such torture. And so we thought it would be very sociable and gracious of you to come for a few days now, with sheep and cattle for company. Later I expect you will be drawn to Frau Schumann's summit,† and we should surrender you with due solemnity to your other real friends. Frau Franz has not put in an appearance, and does not, apparently, desire our acquaintance.

Do me the favour of an immediate post-card announcing your decision, which will, I hope, prove favourable to your faithful

HERZOGENBERGS.

Yes, the Meiningens will certainly be gone before you arrive, and with them, perhaps, all that attracts you to Königssee?‡

---

* Quotation from Hoffmann.
† At Vordereck, near Berchtesgaden.
‡ The Duke had a hunting-lodge on Königssee.

164. *Brahms to Elisabet von Herzogenberg.*

[MÜRZZUSCHLAG, *August* 29, 1885.]

MY DEAR FRIEND,—I seem to miss one opportunity after another of visiting you. Shall I put it down to a languid dread of all the non-acquaintances in the train, and all the crowd of acquaintances in your neighbourhood whom I am also due to visit? Are you staying on? and are you by yourselves again? Might I venture to send you a piece of a piece of mine,* and should you have time to look at it, and tell me what you think of it? The trouble is that, on the whole, my pieces are nicer than myself, and need less setting to rights! But cherries never get ripe for eating in these parts,† so do not be afraid to say if you don't like the taste. I am not at all eager to write a bad No. 4.

That reminds me, when am I to see No. 1?‡ Must I wait for the reason, like the concert conductors?

Is Astor§ not ready yet? I have been much looking forward for a long time to a closer examination of this same No. 1.—With kindest regards, yours,

J. BRAHMS.

* First movement of the fourth symphony in E minor.

† Brahms also considered it necessary to warn his friend Bülow of the acerbity of his new symphony. He says, writing about this time : 'I have often, while writing, had a pleasing vision of rehearsing it [the symphony] with you in a nice leisurely way—a vision that I still have, although I wonder if it will ever have any other audience ! I rather fear it has been influenced by this climate, where the cherries never ripen. You would never touch them !'

‡ Herzogenberg's first symphony in C minor, Op. 50, which was followed later by one other in B flat, Op. 70.

§ Herzogenberg's publisher.

165. *Elisabet von Herzogenberg to Brahms.*

LISELEY, *September* 1, 1885.

DEAR FRIEND,—Yes, you may 'venture' to send that piece of your piece, which—Heaven be praised!—appears to be a symphony. It will make two people very happy. If I had no time, I would make it by some means; but I really shall have time some days, and mean to dive deep into this proof of your kindness. Do please send it soon; you can imagine with what Christmas-y feelings we shall sit and watch for it. It was a real disappointment to us that you could not come. We had everything so beautifully ready—our little house, our two hearts, and some home-bottled wine in our own little cellar, thinking all the time you might drop on us any moment in person, as you did not write. Well, you were evidently better employed. No. 4 in process of construction was better company for you than all of us put together. Send as much as you have, only *at once*. We shall hardly stay later than the 10th or 12th, as we want to spend a couple of days with my parents at Hosterwitz, after which we go forth to meet the great unknown—Berlin, Kurfür-stenstrasse 87! Sometimes I have qualms; then I remember Heinz, and I know that as long as I have him I want nothing else in heaven or earth. Also I have an idea of learning to use the pedals there, and am as happy as a child at the prospect. Heinz, too, is decidedly looking forward to his 'midnight' boys;* and as he certainly has a touch of Dr. Marianus,† he is sure to do well, and I shall be very happy, too. As

* 'Boys, brought forth in midnights haunted' (*Faust II.*, Act V., Scene 7).

† Confuses 'Dr. Marianus' with 'Pater Seraphicus' in *Faust.*

for all the uglinesses connected with it, the malicious tongues which play so important a part in Berlin, and all the various cliques, we shall come to no harm by them, so much faith have I in our power—and in that of everyone whose instincts are for higher, better things—to keep vulgarity at a distance.

To our very happy acquaintance, then, dear No. 4, and a blessing on the dear author for letting us have you at once!

Heinz will send his firstborn* as soon as little friend Astor is ready. We won't inflict the proof-copy, which is full of mistakes, on you.

Fare you very well!—Yours gratefully and most sincerely,

ELISABET HERZOGENBERG.

Frau Franz called the other day ; she is charming.

### 166. *Brahms to Elisabet von Herzogenberg.*

[MÜRZZUSCHLAG, *September* 4, 1885.]

If the piece† should smile on you at all, I should like to ask you to pass it on to Frau Schumann—that is, play it to her. I hope to hear very soon. You will be sure to send me the thing back before you leave ?—Meantime, in haste, yours,

J. BR.

### 167. *Elisabet von Herzogenberg to Brahms.*

LISELEY, *September* 6, *p.m.* [1885].

We lost no time in sunning ourselves in your 'smiles,' my dear friend. The piece arrived to-day, and I

* The symphony.
† The first movement of the fourth symphony in E minor ; also the beginning of the *andante* written on the last page.

ventured to appropriate to myself the precious enclosure which fluttered out from between the pages, as I seem to remember expressing my longing for the two songs* in a begging letter the other day. You are really too good to comply with my request so promptly; I never dreamed of being spoiled to such an extent. The symphony movement has already undergone a fair amount of torture under my clumsy fingers. It is a characteristic piece of ill-luck that we should have arranged to go to Frau Schumann just to-morrow. We cannot put it off, for we leave on the 10th, and have our hands full in the meantime. The piece only came at noon to-day, and Herr von Kaiserfeld† robbed me of the greater part of the short time I hoped to devote to it, so I shall acquit myself badly before Frau Schumann to-morrow, and am not sure that I shall have the face to strum through the little I know. If I had had a little more time, I should have been pleased and proud to play it to her; but as it is, there are certain passages I can hardly make out at all. Unfortunately—and to Heinz's great disgust—I still have difficulty in reading the horn parts, and have to wrestle miserably with those three wicked lines in the score: horn in E, horn in C and trumpet in E. All the same,

* Brahms had enclosed manuscript copies of the two songs which had particularly taken her fancy (Op. 96, Nos. 2 and 4).

† Moriz v. Kaiserfeld, son of the Austrian politician and former Governor of the Province of Steiermark, was devoted to music, and a great admirer of Brahms. When Brahms was about to try over his new quintet in F at Ladislaus von Wagner's house at Alt-Aussee (August 19, 1882), it was found that no second viola-player was forthcoming; whereupon Kaiserfeld, who, though a violinist, had never had a viola in his hand, was persuaded to undertake the part. He acquitted himself so well that Brahms copied into his album the viola theme from the first movement, with the remark : 'First viola, indifferent; second viola, entirely satisfactory.'

I have gained a fair idea of it. It goes best when I
don't think about it, and some parts come out beautifully and fill me with joy. I know exactly how the
whole of the first subject and the second ought to
sound, right down to the smallest details, and will tell
you all about my impressions as soon as I have a
minute. But I do hate parting from it so soon, and
flatter myself that if you knew we were leaving on the
10th you would let me take it to Hosterwitz and send
it back from there on the 15th, on condition of handling
it with the utmost care—'My plaidie to the angry airt,
I'd shelter it, I'd shelter it!' However, it is too late to
ask you now, and I must of course obey orders. After
all, we have plenty to thank you for as it is.

I must do a little more practising, so good-bye in
haste, and a thousand blessings. I love that D minor
in the very beginning,* and all those slurred quavers
on the sixth page† just before the *marcato* (which reminds me a little of the first movement of the B flat
major quartet).‡ The *pianissimo* with the diminished
7th on G sharp and the quaver-figure on the fiddles is
exquisite, and how splendid it must sound with that
flourish on the drum! I hope to write again soon—
Thanking you once more for everything, yours very
sincerely,

E. H.

### 168. *Brahms to Heinrich von Herzogenberg.*

[MÜRZZUSCHLAG, September 30, 1885.]

I have made up my mind before leaving to send you
the Schubert symphonies,§ though without really

---

\* See p. 4 of the score, last bar.
† P. 7 of the score, first and following bars.
‡ P. 8 of the score, first bar.　　§ See Letter 149.

knowing whether you want them! My latest attack was evidently a complete failure—a symphony too!* But I do beg your dear lady will not abuse her pretty talent for writing pretty letters by inventing any belated fibs for my benefit. With kindest regards and best wishes for success in your new surroundings, yours ever,

J. BRAHMS.

### 169. *Elisabet von Herzogenberg to Brahms.*

BERLIN W., *September* 31, 1885.

The enclosed fragment,† dear Friend, was written one evening at Königssee three weeks ago in the midst of packing, but I prudently kept it back because I felt I was quite unqualified to criticize the symphony after such a woefully brief acquaintance, recollecting a certain saying about women's judgments, specially apposite under the circumstances.‡ How glad I am now that I did not air my half-formed impressions, for I know so much more about it to-day—the dear E minor movement—and have played it so often, in imagination and at the piano, devoting to it practically every minute I could snatch from the work of moving in, that it has really become an old acquaintance to which many of the remarks I made the other day seem quite inapplicable. If I send the other shred of a letter all the

* As Brahms had not heard again from Frau von Herzogenberg, he concluded that her earlier remarks had only been a cloak for her embarrassment, and that the symphony had failed to please either the Herzogenbergs or Frau Schumann.

† See the addition to this letter, dated September 8.

‡ 'In their loves and hatreds there is sometimes reason ; never in their judgments and opinions' (Goethe).

same, it is with the idea that you might be interested
in following the workings of a plain person's mind in
chronological order.

I can now trace the hills and valleys so clearly that
I have lost the impression of its being a complicated
movement;* or rather I no longer look upon the complication I read into it as detrimental to its effect in
any way. At worst it seems to me as if a great master
had made an almost extravagant display of his skill!
I was glad to see how great an effect it *could* have
when I played it to my sister at Hosterwitz. She was
quite carried away by the general sound and character
of the movement in spite of the inadequate performance, and she is, I may say, a good example of the intelligent but wholly uninitiated listener. She never
noticed the points with which we were chiefly concerned — the ingenious combination of the themes,
the massing together of separate links, but simply
enjoyed what she heard. Well, and it is the same
with me now that I have duly absorbed it all : it is
all simple enjoyment, and I have a furious longing to
*hear* it.†

I expect wonders from the actual performance, as
a whole and in detail. There is one passage particularly, at the close of the development, where the first
subject makes its entry in semibreves, which I imagine
must sound wonderfully fine and mysterious, not to
speak of its amazing cleverness and delicacy. How

---

* Hanslick had at first the same impression. When Brahms played
it with Ignaz Brüll on two pianos to a few of his friends in Vienna,
Hanslick, who was present, sighed heavily after the first movement,
and remarked : 'Really, you know, it sounds to me like two
tremendously witty people quarrelling.'

† P. 20 of the score, bar 5.

splendid that C major part must be with the quaver-figure !—

Then farther on the (apparent) chord of the 6th on G, which is merely a use of the 3rd, as a basis for the arabesque-like figure with its D sharp and F sharp;† and before that the beautiful section in the development, so exquisitely prepared by these bars,

with which I fall more and more in love:

Indeed, I am enamoured of the whole of the development, with its masculine terseness and intensely emotional character.

The lovely second subject sounds tender and transparent, but I could wish its melodious character were

* The first G sharp in the third bar is a slip of the pen, or a case of defective memory.   It should be G.
† See p. 20 of the score, bar 14.                ‡ P. 16, bar 11.
§ P. 16, bar 15.   The passage is not quoted quite accurately.

not cut short so soon by the touch of agitation in the
new figure:

The coda is no less admirable; the subject in the
bass,† the syncopated chords, the chromatic

working up to the powerful

and, later on, the incisive

(fine!)

all pressing forward to the close with such a fine
impetus, lend the whole movement a massivity for

---

\* P. 10, bar 10.                    † P. 29, bar 4.
‡ Probably p. 29, bar 17.            § P. 30, bars 4 and 5.
‖ P. 30, bar 12.  The various inaccuracies are all due to quoting
from memory.

which one is hardly prepared by the lyric tendency
of the first subject.

But if I were to say everything I should have to
quote from every page, and even your good nature
might find that too great a strain.

I was deep in my letter just now when your strange
post-card to Heinz—written yesterday—arrived. (How
quickly it came!)  What can you possibly mean by the
'complete failure' of your attack?  An exciting Sunday
afternoon spent with your symphony, a sleepless night
and a sunny morning walk with the score in my macin-
tosh (and—in disjointed fragments—in my heart) on
Monday to Frau Schumann's mountain, her dear
flushed cheeks as she listened, and my own agitation
over the mission for which I was so inadequately
equipped—all these form a memory as precious almost
as any I possess, and yet you go and say those horrid
things!  Heinrich sends word that, if he had not such
a talkative wife, he would not forego the pleasure of
thanking you himself for sending us the symphony-
movement; also he begs and implores you to send the
continuation.  He is accustomed to a wider range, and
does not need to concentrate his attention nervously
on the one part, like myself.  Consequently he allowed
himself to fall in love with the beginning of the second
movement, and is clamouring for more.  Surely, having
said A you might as well say B,* particularly when
your name is Brahms!

I hope you will always continue your kindness to
us, dear Friend, for it means so much, so very much,
particularly here where we are like bleating sheep,
straying over the bleak hillside without finding a single

* A common German proverb, perhaps the nearest equivalent to
'C'est le premier pas qui coûte.'—Tr.

blade of grass. It is a great consolation and resource to have Spitta for a neighbour; he is growing so broad and free in his views, and has attained that true liberality of intellect which is the logical development of the one-sidedness of a strong personality. He has mellowed, too, in spite of his stern attitude in matters concerning art, and is altogether a profitable acquaintance.

I played him your two songs,* and he jumped up and began to sing them too,. being quite at one with us in thinking them rare specimens. How glad I am to have them as a gift from you—and how grateful!

Good-bye for to-day. If I did not write sooner, you know me well enough to believe that it was an impossibility. There was too much work to be done. Thank Heaven I am strong, and able to do it! The summer set me up wonderfully. Good-bye. Heinrich looks forward with me to the symphony.

LISL.

[Enclosure.]

KÖNIGSSEE, September 8, 1885.

MY VERY DEAR FRIEND,—We went to Vordereck yesterday, and I played your symphony movement to the dear woman as well as I could. It was much like a bad first reading by a scratch orchestra, but she very kindly assured me she had understood how you meant it to sound, and I felt very glad and thankful. Our outing took up the whole day, and to-day I have been rummaging, and had visitors into the bargain, although I managed to steal a few glances at the

* Op. 96, Nos. 2 and 4.

score. It is gradually growing plainer and more real to me, and I am always making fresh discoveries. I will try and tell you all my impressions, but I am more than ever conscious—as I told Heinz on the way home yesterday—of the cruel fate which robs our opinions of all their delicacy and bloom as soon as we try to formulate them, just as the butterfly will shake the down from his wings, to rebuke his would-be captors for attempting to lay hands on anything so transient, to confine such an emblem of freedom. Your piece affects me curiously: the more penetration I bring to bear on it, the more impenetrable it becomes; the more stars define themselves in the twilight glow, which at first served to hide them; the more distinct sources of joy do I have, some expected, some un-expected; and the more plainly can I trace the great central driving power which gives unity to the complex work. One never wearies of straining eyes and ears to grasp all the clever turns, all the strange illumin-ating effects of rhythm, harmony and colour, or of admiring your fine chisel for its firm and delicate strokes. Indeed, the possibilities are so inexhaustible that one experiences the joys of a discoverer or a naturalist at every new evidence of your creative ingenuity.

But this is just where a vague doubt comes creeping in, and 'just where' this really is is what I cannot clear up to my own satisfaction, much less put it into intelligible language. I have the feeling that this work of your brain is designed too much with a view to microscopic inspection—just as if its beauties were not there for every simple music-lover to see, as if it were a tiny world for the wise and the initiated in which the common people 'that walk in darkness' could have but a slender portion. Many passages I only discovered with my eyes, and had to confess that without that aid I should only have heard them through the medium of my understanding, not through the natural channel of the senses. Even if you ascribe this to the abstract nature of my knowledge of the work, which must, of course, be heard to have all its power revealed, there is still some truth in it—if not, I shall be delighted to be proved mistaken.

Yet it seems to me that, if its actual appeal proves simple and direct, the effect is only gained *at the cost of* all that tangled overgrowth of ingeniously interwoven detail, which must be overlooked if one would taste and enjoy the fruit itself. It means a regular chase after the fragments of this subject or that; we grow quite nervous indeed, and scent a trail even where there is none. We feel we should like to fold our hands and shut our eyes and be stupid for once, leaning on the composer to rest instead of his driving us so relentlessly afield. We know all the time that we are growing under his hands, that no one else has such keen vision, or can exercise our intellects so powerfully; but we have followed him on other occasions when the paths were pleasant as well as steep, and it is of these we dream when we look forward to another journey.

Don't you see, that is why the working out makes the strongest appeal? There one is prepared to find a tangle of heavy undergrowth with spirit-faces (*revenants*) peering through the darkness, to follow the tiny streams which detach themselves and then flow together again; but if the beginning or the end of a movement is decked out with so much elaboration, it loses something of its potency. As an example of

what I mean, take the third page, where the fiddles
are given this scrappy version of the subject:

It sounds very complicated, because the essential is
made to appear accessory to the non-essential, the
principal subject an accompaniment to the new figure
introduced by the wood-wind and violas.

We have barely become acquainted with the
principal subject before we are expected to recognize
it in its changed form and take in the full effect.
There is a similar case at the close of the development, where the principal subject is very difficult to
recognize in the syncopated pizzicato of the fiddles,
because of the distracting crotchet-triplets on the
wood-wind:

which tempt one to repose—and oblivion ! ‡

\*    \*    \*    \*    \*

170. *Brahms to Elisabet von Herzogenberg.*

[VIENNA, *October* 3, 1885.]

My very best thanks. As for my post-card, please
to remember that you were the first, the only people

---

\* See score, p. 5, bar 11.        † P. 18, bar 10.
‡ Here the letter breaks off.

to see the symphony, and that I am far from being so vain as to expect praise. If I could, I would write more; and if I could, I would gladly send you more. But I am writing hard, and shall be able to try the thing over at leisure, and at Meiningen, very shortly. —With sincerest thanks, yours,                J. Br.

### 171. *Brahms to Elisabet von Herzogenberg.*

[Vienna, *October* 10, 1885.]

My dear Friend,—You will now be able to say that gratitude has not vanished from off the face of the earth. At least, I know of no better way to demonstrate the fact than to send you this arrangement.* You will now be able to view the landscape at your ease— through smoked glasses. You will also have a chance of modifying your criticism very considerably!

The Scherzo is fairly noisy with three tympani, triangle and piccolo.

I question whether you will have the patience to sit through the Finale.†

I enclose a second copy, but much prefer to think of you both sitting at *one* piano to play it.

To-morrow I go to Meiningen. It is possible that Brodsky may play my concerto there *as well*.

Let me have a letter there very soon—by special request!

It is very doubtful whether I shall inflict the piece on anybody else after this. Certainly Bülow would like to begin with it at Frankfurt straight away on

---

* Brahms had arranged the symphony as a duet for two pianos.

† The movement is in the form of a strict *passacaglia*, with the eight-bars theme varied in thirty different ways. Brahms himself and others to whom he had shown the movement were afraid it might prove too monotonous as a Finale.

November 3rd.  They choose to announce it here, too, at their own risk.*

And now let me thank you again very much for your most kind letter, which was really essential to me.  I am, you see, much more modest about my things than you imagine.†

I should like to write more—on other topics, too—but have no time.  Besides, I infinitely prefer a comfortable chat, *not* on paper.  I shall surely see you this winter in Berlin.—With kindest regards to you both, yours,

J. BR.

### 172. *Brahms to Herzogenberg.*

[MEININGEN, *October*, 1885.]

DEAR FRIEND,—Many thanks for your kind letter.  My letter-writing pen cannot contain itself for joy at the beautiful example set by your wife.

It dances across the sheet just anyhow; I can hardly control it sufficiently‡ to tell you that I grow more impatient every day to have my things back, one for playing, the other for corrections.§  Sorry to

---

* Dr. Richter had announced it by way of a novelty at the Vienna Philharmonic.

† Brahms had been feeling very subdued in consequence of the lukewarm reception his new and very inaccessible symphony had met with from his intimate friends at a private performance, and was prepared to put it aside altogether should it fail to please at the Meiningen rehearsal.

‡ These two lines are written slanting across the inside of the sheet in the original.

§ Brahms, whose depression had not been dispelled by the rehearsal of his symphony at Meiningen, was again upset by receiving no acknowledgment of the music he had sent Frau von Herzogenberg. He therefore demanded the duet back, and indulged in a little sarcasm about her expected letter which had never arrived. The whole of his letter bears evidence to his irritability at the time.

trouble you to pack them up. But you have often said A before; this is a supplementary B.*—Kindest regards. Yours,

J. Br.

## 173. *Elisabet von Herzogenberg to Brahms.*

BERLIN W., *October 20, 1885.*

MY DEAR FRIEND,—I came home from Dresden— where I had been saying good-bye to the Florentine people† before their long absence—last night, and found your welcome parcel‡ awaiting me. Heinz had told me there was a delightful surprise in store, but without saying what it was. Imagine my delight when —as I could not wait until this morning—he showed me the piano arrangement before going to bed. 'Did you write and thank that dear Brahms at once?' I asked. 'No,' he said, 'for you were to have come home on Sunday.' And that is true; I was obliged to stay and help those infants,§ and here we are at the 20th, and it will be another day before you receive any thanks from the Herzogenberg household, whom you have made happy once more.

Heinrich has been burying himself in your manu- script, and gives the most fantastic account of the finale, which he assures me is unlike anything I have ever seen. He had to go straight to his classes this morning, but we shall both go to the piano after dinner and see what we can accomplish on *one* instru- ment, with good-will and unanimity of purpose. Un- fortunately, we bequeathed that old horror of ours to the *Bachverein*, and it will be a day or two before we

* See Letter 169.     † Her father, mother, and sister.
‡ See Letter 171.     § Meaning her family.

get a new piano in. At worst I can lie down flat on the floor, like Mozart with the Bach cantatas,* and take in both parts at once.

If the fable about ear-burning were true, you must have had a good deal of it while the two Herzogenbergs relieved their grateful hearts by singing your praise, sir. We were so happy to have this proof of your friendship. You evidently think nothing too good for us! But when shall we hear the symphony on an orchestra?

If I might, I should like to ask you to send it to Joachim. After all, his devotion to you is as strong as anyone's possibly could be, and has nothing half-hearted or effeminate about it. He is really one of the few people who have artistic conviction and taste in place of the multiplicity of tastes which has become the rule. B—— is, unfortunately, one of those for whom a novelty has much the same attraction as any red rag for a bull. It is practically all the same to him from which quarter the wind blows it—Brahms or Bruckner, Dvořák, Tchaikovsky, or any other. Now I think that is dreadful. As I often say, of what good to be uplifted by the best things, if you are satisfied with the worst the next moment? But these ideas are out of date, and our convictions, which are of mature growth and religious intensity, are often dismissed as 'one-sided bigotry,' while the pitying smile which accompanies the words may be read as

* When Mozart was at Leipzig in 1789, he heard a performance of Bach's cantata *Sing unto the Lord a New Song*, by the *Thomaner;* and on learning that there was a whole collection of Bach's cantatas there, but no complete scores, he had the written parts brought to him, spread them all around him, and was not to be moved from the spot until he read them all through (see Rochlitz in the *Allgemeine Musikalische Zeitung*, 1799, No. 8).

meaning: '*we* take a broader point of view.' It is
enough to infuriate one sometimes.

But I have never seen a trace of this 'breadth' (trans-
late superficiality mixed with cowardice!) in Joachim,
and I therefore count him among the true Brahms
lovers, as distinct from the other distressingly numerous
class, who merely follow a fashion without possessing a
spark of intelligent interest. Since the Wagner set*
took you up, there has been a serious increase in their
numbers, as you will probably have noticed.

I am curious to know how you will like B.'s playing
of the concerto. We thought his various tricks, his
exaggerated *tremolo* and *glissando* and all the methods
he employs so lavishly to secure melting effects,
rather more pronounced, if anything. It spoils the
pleasure one feels one would otherwise have in such
a genuinely gifted player. But he has always been
worshipped at Leipzig; no one has ventured a word
of warning except Bernsdorf, whose censure is more
likely to strengthen one in crime. If you could warn
him gently, who knows what good results it might have!

But I must stop. You will certainly have no time
for reading letters at Meiningen. How I should love
to be there at your rehearsal, which will be carried
out in such a beautiful, serious spirit, and what would
I not give to hear that theme in semibreves and the
flirtation between C and A♭ major!†

Do tell me your impressions on first hearing it, the
first movement, and whether everything comes out
well—the return of the first subject that first time
with the quaver accompaniment on the winds,‡ and

---

* Refers to Fritzsch, whose paper, the *Musikalisches Wochenblatt*,
strongly championed Wagner.

† Score of the E minor symphony, p. 20, bar 8.     ‡ P. 5, bar 12.

the syncopated passage in G sharp minor (in the development);* and please tell me, too, whether the multiplicity of episodes is as noticeable when hearing as when reading it—ah, when shall I ever hear it myself!—and whether you are duly carried away by the second subject.† And are you not sorry you were in such haste to repent your display of emotion and insert those dotted crotchets‡ to blot out, as far as possible, the *fast zu ernst*§ idea ? For that will always be one of my grievances.

Further, let me say in all humility that the apparent return of the first subject (which leads one to expect the repetition of the first part, though you resisted the temptation out of consideration for Fritzsch ‖) in E minor is, to me, very disturbing, and decidedly weakens the effect of the real E minor when the first subject really comes. Heinrich and I have quarrelled over it every day up to now. He invariably remarks when I am playing it to him, and reach that point : ' You are wrong there ; Brahms would never bring in E minor so soon.' Of course I insist that I am right, relying on my memory, which seldom fails me in a question of harmony. ' I only wish it were not E minor,' I say ; ' but it undoubtedly is.' And you know it does go like this, just after the half-close on F sharp :

---

* P. 18, bar 8.          † P. 8, bar 5.          ‡ P. 10, bar 3.
§ The inscription over the tenth of Schumann's *Kinderszenen.*
‖ The *Musikalisches Wochenblatt* had contained arguments for the rejection of the classical sonata movement, in particular the repetition of the first part.
¶ See score, p. 13, bar 5.

after which the subject enters in full. Don't you think you could do an even finer modulation there, and bring in the E with more blissful, more *powerful* effect ? If I were a Saxon, I should now say, 'please consider this unsaid'; being other, however, and assured of your imperturbable kindness and patience, I will simply thank you again and yet again for everything. As soon as I know the other movements, you will let me whistle my delight in a neat counterpoint to it, I hope.

But please write one little post-card, or else I shall think you are really angry for once.

And please when do you consider we may hope to see you here ? As soon as you are back in Vienna I am going to send you some new songs of Heinz's, if I may. He does not want to be bothering you perpetually, but there is one, a 'Phrygian,' which pleases me particularly.

If you think it at all the proper thing, please present my respects to the family—the friendly members, or at least the Countess, to whom I am really grateful for recommending me the fine Örtel treatment.* It has made me a champion runner!—Yours very sincerely,

E. H.

174. *Brahms to Elisabet von Herzogenberg.*

[MEININGEN, *October 22,* 1885.]

MY DEAR FRIEND,—I wish very much I could hear more, though it would certainly be nicer if you could both go comfortably to the rehearsal with me. You

* Dr. Örtel's treatment was for heart disease.

would be able to listen to the first movement with the utmost serenity, I am sure.

But I hate to think of doing it anywhere else, where I could not have these informal, special rehearsals, but hurried ones instead, with the performance forced on me before the orchestra had a notion of the piece.

There will be a repetition of the symphony here on November 1st, I expect, and at Frankfurt on the 3rd. Please let Frau Schumann have the music by the 1st at latest.

What you say about Joachim is no news to me. I heartily endorse it all, and he knows it. . . .

But I have no more time, as I am due at rehearsal.

Frau von Heldburg is not here, I am sorry to say. She is being nursed at Schloss Altenburg* by the Duke's nurse after a severe illness. But His Highness is expected one of these days, and will come and listen.—With kindest regards, yours,

J. Br.

### 175. *Brahms to Herzogenberg.*

[MEININGEN, *October* 24, 1885.]

DEAR FRIEND,—Please arrange for Frau Schumann to receive the music without fail on Saturday, the last of the month, *at latest!* I don't expect to hear that the piano arrangement has given you much satisfaction, though I think you would have moments of satisfaction here. Be sure you send me the songs to Vienna, the 'Phrygian' included !—Ever yours,

J. Br.

* A slip for Altenstein.

### 176. *Elisabet von Herzogenberg to Brahms.*

[BERLIN W., *October* 30, 1885.]

MY VERY DEAR FRIEND,—The symphony leaves us
to-day according to instructions, and, while shedding
my parting tear, let me thank you with all my heart
for presenting us with the piano score so promptly.
It means seeing it through smoked glass, of course,
but, thank Heaven! we know enough Brahms to be
able to hear it in imagination.  We often felt we knew
just as well what the other movements should be like
as the first, whose real physiognomy has been revealed
to us.

This new manifestation of your power has made us
so happy, dear Friend, and we wish we had the knack
of telling you so in a convincing way.  There must
be many privileged people who can.

The Andante has that freshness and distinction of
character with which only you could endow it, and
even you have had recourse to certain locked chambers
of your soul for the first time.  How free and flowing
it is, too!  Some people will find this a hard nut to
crack,

but to me it is a harshness of the pleasant, bracing
order.  On the other hand, I have qualms about the
passage near the close :

* See score, p. 32, bar 5.

The D sharp in conjunction with the lower D would not matter in itself, but the whole progression of the three upper parts, as against the marked repose in the bass, jars indescribably. *Must* it be, dear Friend? But to return. How exquisitely melodious it all is!—the parting phrase of the theme in E major:

the beautiful way in which the second subject is ushered in by an abridged version of itself! How every 'cellist, beginning with Hausmann,‡ to whom we played it yesterday, will revel in this glorious, long-drawn-out song breathing of summer! And these, I presume, are the cherries which refuse to ripen at Mürzzuschlag!§ The close, too, is delicious, with its modulation to C, which carries one back so happily to the opening bars, with their tinge of the Phrygian mode.‖ The lowered supertonic in the final cadence is peculiarly satisfying, and we rise from this feast in a quiet, happy, satisfied frame of mind, with some desire for an interval in which to attune ourselves for the irresistible rough humour of the Scherzo; but it is

* P. 43, bar 1.　　　　　† See score, p. 41, bar 1.

‡ Robert Hausmann (b. 1852), professor and soloist, a member of the Joachim quartet.

§ *Cf.* Letter 164.　　　　‖ P. 43, bar 7.

not long before we surrender heart and soul to its
versatile gaiety and impetus.

The effect when actually played must, of course,
be very different from the effect produced on that
necessary evil men call a piano. Those semiquaver
chords

on the F are so playful, so frivolous almost, and yet so
lovely as crotchets, farther on, with the syncopated
basses†—the old made new by your great unfailing
skill! How cleverly the *piano* passage

leads up to the second subject, which savours as clearly
of the volkslied as if some tender youth were piping it
on his flute outside! That scale of 3rds§ (obviously
for the wood-wind) in D minor must be droll, too; also
the double 3rds‖ afterwards, which reduce a poor
second-piano player to despair. The *pianissimo* parting
phrase is bewitching,

and the development just after it should be most
effective. How beautiful the soft C sharp minor

* P. 44, bar 6.        † P. 46, bar 7.        ‡ P. 49, bar 1.
§ P. 49, bar 9.        ‖ P. 50, bar 2.        ¶ P. 51, bar 11.

passage is at the end,* when all the gay apprentices slouch home from work, and the peace of evening sets in, while the reminiscence of all this merriment becomes lyrical (*that* subject lyrical!) in D flat;† and, most beautiful of all, the soft entry of the horns and trombones at *poco meno presto !*‡

And now for my one grief with respect to this movement: all that beauty, all that rich tenderness, and then the rapid—almost brutally rapid—return to C major! Believe me, it is as if you had played us some glorious thing on the piano, and then, to ward off all emotion and show your natural coarseness, snort into your beard: 'All rot, all rot, you know!' It hurts so, this forcible C major; it is no modulation, but an operation—at least, so I feel it, Heaven forgive me!

The whole *coda* is exquisite. I look forward to that pedal note§ as I do to Christmas. What an impetus it has, too!—as if you had written it quite breathlessly or in one long-drawn breath. One positively expands and grows stronger while listening.

As for the last movement, shall you mind if I proclaim it my favourite—at least, for the time being? I am fascinated by the theme itself, and the fascination grows as I follow it through its various phases, first in the bass, then in the top part or skilfully hidden somewhere in the middle, and—most impressive of all,

---

* P. 59, bar 3.                    † P. 59, bar 8.

‡ Frau von Herzogenberg was right in her conjecture as to the horns, but Brahms contented himself with bassoons for strengthening the harmonies. There are no trombones in the first three movements. They are reserved for the *finale*, where they bring in the theme of the *passacaglia* with such a shattering effect.

§ P. 70, bar 4.

surely, for susceptible listeners—in its trombone effort
in the golden key of E major.* As my dear Heinz
said at once, when I came home that time: 'If you are
at all like me, you will howl over it!' and, indeed, who
wouldn't? It is the kind of inspiration only a good
man could have. How splendid it must sound—lucky
trombone-players! Didn't the people go mad over it,
and haven't they spoiled you at Meiningen, and congratulated themselves ever so on the success of your
latest effort? And we had to stay at home and content
ourselves with thinking of you. We were really models
of virtue not to pack up and go; but Heinrich really
couldn't leave, and, besides, we are such penniless
wretches with the Leipzig house—for which no tenant
will offer—on our hands.

You asked, the other day, whether I should have
the patience to sit through the last movement. I can
only say I should not mind if it were three times as
long. Surely it must go down with an audience too,
even if they neither understand nor are able to
follow the *passacaglia* form; for there is no laborious
weaving of threads, but a succession of novel combinations, all imbued with a vigour that must have
an arresting, overpowering effect, and one need not
be a musician, thank Heaven! to come under the
spell.

Why, there are certain passages which tug at one's
very heart-strings—that C major, for instance:

* See score, p. 90, bar 6.　　† See score, p. 102, bar 7.

and the way it twists upwards :

which anyone can follow! Who can resist an emotion
strong enough to penetrate all that skilful elaboration!
I call it sheer coquetry to ask if we can sit through it.

But the chief thing is, When are we going to hear
it ? *Joachim is dying to do it.* Won't you let him have
it very soon ? He came to listen to it yesterday, and
once before that, and shared our delight in it. I heard
him do the F major quintet recently, and was again
impressed by his wonderful gift of interpretation.
The close of the slow movement, which forms a link
with the Finale, was a revelation. I grasped its full
significance for the first time, as the D minor hove in
sight, nebulous as an island in the midst of a dream-
like sea.† Heinrich and I, together with many others,
were transfixed with wonder. But enough for to-day,
much as I should like to let my pen run on. My poor
old father is staying with us, and is much in need of
my services as a secretary and as a daughter. I had
really no time for this, and still less for the dear
symphony, which I have not been able to learn by
heart, unfortunately. It costs me many a pang to send
it away to-day.

Good-bye, dear Friend, and send a line to say whether
we may count on hearing the symphony here before
long. Thank you once more, and accept the sincere
devotion of your

HERZOGENBERGS.

* See score, p. 102, bar 7.          † Op. 88, p. 34, bar 12.

### 177. *Herzogenberg to Johannes Brahms.*

[BERLIN (?), 1884.]

DEAR, NOBLE BENEFACTOR,—I must come out of my shell while the memory of our symphony performance* yesterday is still fresh, and thank you most sincerely, not only for your goodness, but for the good symphony. I made over the second piano part to little Wolf,† who is so much better equipped for it than myself, and was able to give myself up to the uninterrupted pleasure of listening. I need not begin at the beginning and describe all the phases of our receptivity, for you are so accustomed to regard my wife's utterances as studies in two-part counterpoint, to which I contribute the steady-going *cantus firmus* while she exercises her discretion on the eloquent, flexible *contrapunctum floridum.* However, they are both one, and lay themselves once more prostrate at your feet, ready to lick the hand that administered the blows, since the effect on their morals has proved so salutary. The truth is, you wield a club which silences all criticism. I have even come to think that the very parts which hurt me before (primarily a result of thumping the piano so hard) now make a great, a very special appeal to me. We were so very sorry we could not go to the Meiningen performance, sorrier than we allowed ourselves to admit. But I am no longer a free agent, and if I were not so happy with it all—why it should be so I can't think—I should be cursing my luck.

Well, and to whose lot is it to fall here? Taubert,

---

* On two pianos at Herzogenberg's house.
† C. L. Wolf (*cf.* Letter 151).

Kadecke, Joachim, Klindworth, or Mannstädt?* And
to whose lot are *you* to fall here ?

I must earnestly request that you do not put us off
with a flying visit, but come and hang up the good old
brown overcoat on its rightful peg.

But my wife will have dwelt on all this at length, no
doubt, and there is nothing left for me, independently,
but to send my very kindest regards.—Yours,

HERZOGENBERG.

But I am forgetting your kind gift of the Schubert
symphonies in my absorption in your own, ungrateful
wretch that I am! They fell, however, on receptive,
fruitful soil. I now realize that the mechanical part
is not so very difficult if only one has ideas to work
on. This trifling point is the crux of the whole
question—whether we succeed in really producing
anything or not. On the whole, I propose to cram
myself—and my pupils—with counterpoint instead of
turning monk!

178. *Elisabet von Herzogenberg to Brahms.*

BERLIN, *November* 4, 1885.

MY VERY DEAR FRIEND,—I had a letter from Frau
Schumann yesterday, from which I gather, to my
horror, that the symphony did not reach Frankfurt
until Sunday morning   To assure you that I did not
disobey your orders, I am writing to say that I took
the parcel to post on *Friday*, the 29th, at 4 p.m., and,
as the Frankfurt express only leaves here at eight,
I was surely safe in supposing it would arrive on
Saturday ? It distresses me more than I can say to

* The names of the various conductors in Berlin at that time.

know that it did not arrive, and that you and Frau Schumann were upset in consequence. You probably thought it gross carelessness or neglect on my part, and abused me accordingly. 'And *that* is the thanks I get for my kindness and generosity!' I hear you say, and I must admit you are justified. It shall be a warning to me always to leave a day's margin on special occasions. I should have sent off the music on Thursday but that Joachim and Hausmann, who particularly wanted to hear the symphony, were not able to come until that evening; and as you had written, 'Saturday at latest in Frankfurt,' we thought there was no criminal risk in posting it on Friday.

Please don't be angry any more. I am, in all seriousness, deeply concerned about it, and regret particularly that Frau Schumann had no opportunity of taking the symphony into her affections before the performance.*

Just a line to set my mind at rest and give us a friendly thought in the midst of all these great occasions. Herr Grosser,† who was at Meiningen— lucky man!—gave such a glorious account of the concert. We were speechless with envy when he told us how incredibly beautiful the symphony sounded. It was at Rubinstein's that he told us, and our poor host must have listened with very different feelings.‡ We are having a little too much of his playing here just now, and are often driven to the sad necessity of quarrelling with him. There is no

---

* At Frankfurt on November 3.

† Julius Grosser (1844- ?), bookseller and journalist, had made Brahms's acquaintance in Vienna.

‡ Anton Rubinstein was a declared opponent of Brahms's music, of which he never played a note in public, the name Brahms being conspicuously absent from his famous historical recitals.

denying that he has a whole orchestra in his fingers, and the most exquisite richness of tone and touch; but he seems to care less and less what piece he is playing, and is letting a certain devil-may-care attitude towards rhythm and other trifling matters grow upon him. One can't help feeling sorry. Are the Leipzigers to be favoured with the symphony? If so, we are going! And Berlin? Well, you won't be angry, will you, but believe in my innocence!—In haste, yours very sincerely,

                                                        E. H.

I may add that the post-office people assured me the parcel would reach Frankfurt on Saturday.


*179. Brahms to Heinrich von Herzogenberg.*

[FRANKFURT-AM-MAIN, *November* 5, 1885.]

The delay of the parcel did not matter to us either here or at Wiesbaden, and we were decidedly more amused than angry. Besides, I owe you many thanks on another score. But to the point! I wrote to Joachim yesterday, but did not know the address, and forgot to ask the Schumanns for it. The letter is accordingly addressed 'Berlin' *tout court*, so Joachim might make inquiries if it does not arrive. There is nothing in the letter but a cheerful 'yes' in reply to his.

I start in an hour's time,* so must ask you to excuse these hasty lines.—Kindest regards from yours ever,

                                                        J. BR.

* To Holland, via Essen and Elberfeld, for a series of concerts in Amsterdam, The Hague, and Utrecht.

180. *Elisabet von Herzogenberg to Brahms.*

BERLIN, *December 2,* 1885.

MY DEAR FRIEND,—You will shortly receive a visit from Frau Prüwer, which please to take with a good grace. We are responsible for the invasion, and I will tell you how it comes about. You will probably have heard of little Julius Prüwer,* who is studying with Professor Schmitt† in Vienna. He has also played from time to time at Bösendorfer's‡ and elsewhere. The parents are poor—he is some sort of minor official—and have taken the boy away from school, and are having him taught at home to give him more time for his music. This has brought them into debt, and they arranged this concert tour with the poor little chap to raise the necessary amount. The attempt has failed, however, for the agent who had talked the mother into it turned out a swindler, and refused to pay at the very first stage, which was Berlin.

Frau Prüwer had a letter to Barth,§ who, together with Rudorff,‖ heard the boy play. They were quite amazed at his talent, and not less horrified at the barbarous method by which he had evidently been taught. The impression made was so powerful, and

---

* Julius Prüwer is described in Theodor Helm's *Kalender für die musikalische Welt* as 'prodigy,' 'pianist,' and (1894) 'concert pianist' successively. He is now conductor of the Breslau Opera.

† Hans Schmitt (b. 1835), pianist and composer, professor at the Vienna Conservatoire, and author of various works on teaching.

‡ A concert-hall in Vienna, belonging to the piano-manufacturer Ludwig Bösendorfer.

§ Heinrich Barth (b. 1847), pupil of Bülow, Bronsart, and Tausig, a professor at the *Hochschule*, Berlin.

‖ Ernst Rudorff (b. 1840), composer, conductor of the Stern Choral Society, and professor at the *Hochschule*.

Rudorff's warm heart was so strongly affected, that he had but the one thought—to take the child away from its surroundings and its teacher. His idea was to interest people here, and have the child properly looked after until it was ready for instruction in the (musically) good and the beautiful, etc., etc. When he came to us, quite full of his plans, and asked us to hear the child too, his youthful enthusiasm quite put us to shame, for we immediately raised an army of objections to damp his ardour. We insisted particularly that, always supposing there were no reliable master in Vienna, it was a great risk to take a child away from its surroundings and set it down to wait until it should be ready to profit by one's teaching; also that general education was of more importance than musical instruction, and other wise axioms. The next day the little fellow came and played—abominably, but with every evidence of great talent. He transposed the C sharp major fugue* into G, or any key required, and, further, played some incredibly neat modulations when I was alone with him, and understood at once what I meant by an interrupted cadence when I dictated it to him by mistake. In short, it is very evident to us all that it is the real thing.

Heinrich and I are more sceptical, in so far that we believe that a talent for music does not necessarily presuppose an artistic nature, and that talents as remarkable have been known to lead to nothing. We are therefore doubtful whether it is worth the risk of transplanting the child into foreign soil, thereby raising the greatest expectations on the parents' part, and fanning the child's ambition. In any case we think it most desirable that the child should be placed

* From the *Wohltemperirtes Klavier*.

in conscientious hands.  So far it can hardly be said
to have had instruction, but a breaking-in at most.
The poor little wretch takes three fingers to any note
he wants to emphasize sharply, and even uses his fist
on occasion.  His wrists are stiff, touch and position
all wrong, and his phrasing bears evidence of the
half-civilized method which aims at effect at any price.
Consequently, in spite of the little performer's childish
personality, it is like listening to a wizened old man,
which is pitiful.  One cannot, being human and a
musician, listen to him without a lively desire to see
the dear gifted child given a healthier existence.  Our
advice was, first of all to send the child back to school
and make music a casual secondary study, partly for
the child's health, and partly to limit the teacher's
influence as far as possible in case no change should
be practicable.  Later on let the boy have a better
master at all costs, the best possible indeed; and this
is where you come in, dear Friend, for everyone knows
you have a tender spot for children.

You can best tell us who would be the safest person
to take him in charge; and as you have had greater
experience than any of us, you will be able to judge
whether it is dangerous to leave him with Schmitt for
the present, if the bond between teacher and pupil
were loosened by curtailing the lessons, etc., for which
a pretext could easily be found.  You will also be
the most reliable judge of the child's musical calibre,
and be able to advise accordingly, and you alone
are cognizant of the facilities Vienna offers.  Does
Epstein do as much now, and is the musical atmosphere there such as to make it desirable to remove
the boy from Vienna later on and bring him here?
The mother was very sensible about it, so much so

that I believe she would be just as easily convinced if anyone were seriously to advise her to the contrary. We—Heinz and I—think the child looks Jewish; a Pole he certainly is. I wish he were German, for the strain is so much purer, after all. We congratulated ourselves on that fact the other day at Rubinstein's Russian winding-up concert. It was all *salon* music, more or less peppered with Nihilists' dynamite, and nothing behind it.

Don't be impatient with this letter, my dear Friend. Most 'great men' are, let me inform you, so selfish that they refuse to be molested or worried with other people's affairs. One loves a child for its own sake; but when it is a question of musical talent too, it has a claim on our consideration even at the cost of some inconvenience. Serious aims and high ideals are, alas! all too scarce in these days; there would be some satisfaction in setting them before anyone so young and malleable, and educating him to that end.

And how is our symphony, and when will your wanderings bring you to Berlin? And do you, in the midst of your conquests, sometimes think of your very faithful old friends?

181. *Brahms to Elisabet von Herzogenberg.*

[VIENNA, *December* 5, 1885.]

MY DEAR FRIEND,—Your little protégé shall be very welcome, though I confess prodigies only interest me in so far as I find their performances entertaining. I have too often seen them do the most incredible things —and it has all ended in smoke!

But who would raise a finger for any youth incapable of inspiring the conviction in himself and

18

all his friends that he is capable of rising to any heights!

Is it possible that I never thanked you for the symphony?* If so, it is because I wanted to say more than just 'thank you,' and I have not your pretty talent in that direction. But I can assure you that no one could bury himself in it with more pleasure or be better able to appreciate and admire all that is good and beautiful in it. How delightful and nice it would be if I could have Heinz here all to myself, and could tell him all I think while it is fresh in my mind!

But as the piece is, above all, so complicated, I find it impossible to go over it in detail just now.

I do think it a great pity (this will make you very angry!) that Heinz should have put such a strain on his audiences in this first symphony. The string trios and quartets had made me hope for better things in that respect. Let us hope it will soon be followed by a second, less calculated to inspire such predominating respect in an audience.

I am sorely tempted to begin at the first bar and chatter to my heart's content. I always feel that I have a sort of claim on anything that interests me so keenly, and may be allowed to take it with me on my walks and think over its possibilities of development.

I have found Rubinstein quite endurable since the Schumann recital here. Have you heard of his latest achievement? He has been giving his fourteen recitals,† two at a time, in Moscow and St. Petersburg

---

* Brahms had taken 'our' symphony (see end of previous letter) to mean Herzogenberg's.

† The famous historical recitals, comprising piano music of all periods in chronological order.

alternately, which means doing the sixteen hours' journey in between fourteen times!

I found a whole stack of letters here when I arrived. I am simply addressing Joachim's to the *Hochschule.*—Yours very sincerely,

J. BRAHMS.

### 182. *Brahms to Elisabet von Herzogenberg.*

[VIENNA, January 1, 1886.]

My thoughts are much with you and the dear one you have lost.* Our meetings have been brief and rare of late years, but each parting left me with the wish to see him oftener and at greater leisure.

With very kindest regards, yours,

J. BRAHMS.

### 183. *Elisabet von Herzogenberg to Brahms.*

BERLIN, February 3, 1886.

MY VERY DEAR FRIEND,—I wanted to write yesterday to tell you what a heavenly evening we had the day before,† but was prevented.

The philharmonic orchestra is good, as you know, but their playing of the symphony was not good, but simply perfection. Joachim had done wonders at the rehearsals. It was a pleasure to see his good-will and enthusiasm; nothing escaped him, no detail was

---

* Her father, who died suddenly on December 29. This brief expression of sympathy was written on a post-card, which is a proof of Brahms's indifference to convention.

† Joachim conducted the E minor symphony on February 1 at the Philharmonic concert, and deemed it wise to call the last movement *Variations*, the theme of the *passacaglia* being printed on the programmes.

beneath his attention. He would take up his fiddle and show them exactly what was wanted; and although the rehearsals ran to a cruel length, he knew how to coax his men to renewed effort and curb their impatience. We felt it growing clearer and more transparent; each beautiful passage shone out more dazzlingly as we listened. I wish you could have been there, and seen our faces, and enjoyed it all with us. My mind, which has been fettered for so long, shook itself free at last. Music has appealed only to my physical side, as it were, all this time; nothing interested me sufficiently to distract me from my grief or to vibrate to it and bring me consolation. But this carried me out of myself, and I realized the inestimable benefit one may receive from great impressions and the liberating power of the manifestation of beauty. You see I owe you very special thanks for bringing my soul this relief.

Yet there were moments in between when I sighed painfully to think that my dear father was past hearing it all. He was so peculiarly receptive to your music. We hardly ever met without his asking me for *Feldeinsamkeit, Über die Heide hallet mein Schritt,** and various other things. You would have had some pleasure yourself in seeing him turn young as he listened, the dear old man! But your wonderful symphony was to be my theme, not this. The effect was *overpowering*, beyond all we had imagined, though we were prepared for something very beautiful. I was moved to tears—happy tears—by the Andante. The way that E is held on after the first powerful quasi-Phrygian summons, and the soft entry of the G sharp, and finally the lovely E major itself, sounding like an organ in the

* Songs from Op. 86.

distance*—I know of no other orchestral effect to compare with it. It is one of the most affecting things I know, and, indeed, I should chose this movement for my companion through life and in death. It is *all* melody from first to last, increasing in beauty as one presses forward ; it is a walk through exquisite scenery at sunset, when the colours deepen and the crimson glows to purple. We exchanged glances at the return of the second subject in E major,† and our hearts thanked you. How healthy it all is, too! Its pathos comes from a pure source, and is inspiring in the best sense—never excessive or ecstatic, as is the present tendency. One can listen with a good conscience, that is, and submit *voluntarily* to the magician's spell. The two pulsations on B‡ for the drum at the end are deliciously thrilling, and, indeed, the whole passage

based on 🎼 is so exquisite that one ends by

withdrawing the objection to 🎼 §, since it

comes from *you*, and the rest of you is so nice! The Scherzo is one string of surprises. Who can describe the effect of it all, its purely orchestral origin! Such passages as——

But I really must not bore you with my everlasting examples. It all comes from wanting to add conviction to my assertions that nothing is lost upon us, but that we take it all in with delight. We shall be able to tell you everything better at Leipzig—where I hope we are to meet on the 18th ?—the beloved score in hand.

---

* See score, p. 32, bar 3.    † P. 41, bar 2.    ‡ P. 42, bar 7.
§ Referring to the powerful dissonance referred to in Letter 176 (p. 43, bar 1).

Joachim was so kind as to leave it with me for a couple
of hours, having first extracted a solemn promise from
me; but it was just dinner-time, and I had only time
to play the second movement through to Johannes
Röntgen and Thomson* before taking it back, which
was worse than nothing. When shall we have a
chance of seeing it, and is there no possibility of
reclaiming the two-piano arrangement which the lucky
Frankfurters have had for so long? Barth is so keen
on studying it with me.

Speaking of Barth reminds me of Bargiel,† who was
quite carried away by your symphony. He completely
thawed, or perhaps the iron band about his heart split
in two like Iron Heinrich's. He almost embraced
Joachim after the symphony—and, indeed, the man
deserved embracing! I was sorry I had not the
courage for that sort of thing, for he was so splendid
in his sacred ardour, so happily and devoutly absorbed
in your music. Both he and his orchestra were roused
to the highest pitch of excitement in the last movement,
and really there was not a single mishap, not a moment
when the effect was unfavourable; nothing in the
whole symphony went wrong—a rare achievement
in the case of a new work! The trombones played
their E major variation superbly, and the flute its
lovely monologue likewise.‡ Above all, the performance brought out clearly the unity, which is the most
admirable thing about this movement, making of the
whole one stately progress, a *finale* in which the ' varia-

* César Thomson (b. 1857), violinist, conductor, and professor at
the Conservatoires of Lüttich and Brussels.

† Woldemar Bargiel (1828-1897), composer, stepbrother of Frau
Schumann's.

‡ See score, pp. 90 and 88.

tions' assume their due proportions as hills and hollows in the vast picture. And Herr Gumprecht* thinks it instructive, a scholastic experiment! Why, it is just the opposite!

Well, are you really coming to Leipzig on February 18th? May we look forward to it? Heinz will be able to get one or two days' leave.

Good-bye. The said dear Heinz sends kindest remembrances. He is writing such nice things just now, and is very happy. Kindest remembrances also from Johanna.† I suppose our telegram never reached you. I only heard yesterday from Joachim that you were at Cologne.‡ Please send me a line, and you might take a whole sheet of paper this time, even if you can't fill it. I only want to know if you are really coming to Leipzig on the 18th, and if you still like us a little. I sometimes fear you may lose the art, now that we so seldom meet and you have so many friends. But we must keep your friendship; we need it so, and you well know our feelings towards you now and always.

Remember us to Wüllner. Can't you cure him of Bruckner, who has become as much of an epidemic as diphtheria.

Fritzsch's paper§ has really become impossible. If I were you, I should refuse to be praised by him any more.

And now really good-bye. Johanna says: 'Say

* Otto Gumprecht (1823-1900), music critic of the *Nationalzeitung*, known as the 'Berlin Hanslick.'

† Frau Röntgen.

‡ Brahms conducted his E minor symphony, the *Song of Destiny*, and played his D minor concerto, at a Gürzenich concert on February 9.

§ The *Musikalisches Wochenblatt*.

something nice to him from me.' She is really one of the faithful.

Just a little line, then, to your faithfullest

E. HERZOGENBERG.

### 184. *Brahms to Elisabet von Herzogenberg.*

[COLOGNE, *February* 7, 1886.]

MY DEAR FRIEND,—The general confusion here makes it impossible for me to do anything but send my best thanks for your kind letter and your most kind intention of coming to Leipzig. I have still to get in a quartet this morning. Then comes a big dinner-party, afterwards a grand celebration at the conservatoire with quantities of music, and another in the evening at the *Männergesangverein !*

Can you expect more than a cheery *auf Wiedersehen ?* —Very sincerely yours,

J. BR.

### 185. *Brahms to Herzogenberg.*

[VIENNA, *February* 24, 1886.]

MY DEAR FRIEND,—Do tell me whether you have anything in Beethoven's handwriting.* If not, I will enclose a slip (by way of interest) when I return your Schuberts. I wanted particularly to tell you, too, that Frau Gräfin Wickenburg† is selling her Schuberts! So far as I know, she has only some overtures as duets and a few transposed *Müllerlieder* besides the trio in E flat.—With kindest regards, yours,

J. BR.

---

* Brahms's collection of autographs included nearly thirty loose pages and the sketch-book to the sonata, Op. 106, in Beethoven's own hand.

† Gräfin Wilhelmine von Wickenburg-Almasy (b. 1845), poetess.

186. *Elisabet von Herzogenberg to Brahms.*

BERLIN, *February* 26, 1886.

MY VERY DEAR FRIEND,—I really needed your kind post-card, for I came back from Leipzig* in a fit of the dumps in spite of all the E minor glamour. The scanty rations on which I had to exist quite failed to satisfy me after the good old times, and I felt as if I had been deposed from a very pleasant post. O Humboldt-strasse! O Zeitzerstrasse, even! How shady were thy branches!† It was too depressing to be jostled about as a visitor in the grimy town with never a claim on the dear person at Hauffe's Hotel—no possibility of looking after him at home, or making his coffee, or having him all to one's self for a cosy chat. I felt too lost even to enjoy that precious dinner-hour at the Wachs' with you as I should have liked. Worst of all, I never seemed able to get near you with my enthusiasm for the E minor, when on other occasions I have always succeeded, after much perseverance, in penetrating your defences, and bringing home to you little by little all I felt. I admit that in this case you knew it all—for have I not written it more than once ?—but it is a satisfaction to say it, and to thank you by word of mouth and a grip of the hand as you deserve. But with you one must watch one's opportunity, and then attack boldly ; there is no taking you on the wing, least of all for a bungler like me. You know I am very much in earnest about it, and I

---

* Brahms conducted his E minor symphony at the Gewandhaus on February 18. Brodsky played the violin concerto at the same concert.

† 'O Tannenbaum, O Tannenbaum, wie grün sind deine Blätter ' (popular song).—TR.

wish I could have thanked you worthily for enriching
our lives as you have done by producing this latest
work.   However, I will set it down here instead, and
like to imagine you will read it with one of your
kindest smiles and be happy to think of our happiness.

You took all that about Schubert too seriously.   Do
consider how it flattered the little school-girl I was
then to possess anything you should think it worth
while to steal!   Had I been able to give you it (as
I did actually give you *Anselmo*),* it would have been
better still.   But I do beg you will not send it back
now, for I should really be hurt.   Won't you send me
a nice Brahms manuscript instead?   You see I am
ready as ever to take all I can get—and why not?
You have already given me so much that I have
exhausted my blushes.   I am a veritable marmot: the
more you heap upon me the happier I am.   But there
shall be no reason to complain of my ingratitude.
How should a waif like myself possess a Beethoven
manuscript!   But ought I really to accept it, and do
you know of nothing that I could give you beside
my boundless admiration, which leaves you so indifferent?

I am not surprised to hear that the Wickenburgs
are selling their Schuberts, for this generation knows
no piety, no scruples.   Have not the Orsinis sold
Benvenuto Cellini's own doorkey, and are there any
treasures still in the hands of their original owners?
But the Wickenburgs have, after all, no particular
musical traditions, and I shouldn't mind if only they
had *given* them away.   Perhaps their circumstances
did not admit of that ; people with children never can
do anything nice and unpractical.   That is the one

* The manuscript of Schubert's song *Am Grabe Anselmos*.

thing that makes us almost glad we have none sometimes, for we can at least be unpractical to our hearts'
desire—and are!

Yesterday at Joachim's I begged for my favourite
little bit out of the concerto :

which B. does not come anywhere near playing! He
played it fairly well as long as you were there and
could tell him, but he is not a refined player, for all
poor Fritzsch declares him to be '*absolutely* the most
congenial interpreter' of your concerto. It always
makes me furious to hear facts so grossly misrepre-
sented, just as it does to watch the growing Bruckner
craze, and I admire you for keeping a cool head. It
is a wonder you do not descend on these people like
a St. George, and storm at them. We played Joachim
a page or two of Bruckner's E major—by request—but
soon had to stop out of compassion. To show you
how firmly the disease has taken hold, a young musician
from Vienna who is studying with Spitta was complaining bitterly to him the other day of the injustice
of the world's judgment in making Brahms a little
god while he was still young, while Bruckner's great
genius received no recognition even in his old age!
And he is in other respects very nice and a keen
worker.

I am telling you this in the hope of arousing a little
holy indignation.

Farewell, dear, dear Friend. When summer comes—
summer!—please remember that we have a little house,

* See score of violin concerto, p. 60, bar 3.

and that we should like to be allowed to make a little fuss of you, if only you would let us.

Heinrich's love.  He sat behind me at the Gewandhaus concert, and I turned round so much at all the very particular passages that people must have thought us crazy.  We happened to be sitting in the most 'correct' corner, where it is bad form to show any interest.  At the opening of the new Gewandhaus last year, a Leipzig girl, one of your great admirers, overheard another girl say, 'You really enjoy music twice as much *décolletée !'*

With this choice piece of folly I will close, for I *could* hardly improve on it.

Think kindly now and always of your old

HERZOGENBERGS.

187. *Brahms to Elisabet von Herzogenberg.*

[VIENNA, *February* 28, 1886.]

Your anecdote is charming, and I shall, as usual, go on telling it until it becomes quite stale.  You will have to accept the manuscripts* as my gift now, for they certainly are mine to give.  *Anselmo* figures in my catalogue as your present, January '77 !  But you know I have a fair assortment.  Don't fall a victim to the collecting mania, but take an innocent delight in odd specimens, as I do.—With kindest regards, yours,

J. BR.

I go to Frankfurt, and the manuscripts to Berlin, this very day.

* The Schubert and Beethoven manuscripts (*cf.* Letter 186).

188. *Elisabet von Herzogenberg to Brahms.*

BERLIN, *March* 12, 1886.

MY VERY DEAR FRIEND,—All this time I have never thanked you for the Beethoven, and yet it was as if I had come into some property. You must certainly like me a little to part with such a treasure, and that is what delights me most.

Heini thinks it must be a copy of some old piece—but which?

It is all the same to me what it is, for it is undoubtedly genuine, and therefore sacred. I am so glad it came to me through you; it is a double pleasure to receive very special things from very special people.

But I can neither appreciate nor enjoy the Schubert manuscripts.* How shall I look this restored gift-horse in the mouth! I said I did not want the *Ländler* back, and particularly the *Anselmo*, which I presented to you deliberately and with great pride that time. You evidently lack that sixth sense of consideration for lesser mortals and their pardonable sensitiveness! I shall simply pester you—I put it fairly plainly the other day—into giving me one of your own manuscripts in exchange. You might really give me this gratification, for I am so happy and proud to possess any sheet, any tiniest scrap, of your writing. I will keep these, but merely as securities, until you do.

You will soon be going to Dresden.† How blissfully happy my dear old brother will be to hear the

---

* Besides the song *Am Grabe Anselmos*, Frau von Herzogenberg had presented to Brahms a set of Schubert's *Ländlers*.

† Brahms conducted his E minor symphony in Dresden on March 10.

symphony and to see you! If we only could, we would run over, too, and sun ourselves a little in your presence!

Where shall you be at Whitsuntide?

They are doing your symphony at the Singakademie to-day, but I have to stay miserably at home because of my cough, after counting on it for months. Heinz came back from the rehearsal in bad spirits, by the way. . . .

Good-bye, dear, perfect Friend. It is good to feel you are there!—Your devoted     HERZOGENBERGS.

### 189. *Brahms to Herzogenberg.*

[VIENNA, *October*, 1886.]

MY DEAR FRIEND,—I think you and Joachim will derive considerable pleasure and interest from the enclosed.

It is an exact compilation of the printed score and the original concept of Schumann's D minor symphony, modestly and, I think, unjustly described by the composer in his introduction as a rough sketch. You are, of course, familiar with the state of affairs, which is quite simple.

Schumann was so upset by a first rehearsal, which went off badly, that he subsequently instrumentated the symphony afresh at Düsseldorf, where he was used to a bad and incomplete orchestra.

The original scoring has always delighted me. It is a real pleasure to see anything so bright and spontaneous expressed with corresponding ease and grace. It reminds me (without comparing it in other respects) of Mozart's G minor, the score of which I also possess. Everything is so absolutely natural that you cannot imagine it different; there are no harsh colours, no forced effects, and so on. On the other hand, you will no doubt agree that one's enjoyment of the revised form is not unmixed; eye and ear seem to contradict each other.

I cannot resist pointing out pp. 20 (horns), 25, 30; 128-9 (violins and double basses); 141-2 (1st and 2nd violins); 148-9, 163-4, although it is quite superfluous, for you will enjoy every page.

Had the Meiningen quartet been more reliable, I should have tried it there long ago. How is Joachim off for strings?

Now comes the question whether you agree with me that the original score should be published? Will you, in that case, see to it? But please return this copy as soon as possible, as it is not mine.

I can only thank you very briefly for the parcel you so kindly sent—I should have to cut a new quill to do it adequately—but I am expecting Hausmann any minute, and am looking forward particularly to many parts of the Finale,* although I may want to omit the first two pages!

Kindest regards to you both, and let me hear from you now and then.—Yours,                J. Br.

### 190. *Herzogenberg to Brahms.*

BERLIN, KURFÜRSTENSTRASSE 87,
*October 26, 1886.*

MY VERY DEAR FRIEND,—We were delighted to have your parcel and letter. I have learnt so much from the two versions,† both on general lines and in detail,

---

* Probably the Finale of Herzogenberg's 'cello sonata, Op. 52, which is dedicated to Hausmann.

† The Schumann symphony (*cf.* Letter 189).

and am so glad I have you to thank. Joachim would very much like to hear the earlier one. May we have the parts copied, and how long can you spare the score?

But perhaps the owner of the score has also provided copies of the parts, or would do so?

Hausmann, dear fellow, came back from Vienna in a just-after-confirmation frame of mind. You must have shown him some beautiful things. He raves most about the whole of the 'cello sonata* and an Intermezzo in the violin sonata.† He is coming here this evening, and will have much more to tell us.

I can't make out from your letter what it is you don't like about the introduction to the *variations* in my sonata, and I should so like to know. Meanwhile you have my formal permission to consider it non-existent. To you, anything one of us writes can only be well-meant feebleness, so why trouble about a few bars more or less if only you are inclined to be nice about the remainder!

Please send a line to say whether we are to copy the score or send it straight back.

You might really pass through Berlin, or come to stay, in the flesh, this winter. You could then hear the D minor‡ played by our good little school orchestra or the Philharmonic, and we could have a few days together.

All kindest messages from myself and my wife.—
Yours ever,                                    HERZOGENBERG.

* Brahms's sonata for violoncello in F, Op. 99.

† Sonata for violin and piano in A, Op. 100, composed at Thun in the summer of 1886, as also the 'cello sonata. By Intermezzo the Andante is probably meant.

‡ The Schumann symphony.

191. *Brahms to Heinrich von Herzogenberg.*

[VIENNA, *October* 28, 1886.]

Very well, have the parts copied! I will see Herr Mandyczewski,* whose diligence is responsible for the compilation, about it. It would be very nice to hear it properly played.—Sincerely yours,

J. BR.

192. *Elisabet von Herzogenberg to Brahms.*

BERLIN, *December* 2, 1886.†

. . . . And now to change the subject, dear Makart,‡ let me thank you for the dear, beautiful sonata, which I am most anxious to study thoroughly. It is far from satisfactory to shuffle through it twice with Hausmann, for while it is still so new the excitement of listening is so great that one fails to take it in. It is impossible to settle down to serious enjoyment of a novelty of this order, because of the ferment, the tumult of emotion, glorious in themselves, which inevitably possess one. So far I have been most thrilled by the first movement. It is so masterly in its com-

* Professor Dr. Eusebius Mandyczewski (b. 1857), composer, writer, editor of Schubert's works, librarian of the Vienna *Gesellschaft der Musikfreunde*, was, during the last ten years of Brahms's life, his untiring amanuensis and most faithful musical adviser.

† Frau von Herzogenberg's correspondence with Brahms had ceased abruptly in March, 1886, on account of a report spread by some busybody, which afterwards proved to be quite unfounded. Brahms either ignored the fact or pretended to do so. He sent her the 'cello sonata, however, unaccompanied by any sort of message.

‡ The painter Hans Makart, who was famous for his taciturnity, was once at a dinner-party, when his neighbour, Josephine Gallmeyer, after one of his long silences, turned on him with, 'And now let us change the subject, dear Herr Makart.'

19

pression, so torrent-like in its progress, so terse in the development, while the extension of the first subject on its return comes as the greatest surprise. I don't need to tell you how we enjoyed the soft, melodious Adagio, particularly the exquisite return to F sharp major, which sounds so beautiful. I should like to hear you play the essentially vigorous Scherzo—indeed I always hear you snorting and puffing away at it*—for no one else will ever play it just to my mind. It must be agitated without being hurried, *legato* in spite of its unrest and impetus. I wish I were able to practise it, and really master the last movement too, with its quasi-lyrical theme, which seems to me almost too violent a contrast to the 'grand' style of the others. But, as I said, I want to hear it again and learn how to play it.

I have not seen Hausmann since his return, unfortunately, but I shall no doubt hear when he expects to receive the sonata. And what about the violin sonata? Why doesn't it come? Have you really so many acquaintances left in Vienna who have not heard it, that you cannot spare it for a few days? And don't you rather want Joachim to have it soon? And do you never think how he must secretly long for it? I say nothing of my own craving, which is second to nobody's, but how can you keep him, Joachim, waiting so long when surely he has first claim to it? It is really rather cruel, and I think you ought to find a large envelope with all speed and send it him.

I will now confess, with your permission, that I

---

* Brahms often accompanied his playing by uncouth noises, which were sometimes so loud as to be audible to a concert audience.

made copies of both the Spies contralto songs,* and
am much attached to them, although, with my usual
effrontery, I am anxious to voice two objections. Do
you really like all those chords of the six-four in
succession in the C sharp minor song,† particularly
in the second verse—G major, B flat and D flat, one
after the other, and all second inversions? You
surely never wrote anything of the kind before? I
know of no other passages to equal it for harshness in
the whole of your music, and flatter myself you will
find some other means of expressing the passionate
yearning of the poem at that point. It is quite clear
what impression you wish to give, but the actual
result is so much less beautiful than Brahms usually
is that it positively gave me pain. It is such a pity
to spoil a soft, dreamy song with these sudden shocks.
I love the warm flow of melody in the A major, with
its abstract text,‡ and sing it with the greatest pleasure.
But in this, too, the final cadence will not seem right.
I have played it over and over until I got used to it
and *felt* it as A major, but at first I never could work
myself up to it. The A always seemed more like the
dominant of D. Have you any more songs in your
drawer, I wonder? Should you not like to wrap up
one of them in some of the Strauss waltzes which you

---

* Brahms had not given Hermine Spies permission to sing in
public the two songs, composed at Thun in the summer of 1886, of
which he had sent her copies — *Wie Melodien zieht es* and *Immer
leiser wird mein Schlummer* (Op. 105, Nos. 1 and 2)—but Frau von
Herzogenberg had been allowed to see them (*cf.* Hermine Spies,
*Ein Gedenkbuch*, p. 303).

† *Immer leiser wird mein Schlummer.*

‡ The words of the song *Wie Melodien zieht es* are by Klaus
Groth. Brahms often succeeded in setting an abstract poem to a
charming melody. Another example is Rückert's *Mit vierzig Jahren*,
Op. 94, No. 1.

always have at hand for the purpose, as in the good
old times ?  Come, do spoil me again a little; you
know how happy it makes me.

Good-bye, dear, dear Friend.  I should like to send
you something — a few of Heini's latest *a capella*
choruses, which seem to me particularly good.  But
should you really care to see them ?

Please spare me a kind word and a quiet thought,
such as I have so often coveted during this long, long
silence.

As of old, your devoted

ELISABET HERZOGENBERG.

How did Spies sing in Vienna ?    I can't help feeling
strongly that she is not developing at all.  When I
think of Frau Joachim* and the way her voice grew
steadily fuller, it seems to me that concert work and
tearing about is, on the contrary, making this one more
casual.  She sings so many things as if she were
reading at sight, and I do so wish someone like you
would warn her, nice and—at bottom—serious girl
that she is.  I have never seen enough of her to
venture; for she gets terribly spoilt, and understands
no hints.   It would have to be put very plainly.†

---

* Amalie Joachim (*née* Schneeweiss, 1839-1899), whose professional
name before she married was Amalie Weiss, was a contralto engaged
at the Hanover *Hofoper* from 1862.  She subsequently became famous
as a *Liedersängerin*, and was unrivalled in her interpretation of
Schumann's songs.  In 1863 she married Joachim.  They went to
live in Berlin in 1866, but separated in 1882.—TR.

† Brahms had forestalled this request, in a letter to Hermine Spies
on November 4, by writing, half in jest, ' I actually dreamt that I
heard you skip half a bar's rest, and sing a crotchet instead of a
quaver,' to which the singer replied, ' It is very kind of you only to
dream that I am unmusical.  I have not only dreamt it, but known
it for ages.'

### 193. *Brahms to Elisabet von Herzogenberg.*

[BUDA-PESTH, *December 22*, 1886.]

MY VERY DEAR FRIEND,—I have been a long time writing to tell you how pleased I was to have your kind letter, and how unwillingly I have dispensed with your correspondence all this time. But as I am so sadly behindhand again, and as you express some desire to see some of my things again, let us come to an agreement: I will send you something from time to time without writing, and you shall write me nice things in return—particularly any nice scruples you may have!

I hope to send something very shortly, and hope it will reach you when you have some free time, so that you can return it quickly, accompanied by the said scruples. I need not really have as many qualms as usual, for your kind, long letter was, I regret to say, three-parts taken up with that good-for-nothing fellow.*

I am sorry I have not your letter by me, otherwise I could answer it better; that is to say, agree with some of your remarks†—as to Fräulein Spies, for instance, and Frau Joachim's undeniable position in the very front rank. The other will never be able

---

* The person responsible for the breach in their correspondence.

† It is doubtful whether Brahms agreed with her objections to the chords of the six-four in *Immer leiser*. He evidently wrote them deliberately, because they seemed to him a fitting expression for the feverish exaltation of the song. Hanslick had suggested the poem (by Hermann Lingg), but at first neither contents nor form appealed to Brahms. The breaks in the song after '*singt im Wald*' and '*Willst du mich*,' which are really inadmissible, may be explained as expressing the failing of the invalid's voice, which is making its last desperate efforts to be heard before sinking into a last sleep. Sung by an ideal

to catch her up, for various reasons, but she has just those qualities which tell in a concert-hall rather than in a room. We get very little good singing in Vienna, and her success there is very natural and desirable. I am most looking forward to the new symphony among Herr Heini's new things. I still consider the two string trios and the three quartets\* his high-water mark more or less, and I want to see him reach gaily beyond it.

If I do send, I shall only enclose the violin part with the greatest reluctance.† Reading together at sight from the manuscript is usually very unsatisfactory. As far as enjoying it goes, it is much better to play it through comfortably alone.

I must go to rehearsal,‡ and will only add best wishes for Christmas. Have I your address?

Well, 'until presently,' as they say on the Rhine.— With kindest regards, yours very sincerely,

J. BR.

---

interpreter, the song should produce the impression that it is costing the singer her life : for in response to the dying girl's call comes, not her lover, but Death. Billroth, to whom Brahms sent the song on August 18 from Thun as 'the work of one of your old colleagues' (Hermann Lingg being a retired Bavarian army doctor), replied : 'H. Lingg's poem about the dying girl in your illuminating setting affected me most of all. I imagined it sung quite simply in a touching girlish voice, and I am not ashamed to say that I could not finish playing it for weeping.' The ultimate success of this particular song justified Billroth's choice, and the chain of chords of the six-four will go down to posterity unchallenged.

\* Herzogenberg's Op. 27 and 42.

† The A major violin sonata.

‡ Of his fourth symphony, which he was conducting at Buda-Pesth on the 22nd.

194. *Elisabet von Herzogenberg to Brahms.*

[BERLIN, KURFÜRSTENSTRASSE 87,
*December* 28, 1886.]

MY DEAR FRIEND,—Was it of your own devising
or by a lucky chance that your letter arrived on
Christmas Eve, the first and most precious of Christmas
presents? It meant much to me to read my name in
your dear writing again at last, and if you would take
that to heart you might be less chary of setting pen to
paper. It is a pity, for you used not to be so lazy;
indeed, you honoured me with many a nice long letter.
However, I am well satisfied with the contents of this
one, and can hardly fail to agree with your proposal to
send me music now and then 'without writing,' while
I find 'nice things' to say in reply. Please do not
forget this delightful compact, but act upon it soon!

I thought we should probably agree about Fräulein
Spies. Yet it seems to me something might be done
by an impressive word in season; but it must come
from a musician, and you are the only one to do it.
Her talent is such as to make it worth while to warn
her against resting on her oars too much. There may
always come a turn in public opinion, and I do think
she *might* become more serious. She sang your two
songs here as if she were reading them, and I only
consider her light head-notes really beautiful, quite
bewitching indeed. The lower notes are inclined to
be thick, and the high ones hollow and harsh. If
only I dare tell her—but I cannot venture, whereas
you could and ought.

To-morrow evening we shall hear Joachim do your
B flat sextet,* and I have it with me at the piano now,

* Op. 18,

so as to have it all fresh in my mind.  You see we
have a good deal of you here, and you are in good
hands.  The other day, at the end of a long concert
which we only sat out with difficulty, they sang the
*Liebeslieder;* * and when Hausmann's head appeared
suddenly in the background, we recognized him, and
he us, by sheer force of the animation the beloved
things had aroused.

Last year I even made an acquaintance on the
strength of your music.  It was when they did the
E minor, and Frau Hartmann† and her son were
listening with such unusual keenness, that I introduced
myself, thinking I really must know her ; but I really
loved her before I spoke for her thoughtful face and
her intent way of listening.  I realized the beautiful
meaning of the word 'community,' and Goethe's
charming lines came into my head :

> ' Was ist heilig ?   Das ist's, was viele Seelen zusammenbindet
> Wär's auch nur so leicht, wie die Binse den Kranz.' ‡

Good-bye, dear *Binse.*—With kindest remembrances,
your affectionate and devoted
HERZOGENBERGS.

How your letter in La Mara§ did amuse us !  She
evidently does not see what a reflection it is on her
book.  Your letter, by the way, gave no clue to your
present whereabouts.

---

* Op. 52.

† Frau Bertha Hartmann, widow of the poet Moriz Hartmann, of
Vienna, and a friend of Billroth's.

‡ From Goethe's *Seasons* ('Autumn,' No. 69).

§ See Letter 149, note.

195. *Brahms to Elisabet von Herzogenberg.*

[VIENNA, *December* 31, 1886.]

I am sending off sonata and trio* to-day. Please let me have a line to say they have arrived safely with their wrappers† in spite of its being New Year's Eve. I hope the festive season will leave you some free time, so that you can write me the few nice things—and your scruples. It goes without saying that I want them back as soon as possible! Will the Schumann symphony soon come, and have you arrived at a rehearsal?‡—Yours,                     J. BR.

196. *Elisabet von Herzogenberg to Brahms.*

[BERLIN] *December* 31, 1886.

MY DEAR FRIEND,—We were at dinner, Joachim with us, when your two registered packages arrived. Naturally, we finished with all speed and fell to on the sonata. I assure you the trial performance was anything but unsatisfactory.§ Thank Heaven, the thing

---

* Op. 100 and Op. 101.

† Brahms always sent his manuscripts in an ordinary wrapper by book-post, if possible. Once, in Vienna, a friend brought him back the score of the E minor symphony which he had had to look at, and was horrified to see Brahms hurriedly tie it round with a piece of tape, and address it to Joachim just as it was. On his friend's entreaty that he would register it, Brahms replied: 'Nonsense! Stuff like this doesn't get lost. If by chance it should, why, I should write out the score again, that's all. All the same, I will be good, and register things in future.' To send off a parcel with all the attendant formalities of sealing, filling in declaration forms, etc., was really a nightmare to the impatient composer. Pohl, and later Mandyczewski, were always willing to take it off his hands; but he did not care to give them the trouble, and always tried to despatch his things in the quickest and easiest way.

‡ *Cf.* Letters 189-191.                     § *Cf.* Letter 193.

is nothing like so difficult as Frau von B—— told me
in her letter. It was only in the last movement that
I had some trouble with the rhythm. But what a
charming, happy inspiration of yours it is ! The whole
piece is one caress. How delighted I was, too, to meet
and embrace the melody of the Klaus Groth song* in
the first movement ? The first movement is so clear
and sunny, the *pastorale* in the second so lovely (we
played it quite beautifully straight away), and the third
will end by becoming my favourite. You see what
pleasure you have given us, but why, oh why, did you
disappoint us so grievously by not sending the parts
of the trio ? If you want to begin the New Year well,
please forward them at once. Joachim implores you !

Please put up with this shortest of notes. It is
merely a form of receipt, given at Berlin W., on the
31st inst. at 8.30 p.m., still warm from the excitement
of playing and enjoying the new acquaintance.

Please, please send the parts of the trio. We shall
have time, and you will have everything back very
quickly.

Your piece is so lovable, you must be the same, and
make us happy with those trio-parts.—Your grateful
and happy

ELISABET HERZOGENBERG.

The symphony† is to be played shortly. The only
reliable copyist took such an age to write it out.

---

* The second subject of the sonata in A (Op. 100) is a variant on
the theme of *Wie Melodien zieht es,* and at the same time an affectionate remembrance of Klaus Groth. The song was composed
before the sonata, and stands in the same relation to it as *Regenlied*
(another Groth song) to the violin sonata in G. There is another
reminiscence in the A major sonata—the touch of *Auf dem Kirchhofe*
(Op. 105, No. 4) in the last movement.

† Schumann's D minor symphony in the original version.

197. *Brahms to Elisabet von Herzogenberg.*

[VIENNA, *January* 8, 1887.]

To-day is Thursday, so I can give you till Monday. Please remember me to your guests and your musicians.

I should think the trio Finale requires, first very careful handling, then the reverse!—Ever yours,

J. BR.

198. *Elisabet von Herzogenberg to Brahms.*

BERLIN, *January* 9 *and* 10, 1887.

MY VERY DEAR FRIEND,—I will pack up your music to-morrow first thing, but must get a little note written to-day, which shall at least tell you of our delight in the new pieces, if nothing else. It would be even more idiotic than usual if this poor little midge should set herself to catalogue her impressions, and attempt to explain why it is all so beautiful. I could not do it with any conviction, if I would; for I confess I think the particular success of these compositions is due, not to any particular features one could point out, but to the fact that they were evidently inspired from above. You were indeed highly favoured! Few things, I imagine, have ever been so perfectly proportioned as this trio, which is so passionate and so controlled, so powerful and so lovable, so terse and so eloquent. I suspect your feelings as you wrote the last bar were very much those of *Heinrich der Vogler*, in his prayer: 'Thou gavest me a goodly haul, for which I thank Thee, Lord'

I find all the four movements fascinating, but the

last proved the most exciting, as, indeed, a Finale should.  It does not make the others less beautiful. Could anyone imagine anything more lovely than the gentle Andante with its tender duologue between piano and strings ?  The first movement is glorious, with its exquisite second subject and the working-out, as fine as it is short.  One can find no fault with it until the end, and then only because it is over and one would like more   But the pearl among them all is of course the second, muted movement, which is truly irresistible. Its ghost-like figures ('lovely phantoms,' as Heinrich says) are so tangible in their beauty.

If you knew, dear Friend, how happy this piece has made us!  We have no greater pleasure in the world than that we derive from your music.  You will not feel aggrieved, I hope, if I fail to manifest any of the scruples you so kindly ordered.  I really cannot discover any, and should have to be a very punctilious person to find anything to complain of.  We were all surprised to find you did not give us a second subject in the last movement; but, after all, the good God makes some flowers with five sepals and some with more, and they invariably turn out well, His flowers! And if you can produce such a flow of movement without a second subject, why should we dictate a different method to you ?  It is only that we are such creatures of habit, and you so seldom swerve from tradition in these matters, that it comes as a shock. At the close of the trio Andante you have varied the passage shared by violin and 'cello—the violin in double notes.  The first time it comes it is :

*January* 10.

I was interrupted last night, dear Friend, by the arrival of the Wildenbruchs,* and refrained conscientiously from even glancing at the music this morning, for fear of delaying it; so, as I cannot quote it accurately from memory, I will only say that the first version is quite easy, according to Joachim, and much nicer than the second, where you crossed out the middle parts. He thinks, much better leave it as it was. Your music has made us all blissfully happy. We are so full of it, we can talk of nothing else. The Wildenbruchs were delighted too. He is hard of hearing, by which I mean hard to move to enthusiasm in respect of music; but yesterday he quite melted, and opined that the trio was a perfect expression of your character. I quite agree; indeed, it is better than any photograph, for it shows your *real* self.

I did so want to address your music to Frankfurt.† I have quite a bad conscience when I am allowed to see any of these things—even though it be by the merest chance—before that dear, blessed woman over there, who has first claim to all the good and beautiful things in the world, and especially to your music. I know how she is longing to see them, and I am sure you will be kind—kind and sweet as your kindly A major sonata—and send the things to Frankfurt at once if you can possibly spare them. And please send *me* that new thing for chorus.‡ I am so eager to see it, and you must be in a generous frame of mind, induced by all the glorious music you have composed; so strike the iron (of kindness) while it is hot, and

* *Legationsrat* Ernst von Wildenbruch (b. 1845), poet and novelist. —Tr.

† To Frau Schumann.   ‡ *Im Herbst*, Op. 104, No. 5.

put a wrapper round that chorus piece, won't you, please ?

No one could open it with keener, thirstier, more loving looks than Heinrich and myself.  I think I am safe in claiming that the said Heinrich constitutes your very best public, for nothing could exceed his delight, his dear, intelligent, sincere delight in any new, beautiful work of yours.  How I pity the musician who, incapable of such enthusiasm, is peevishly occupied in recording or defending his own successes, great or small !  Think if I had married X, or Y !  I should never have survived.

But good-bye now.  If you send the chorus, please enclose Heinrich's four madrigals (I packed them up with my own hands).  I hope you liked them a little. We heard *In der Nacht\** here, and it really sounded like velvet—or so his wife thinks.  The entries of the basses at the end are magnificent.

Be nice, and send us something else to occupy our affections soon.

I should so like to make up my mind about the *tempi* in the last movement of the trio.  When, when shall we see it again !—Your grateful friend,

Elisabet Herzogenberg.

### 199. *Herzogenberg to Brahms.*

[Berlin] January 9, 1887.

Dearest Friend,—Your last chamber-music pieces proved a positively royal gift, not only to my wife, but particularly to us men—Joachim, Spitta, Hausmann, and myself.  They are constructed in the plainest possible way from ideas at once striking and simple,

---

\* Published later among the *Sechs Gesänge für gemischten Chor a capella*, Op. 57.

fresh and young in their emotional qualities, ripe and
wise in their incredible compactness. The result is
some of the most convincing music I know, and the
general tendency of the form is as surprising as it is
instantly satisfying.

We had a foretaste in the 'cello sonata,* and now
the violin sonata and the trio† seem to us the perfect
development of this new drift. No one, not even
yourself, can say what it will lead to; let us hope it
will clear the field and leave the giants in possession.
Smaller men will hardly trust themselves to proceed
so laconically without forfeiting some of what they
want to say. We felt almost like the Fisherman in
the *Arabian Nights*,‡ out of whose tiny box an
enormous genius sprang, the difference being that
we could hardly feel surprise at the contents of the
box, though we were the more amazed at the small
space in which they were confined.

And where shall I begin to quote examples? The
second movement of the trio remains the most
marvellous, for there you strike an entirely new note;
and yet its character is so well established by the first
few bars that one feels it to be an old acquaintance.
Not until the whole short movement has flitted past
us do we realize that it is the clear-cut outline which
enabled us to grasp it *instantaneously*. Then the
Andante from the violin sonata! We fell in love
with it on the spot, of course. At first I did not
quite like the idea of the lovely F major lady's
betrothal to that melancholy Norwegian jester ;§ how-

* Op. 97.                    † Op. 100 and Op. 101.
‡ The adventures of Diandar, the fisherman.
 § Herzogenberg means the D minor *vivace*, which alternates three
times with the *Andante tranquillo* in F major, and eventually closes
the movement. It is slightly reminiscent in general colouring to
Grieg's violin sonata, Op. 8.

ever—so long as the union turns out well, and they have plenty of children!

The Finale of the violin sonata affected us curiously. Joachim and I did so want a second subject, just where you reach the E major chord through the dominant 7th on B, after those long, winding arabesques.* We listened open-eared and open-mouthed; but the moment passed, and the principal subject, which is really exquisite, made its reappearance. We pedants should either have regained the dominant of the principal key by an interrupted cadence, or by a full close leading to some new combination, or at least introduced a long pedal note on E with $\frac{7}{E}$ forming the bridge into A major.† Ah yes, we pedants! And what avails all our learning against your determination, when the one is as completely at your disposal as the other is beyond our reach! The first movement of the sonata has a very special place in our affections. The effect of the unconcerned lapse into C sharp minor (in the development)‡ is original and very charming, also the gay re-entry of the first subject in A major, which has the air of shaking itself free of the development section with a smiling 'Well, that's over, my friends; now let me go my ways in peace.' To return to the trio, that cleverly dissected $\frac{7}{4}$ bar§ is bewitching; and so is the manner in which the two choruses relieve each other, changing over as easily as if they were three people rehearsing a well-known piece and picking up their cues from memory. You, meanwhile, betray not the faintest

---

* P. 48, bar 18.    † P. 8, bar 1.    ‡ P. 8, last bar.
§ Brahms divides it as follows: $\frac{3}{4}+\frac{2}{4}+\frac{2}{4}$ (*Andante grazioso*).

interest in your puppets, but leave them to their own devices. Your big paw comes down heavily with the very opening of the Finale, however, and one sees stars, and begins to count the slain; at least, it nearly proved the death of my wife, that stormy semiquaver passage* in particular. How splendid the *pp* subject is, with chords for the strings and splashes for the piano,† and then the coda in C major with the subject played *legato*,‡ and finally the tremendous jubilations,§ where the rhythm would not come right—not that it matters! And here I am on the point of forgetting the second subject in the first movement,‖ for which I could kiss your hand if you were Liszt, but then you would never have had the inspiration!

Well, if the blessings and thanks of an old cackler like myself are of any account, I hope you will accept them, together with my apologies for failing to provide a more suitable wrapper for the music.¶—Ever yours sincerely,
                                        HERZOGENBERG.

### 200. *Brahms to Elisabet von Herzogenberg.*

[VIENNA, *January* 15, 1887.]

MY DEAR FRIEND,—I have to thank you for a pleasant evening and a pleasant morning; the one brought your letter, and the other the many enclosures which I unfolded one after the other from your rolls—to my delectation in every respect.

The 'night-song'** sounded like velvet in my ears

---

* P. 27, bar 15.      † P. 26, bar 11.      ‡ P. 34, bar 6.
§ P. 35, *tempo primo.*                          ‖ P. 4, bar 3.
¶ Herzogenberg's own compositions.
** Herzogenberg's chorus *In der Nacht*, from Op. 57.

too, and I secretly wished a certain pretty little woman were coming to play it with me *à quatre mains*. I think I liked that one best. It is the first time, however, that I have desired or needed a lady's assistance, for I invariably play duets by myself. So far the violin sonata appeals to me least; it smacks more (so far) of Berlin streets than of lovely Berchtesgaden walks.

I consider myself a very knowing fellow, by the way, to think out tunes and develop them while I am out walking. Heinz's things, more than anyone else's, make me think of myself, and recall the scene and the manner of my own struggles to learn and to create.

He really knows and understands, and that is why I treasure and depend on his approval (with yours thrown in).

His knowledge is wider and more accurate than mine; but that is easy to explain. What I do envy him is his power of teaching. We have both trodden the same steep paths with the same plodding earnestness. Now he can do his part to spare others the weary effort. Berlin is responsible for much talk and much bad method, but better days seemed to have dawned there for the present generation.

You must forgive me for replying to so much else with a hasty 'thank you.'

It is to be hoped you can guess how much nicer I really am than I appear.—Kindest regards. Yours,

J. Br.

201. *Elisabet von Herzogenberg to Brahms.*

Berlin, *March* 1, 1887.

My dear Friend,—I am returning you the Schumann symphony with many thanks. You will think it a nuisance, because there is duty to pay on it, but I dare not send it by book-post.

Your charming letter in response to my fat parcel gave us indescribable joy. It means more to Heinrich to have you write like that than to receive an order *pour le mérite*, and he sends his warmest thanks. His only hope is that you will not find the violin sonata so *Berlinerisch* on closer acquaintance. I think you would not say that of three big things for chorus, which you have not seen yet. Oh, why can't we be together sometimes! Heinrich so longs for it, and it would mean so much to him. And you would have some pleasure in our company too, when you read in our faces our delight in yours. Oh that trio! I wrote out a whole heap of the C minor movement for our angel,* and the Andante too. They two will sit at the piano and enjoy the beautiful fragments, while he, the favoured one who heard the trio at our house, will discourse learnedly about it. Those are the sort of people one would rather have here than at Utrecht. . . .†

Hausmann is playing Heinrich's sonata on the 16th, and—can you believe it—with me! He has invited none of the critics, and I therefore took courage, for we really agree about the piece and play it well together. I even cherish the secret desire to play your sonata! I should not breathe this to anyone else, but I know you will only be good-naturedly amused at my presumption. And now I have still to ask you to put those choruses‡ into an envelope—will you?

* Frau Engelmann.
† The passage omitted consists of a violent tirade on the indecisive, opportunistic attitude of the *Musikalisches Wochenblatt*, and an urgent request that Brahms would interfere and set everyone to rights.
‡ Herzogenberg, Op. 52.

But I should have congratulated you on your Order *pour le mérite.** The truth is, I can't help feeling more inclined to congratulate the Order in a case like this; for it may flatter itself on having come to the right person for once.

Last of all, I should like to suggest that when you put Heinrich's choruses into their cover you might slip in something else besides. I know you have written some choruses yourself,† so why not show them to a pair of lovers like ourselves, who are yearning to see them?

Be a nice kind person and think of us occasionally.—
Your very devoted
HERZOGENBERGS.

### 202. *Brahms to Elisabet von Herzogenberg.*

[VIENNA, *March*, 1887.]

Alas, dear friend, newspapers have become a necessary evil, and I fear the habit of reading even musical gossip has grown too strong. Admitting this to be so, I consider Fritzsch's the most practical and tolerable—I hesitate to say the best. As to the others, from the *Signale* to Chrysander, I can call them bad—without hesitation.

As for the violent tone, I hardly think that a disadvantage; it rouses such readers as take it seriously to closer attention and to protest. You know you would never touch a flabby thing like the *Signale* or the more ambitious . . . ?

Fritzsch does not rouse me to protest, principally

* Brahms had just received this high distinction. The Order was founded by Frederick the Great, and has rarely found its way to the 'wrong' person.

† *Fünf Gesänge für gemischten Chor a capella,* published 1889.

because he deals with us mortals of to-day and yesterday. Now Chrysander succeeded in enraging me to
the point of protesting. I could not stand the way he
advertised the Mozart things, for instance, without
a trace of affection or piety, and distorting the facts
to suit his own preconceived notions. Yet we allowed
this treatment of our glorious Mozart to pass, and con-
tinued to respect Chrysander, as indeed he deserves!

Again, it is a matter of supreme indifference to
friend Fritzsch whether we respect him and his paper
or not.

By which I merely mean that a journalist is in
much the same case as a parson. If you must protest,
why stop at defending Heinrich and abusing Fritzsch?
Look at your Berlin papers and your Berlin public
next time the latest filth from Paris arrives, and then
look at the interest and attention men like Heyse,
Keller*—and greater than they—receive! And do
you really believe they would play one note of my
music in Berlin if French composers of to-day had
a shade more talent?—and so on, and so on. I only
wish to persuade you to let it pass, remembering that
Fritzsch is a decent, well-meaning fellow in himself,
and that by going over to the *Hochschule* you have,
after all, come within his legitimate line of fire. . . .

But I cannot write any more, and would much
rather have written of other matters.

Fortunately my sheet is full, and I must not spoil
the sweet picture.†

So good-bye.—With kindest regards, yours,

J. BR.

* Paul Heyse and Gottfried Keller were among Brahms's favourite
poets.

† A portrait of Hans von Bülow adorning the note-paper.

### 203. *Brahms to Herzogenberg.*

[VIENNA, *April*, 1887.]

MY DEAR FRIEND,—I am going to Italy,* and shall be at Thun from about the middle of May onward.

As I shall be making no music myself, you might send me your new things to look at there. They will sound very beautiful with the ripple of the river coming through the open window.†

If it were not too lengthy, I would tell you in detail how the warning which you thought so desirable has descended on Fräulein Spies, and how well Hanslick,‡ who felled the blow, came out of it all—as usual.

But I have all my belongings to pack up. A line here would still reach me, as I start on the 26th. Once I am at Thun, however, I appeal to your charity for a good supply of summer reading.—Yours,

J. BR.

* Brahms's companions on his fifth Italian tour were Fritz Simrock, his publisher, and Theodor Kirchner, who came as Simrock's guest. Writing to Bülow, Brahms says: 'Simrock's happy thought of giving Kirchner a glimpse of the promised land delighted me, but I now fear it is at least twenty years too late. At least, I suspect he only feels really at home when he sits down to dinner or supper, and can chat about the Gewandhaus and other splendours.' The outward tour included Verona, Vicenza, Venice, Bologna, and Florence, the return being made by way of Pisa, Milan, and the St. Gothard to Thun, where Brahms arrived on May 15 for the summer.

† Brahms's summer house at Hofstetten, near Thun, was beside the River Aar, at the point where it bends to flow into the town. There is a picture of the house, with its commemorative tablet, on plate xxv. of the *Brahms-Bilderbuch*, edited by Viktor von Miller.

‡ Hanslick had raised a warning voice in the *Neue Freie Presse*, drawing the singer's attention to various defects of style. It is true she had fallen a victim to an 'East Prussian catarrh' in between, and her voice had suffered considerable injury.

204. *Elisabet von Herzogenberg to Brahms.*

[BERLIN, *May* 16, 1887.]

MY DEAR FRIEND,—At last we know where to find you again, and I am writing without delay at my poor Heinrich's request. He has been seriously ill for nearly six weeks now, and I have had an anxious time; I can hardly say it is over yet, although I am no longer so alarmed.

We took advantage of our short Easter holiday of seventeen days to pay a flying visit to Florence too, for the sake of my dear old mother, who was anxious to see us. It is only a day and a half's travelling, and we can stand these enforced journeys very well; but, unfortunately, the weather was icy, and one so easily takes cold there with those wicked stone floors and those tricky little alleys which are so villainously draughty. Poor Heinz fell a victim to a sudden attack of rheumatism towards the end of our stay, and had to make the journey back under painful conditions. Once here, he developed something more serious, and was soon unable to put his right foot to the ground. He was kept in bed suffering intensely, and, worst of all, the doctors (for I had to call in a second) were at a loss, and could neither tell how serious it was nor what course the disease was likely to follow. It seems the symptoms were strangely contradictory. They finally diagnosed an inflammation of the *os sacrum*, but the application of ice-bags increased the pain to such an extent that they had to reject the theory. Our own dear doctor from Leipzig, who hurried over unprofessionally to reassure himself, took it to be inflammation of the hip-bone; but that had to be given up too, and we now call it muscular rheumatism!

All this would be more comic than tragic were it not for the uncertainty of the treatment. The pains have yielded to morphia injections, thank Heaven! but he makes no progress in walking. For the last ten days he has been able to hobble about with crutches, but only a few steps at a time and with great difficulty. He was always so gay, and has not been ill once in all these eighteen years, which makes this suffering and enforced idleness doubly hard to bear; even his patience is not equal to it. Yesterday, for the first time, we were able to cheer him a little with some music. We played him your trio, your glorious trio, beloved above all things, and the effect of it, together with the society of the two players, was a great improvement in spirits. He sends a thousand thanks for the precious gift and the kind thought which prompted it.*

He also thanks you very much for the parcel sent before you left, with the interesting photographs. We had not seen that lovely van Eyck before. Fräulein Spies told me how good you had been to her, and how glad she was you spoke to her. She was quite willing to take anything from me too, and expressed herself to that effect in a very nice letter. But I was tied by my husband's illness, and she was unable to keep the appointment we made.

We searched that envelope in vain for the chorus,† to which we are looking forward so eagerly. Now that Heinz is so ill, and sadly needs distraction, you will send him it, however, won't you, dear Friend? We will then write you a nice long letter, and sing your praises and praise your kindness. Do, do send

---

* Brahms had sent them a printed copy of the trio.
† *Im Herbst*, Op. 104, No. 5.

something. To-morrow I am to play your sonata*
with Joachim by order of Heinrich the hungry. Then
comes the turn of the 'cello sonata, and after that we
start on the old beloved round again.

Heinrich sent you his two new choruses† through
Astor,‡ and begs you to say a kind word about them.
He is longing for it. So you are in Switzerland again,
far away from us, and I suppose we shall not see you
again all our days, which is a sad thought!

We are only staying here as long as we are absolutely obliged. As soon as Heinrich is equal to sitting
in the train, we shall go to Nauheim (between Frankfurt and Giessen), and try what vigorous treatment
will do towards driving out the rheumatic pains.
After that we hope to be different beings, and propose
to rest from our labours at quiet Liseley. I am keeping exceedingly well, and my capacity of nurse calls
out all the strength of which I have a store in reserve
against emergencies.

Good-bye, dear Friend, and send something nice for
my poor cripple.

All happiness and prosperity to you throughout the
summer—the reflection to fall on your ever faithful

HERZOGENBERGS.

### 205. Brahms to Elisabet von Herzogenberg.

[THUN, May 26, 1887.]

Our friend Astor has just sent me the sumptuous
sequel to your letter, and I must send a word of
thanks at once, also my heartfelt sympathy to Heinz.

* The A major sonata.
† Der Stern des Lieds, ode for chorus and orchestra, Op. 55, and
Die Weihe der Nacht, for contralto, chorus, and orchestra, Op. 56.
‡ Of the publishing firm Rieter-Biedermann.

I know of a similar case here, about which I will tell him when his speedy recovery is an established fact. Had I anything remotely approaching these things of his to send, I would not keep you waiting.* But there is nothing that is any good, and I don't know what ground you have for your kind supposition.

Don't leave me without reports of Heinz, however brief.

J. Br.

### 206. Brahms to Elisabet von Herzogenberg.

[Thun, July 20, 1887.]

Poor Heinz! and poor Liseley and poor Lisel into the bargain! How sorry I am about it all, and how I wish I may very soon be able to send you another reminder, and thus enjoy the feeling of being present with you! This is an occasion for writing or sending something really pleasing, but, alas! I can neither send a lot of beautiful new compositions, like Heinz, nor acknowledge things in more beautiful words like you. I can but keep my pen going a little, begging you to recognize my good intentions, and this exchange of coin may prove profitable to us both.

The best thing that came my way this summer was a delightful couple of days spent with Frau Schumann.†

* He was probably not satisfied with his new compositions, and wanted to improve them.

† Brahms had promised his friend Wüllner, much against his will, as he insisted in a letter of many pages, to go to Cologne for the twenty-fourth *Tonkünstler-Versammlung*, where the following of his works were performed : *Darthulas Grabgesang* (from Op. 42), the *Triumphlied*, the violin concerto (Brodsky), and the new C minor trio, in which Brahms was associated with Holländer and Hegyesi. Richard Pohl, who plumed himself on 'discovering' Brahms on this occasion (*cf.* Kalbeck, *Brahms*, i. 216), described the trio in the *Wochenblatt* as ' hardly among the most striking of his chamber-music

I must at least give you that information, and tell you how entirely I agreed with your words of some time back. But I can give you nothing worth calling information about the undersigned musician. True, he is now writing down a thing which does not yet figure in his catalogue—but neither does it figure in other people's!* I leave you to guess the particular form of idiocy!

If I were able to talk to Heinz, I should have a great deal to say about his chorus works; but I should never be able to write it all. A mere '*bravo!*' won't do it. You know well with what pleasure and interest I look at the things. I am sure none of their beauty and delicacy escapes me, and I am often vastly entertained by Heinrich's skill in adapting difficult words in the text.

But that is just it: I am obliged to protest against the poems† (as is so often the case with new compositions), which are totally unsuited to a musical setting both in form and contents.

Of course one ought to hear these things first to find out if it is, after all, possible to enjoy them.

Reading them is quite another matter, and has its advantages as well as its disadvantages.

I can see Heinz's admirers (Spengel‡ in Hamburg is one) waxing enthusiastic over *Nachtweihe.*

---

works. On the way Brahms called on Frau Schumann, and removed a slight misunderstanding which had clouded their friendship temporarily.

\* The double concerto for violin and 'cello.

† The words to *Stern des Lieds* and *Weihe der Nacht* are by Robert Hamerling and Friedrich Hebbel respectively.

‡ Julius Spengel (b. 1853), composer and conductor of the Hamburg *Cäcilienverein.* In 1898 he published an interesting character study of Brahms, and in 1897 an essay, *Heinrich von Herzogenberg in seinen Vokalwerken,* published later by Rieter-Biedermann.

I fear the words would prevent me, however fine the music.

For instance, take '*Ich hatte viel Bekümmernis*';* you may repeat it (in music) as often as you like. I shall understand it and follow it with interest until you arrive at *Tröstungen.*

If, on the other hand, you begin by treating '*Was da lebte*'† fugally, I have no clue for the time being. Your next phrase—'*was aus engem*'—is no more enlightening, and by the time the sentence is finished I find I have been listening solely to the music, and am still not much the wiser. If, on the other hand, you attempt a whole sentence as in '*Seele, du,*'‡ I see, of course, that you are taking pains to speak plainly; but the music confuses me, and I still do not know what I have heard.

Only, please remember, all this has first to be proved.

Hamerling's plaint is the kind of poem that does not attract me particularly. All the same, I would write music to it with the greatest pleasure—if I were inspired to anything like the cheerful, festive march in E flat from *The Ruins of Athens.*§ The 'chosen one'‖ should hover in the air to just such music— but I should laugh the poet Hamerling to scorn at the same time. Even more than in the other song, I am conscious here of the tendency (often unavoidable) to turn every comma into a (musical) full stop.

* Bach cantata.
† The whole sentence reads: 'Was da lebte, was aus engem Kreise auf ins Weite strebte, sanft und leise sank es in sich selbst zurück' (Hebbel).
‡ '*Seele, du wachst noch*' (Hebbel).
§ Beethoven. Brahms places Hamerling's ode on a level with Kotzebue's poem *d'occasion*, which Beethoven set to music.
‖ 'Mag freudenleer hinziehn ein *Erkorener.*'

In between I have been out for an hour's walk. I
would really rather send the nearest empty sheet with
a simple greeting than this confused twaddle. But
you must believe I mean well. My greetings are the
same as of old, I am the same as of old, and ever yours
sincerely,
                                                    J. Br.


207. *Brahms to Elisabet von Herzogenberg.*

[Thun, *July* 23, 1887.]

I am feeling most rueful about my very unseemly
and superfluous chatter the other day. It would be a
real consolation if you would write just a line to say
that you, at least, took it for chatter and nothing else.
We have all sinned, and fall short of the glory of
God!

Well, I can only say I shall not succumb to the
temptation of a sheet of note-paper again for some
time!

But I wish you all things good and beautiful. You
can leave grumbling and its consequences to yours
very sincerely,
                                                    J. Br.


208. *Elisabet von Herzogenberg to Brahms.*

Liseley, *July* 27, 1887.

My dear Friend,—You need not feel rueful. We
are glad to have either your grumblings or your
flattery, and when you combine the two, as in your
very nice Munich letter,* Heinrich is the first to say,

---

\* The letter bore the postmark Thun; but Frau von Herzogenberg
was at Munich when it came, and therefore calls it a Munich letter.

'God bless you'! Naturally he would have been pleased, poor devil! had you been able to say of any one movement: 'I like that.' You know yourself what a difference that makes, and you are spoiled while he is not—consequently it means a hundred times as much to him. But these are merely my remarks—his wife's, who alone has the right to make them. He sends many, many thanks for your kind letter.

I can give no good account of my poor dear. The famous Ziemssen* held out small hope of a speedy recovery when we were in München. He took it to be an obstinate muscular complaint (his nerves seem only indirectly affected, as they would be in any illness), and was of opinion that a strict course of treatment, after a few weeks of rest here, would be absolutely necessary. We shall probably have to go to a hydro where Heinrich can be treated by electricity, massaged, wrapped in wet cloths, and taken in hand in every possible sort of way. Ziemssen insists on hot sand-baths and plenty of gymnastics as being of primary importance, and hopes for some visible result from this polyphonic *Kur* after six weeks or so.

So we shall hardly be able to return to Berlin in October. Heinrich's patience is incomparable, really splendid, and how can I complain, with that before me?—not to speak of the advantage I have in being actively employed in his service. I have to plan out everything; to nurse him, electrify, bandage, dress and undress my sick child, and there is no time left for brooding. Also, thank God! I am an inveterate optimist, which is a help both to him and myself. But

* H. W. von Ziemssen, a Munich specialist.

it is not an easy time, all the same, and I shall heave a very special sigh of relief when I can say: it lies behind me.

Naturally, we are quite of your opinion as to Hamerling's text. We never liked it, but it is tempting to set to music; and if one can only forget the author, it even strikes one as beautiful in places. If you do happen to be keen on writing for chorus, and feel you must unburden your soul by composing in that particular form, you end by making a compromise. You can like a text on so many different scores. Very often it does not show to advantage until it is seen in its musical setting—as, for instance, your *Nachtwandlerlied*,* which I should consider far from edifying, were it not for your music.

Well, when you see the psalm† I really think you will be satisfied with my Heinrich.

I must really close. Please excuse this unsatisfactory letter. I never have more than five consecutive minutes at my disposal, now that I am a perfect slave, more like a human sponge than a human being; a bad friend and a worse correspondent.

Write again soon and send that chorus, for I happen to *know* that Billroth has seen it.‡—Your old friend,

L.

* Op. 86, No. 3. Text by Max Kalbeck.
† Ps. xciv., for four soloists, double chorus, orchestra, and organ (Op. 60).
‡ As a matter of fact, Brahms had sent the much-discussed chorus, together with other new compositions, to Billroth from Thun on August 18, 1886, Billroth being one of the few privileged to see his works before they were printed. Frau von Herzogenberg may have had her information from Frau Hartmann.

### 209. *Brahms to Herzogenberg.*

[TELEGRAM FROM BADEN-BADEN,*
*September* 25, 1887.]

Neuwittelsbach Hydropathic, Neuhausen. Expect me to-morrow morning.—BR.

### 210. *Brahms to Elisabet von Herzogenberg.*

[VIENNA, *October* 15, 1887.]

Epstein has just sent me your card, which grieved me very much. How I wish I could offer you any little pleasure or distraction! The concerto† could only be the latter at best. Perhaps I may send it you from Cologne, which is my destination to-day.

All kindest messages to your dear invalid. Keep up your own natural gaiety, and hope confidently for better times soon.—Ever yours,

J. BR.

### 211. *Elisabet von Herzogenberg to Brahms.*

[NEUWITTELSBACH, NEAR MUNICH,
*October* 18, 1887.]

MY DEAR FRIEND,—Your dear kind post-card did me so much good, and recalled so vividly the hours you spent here with us. I should have written long before

---

* Brahms had gone to Baden-Baden to meet Joachim and Hausmann on September 19, and rehearse the double concerto for violin and 'cello with the municipal orchestra at the *Kurhaus*, and also, as he expressed it in a letter to Frau Henriette Fritsch at Marseilles, to ' practise hard.' The first performance was announced for October 18 at Cologne, the second for November 18 at Frankfurt, and the third at Basel.

† Op. 102.

this to thank you anew for the precious gift of your friendship, had we not been so far in the depths ourselves that my courage failed and my heart despaired. It is no better now; each new day is inexorable in bringing the old pains, added to which I am bedridden myself. It was all through the doctor's too vigorous application of cold water bandages for bronchial catarrh (before you came), the result being a skin affection, an artificial illness induced by the remedy for a natural one! It began to spread so alarmingly, and the pressure of my clothes made it worse. So I could not stay up any longer, and here I am useless, a creature of luxury—and my poor dear wants help so badly. Our only distraction is the snow, which has been falling steadily in huge, noiseless flakes for three days; our consolations, a splendid little stove and a good room, with windows facing south, although no sun comes in through them; our pleasures, an occasional kind letter (Joachim's the day before yesterday, for instance, with the three first quartets), and your card with its enticing promise! Our dear old mother, who nurses us devotedly and reads to us, is also a blessing. After all, there is no comforter like a mother.

You will send the concerto, won't you? It will cheer our very souls, and prove the best possible medicine.

Remember us to Joachim and Hausmann. Have a good time, all of you, and think of these poor wrecks,

THE HERZOGENBERGS.

Remember us kindly to the Wüllners, too, please.

### 212. Brahms to Elisabet von Herzogenberg.

[VIENNA, *November* 4, 1887.]

I shall not worry you to return the score in any haste. I only wish it were something better, something that would make you forget all your sorrow and pain for a little. I don't know why Wüllner did not send it a fortnight ago. However, he will conduct your choral piece all the better at the next concert.\* You may feel quite comfortable about it, and follow an excellent performance in imagination. Be sure you keep me posted up. You don't know how much my thoughts are wrapped up with you. I hope you will soon be able to write more cheerfully, and tell me that you are able to go South.—Ever yours most sincerely,

J. BR.

### 213. Brahms to Elisabet von Herzogenberg.

[VIENNA, *December* 16, 1887.]

MY DEAR FRIEND,—I can only send a line in haste to ask you to forward my score to Meiningen. I go to Pesth to-day, then to Meiningen, and then to Leipzig for the New Year's Day concert. Everything has to be done post-haste, or I would have written more leisurely. But you must forgive me, and be sure to send a line to say how you and Heinz are. I did hear of some improvement, and hope you will confirm it. Joachim and I talked much of you on our travels. You may have heard of our doings from Volkland and

---

\* Wüllner performed Herzogenberg's *Die Weihe der Nacht* at the third Gürzenich concert, Cologne.

others.* I hope to be back immediately after New Year, and should be uncommonly grateful for any letters!—Most sincerely yours,

J. BR.

214. *Elisabet von Herzogenberg to Brahms.*

MUNICH, HESS STRASSE 30,
*December* 30, 1887.

MY DEAR FRIEND, — This is only a greeting — a melancholy one—to show you my frame of mind when I think of you all together at Leipzig,† while we are so far away in a strange town. O Humboldtstrasse, O Zeitzerstrasse, 'how shady were thy branches!' Ah yes, those happy days have faded, together with all our youthful courage! Now we live by hope only, with patience and resignation for our daily bread. Sometimes I think it never will be the same again, and down goes my head into my hands, while the tears—which I can generally control—trickle down. So long as you feel you have it in you to be happy, gay, even young again, it is really too soon to give up all the good things of life and sign a compact with grim care.

God grant we may soon see better days. I sometimes feel my strength failing me, my natural gaiety, as you call it, vanishing beyond recall. My invalid is, on the contrary, amazing, and quite himself the moment the pains abate. His mind is quite clear too. He made an elaborate speech on the use of the sub-

* At Meiningen, on December 25, Brahms conducted his Haydn *Variations*, the third symphony, and the B flat major piano concerto (D'Albert). On January 3 the double concerto was played there for the first time.

† Joachim and Hausmann played the double concerto at the Gewandhaus on January 1, Brahms being the conductor.

dominant and its substitutes the other day, and is able to enjoy the score of your concerto, which so often lies open on his bed.  As I told you, he could never have done that at Neuwittelsbach, and I have therefore every reason to believe he is making progress.  Yet the actual disease—which is the main thing—is distressingly immovable, and the doctor has prepared us to expect nothing good from the winter.  After that we are to consult him again; and will it be any better even then?

I don't need to tell you how much I have thought of you and the friends in Leipzig.  How they must be looking forward to seeing you and your new piece—the dear Engelmanns and the Röntgens, for instance!  What a delightful fuss they will make of you!  If only I could hear just the rehearsal to-morrow, I should have a general idea of the concerto, whereas I can only take in fragments of it.  That most lovely Andante is easy to grasp as a whole, of course, but I had no time to study the other movements properly.  If I am able to write to-day to all my dear friends assembled in Leipzig, it is only by giving up my constitutional (on which the doctor rigidly insists), and thanks to Fillu's* help in housekeeping.  She has been with us since Christmas, but leaves to-morrow, unfortunately.

Farewell, dear good Friend.  You know our red-letter days at Leipzig were those of your visits, and the very keenness of our pleasure then makes our absence this time doubly hard, especially under such circumstances.  My poor Heinrich sends you kindest messages, as does your old friend,

ELISABET HERZOGENBERG.

* Fräulein Marie Fillunger.

### 215. *Brahms to Elisabet von Herzogenberg.*

[VIENNA, *February*, 1888.]

MY DEAR FRIEND,—I often reproach myself for not writing to you, yet I find it impossible. In the ordinary way I can think of you hopefully, but once I sit down to write, with the idea of saying something comfortable and hopeful, all my thoughts turn to sadness. I don't care to ask for news, for as soon as you can report any improvement you will not fail to communicate with your friends. How I look forward to some such cheery message!

You will have heard from plenty of sources that you were never 'absent' from our little gatherings. It is the same here—your picture stands on my writing-table *—I never see any of our mutual friends but the conversation turns upon you; particularly is this the case with friend Epstein.

Can you not at least make your plans for spring and summer?

I mean to write to you frequently if briefly. Perhaps I may then find it easier; for now, as I turn the page, I find I cannot go on. I have no desire to start a fresh subject, neither can I worry you with questions.

If you are able to write at all, remember no one could be more sincerely pleased to hear than myself. Remember me most kindly to your dear Heinz, and, if possible, tell me a little how things are. I often wonder, for instance, whether you have a piano, and can play and sing to him, also whether you have any nice friends in Munich?—As of old, your sincere friend,

J. BR.

* Brahms kept her photograph there until his death.

### 216. Brahms to Elisabet von Herzogenberg.

[VIENNA, *February* 15, 1888.]

When your message (for which I here tender sincerest thanks) was delivered to me, I heard that Frau Franz had tried to send you some very beautiful flowers (bulbs). The parcel was returned, however, and the most tiresome formalities ensued, all because there was no accompanying form to guarantee the absence of *Phylloxera vastatrix!* Are they secretly planting vineyards in Bavaria, or does the little beast like beer too!

Anyway, you can see that we think of you in Vienna, including myself, even if I don't send flower messages. —Kindest regards. Yours,

J. BR.

### 217. Brahms to Elisabet von Herzogenberg.

[VIENNA, *March*, 1888.]

DEAR LADY,—I think you may be glad that I am less delicate in my feelings than Frau Franz, to whom the idea of your dear little house* being let to strangers was sacrilege.

I am probably too late to put in a word for her, but should like to propose Professor Gomperz,† who would be, I imagine, a good tenant.

To balance this, I have refrained from the still greater indelicacy of sending you some excessively gay stuff‡ of mine, which a few people here are very

* 'Liseley,' the house standing empty at Berchtesgaden.
† Dr. Theodor Gomperz, Professor of classical philology in Vienna.
‡ The *Zigeunerlieder* for vocal quartet, with pianoforte accompaniment (Op. 103).

fond of singing and hearing. I should never keep
back from you anything more serious or enjoyable—
had I but an inspiration!

But I do so want a line from you. I suppose my
letter* was not of the sort to deserve a reply.

It is not, alas! by writing letters that I can hope to
gain anything.—Yours most sincerely,

J. BR.

### 218. *Elisabet von Herzogenberg to Brahms.*†

MUNICH, HESS STRASSE 30,<br>
*February* 16, 1888.

MY VERY DEAR FRIEND,—It did my heart good to see
your handwriting again and have your letter of three
pages and a half,‡ with its after-drip of a post-card
to-day telling me of Frau Franz's glorious flowers.
They are quite mad on the subject of the *phylloxera*
here. Some years ago we wanted to transplant two
harmless carnation cuttings from Bozen (where they
grow particularly fine) to Berchtesgaden, and were
treated like thieves and murderers when we reached
the Bavaria frontier. The flowers were escorted back
into Austrian territory by our kind Salzburg coach-
man, and after much controversy (for naturally I
refused to yield an inch) they came back to us, labelled
with their Bozen medical certificate, but twisted and
pulled about, and quite worthless, having cost us
roughly about ten gulden. It is a wicked, senseless
imposition. I am miserable to think that Frau Franz's
kindness should meet with such a reward.

* Refers to Letter 215.
† This letter, begun on February 16, was set aside, resumed on
March 6, and finally despatched on March 9.
‡ Refers to Letter 215.

And now thank you for your kind little letter, dear Friend—whose questions I am always glad to answer, even if the answers cannot be cheerful. Heinrich's condition is such that we can only make negative plans at present. We know all the things that cannot happen—as, for instance, no Liseley for us next summer, no return to Berlin in the winter, for the whole of that season will have to be spent in 'consolidating' the convalescence which favourable circumstances may have brought about. The disease makes such frightfully slow progress, and in any case Heinrich could never risk another northern winter again so soon; it might undo all that we hope the summer may do for him. This is the opinion not only of our present medical attendant, but of our kind Leipzig and Berlin doctors, who continue to take the kindest interest in us. So the prospect is dreary enough! Heinrich has been in bed nearly five months now without a break, for his right leg is so twisted and stiff that he cannot even sit in an easy-chair. The monotony of such an existence, not to speak of actual pain and inconvenience, is terrible to anyone as gay and lively as Heinrich, who, in spite of the psalmist's warning, 'taketh pleasure in his legs,'* his nimble, indefatigable legs. This mental inactivity too! Who would not be rebellious and despairing? I will spare you the description of our dark hours together, when my poor dear gives way to despondency.

But we do have bright moments in spite of our misery. Heinrich is so good in meeting every pleasure, every distraction, with open arms, so far as his physical condition allows. He hears, for instance,

---

* 'He delighteth not in the strength of the horse: he taketh not pleasure in the legs of a man' (Ps. cxlvii. 10).—Tr.

a little music very occasionally—it is often too much for him—played by me, three rooms away. The last new Bach volume* gave us great joy; the last *aria* for contralto,† particularly, with the lovely poetic vision of a dwelling in Paradise, 'where I shall find rest,' charmed us each time afresh. The cantata *Come, let us go up towards Jerusalem,*‡ in the volume before this, was very touching and beautiful. What a prophet, what a poet this Bach of ours was! Every Bible verse was to him a picture, a complete incident. It is always a fresh surprise, however well one knows him.

*March 6.*

My dear Friend, I am really ashamed to take this embryo letter from my case, where it has grown old; yet I am not inclined to suppress it, for you will realize how tied I am by the fact of my being content to patch up this feeblest of letters when I can scribble so rapidly at other times. You dear, kind Friend, *indeed* your letter was 'of the sort' to deserve and inspire a far speedier reply, only you see how I am fixed. I have just had an unusually bad time, which cooled all my ardour and scattered my thoughts. You would not believe how terribly a long illness and nursing absorb and stupefy both patient and nurse, nor the amount of effort any communication requires when the person addressed has no idea of the writer's condition—and that you cannot have! When you in your kindness came to see us at Neuwittelsbach, everything was mild by comparison. This is Heinrich's sixth month in bed

---

* The Leipzig *Bachgesellschaft's* publication.

† From the cantata for contralto solo, *Vergnügte Ruh'*, in the seventeenth book of cantatas.

‡ Vol. xvi., No. 159.

—an illness in itself apart from pain! You inquire so kindly after our life outside, and whether we have a nice 'circle' of friends. I could not help laughing, for we are literally as solitary as Florestan;* and yet not quite literally, for we have Dr. Fiedler†—a splendid, really exceptionally fine man, rich in ideas, delicate, high-minded, and exceedingly sympathetic in manner: we value his acquaintance greatly, and are much touched by his persistence in coming to see us. Then there is his wife, a bright, kind-hearted woman whose devotion to Wagner forms rather a bar to closer intimacy, however; also Levi,‡ whom one can't help liking, in spite of constant wrangling. He is, after all, upright and genuine, and, given those qualifications, one can put up with most things. He is like a Jesuit on the track of heretics, and is for ever preaching to me the one and only chance of salvation. Fanatics invariably practise on us poor women, who are supposed to be incapable of resistance! However, as I have parried his blows so far, and kept myself well in hand, we have settled down amicably to a state of honourable feud. How Levi, with his fine musical feeling, could be victimized by so many coarser natures is a mystery to me. It is not so much his Wagner worship, for he is one of those who need a deity before whom they can prostrate themselves, but there are various side-issues where his usually keen discernment is quite at fault; and his *unconditional* devotion to Wagner, his insensibility to the weak places in *Parsifal* and other things, are

* The hero in *Fidelio*, who was left to languish in a dungeon.

† A literary man, living at Munich, whose wife afterwards married Levi.

‡ Hermann Levi (1839-1900), *Generalmusikdirektor* at Munich, was intimate with Brahms in the 'sixties and 'seventies.

hard to understand. Well, at least he did not defend the symphony* when I abused it thoroughly as being really *remarkably* meaningless!

I have heard next to nothing this winter, as my 'outings' have to be few and far between. Since the middle of December I have not left the sick-room for a single evening, in spite of the doctor's frequent remonstrances. Who could think of their own amusement with anyone so dear as my Heinz is to me on their hands, especially in the evening, when he depends on me so entirely to read aloud to him or encourage him. Some time ago I went out of curiosity to see Zöllner's *Faust*.† Of course the whole thing is monstrous from an artistic point of view, an incredible undertaking; but there are occasional signs of a remarkable talent gleaming out of the mass of shallow insipidity. Gretchen's description of the graves and the mother's head-shaking are really thrilling, while the beggar's song is so charming that I wrote it down. The figure of Faust is deadly dull throughout—how should it be otherwise? Where is the mortal who could produce a musical embellishment worthy of such words, such gold from heaven? And, indeed, who would desire anything so sumptuous? There is, as Hanslick points out, little enough of 'infinite melody' in this work. It is rather Schumannesque than Wagnerian, with the exception of the love-scene, where the fiddles become duly ecstatic and semi-hysterical; for no one seems to venture any variation from the Wagnerian tradition in describing

* The symphony composed by Wagner in 1832 (*cf.* Letter 45, postscript).

† Heinrich Zöllner (b. 1854) produced a musical drama, founded on Goethe's *Faust*, in 1887.

the tender passion. Indeed, one of the most pernicious results of Wagner's influence is this rejection of the fresher, more innocent conception of sensuality for a sultry, oppressive atmosphere of supreme desire which arouses a kind of evil conscience in the listener—a feeling that his presence amounts to an impropriety.

We are most grateful to you, dear Friend, for trying to find a tenant for our poor Liseley. I am enclosing a small plan, which I will ask you to give to Professor Gomperz (he is not the one Fräulein Bettelheim* married, surely?). If they seriously consider taking the little house, I am of course willing to supply any information. You might mention that there are eight beds and bedsteads complete, and that we have fixed the rent at forty pounds. Frau Franz's delicacy is touching, but excessive sensitiveness is a luxury we cannot afford—an illness is far too expensive a matter.

I am cherishing the hope that we may meet this summer, perhaps stay somewhere together. As we have to choose as dry a climate as possible, we may happen on Switzerland, which you seem to have chosen as your headquarters. How I wish I dare count on it!

*March 9.*

There is to be a consultation one of these days with the most famous surgeon in Munich—Professor Angerer—as to the best treatment for the right leg, which now shows unmistakable deformation, and can only be put right by mechanical appliances, such as

* Karoline Bettelheim, operatic singer, married Julius von Gomperz, President of the Chamber of Commerce at Brünnaud, brother of Professor Gomperz.

splints. Heinrich's own wish is for energetic handling under chloroform; but our own doctor is afraid of the result, as it is impossible to ascertain whether the knee has lost all tendency to exudation. In any case, poor Heinrich has more trouble before him and a lingering malady. Even if the leg can be straightened, it can hardly become supple again. You might ask Billroth for his experience of mechanical contrivances in cases where deformation has set in. I am not hopeful! Professor Angerer is considered a great authority, and I shall soon know his opinion. I will then write again, my dear Friend, assured as I am of your constant, loving sympathy.

One thing more about Liseley. I suggested to Minna Wickenburg* that she might take it—she wanted to find something fairly near Munich—and am expecting her reply daily. I hardly think it will suit her, but I should have to give her the precedence. I am writing to-day to tell her she must decide, and let you know. Her reply will soon reach you, as she is at Gries.

The Kaiser's death† was a great shock to us. His venerable figure had come to be so much a part of our lives that we shall find it hard to realize that he has left us. I remember so well standing in a close crowd in front of the *Friedrichsdenkmal* on the 22nd last year.‡ All at once his figure appeared in the corner window, and a chorus of cheers went up. We saw nothing more, for the tears stood in our eyes as we told ourselves it was probably the last time. Now

---

* *Gräfin* Wickenburg (*cf.* Letter 185).

† The death of Kaiser Wilhelm I. (March 9, 1888) had affected Brahms deeply also.

‡ The celebration of his birthday, March 22.

he is dead, and the poor Crown Prince\* as good as
dead.  How terrible to enter upon such a heritage in
his condition!  To have spent a lifetime in expectation
of this moment, and then to be unable to say, 'Stay!'
It is one of the saddest things the world has ever
seen.

It is strange how nearly these things affect one—
affect all of us.  The proof that we do feel a close
connection is, after all, consoling.  I really pity French
people.  Who is there whose death could affect them
to the extent of a single tear?

But now good-bye.  Please do not let your delicacy
deprive us of the 'excessively gay stuff'† any longer.
It is the very thing to cheer us poor things, for I will
admit—in confidence—that we have sunk very, very
low.

You know how happy we used to be; for in spite
of the one great thing fate denied me,‡ we were
content, and our minds were as perfectly in accord as
any two-part harmony.  Then came our trial, this long
bondage—stifling all our freedom and light-hearted-
ness—from which we find no release.  It is not easy
to keep up, but I try hard; for what would happen
if I had not courage for two!

Good-bye.  Unmarried people are in so far enviable
that they have only their own calamities to suffer, yet
I would not change with anyone.

Write soon, and keep us in your affections, please.
You know our devotion.

ELISABET H.

\* Kaiser Friedrich.
† The *Zigeunerlieder*, Op. 103.
‡ She refers to her childlessness.

### 219. *Brahms to Elisabet von Herzogenberg.*

[VIENNA, *March* 11, 1888.]

MY DEAR FRIEND,—What you tell me is all so very sad. Let me sympathize in silence, and hope as silently. I should have been glad to speak to Billroth, and still can; but it is practically no good, as I know from experience. Not knowing and not having seen the patient, he will say anything, just as we do when people ask us about some young artist whom we do not know.

One thing did delight me exceedingly, and I beg you to keep it well in sight—your idea of spending the summer in Switzerland too. Could you not say Thun at once? I never noticed any dampness there, as at Ischl. Not only I, but other people, sit out of doors every evening.

My house there, which is exceptionally charming, and might have been made for you, is at your immediate disposal. I shall easily find a lodging elsewhere. Be sure and tell me what you propose and finally decide to do with regard to this.

I should be glad to think the enclosed* had provided you with an hour's amusement, but I fear the humour will prove too violent in the quiet, subdued atmosphere of your room. But apart from that, I wonder whether you will dislike the things? In any case, please keep them quite to yourselves. When you return them, I shall certainly be able to respond with some small things that are less crude.

I saw Allgeyer's fine essay,† and also the Feuerbach

---

* The manuscript of the *Zigeunerlieder*.

† Brahms had persuaded Julius Allgeyer to write an essay on their mutually esteemed friend, Anselm Feuerbach, the painter (1829-1880).

sketches published recently. Allgeyer will have shown you them, no doubt.

\* \* \* \* \*

I have, of course, been much affected by the startling events in Germany. It is all on a scale—a tragic scale at present—unparalleled in history.

Kindest messages to poor dear Heinz, and let me have a line soon.—Most sincerely yours,

J. BR.

### 220. *Elisabet von Herzogenberg to Brahms.*

MUNICH, *March* 25, 1888.

MY VERY DEAR FRIEND,—I told you, of course, of the expected consultation with the principal surgeon here, Professor Angerer. It took place on Monday evening, and Angerer's verdict was as follows: It can only be cured by resorting to operative measures—not the slow process of bandaging, nor by forcible extension (*prisma forcé*), but simply and solely what they are pleased to call *resection*. He considered the knee to be in a very serious way, the kneecap partially destroyed, and, in short, so far past curing by any other means that it had become necessary to employ the only radical method. You can imagine how I felt! But Angerer announced his views with such conviction, and was so reassuring, so certain as to the result, that I immediately felt courageous enough to persuade Heinrich. But he hardly needed persuading. One short, touching struggle with himself, and the next morning, when the doctor came, he was able to consent.

---

The essay, which subsequently served as a foundation for Allgeyer's biography of Feuerbach (1894), was printed in the *Austrian Weekly Journal of Science and Art*, edited by Bruno Bucher, a friend of Brahms's.

They came on Friday morning at 8.30—four strong—
to butcher my poor lamb. The drawing-room was
arranged as an operating-room. I was there when
they sent him to sleep; but then they carried him
away, and I was not allowed over the threshold of the
torture-chamber. The wife was left to bear it as well
as she could.

Then a strange thing happened. I was prepared
for the operation to last two or three hours. For the
first three-quarters there was not a sound from the
other room, and I thought they were merely preparing
for the real horror, when suddenly the door opened
(at 9.30), and the doctors brought him back all neatly
bandaged. I had a terrible fright, thinking something
dreadful must have happened to interrupt the operation. However, thank God, it was all happily over,
and Heinrich came to himself again gradually in bed.
When he asked for our doctor, who had left the room
for a moment, and I told him how glad he was that
it had all gone so well and so quickly, the poor fellow
exclaimed, 'What, is it all over?' and on receiving
my assurance he burst into tears of joy. You can
imagine, dear Friend, how one feels at such a moment;
it makes up for all the trouble and heartache without
which one would never have this precious experience.

Angerer says the operation established beyond all
doubt the necessity for action, for it showed the worst
possible necrosis of the kneecap. Part of the *patella*
had to be removed too, as the joints did not fit in
properly; in short, the leg was doomed in any case.
Now, if it heals all right, it will be perfectly straight, if
a little shorter; stiff it is bound to be. But an illness
of these dimensions makes one modest, and we are
grateful for even this much. Heinrich has recovered

from the operation astonishingly well. His heart and his stomach fulfil their functions excellently, and this fact stood him in good stead. He has hardly any fever, and the doctors are well satisfied. Please tell Billroth about it. He will be able to tell you better than I how they manage 'resections.' The joints are sewn together with catgut, which gradually becomes absorbed. That amused Heinz somewhat. He sends his very kindest regards. Your dear songs* were a great pleasure to him just before. Send something else soon. Please tell me where you found the words.†
The line of the melodies often strikes me as being more Bohemian-Dvořákesque than Hungarian.

Please give our good Epstein the news, also Frau Franz and the Fabers.—As of old, your devoted

E. HERZOGENBERG.

### 221. *Brahms to Elisabet von Herzogenberg.*

[VIENNA, *end of March*, 1888.]

MY DEAR FRIEND,—I rejoice with all my heart to hear that you are at last relieved from your terrible suspense, and, I hope, from all your misfortunes and troubles. He has come out of it all with one leg shortened and crippled—well, I think I could accept that legacy without any particular grief, only spare me the operation and the season of terror beforehand!

---

* The *Zigeunerlieder.*

† The words were taken from Hungarian volkslieder, and transcribed into German rhyme by Hugo Conrat, whose house in Vienna Brahms frequented a good deal at the time. The original melodies, with Conrat's words underneath, were published at Buda-Pesth under the title *Ungarische Liebeslieder : 25 ungarische Volkslieder für mittlere Stimme. Klavierbegleitung von Zoltán Nagy.*

The other is bearable, and again I rejoice for you that the worst is over.

Thank you also most sincerely for letting me know at once, and for your devotion in detailing it all so that I can follow in imagination. I shall now be able to discuss it with Billroth.

I suppose your plans and prospects for both summer and winter will now change for the better?

I am of course glad for the coming symphony-composers in Berlin,* but most of all do I desire to learn your summer plans. Please tell me as soon as you can. I expect Berchtesgaden smiles on you again and Thun is quite dropped?

Billroth was here just now, and I read your letter through with him, and learned, for instance, that *patella* meant kneecap. It is as well though, on the whole, that I am not required to set down all his learned remarks in writing! Other news next time. For to-day kindest remembrances from your overjoyed

J. BR.

I will give Epstein your letter to read this evening.

### 222. *Elisabet von Herzogenberg to Brahms.*

[MUNICH] March 28, p.m., 1888.

MY DEAR FRIEND,—Thank you for your kind letter and your charming eagerness in arranging summer plans for our benefit, even to the extent of making over to us your lovely house at Thun. But, alas! we are still far removed from planning anything definite. For the present we have to wait patiently for this big wound to heal (so far we have reason to hope for the

---

* Meaning Herzogenberg's pupils.

best); then comes the very slow process of coaxing
the stiff leg to walk, which will be a matter of weeks;
after which we shall find some hot springs to strengthen
the system and do battle with the 'residue' in the left
arm and back of the neck—in short, drive out the
seven devils for good. Not till then can we think of
a thorough rest. We hope the doctors may advise
Switzerland, on account of you and my sister and the
Wachs,* but it is still all so uncertain, and we are
entirely in the doctors' hands. So take possession
of your own beautiful house without considering us
further, dear Friend. Thank you for the very kind
thought. Think of us still, but do not count on these
miserable friends of yours for anything.

These have been dark days for me. The energy
one summons up to meet the occasion leaves a feeling
of exaltation to balance one's shattered condition—
then comes the reaction. The solemn exaltation, which
attends any great trouble, wears off, and the wearisome
daily round sets in. Heinrich's excellent constitution
is my greatest comfort through all this misery. He
pulled through amazingly after the operation—free
from fever the third day!—and is quite normal in
his appetite and everything; but what a mountain of
patience we need to meet all there is to come! Think
of the misery of having no rest for another nine or ten
weeks *at least* after being in bed so long, the frightful
pain of sitting down, caused by the continual pressure,
and the soreness of the heel resulting from his present
position and the operation. We are, to make it worse,
left quite to ourselves. The Fiedlers and Levi are
away, and our friend Allgeyer has no use for any but
healthy—and wealthy!—people.

* Professor Adolf Wach had gone to live near Interlaken.

On April 4 our doctor forsakes us too, so poor
Heinrich will be quite dependent on his Fidelio, who
has frequently to jog her own elbow to keep up to the
mark.

So you see we are not exactly gay here.

Why don't you write something nice for the dear
old Kaiser, so that there may be some music worthy
to honour his memory! Poor Heinz was to have
written the music for the academic celebrations on
the 22nd, had the Kaiser lived; of course he gave it
up regretfully months ago, and now it would have
been useless. But how many things an invalid does
have to give up!

Please tell me at your convenience—first, whether
you know Wilhelm Hertz's *Spielmannslieder* and
*Tristan\** (written in delightfully pure, healthy German
that does one's heart good); and, second, Stauffer-
Bern's† etchings.

What precious moments of enjoyment one may have
in spite of everything! We had saved up *Martin
Salander‡* to read until it came out separately, and
how we revelled in it! The power of the book reveals
itself in the ever-increasing sweetness and mellow-
ness which mark its progress to the end. Where
should we be now but for these bright spots in our
lives?

* Wilhelm Hertz (1835-1902), Professor of Literature at the Munich
Polytechnic, was a member of the Munich 'Crocodile,' a group of
poets headed by Geibel, Heyse, and Lingg. His *Spielmannsbuch*,
*Marie de France*, and *Tristan und Isolde*, were free adaptations in
verse of old romantic and German originals.

† Karl Stauffer-Bern (1857-1891), painter, poet, and etcher (see
Otto Brahms's *Karl Stauffer-Bern: Sein Leben, Seine Briefe, Seine
Gedichte*').

‡ Novel by Gottfried Keller, which had been coming out in the
*Deutsche Rundschau.*

Please find something new to send us. I am at last returning the songs (to-day),* for which many thanks.

Let me know soon what Professor Gomperz decides, as I must look round for other tenants if he scorns the little house.

Sincerely, as ever, and with every kindest message from my dear, good patient, yours,

ELISABET HERZOGENBERG.

The colouring of '*Horch, der Wind klagt*' (the G minor song)† is very orginal and charming. I should love to chatter my fill about your lovely music, but in this, as in so many other matters, I am not my own mistress. I have not time enough for the necessary things. But send us something nice again soon, won't you?

### 223. *Brahms to Elisabet von Herzogenberg.*

[VIENNA, *April* 22, 1888.]

I am sorry to say the Gomperzes are not considering it, but anyway you cannot be waiting to offer it to other people! I assure you I am always telling people about the little house, and I had hoped the Meiningens would take it for the greater comfort of the ladies of their Court. I wish I had anything nice to amuse you with, either my own or anyone else's; but wherever my glance strays I see waste and desolation. A thousand good wishes for May Day and the whole summer. —Sincerely yours,

J. BR.

* *Zigeunerlieder.*          † No. 8.

### 224. *Brahms to Elisabet von Herzogenberg.*

[THUN, *June* 7, 1888.]

Are you still at this address,* and how is Heinz? Since I wrote I have had the most beautiful time in Italy, on both coasts and in Rome.† If I had not such endless letters and things lying before me, I would tell you how splendid it was. I want so much to know how you both are. Do write—as much as you can spare time for (address Thun, simply). I am installed in my old pretty rooms, which always seem to me to be made for you.—Ever yours,      J. BR.

### 225. *Brahms to Elisabet von Herzogenberg.*

THUN, *June* 12, 1888.

Had I known sooner of your plan of going to St.,‡ I should have been much tempted to go there myself. As it is, I must content myself with urging you to carry it out, which I can do the more happily for knowing how many old friends you will meet there.

I can tell you nothing definite, except that the concerto§ will probably be put into the second day. After that it will find its way to you at home. It has been too shy to go before.

* The card is addressed to Munich, Hess Strasse 30.

† Brahms had spent the month of May in Italy. It was his sixth visit to that country. He met a friend, Widmann, at Verona, who was able to act as guide to many hitherto unexplored towns. Brahms then returned with him to Thun for the summer. Widmann's *Brahms-Erinnerungen* (pp. 144-158) includes a charming description of some incidents of their travels through Bologna, Rimini, San Marino, Ancona, Loretto, Rome (Frascati, Tivoli, and d'Anzio), and Florence.

‡ Stuttgart.

§ The double concerto (Op. 102) was performed by Joachim and Hausmann on the second day of the festival (June, 1888), under Immanuel Faisst's direction.

Do arrange accordingly, and permit yourselves this recreation and change at Stuttgart.—Kindest messages to your Heinz, and drop a line later on to yours,

J. Br.

N.B.—I have been away for a few days.


### 226. *Brahms to Elisabet von Herzogenberg.*

[VIENNA, *September*, 1888.]

DEAR LADY,—Your letter found me here in Vienna. It was at Thun—and you at Basel—while I was pottering in Berne and Zürich on the way home! But I will not pursue this unprofitable subject. It is all too annoying. Your card means a long farewell, and letter-writing is, as far as I am concerned, a poor consolation.

But I must have your address in any case, and— but I think you will agree with me that it is never any good talking. Only let me know how things are occasionally. Everyone who knows you is full of interest and sympathy. As for me, I rank with the keenest.

If I should be sending you a few worthless books of songs, you may leave them behind when you go away. It will perhaps interest you to know that I have again collided with Heinz—I have been trying my hand at Groth's *Herbst.** It is a difficult thing to tackle—difficult and dull!

I am unpacking and confusion reigns; forgive this untidy sheet. Do please send word to, and think as kindly as you can of, yours very sincerely,

J. Br.

* *Im Herbst*, Op. 104, No. 5.

227. *Elisabet von Herzogenberg to Brahms.*

LUGANO, *September 22,* 1888.

MY VERY DEAR FRIEND,—Your kind words, forwarded to me here, where we are making a halt, have made me very sad and reflective. You cannot feel as vividly as we can (or perhaps you can ?) how unreasonable it is that we should spend so little of our short lives together. Don't think me presumptuous, please, if I choose seriously to think you cannot have many friends who have a *much* greater claim to see a good deal of you. Certainly no one is better able to appreciate you, both from the artistic and the human sides, and yet, when at the end we come to add up the days we have spent together, what will the total be ? If an improvement were possible, if you were inclined to regret it, too, sometimes, ways and means might be found. We relied on your writing to us before going home, and it is a real grief to find we missed you at Basel.

Our address at Nice is Boulevard Carabacel 27.

We found a particularly well-recommended house there, facing south and properly heated, and that was mainly what brought us to this sudden decision. I hope soon (we shall be there the day after to-morrow) to receive your songs, and shall then—if I may— chatter to you a little, although you did give me a plain hint to-day that it was 'never any good talking.' If only you were not quite so convinced of that! If you knew how one learns to appreciate real worth, kindness, and affection, in such hard times as we have been through, you would not be so chary of your words, but would let us hear your written voice a little oftener. You must know that you write not only easily, but well, and that every letter you send us is a precious gift. The fact is, we love you very much, dear Friend; and that being so, you might really take your share of the inconvenience!

You will send the songs as soon as possible, then, and I may hold forth at will? I have much more time now. The man we have had to engage proves—almost to my sorrow—to be an excellent nurse, and relieves me of all my duties. Heinz is slowly learning to use crutches, and is, as usual, trying to make the best of things. I fear I sometimes feel like crying for the moon. I am of the earth earthy, and can't help longing to be happy and light-hearted again. This craving for happiness is after all a common instinct.

You go to Italy every year; could you not come to Nice? How happy you would make your faithful

HERZOGENBERGS!

## 228. *Elisabet von Herzogenberg to Brahms.*

[NICE, BOULEVARD CARABACEL 9,
*October*, 1888.]

Is it my imagination, or am I right in thinking my letter to you from Lugano was of the sort that a nice person would answer—unless, indeed, he wished the poor writer to think she had gone too far, been guilty of presumption, and reckoned without her host?

You might have found time to send me a line, dear Friend. I shall soon begin to think all sorts of things! I do so want to be assured that you still like us, and mean well by us. And where are the songs which I am so looking forward to trying over on my Erard?

You will send a kind message and a beautiful song and a clasp of the hand, won't you? to yours always sincerely,

ELISABET HERZOGENBERG.

## 229. *Brahms to Elisabet von Herzogenberg.*

[VIENNA, *October*, 1888.]

DEAR, DEAR LADY,—Every letter of yours is of the sort that—one is overjoyed to receive, and would certainly like to answer as it deserves. But did I really not label my note 'preliminary'? Then I will do so now; and let me insist that, whatever I do, no one has the right to take offence, little as I deserve such kind consideration.

Again, one might go on feeling injured for ever, so much better not begin.

But you ought to know and believe that you are one of the few people one likes more—as your husband is sure to see this—than one dare say. But, then, he is also one of the said few!

And, by the way, Karl Spitteler* was complaining in the summer that you had not replied to some parcel or letter of his, and that he did not care to write again in consequence! Let him send you his article on Schubert's sonatas,† which is not at all stupid.

Your good intention of writing me at length on the receipt of my next parcel will probably be frustrated by the nature of the latter. How I should like to be

---

* Karl Spitteler (b. 1845), a Swiss poet, writing under the pseudonym 'Felix Tandem,' had published several poems, and (since 1866) edited the *Schweizerische Grenzpost* at Basel. He made the acquaintance of Brahms through their mutual friend Widmann.

† The essay appeared in the *Grenzpost*, and was included later in Spitteler's book *Lachende Wahrheiten*.

thanking you for a lengthy epistle! But you will not even find anything to scold me about.

I don't know Nice and your part of the Riviera at all, but only the other side. Nice does not count as Italy, or come into an Italian tour, though, and to me its extreme fashionableness would make it impossible.

But I may think of your stay there as the pleasantest and most cheerful you have had anywhere for a long time.

Make some real nice plans for the summer, choosing some beautiful Austrian place, if possible. In which case I hope to be there.—Yours most sincerely,

J. BR.

## 230. *Elisabet von Herzogenberg to Brahms.*

[NICE] *October* 13, 1888.

There was a nice kind letter again! It made me so happy. Thank you more than I can say for every kind word. You don't realize how important it is not to avoid the obvious too scrupulously. Life would be greatly impoverished if everyone practised this saving plan, already adopted by so many! You do not hesitate to use the same beloved formulas again and again in your art, yet in human intercourse such a craze for brevity prevails that it requires something like courage to be as persistently loquacious as I am. Therefore I must thank you again for your eloquent letter and for counting us among 'the few.' Believe me, your confidence is not misplaced.

Karl Spitteler is no friend of mine. How can you bring him into the comparison? I am nothing to him! I admit, though, there is the more need for politeness on that account. But in such dark days as those at

Wittelsbach one gives no thought to superficialities, but reserves any leisure and spirit one has for real friends. To set matters right, I did look him up at Basel, but he was out. When he returned my call, I was again quite at a loss to place him. I have rarely seen such a chameleon. He appears to have absolutely no refinement of speech, and yet there is something in his writing which betrays a highly cultivated mind.

Your delightful big parcel of music came to-day, and will soon produce a letter in which I shall say anything that comes first, just as I feel it. How splendid to have all this pile to look through and appropriate to oneself! I value the *Zigeunerlieder* twice as much for having seen them in undress first. If you would but give me that pleasure oftener!

Amanda Röntgen* is one of our household here; that is, she has the rooms above ours, and will join with us in the new Brahms orgy. The poor little woman is hoping to cure her affected lung here, and later at Ospedaletti. Our dear Dr. Schmid,† who attended us at Munich, is here just now, and has examined her. Unfortunately, he was only able to confirm the unfavourable report of her other doctors. Poor things! it is terribly sad to see this cloud on their young happiness. She is so forlorn with it all, so helplessly ignorant of all the practical side of life, a lily of the field, set all at once to sow and reap. I am glad I was permitted to take her under my wing here; it made the beginning less hard for her. Really, I am so amazingly robust myself that I can risk any worry, any exertion, now.

* Wife of Julius Röntgen. Her illness proved incurable.
† *Hofrat* Dr. Adolf Schmid.

Nice fashionable? So much so that I go marketing every morning with an empty basket, as my cook has not time, and return with an armful of glorious vegetables and fruit, from under which, as often as not, a sturdy chicken leg peeps out. So fashionable is Nice! and so well am I in this steely and yet mild air, that I am equal to that and much more; whereas before I could not carry a pound's weight without gasping. I will not expatiate on the beauty of the neighbourhood, as I am bad at descriptions, but will only say I never saw anything to equal it. It might be stage scenery for Gluck's operas! But the figures for such a landscape should be of noble build, draped in flowing garments, or lovely naked Cupids, Bacchus trains— anything to heighten the natural picturesqueness—not the feeble, oppressed race one actually sees here. It seems the real population, the influx of visitors, has not yet arrived. We never see anyone when we go through the town, but one is conscious of all the lurking ugliness and deformity, which would be depressing enough if one thought about it. But the dazzling, indestructible beauty of the place is far too absorbing, and at present we are constantly agape with delight. Indeed, we should be almost happy but that poor Heinrich is half a cripple, dear Friend; and if his condition remains unchanged we shall hardly have reason to be gay. But Dr. Schmid, my consoler, hopes *for certain* that much more may be done by mild, or possibly vigorous, treatment. The deformations in the neck and the left arm will have to be fractured, but I shall soon hear more definitely from Schmid.

Believe me, it is difficult to bear up. I could tell you of nights spent in misery; but I want to keep

the bright side uppermost as far as possible when I
tell you of ourselves.

Good-bye for to-day, and *auf Wiedersehen* this evening at the piano, when I dive into your dear music.
Think of me occasionally.—Your devoted

LISL HERZOGENBERG.

Please tell me our good Frau Franz's address.

### 231. *Brahms to Elisabet von Herzogenberg.*

[VIENNA, *October* 21, 1888.]

Frau Franz lives at No. 8, Elisabetstrasse. Many
thanks for your kind letter. I am tempted to send
you another trifle 'in undress.' But are you sure you
don't mind packing it up and returning it? And
really, this time, it is not worth the trouble. So
Frau Röntgen is with you! Please remember me
very kindly to her. Useless to enclose a violin part
for her, I suppose?* Fate might have dealt more
kindly with that poor little couple. They cannot,
like Frau Schumann, look back triumphantly on a
long life and some very hard blows. I am afraid he
will not get on any better in Amsterdam this winter.
Billroth tried to find you at Munich; he wanted to
view the landscape of leg and arm.

Forgive me, and accept kindest remembrances from
yours,

J. BR.

* He sent both the violin part and the piano score of the violin
sonata in D minor (Op. 108). It had been completed at Thun in 1886,
but Brahms chose to hold it back. It was published in 1889, with a
dedication to Bülow.

*232. Elisabet von Herzogenberg to Brahms.*

NICE, *October* 28, 1888.

MY DEAR FRIEND,—If I sit down to-day to talk about
your last parcel of music, it is in the confidence that
the person for whom you professed a liking in your
last charming letter may allow herself some liberties,
and that you will prefer even the most misguided of
her remarks to pretty speeches. I am so fond of you
and your music that I am incapable of humbugging
you ; consequently I am reduced to blurting out all
I have on my mind. You see, I have no greater
pleasure than the enjoyment of your music, and when
I cannot enjoy it I feel as if I had been done out of
something. You cannot take it as presumption if I
am quite open about it, and you must please believe
that any other course is impossible to me, if only for
my own sake. I should not dare to dwell on the
things which arouse my enthusiasm among the
selection,* were I to be silent as to those which fail
to touch me. I have played them all many times, and
each time the impression grew in intensity. I will set
it down just as it came to me.

In Op. 104 we both fixed on the second *Nachtwache,†*
at the first glance, as a pearl among the part-songs,
and it found its way right into our hearts on hearing
it. It is inspired from first to last, warm with the
glow of sunset and the ring of bugles; the entry of
every fresh voice is a delight in itself, and its soft
fulness, combined with its austerity, makes it a perfect
jewel. Our next immediate favourite is *Im Herbst,‡*

* Songs, Op. 104-107, published in 1889.
† *Fünf Gesänge für gemischten Chor, a capella,* Op. 104, No. 2.
‡ Op. 104, No. 5.

with its thrilling third verse. How beautifully you treat 'er ahnt,' how satisfying is its progress, and how daring from the point of view of harmony! Then the whole piece is so concentrated, the tone so well sustained. On the other hand, the little string quartet in D minor* quite eludes me. It fails to charm from any point of view, and the seventh bar on the first page (or the third, on the last but one) positively hurts me; the E flat, which the two outer parts reach simultaneously, strikes me as cruel, although I can imagine you intended a comma between the second and third crotchets, and considered the E flat merely in its relation to the next bar. But an ordinary mortal (not Bülow-Riemann†-Westphal‡ trained) gets a shock from which he takes time to recover. The first *Nacht-wache*§ would have more chance if she had not so dangerous a rival in the second, which promptly spoils one for anything less perfect. And here is another case where the critic within pricks up his ears, and asks whether these delicate but rather pianistic than chorally inspired entries will ever sound perfectly in tune and natural. Now, in the other, one has never a moment for criticizing; the feeling of pure enjoyment in the possession of such beauty and originality is too strong. 'This is the Brahms I like; I can surrender wholly to a mind

* '*Verlorene Jugend,*' Op. 104, No. 4. By the expression 'string quartet,' the writer conveys her disapproval of the instrumental rather than vocal treatment of the voices.

† Hugo Riemann (b. 1849), theorist and lexicographer, well-known writer on music, published in 1884 his *Musikalische Dynamik und Agogik* (strongly influenced by Westphal's *Theory of Rhythm since Bach*), followed by *Praktische Einleitung zum Phrasieren* in 1886 and a textbook on harmony in 1887.

‡ Rudolf Westphal (1826-1892), theorist and writer on music.

§ Op. 104, No. 1.

23

like this.'* But this same Brahms is not quite himself in the other one, or else I am lacking in the
particular sense needed to take it in. ' *Letztes Glück*'†
is another that gives me little satisfaction, although I
think I am able to appreciate every finely worked out
detail : the tenor catching up the theme from the
soprano, the sighing quaver-rests, and the charming,
subdued tone of the whole. But if you will spoil us
so dreadfully with your very best, how can we do
justice to anything falling short of that perfection !
And why don't you indulge in a hideous harmony,
like this one at the end,

oftener, so that our ears might grow accustomed to it !
You have trained us to think a simple chord of the
7th, with a single, not double, suspension on the G,
more melodious and satisfying in a case like this.
Can you blame us for applying the same standard to
every new work of yours, particularly when, as in
the *Nachtwache*, you give us a fresh glimpse into the
highest spheres.

It is the same with the other songs. Now tell me,
is it really all our fault if the *Kirchhof* song § provokes

* A paraphrase from Faust's last monologue (II.).
† Op. 104, No. 3.        ‡ P. 17 of the above, bar 10.
§ Op. 105, No. 4.

a burst of enthusiasm while the rest receive but a chilly welcome? Believe me, dear, dear Friend, your truest friends are not those who greet every new volume of your music impartially, with rapture, before even scanning the contents. I know some of these indiscriminating *Brahmsianer* who go into ecstasies at the very sight of your name on the cover; they must have some fetish to worship, poor things! even though they have no intimate connection with it and are often without a glimmering of its real significance. Now I know that your music is a real force which has found in me 'an abiding city,' and just because of this inviolable possession, just because I look up to you with such intense gratitude, I find the courage to tell you when I am unable to follow, when your music awakens no response. And just because I am so strongly predisposed to enthusiasm, so hotly prejudiced, I might say, in favour of this same Brahms, I often ask myself—softly, discreetly, but I do ask—whether he does not sometimes produce things born, not of his heart's blood, but only—as I ventured to say once before—of his cleverness, his routine, his supreme skill; while the impulse which stamps the thing produced as inevitable, enduring for all time, is entirely lacking.

Believe me, I do not write without deep emotion, without the fullest consciousness of the liberty your great kindness and friendship so graciously extends to me; believe, too, that I never respect you more sincerely than when I say these impossible things! But to return to the *Kirchhof*, I must say some more about the glorious thing, with its distinctive colouring, its perfect co-operation of words and music. The harp-like pathos of the very opening bars gives the key to its character. The declamation of the first verse is perfect, and how touching is the phrase '*überwach-senen Namen*,' how intensified the accent at '*gewesen*,' where the modulation is as surprising as it is legitimate! Then comes the delicious lull where it falls into C major* with those even crotchets; that pause on '*schlummerten*'; that exquisite lift at '*still*,' the exquisite line of the whole melody—all this is so powerful, so original, and so mature, such real music of so superior an order, that one would be content to hear nothing else for a long time. But to turn the page and be confronted with that *Mannsbild*,† that skulking figure of a man, is to be brought back to earth with a thump. Oh, how could you think this poem worthy of being composed by you! I cannot understand. An unattractive, dry, cheaply popular ditty with its barren heath—barren enough it seems to me! Are all the good poems really so used up that you must fall back on such skim-milk or on Lemcke's 'cold devils'?‡ How glad I am to think that I always detested Lemcke; I now know why. Heyse's little *Mädchenlied*§ is Goethe by comparison, and one can breathe sweet, pure air again. What sweet music you have woven about it, too! It is all so fine and dainty, so exceedingly attractive to the musician, with its tonic turning into a dominant in the last bar of the melody. Its plaintive yearning is so pleasing, and our ears are flattered by a newness which has yet nothing strange. The one in E flat‖ immediately before it is sure to be

---

* P. 15, bar 9. The writer does not appear to be aware that this is taken from the chorale '*O Haupt voll Blut und Wunden*.'

† *Verrath*, Op. 105, No. 5, '*Mein Schatz liess sacht ein Mannsbild 'raus*.'

‡ *Salamander*, Op. 107, No. 2. Words of both songs are by Karl Lemcke.

§ Op. 107, No. 5.          ‖ *Maienkätzchen*, Op. 107, No. 4.

popular, as such contrasts always are; similarly the Swallow song,* the words of which are again spoilt for me by that '*alter Mann.*' It makes a pretty enough piano piece, however. The 'proud' one† gives me the unshakeable impression that old Flemming conceived of her as quite a different person. I can't reconcile words and music.

*Meine Lieder*‡ is quite my favourite in Op. 106. Who could resist anything so dainty, its fine gold tracery and the added fervour which those sustained bass notes give to the closing sentences—an effect which never fails with me! I do so enjoy anything like that. The *Wanderer*,§ again, is one of those I am too cold-blooded to accept entirely, in spite of the beautiful modulation on the second page. I can't help complaining that I have heard some Brahms like it before, though more vigorously and convincingly expressed—when to please me he ought to surpass himself each time. I am as ambitious as Macbeth for those I love, you see. Amanda Röntgen and I play *Auf dem See*‖ together; it sounds charming on the fiddle—better then sung, I almost think. That must be a slip on the last page, where there is a D sharp in the second bar? Surely it should be D natural?¶ Rocky as this particular part is, I expect everybody will play D sharp, and few will rejoice in it. For my part, I should picture a 'floating Eden' less bristling and without this array of obstacles in the harmony.

---

* *Das Mädchen spricht,* Op. 107, No. 3 ('*Schwalbe, sag' miran, ist's dein alter Mann ?*').

† *An die Stolze,* Op. 107, No. 1. Words by Paul Flemming.

‡ Op. 106, No. 4.　　　　§ Op. 106, No. 5.

‖ Op. 106, No. 2.

¶ P. 10, bar 2. Brahms subsequently inserted a natural before the D in his own copy.

What shall I say about *Ständchen?*\* As I glance
over it, I see it stamped with the charm and originality
which you are always able to impart with a turn of
the hand; and yet it seems more of a Brahms manu-
facture than a Brahms inspiration. I cannot warm
to it—as I am obliged to confess, now that I am on
the stool of repentance. In Klaus Groth's '*Es hing
der Reif*'† I find the $\frac{3}{4}$ rhythm disturbing; heard in
conjunction with the never-failing minim, it gives an
effect of indolence and immense difficulty. Try singing it yourself, very *legato*, and you will see what I
mean.

There still remains to say that I like No. 3 in
Op. 105‡ very much. The two first are, of course,
old favourites—not that I shall ever be reconciled
to that succession of chords of the $\frac{6}{4}$ in the C sharp
minor!§

The more I play the *Zigeunerlieder*, the more I love
them. You were quite right in thinking I should not
be able to put enough fire into them in the sick-room
to enjoy them thoroughly. They are so gloriously
alive—rushing, throbbing, stamping along, then settling
down to a smooth, gentle flow. We cannot try them
properly in this beautiful uncivilized spot, and it is
a sore deprivation. Yet I have a vivid idea of how
they all sound; the two first numbers aglow with
life, the charming humour of No. 6, the adorable
melancholy fervour of the next one in E flat—I am
always moved to tears in the second part, then the
whispering G minor with its strange colouring! How
opportunely the solo voice separates itself from the

---

\* *Der Mond steht über dem Berge*, Op. 106, No. 1.
† Op. 106, No. 3.                          ‡ *Klage.*
§ *Immer leiser wird mein Schlummer.*

rest, and how refreshing is the re-entry! How delightful it would be to arrange a really good performance of this fine work by a few music-lovers! I look forward to next winter for this sort of enjoyment.

Dearest Friend, I know I ought to stop, but let me sum it all up once more: I love and admire your music more than ever, but my very admiration leads me to ask why one who has coined and still can coin such gold (*Nachtwache, Kirchhoflied*, etc.) should be so sparing with it, and why we should be put off with silver—music that is never devoid of worth and charm, considered on its own merits, but unsatisfying in that it comes from the magician who has accustomed us to the very best.

One thing more. If my letter angers you, fling it into the darkest, dustiest corner of your room, but not the writer along with it! Or if you should do so on the impulse of the moment, fish her out again after a time, and tell her that you have not quite lost patience with her, and are not going to withdraw your friendship—have even, perhaps, no desire to do so.

Yesterday I bought a Reclam edition of Platen,* and rejoiced in the two or three glorious poems in the collection. I took '*Wie raff' ich mich auf*' to the piano, and there I recalled your exquisite song† note for note, to my joy and happiness. I have, of course, practically no music here, and can have none sent, as it is all stored away in the attics in Berlin. Under these conditions I make bold to ask if there is anything you do not want—songs, or the G major sonata

---

* Graf August Platen (1796-1835), poet.
† Brahms, Op. 32, No. 1.

or *anything whatsoever*—which you could pack up and
send to Nice, thereby making us very happy? Some
things I cannot remember, and I rack my brains
distractedly. Nothing is to be had here except the
Hungarian Dances—and any amount of French trash.
Bizet excepted, it is all so impossible to us; even
the more modern Délibes* is dreadful. Thank God
one belongs to Germany and is your countrywoman!
—Your most faithful and devoted

L. H.

### 233. *Elisabet von Herzogenberg to Brahms.*

NICE, October, 30, 1888.

MY DEAR FRIEND,—This 30th of October will long
be green in my memory. I cannot tell you how I felt
when the dear, fat roll of music† was brought in this
morning. We were still at breakfast, and my heart
beat fast as I cautiously extracted the kernel from
its shell. Heinrich wanted to tear the manuscript
from me; but I held it tight, and ran straight up to
Amanda's room, where—more or less *mal coiffées*, but
full of joyous expectancy—we sat down to play it
at once.

We got into the spirit of it immediately, feeling your
spell upon us. Our eyes flew from bar to bar, our
zeal and delight grew from page to page, our fingers
tackled every difficulty with such success that I hardly
knew myself. We grasped each successive beauty,
feeling quite at home in spite of the startling sense
of novelty which a first movement invariably produces.

---

* Léo Délibes (1836-1891), composer of opera (*Le roi l'a dit,
Lakmé*, etc.) and ballet (*Coppelia, Sylvia*).

† The manuscript of the violin sonata in D minor, Op. 108.

At the opening of the development* we quite caught our breath. How new it is, with that exquisite pedal-note absorbing everything! How our surprise and delight grew and grew as the A showed no sign of giving way, but held its own through all the glorious tissue woven above it! How my left thumb revelled in the pressure it had to exert! And that F sharp minor on that Proteus A,† and the gradual ebbing until the theme's subdued return—*molto legato*. O my friend, that was indeed one of your moments! Not that you ought to take all the credit, for it was borne in to you on that tide '*das flutend strömt gesteigerte Gestalten.*'‡ How happy, how happy this piece makes me! I feel so glad, too, that I kept back nothing of what I felt the other day, for it gives me the more freedom to express all my present delight.

It is still too new to write quite fully, but I must dwell on one or two points; the delicious *tranquillo* of the *coda*,§ and the shorter pedal-note‖ at the end, emphasizing the structure of the sonata-form and welding the two pedal-notes, A and D, into one golden ring. And how one's heart goes out to the last page; to those sustained notes on the violin which combine with the left-hand minims on the piano in such beautiful contrary movement! How it vibrates with emotion, how it grows in intensity at the *ritenuto*, reaching its climax where the pedal-note ends and the violin becomes chromatic! When we had reached that point we exchanged comprehensive looks, we three, and our looks would have told you much that you would like to hear. Would that I had you here and

* P. 6, bar 13.                    † P. 7, bar 19.
‡ Goethe.                          § P. 12, bar 19.
‖ P. 12, bar 19, etc.

could press your hand in gratitude for this great gift, and seat you at the piano to hear you play it through to a fine rumbling accompaniment of your own making! What delights me so in this sonata is its wonderful unity. The four movements are so unmistakably members of one family. One purpose dominates them, one colour scheme embraces them all; yet their vitality finds expression in such various ways.

I rejoiced to find the Adagio undisturbed by any middle part, for, as I have often admitted, however nice the middle parts are, I never can enthuse over them. That kind of contrast almost always strikes me as artificial, and my chief pleasure in an Adagio is its continuity of emotion. For that reason this compact movement, so expressive in its contracted form, pleases me particularly. What a fine contrast those clashing chords form to the broad flowing line of the melody, and how beautiful it *sounds!* How comical (in the best sense, for one laughs for very pleasure) is the Presto! how amazingly original in its breathless hurry, how merry, how humorous and how rich in every line! The piano part is so charmingly written, a pleasure from first to last, and so playable, with all its colour-effects, that one can almost manipulate it at the first reading. We literally laughed for pleasure over this movement, and yet how perfectly in keeping with the rest it is! It does no violence to one's mood, but is the natural relaxation of a mind which has just been strained to the utmost seriousness. The *presto* of the Finale is the most difficult to grasp at first, but one feels at once how good it is going to be and how fitting a crown to the whole; and it has in the highest degree the one quality essential to a Finale—an irresistible impetus. It tears along like Aurora's steeds in the glorious picture,* and gives one no rest until the soothing second subject comes in with such fine solemnity. Short as my acquaintance has been, I took in that beautiful passing-note D, where the violin comes in in the third bar, from the first;† also the lovely *pp* passages and the *crescendo* in the development. How delightful they are to play, too, excepting the last bit, which is rather cruel! We played on and on in a tumult of delight, and paused at last with flushed cheeks, restraining ourselves with an effort from beginning all over again. We could not have done it on Amanda's account; that is reserved for this evening, and we are rejoicing in the prospect meanwhile. I had to write you these few words, which are at least better than a telegram, to let you know what a festival we are having to-day.

Let me thank you, dearest Friend—thank you for your good deed in *sending* us the sonata, and thank you for *writing* it and giving us *only* of your best. Even Lady Macbeth's ambition is satisfied!

You are not angry with me for the other day, are you? And you do understand that it is just my very sincere admiration for you which makes it impossible for me to do otherwise? All the more do I delight in my feelings to-day.—Your grateful and devoted

LISL HERZOGENBERG.

You will forgive the slovenliness of these *prestissimo* scribbled lines? I could not wait to think over what I should say, and the result is a mass of slips and smudges.

* Guido Reni's fresco in the Rospigliosi Palace in Rome. Brahms had a copy of Rafael Morghen's engraving in his music-room in Vienna.

† Op. 108, p. 24, bar 30.

## 234. *Brahms to Elisabet von Herzogenberg.*

[VIENNA, *November* 3, 1888.]

DEAR LADY,—A thousand thanks; but greatly as the sonata letter delighted me, I am far more inclined to be suspicious about it than the other;* neither did I expect to hear you say such nice things about the *Zigeunerlieder.* I prefer to consider it an error of judgment rather than a case of hypocrisy, however, so for the present accept my sincere though hasty thanks.

I have just written to Frau Schumann. In case she should want the sonata, please send it her *at once.* We can see about a copy afterwards.

I doubt whether there is anything you would care about among my things. I have only a few trans-positions and arrangements lying by. If you will mention any special piece (as the first violin sonata), I will try and get it. It would be easier for you than for me to ask Astor for the Platen† things.

Once more best thanks, and if you should have made the last letter too sugary from sheer kindness, send the pepper-box after it.—Your grateful

JOH. BR.

## 235. *Elisabet von Herzogenberg to Brahms.*

[NICE, *November* 6, 1888.]

MY DEAR FRIEND,—I am quite touched by the arrival just now of the dear old G major sonata.‡ It is surely

* Letter 232.

† Op. 32 (including Platen's '*Wie rafft' ich mich auf*,' to which reference is made in Letter 232) was published by Rieter-Biedermann (Astor).

‡ Op. 78. Brahms had sent it off before his letter on the 3rd.

a sign that you are not angry with me, after all.   My very best thanks.

I know the D minor sonata by heart now, to my great joy.   It is an indescribable pleasure to absorb it into one's self and then play it quite out of one's head. Amanda Röntgen and I kept on smiling at each other when we found we knew even the last movement to-day.   But the development gives us considerable trouble, and I do beg you will look at those syncopations* again, and see if you could not alter them a little; I mean from B flat minor onwards, and particularly the bars where the bass has the theme in C sharp minor.†   It is more comprehensible in the big *crescendo* afterwards, where the swing and breadth of movement are a help.   But the C sharp minor part is complicated by the unfavourable position of some of the important notes of the harmony given to the fiddle.   It is really quite a blot on the movement, which is so glorious and so effective as a whole.   Then, again, one has to struggle and pant to keep in, because there is so often nothing to mark the strong beats in those bars.   It would be just the same, I believe, no matter how good the violinist, and it is such a pity to let that one place spoil the effect, when the rest of the movement sounds so well.   It is one of those episodes that only musicians will understand, and that is not desirable, is it ?

I have one other proposal: that you should make the chords in the Scherzo *pizzicato*.   It sounds as well again.‡   Played *arco*, that part becomes abstract too;

---

* Op. 108, p. 28.

† P. 28, bars 1 and 9.  Brahms did not alter this extremely difficult passage.

‡ Brahms followed this suggestion in part.  In the repetition (p. 20, bar 21) the violin chords are marked *pizzicato*; on the other hand, the violinist finds special legato marks in the beginning to show

you hear notes, but no connected sound, and it makes it difficult to trace the continuation when the whole passage is so complicated in itself. I always add the top note on to my own chord, which makes it much clearer. Here at Number 27, Carabacel, it does not seem to matter if I take such liberties!

If it is left to the violin it is all too shadowy, and although it sounds more real played *pizzicato*, the doubling does no harm even then. Please tell me if you agree about the *pizzicato*, or if you think it all nonsense?

Let me thank you once more for this glorious piece, whose beauties now lie fully revealed before me. The construction seems to me more and more wonderful. If it were not so exquisitely compact, proportioned like the façade of some romanesque church, how could one commit it to memory so quickly? . . .†

### 236. *Brahms to Elisabet von Herzogenberg.*

[VIENNA, *November* 6, 1888.‡]

It seems I did not write clearly to Frau Schumann. She asks me to request you to send her the sonata

---

that the chords are to be played as broadly as possible, and, of course, with the bow. It is perfectly in keeping with the *con sentimento* which modifies the *un poco presto* of the signature.

  \* P. 17, bar 9.—TR.

  † The second sheet of the letter is lost.

  ‡ Letters 234 and 235 appear to have crossed in the post.

*immediately*, which I now do, with a *sffz** by way of emphasis. She is going to Berlin very soon, and would like to play it with Joachim; and she is so conscientious as to want to prepare it thoroughly.— Kindest regards to you all from yours,

J. BR.

### 237. *Elisabet von Herzogenberg to Brahms.*

[NICE, November 8, 1888.]

MY VERY DEAR FRIEND,—Forgive me for bothering you again so soon, but I *must* ask whether the discrepancy between the original 'bridge' leading to the second subject and the parallel passage later is deliberate or accidental? You remember, the first time it is—

and the second time, where, to be consistent, B flat major should be followed by C, the sentence begins with A major.‡ Please do you mind explaining? I still have no message from Frau Schumann, so am keeping the sonata; but ought I to have despatched it to Frankfurt before? If only Joachim might have it soon! I cannot say how badly I have wanted him just now, with all due respect to the musical Amanda.

One thing more: in the 6th and 7th bars of the Finale you change the harmonies in the piano part,

---

\* To indicate the strongest possible *sforzato.*

† Op. 108, p. 4, bar 12.　　　　　　‡ P. 10, bar 3.—TR.

but *not* in the parallel passage.* I thought I would
just tell you.  Personally I am glad, and should even
prefer a simple augmented triad (F, A, C♯) to accompany the F on the fiddle, instead of that E, which
always sounds like a mistake.  Until you forbid me,
I shall continue to play—

The more I play the Finale, the more hopelessly do
I fall in love with it.  *'Wind und Ströme, Donner und
Hagel rauschen ihren Weg.'*† I hardly know anything
else that tears along with such spirit.  I always
wonder how you felt when you tried to fetter the
mental picture and shape it in artistic form.  How
glorious it must be to feel it has lost none of its
original power in the process of development, from
that first conception to its present elaborately worked-
out form! It has preserved all its natural flavour,
and yet every little note plays its allotted part in
building up a masterpiece.  How often must even the
greatest composer find the cherished vision he is
striving to capture 'melt like a cloud of mist and
vanish like a breath,'‡ or appear as a lifeless reproduction! But this is so warm with life, so full of fire
and vigour, so direct and sincere in its appeal, that
the consciousness of any intermediate stage is entirely
absent.

Had I but the gift of eloquence to tell you really
and truly all I feel, and how entirely this great, this
beautiful work has won our hearts! . . .§

* Op. 108, p. 27, bars 3 and 4.        † Goethe, *Das Göttliche.*
‡ Quotation from the song ' *Wie Melodien zieht es,'* Op. 105, No. 1.
§ The letter is incomplete.

238. *Brahms to Elisabet von Herzogenberg.*

[VIENNA] *November* 10, 1888.*

DEAR FRIEND,—Quite as much depends on the way a letter is read as on the way it is written.

In my reply to your letter there is not a word of untruth, nor did it ever occur to me to write one. I should be incapable, for very shame, of responding to you and your genuine, well-meant criticism otherwise than with the utmost sincerity and gratitude, even though I might consider I had the right to contradict you.

It was not right of me to reply to your long and careful letter with that hasty, casual note, which was probably responsible for your misapprehension. It must have sounded confused to a degree, for I had all sorts of things in my head just then, and intended writing more fully another time.

I have often told myself I should do better to give up corresponding with my friends altogether. I generally manage to go wrong somewhere, and if I don't, my correspondent infallibly does in reading it!

I hope you really sent off the sonata on the spot? You know Frau Schumann is very touchy!—Kindest regards to all three of you,

J. BR.

(Do you ever meet the great Nietzsche† on your marketing expeditions, and read him when you get home?)

---

* The date was noted by Frau von Herzogenberg, and marks the *arrival* of the letter.

† Friedrich Nietzsche (1844-1900), the philosopher, had spent the previous winter at Nice, but was then in Turin.

### 239. *Elisabet von Herzogenberg to Brahms.*

[NICE, *November* 10, 1888.]

Thank you, dear, dear Friend, for your good letter just received. Believe me, if I misread the other, it was not lack of modesty which influenced me, but a not unnatural diffidence. And how, pray, was I to take that remark about your being 'more inclined to be suspicious' about my second letter than my first?*

Only consider what a perfect right a man like you has, after all, to grow impatient with a woman like myself, and simply say, 'Hold your tongue, goosey!' I had, after all, every reason to fear your wrath, in spite of your friendship and all the indulgence it brings, and your note the other day was so 'enharmonically' ambiguous that I really had some ground for bothering you again with my inquiries.

Set your mind at rest; the sonata went off yesterday by the first post. Frau Schumann has surely not had time to be angry yet? In any case I am innocent; yet the fact that she did not write to *me* for the sonata looks rather suspicious. She must be jealous of our having had the pleasure first, but poor Heinrich might really be allowed this special favour. When I think how rich all your lives are compared with ours, which is one struggle against overwhelming odds! If we do contrive to be fairly happy sometimes, it is hard-earned happiness, and people who still show us a little extra kindness will find that it is not wasted.

I have already abused Nietzsche with some vigour, and am always lamenting that such an intellect should have gone to the wrong man. For I do think him ex-

* *Cf.* Letter 234.

tremely clever despite all his vagaries, his paradoxes, and his boundless exaggerations.  I have seldom been so fascinated by any book as by his *Genealogie der Moral*,* for instance, and I would rather disagree with one of his calibre than agree with many others, who are more orthodox but have less to say.  And in his *Der Fall Wagner*† his description of Wagner's style is excellent, better than anything else I have read— don't you agree ?  But when he goes on to discredit the worth and the style of another composer,‡ so precious to us, dismissing the subject with careless levity, I simply ignore it as I do his flippant, short-sighted depreciation of Christianity and many other things.  One has to sift the wheat from the chaff as one reads, and exercise much toleration; but the remainder is worth it, and there are certain things no one but this odd person is able to say, it seems to me.  His remarks on music in *Jenseits von Gut und Böse*§ are incredible and incomprehensible in relation to the rest.  The best, from a humorous standpoint, is his allusion in the latest pamphlet to the only man living who can write an overture—*i.e.*, Nietzsche,‖ 'who has given to mankind

* Appeared in 1887.

† *Der Fall Wagner, Turiner Brief vom Mai,* 1888.  In this letter Nietzsche turns and rends his former idol.  He concludes the letter with an attack on Brahms, culminating in the sentence (often misquoted) : 'His is the melancholy of impotence.'  But Nietzsche's judgment was biassed by personal considerations in each case.  Neither Wagner nor Brahms approved of his compositions.

‡ Brahms.                      § Published in 1886.

‖ Nietzsche alludes to his friend Peter Gast (Heinrich Köselitz, b. 1854), composer of various operas, orchestral and chamber-music works.  On June 28, 1888, Nietzsche expresses himself in a letter to the effect that Gast is the only man left whose music finds grace in his eyes, and that his opera (*The Lion of Venice*) is the first of modern operas—gay, emotional, and masterly in style, not amateurish like Wagner's.

the most profound books it possesses'! But Volkland knows a composition of his which is beneath criticism.*
Really, this man's vanity will bring him to a lunatic asylum yet! All the same, it would amuse me to meet him and have a tussle. Is he really here?

Heinz climbed the *Schlossberg* with me this morning, a very creditable performance even for normal people. Wasn't it good! By the way, please thank Billroth very much for his intended call. It was exceedingly kind of him to think of my Heinz.

Farewell, and thank you once more for the good letter. My soul was indeed 'cast down and disquieted within me'! Let me see what dear Frau Schumann says to you about the sonata. I wish I could be there when she plays it with Joachim. Another thing I wanted to say—if doing up parcels is not too terrible a nuisance, I should welcome anything, arrangements, transpositions, etc. I know the original keys, and can adapt the transpositions accordingly.

It will all come in useful for Liseley later on!

Remember me to Frau Franz; she wrote such a kind letter. I shall be writing to the Fabers.—Your old friend and admirer,

LISL HERZOGENBERG.

What is the name of Epstein's street again?

240. *Brahms to Elisabet von Herzogenberg.*

[VIENNA, *October* 14, 1888.]

Epstein's address is I. Rudolfsplatz 13. Nietzsche's was Hôtel de Genève a short time ago. He is said to

---

* *Hymnus an das Leben,* for chorus and orchestra, which Nietzsche had sent to Brahms with a dedication. Brahms, however, declined the honour, sending a polite message on his visiting card.

be a fitting illustration of his *Jenseits von Gut und Böse*. His piece for chorus* has been printed by Fritzsch, and is much the same as any young student's effort. Don't waste the precious daylight too often by reading such things, and remember the saying: 'The reverse may be true.'† Labor‡ gave an excellent rendering of Heinz's E flat sonata with a good violinist at the *Tonkünstlerverein* the other day. He has a splendid touch, fire, energy, and everything desirable.—Kindest regards,

J. BR.

### 241. *Elisabet von Herzogenberg to Brahms.*

FLORENCE, May 14, 1889.

DEAR, DEAR FRIEND,—We were glad to have your message through Frau Schumann, and the good news that you would like to see us, and would even face a journey to that end. You offered so kindly to come to Graz in case we should pass through, and were equally willing to go to Berchtesgaden, which would not be far from your summer home this year. We shall hold you to it, and beg you to be sure and

---

\* *Cf.* Letter 239.

† 'Perhaps the reverse may be true' is a remark of Beethoven's at the age of twenty, recorded on a sketch page for the music to Hölty's '*Klage*' (in possession of the *Archiv der Gesellschaft der Musikfreunde*, Vienna), as the result of a long debate on the relation between the method of notation and tempo. Brahms gleaned the phrase from a supplementary volume to the complete Beethoven edition, published in 1888, and was fond of using it to dispose of any sophistries and equivocations attributed to philosophers of the day. It is characteristic of his general attitude that he did not think it worth while to mention the incident between Nietzsche and himself.

‡ Josef Labor (b. 1842), Court organist, pianist, and composer, in Vienna.

act upon your charming resolve. We should have infinitely more of you at Liseley than at Graz, where we are only paying a short visit to our relatives, and shall hardly have a room to ourselves; whereas at Liseley we can offer you a nice room and an excellent bed. It would be such a joy to welcome you there at last. We move in at the end of June or beginning of July, as our dear Dr. Schmid, the ruler of our destiny, makes no objection. I shall write promptly, and hope to hear from you in the meantime.

We have so enjoyed having Frau Schumann here and at Nice, although we wish she could enjoy all the beauties of the place more at the cost of less exertion. The dear thing has ten years too many on her shoulders, and has not the elasticity of temperament which one must possess if one would be perfectly happy among the Italians in spite of the dirt, fraud and general discomfort. Also one needs more leisure to absorb so many new impressions, striking as they may be, than her circular tour ticket—that ghastly invention!—allowed her. Once or twice we found her miserably seated on her camp-stool before some Signorelli or Verocchio, rubbing her hands nervously and trying so hard to feel some enthusiasm. But nothing would come and carry her off her feet; nothing awoke a response in her, receptive as she undoubtedly is. The truth is, one can only appreciate the best in art after a thorough apprenticeship; we have to serve our seven years for so many things in this world! But when the glorious soul did take in anything quickly, her beautiful grey eyes, dim with emotion, would light up with youthful fire, as we all love to see them; and how we rejoiced in these rare moments of happiness for her! She always enjoyed

going to see our dear Hildebrand* at San Francesco,
and seeing his fine new things. You must really meet
him and get to know and admire his work.

You can imagine how much we talked about your
D minor,† each taking the words from the other's
mouth. Frau Schumann played the precious thing
with Amanda Röntgen, and was very pleased with
her.

They sang Heinrich's psalm‡ at Leipzig yesterday,
dispensing with an orchestra, but putting all possible
good-will into the performance ; and Heinrich—who
is not spoilt—was much pleased by a telegram
from the *Bachverein* a yard long. He has never
heard a syllable from you on the subject, however,
and that would please him far more. Rudorff's performance in March§ was very good, they say.

I must stop. I have very little time here. Kindest
messages from Heinrich, who is wild with delight at
the thought of having you at Liseley. Let us know
when it would suit you best. It is too nice of you to
come to our mountains again, and leave superior
Switzerland to look after itself.‖—Give a kind thought
to your most devoted

HERZOGENBERGS.

VIA PONTA A EMA 51,
    RICCORBOLI.

* The sculptor, who had been living at Florence since 1874.
† The third violin sonata.        ‡ Herzogenberg, Op. 60.
§ At the Stern *Gesangverein*, Berlin.
‖ Brahms's house at Thun had been spoilt for him by a newly
laid-out promenade on the bank of the Aare, which ran immediately
under his windows. Strangers, especially English tourists, insisted
on stopping to listen when he was playing.

## 242. *Brahms to Elisabet von Herzogenberg.*

ISCHL [*May* 23, 1889].

DEAR LADY,—I do wish I could have the pleasure of seeing Frau Schumann enjoy Italy.

But it is too late now, and your letter, in describing the pathetic side of it, proves that I was right not to attempt it. It could have been no satisfaction, since it fell so far short of what one hoped and desired for her.

I don't understand your movements, given the supposition that good air is what Heinz needs. Both your present stay in Florence and the projected visit to Berchtesgaden are inexplicable. However, the prospect of our long-postponed meeting is clear to me, and makes me as happy as a king.

I have still to thank you for certain dear old friends in their smart new Rieter dress.* No one could receive and examine your husband's things with greater eagerness and affection than I. Yet you must not expect any further comment, for I simply cannot see my way to it. For one thing, we have both much the same ambition in this case, so that I am led, involuntarily, to compare my own point of view. My only safe outlet would be a cheerful attack on the texts, which would bring me no honour and glory; for it only means that I am lazier than Heinrich, and wait until something turns up to attract me. The words of his psalm never would! They remind me of a fanatical religious war, and that is no subject for music.†

* Herzogenberg's compositions—in particular Ps. xciv.

† The psalm begins, 'O Lord God, to whom vengeance belongeth,' but closes with the words, 'Yea, the Lord our God shall cut them off.'

Well, I wish you all things good and beautiful, with
my visit to Berchtesgaden as an intermezzo!

I dare not ask to be supplied with news occasionally;
I am so far from deserving it.—With kindest regards,
yours,

J. Br.

### 243. *Brahms to Elisabet von Herzogenberg.*

[ISCHL, *June* 28, 1889.]

This is just to say that I have made no plans, and
shall look forward eagerly to your next letter. You
know Ischl and the 'Post,'* or perhaps some of the
other better-class inns? It is foolish to venture an
opinion without knowing the circumstances—but I am
glad, all the same, that you are not going to Berchtesgaden.

Good-bye then, with best thanks for the delightful
prospect this opens up.—Yours always sincerely,

J. Br.

### 244. *Brahms to Heinrich von Herzogenberg.*

[ISCHL, *July* 29, 1889.]

Your parcel arrived with the post-card, though I
only saw and read the latter afterwards. And what
a disappointment! No piano concerto of yours for
me, but what I take to be a violin concerto of your
wife's for Joachim†—and not even permission to open
the fat parcel! Now, of course, I shall not be able
to enclose anything for eight voices;‡ I confess it is

---

* An inn at Ischl.

† The music sent was probably Herzogenberg's *Legenden* for piano
and viola, Op. 62, dedicated to 'his Friend, Josef Joachim.'

‡ Three motets for four-part and eight-part chorus *a capella*,
Op. 110, which Brahms had shown them on their visit to Ischl.

not copied out yet, and will come in nicely to send along with a letter of thanks for your most kind visit. You will enjoy staying there,* I feel sure, for it is a glorious spot.  How you will revel in those woods!— Sincerely yours,

J. Br.

### 245. *Elisabet von Herzogenberg to Brahms.*

Berlin, December 26, 1889.

Dear, dear Friend,—It would be difficult to give you any idea of my pleasure in receiving your parcel —a precious gift in every respect.  I am writing at once to ask you to set my mind at rest on two points. First, I usually look upon anything that arrives on Christmas Day as a present; but may I really claim these polonaises, interlarded with *such* truffles,† as my own?  Can you really have intended anything so delightful?  Then—and this agitates me even more —the end of the piece is missing!  It only goes to page —, so the rest must still be in your possession, and not, surely, by your own intention.  You would never be so inhuman as to 'put asunder that which God hath joined' just for the sake of keeping another piece intact!  I would rather resign mine in that case, if the other happier solution is impossible.

In any case I want a line to reassure me, and if possible the missing pages.  I leave you to imagine the bliss with which I sat down to the piano with the mildewed‡ manuscript, the delight with which

* At Baden-Baden.

† The motets mentioned in Letter 244.  Brahms had followed his usual method of wrapping the manuscript in old Viennese dance-music, probably the polonaises referred to.

‡ It is evident from this that Brahms had again indulged his passion for using old waste-paper.

I hailed each fresh entry,* my absorption in the
exquisite passing-notes, and my renewed wonder at
the unfailing terseness and vigour, the delicious
warmth of feeling in every bar—and finally my
gratitude for being permitted to see and enjoy it.

You have again made me exceedingly happy.

More later on, when I am reassured as to those
missing pages.—Your old friend,

LISL HERZOGENBERG.

P.S.—I can't tell you the page, as you have only
numbered the sheets. Those I have are 11, 12, and 13.

### 246. Brahms to Elisabet von Herzogenberg.

[VIENNA, December 29, 1888.]

DEAREST FRIEND,—For to-day let me simply notify
you that the last page contains nothing more valuable
than a few closing bars. It was left behind from
absent-mindedness, like the commonest umbrella. As
soon as I can find a nice diagonal wrapper† I will put
it in.—With kindest regards, yours,

J. BR.

### 247. Elisabet von Herzogenberg to Brahms.

[BERLIN] BURGGRAFENSTRASSE 4,
March 17, 1890.

DEAREST FRIEND,—I hope you are not angry at
receiving no acknowledgment of the patriotic *Gedenksprüche* and motets ;‡ but we received them a fortnight
late, as we now see from the enclosed bills of consign-

---

\* Of the different voices in the choruses.

† Meaning another page of old dance music.

‡ *Fest- und Gedenksprüche*, Op. 109, and *Drei Motetten*, Op. 110,
published by Simrock early in 1890.

ment, dated February 21 and March 10, owing to some oversight at Simrock's. Since then Heinrich has been hoping from day to day to write to you himself—an intention of long standing—and thank you properly for this delightful present. Instead, he is condemned to sit idle, with the further complication of a painful and troublesome inflammation of the eyes—so his wife must again be the speaker.

We take the deepest pleasure in these choruses. Your choice of the glorious, strengthening words, designed to enhance the splendour of these solemn festivals, is not happier than the note you have chosen for their musical setting. It is so precisely right— edifying, simple, pithy, unsentimental, and yet glowing with inward fervour. I wish I could hear them soon, rendered in the spirit in which they were conceived. A composition written in a serious mood should be performed with equal seriousness, not thrust upon concert-goers whether the rest of the programme is suitable or not. Although I now have my motets* in print, with the addition of a most insulting piano arrangement (a severe reflection on present-day choir-masters, by the way!),† I want that *last page* of mine more than ever. You really must not keep it back any longer. Please smuggle it neatly in with some delightful thing or other, and send it me very soon.‡

* '*Wenn wir in höchsten Nöten seien,*' and Op. 110, No. 2, '*Ach arme Welt, du trügest mich,*' which Frau von Herzogenberg had appropriated as a Christmas present to herself.

† The piano arrangement is duly explained in the score as a ' possible help in rehearsing.'

‡ Brahms could not be induced to give up the missing page. Frau von Herzogenberg's manuscript was found incomplete after her death.

Don't be so sparing with the use of your pen! It used to be much more diligent on my behalf. In sorting out my letters, I was touched to find I had quite a respectable fat bundle in your handwriting to tie up and pat, and the thought would come, Why does he grow more monosyllabic? why does he only send post-cards when he writes at all—these lamentable substitutes for closed and therefore precious letters? That you *can* write charmingly I realized again with joy on perusing these letters—of, alas! such ancient date!

You used to demand an epistle from me now and again, too; but one drops into silence after a time when no sound penetrates the dear, beautiful forest in which one wanders. It is a pity. Our pleasures are not so numerous that we can afford to be wasteful, and even you cannot have many such devoted friends as ourselves, in spite of the new communities which are springing up all around you.

We often long for the B major trio,* and the press notice you were so kind as to send increased our curiosity.† Don't keep us waiting too long.

Good-bye for to-day. I should like to write a good deal more, but don't know whether you would care for it.

---

* Brahms had thoroughly overhauled an early work (Trio in B, Op. 8), and brought it out in its improved form as a 'new edition' (see Kalbeck, *Brahms*, i. 156-163). He played it on February 22, 1890, in Vienna with Rosé and Hummer, and before that in Buda-Pesth with Hubay and Popper.

† Probably an anonymous discussion which appeared in the *Deutsche Kunst- und Musik-Zeitung*, a very inferior paper. The article, which was remarkable for its intelligence, took Brahms by surprise, and he praised it to a few of his friends. Among these was Mandyczewski, the writer of it; he kept his secret, however, so as not to spoil Brahms's pleasure.

Let us hear from you soon. We are not always bright and cheerful, and can do with a little friendly encouragement.—Yours ever,

LISL HERZOGENBERG.

Please remember me to Frau Franz and the Fabers —who have had trouble again!


248. *Brahms to Herzogenberg.*

[ISCHL, *May* 23, 1890.]

DEAR FRIEND,—I wished, even before leaving Vienna, I could borrow your wife's graceful pen to fill this envelope. I wanted to thank you for your last bulky parcel, and express my pleasure and thanks at my ease.

But I never could manage it. One thing in particular restrained me: I have been more than usually impressed this time with the great similarity of our work! In looking over the *chorales*, the quartets, and the songs, I was quite agitated to find how vividly they recalled all sorts of efforts of my own. May your own agitation, when you have occasion to indulge in a similar retrospect, be of a more pleasing order than mine!

But I am not going into the question of our music to-day and in these surroundings. I am merely curious about something.

I read a notice just now to the effect that you were to be at Hamburg *to-day*.* That is a pleasanter sort

* Several of Herzogenberg's compositions were performed on May 23 at the Hamburg *Tonkünstlerverein*, among them a string quartet (Op. 42, No. 3), the waltzes for pianoforte duet (Op. 53), and choruses for female voices from Op. 26 (performed by the *Singakademie* choir under Schwencke). The Herzogenbergs had gone over specially for this concert.

of agitation, and I am particularly anxious to hear more about it—a full account. The town may have pleased you, if it happens to have exerted itself for once to secure a fine day. Our worthy colleagues have as usual exerted themselves to no effect, I imagine? Mediocre as ever? I miss Spengel's name among the parties concerned, yet he is the leading spirit where you and your music are in question!

I hope you will be inclined for a little chat. I need not say how specially interested I am. And what are your summer plans? Send me a few lines to Ischl. —With kindest regards to you both, yours,

J. Br.

### 249. *Herzogenberg to Brahms.*

BERLIN, *June* 8, 1890.

DEAREST FRIEND,—I might find your 'agitation' (that for which my last parcel of music was responsible) infectious, could I but make sure what you mean by it. I could read *every* meaning into your mysterious words—pleasing or painful according to the way I turn them about. The process of my development reminds you here and there of your own. Is it the chaff or the wheat that gives the resemblance? Or merely the restlessness of my millstones? You know that every least sign from you has been of value to me, not merely because I was able to grasp it instantly, but because I always tried to turn it to practical use; and you must not withdraw your help now, whether you think me fully fledged or a hopeless case. I do not consider myself 'finished' in either sense.

We spent some pleasant, invigorating days at Hamburg. We were quite unprepared for the imposing and

stirring aspect of your native town.  It makes Berlin
seem like a haphazard conglomeration of material,
which might any day be taken to pieces again.  How
fascinating it is to stroll down to the picturesque
harbour in the morning, prowl about the quaint,
serious old streets, and float peacefully down the
Alster past all those serene old houses which have
such a proprietary air!

The only dissonant note (badly prepared and impossible to resolve!) was X.'s terribly flowery speech.
The rest of the evening passed off agreeably.  The
performance was excellent, and the audience patient
and well-disposed.  We made some charming excursions through the beech-woods at Reinbeck to the
Spengels (what a delightful woman she is!), and to
Chrysander, whose alertness we found most refreshing.  The double life he leads struck us as so well
ordered, so natural.  From the greenhouse we passed
into his music-printing room; from the cowhouse into
the library—and what a library!  We gleaned the
latest authentic news of his great neighbour,* of
course, and were more than ever nonplussed by the
recent turn of events and the attitude of the Almighty
in countenancing them.

Before this we had to superintend the sale of
house and furniture at Berchtesgaden, taking our
last farewell with heavy hearts though not heavy
purses!

We shall spend July at Wildbad, part of August at
Sylt; so you see we mean to do our best—

Also for the coming generation of composers, but I
am still on the lookout for a pupil possessed of talent
at least!  Has no one come your way whom you could

* Bismarck, who was then living in retirement at Friedrichsruh.

pass on to me? Kahn* is a real joy to us. He seems to improve as if by instinct, and I have no fear that any seed of his ability will run to waste. That is the right sort! Like stags, they select the food that suits them, and don't wait to have it thrown to them in their stalls like cows. But could you not scatter a grain of manna in my path again occasionally, as before? I should not be stingy and store it in sacks like the Jews, but use it to feed my own soul.—With kindest regards from my wife and myself, yours,

HERZOGENBERG.

### 250. *Brahms to Herzogenberg.*

[ISCHL, *June* 14, 1890.]

MY VERY DEAR FRIEND, — I must just thank you for your very kind and charming letter, though I will not attempt to answer it, being even worse at writing words than music — for at least I don't begin to dislike the latter until the day after it is written!

I am glad my last letter shone in two colours—grey for me, sky blue for you!

Liseley stood for a sentimental chapter in your family, and it is grievous to hear that it has come to an end.

May the summer bring you good luck in other respects, and the winter good pupils. I should be

* Robert Kahn (b. 1865), composer and conductor, pupil of Vincenz Lachner, Kiel, Rheinberger, and Herzogenberg, at present Professor of Theory of Music at the *Hochschule*, Berlin. In the 'eighties he had the benefit of some lessons from Brahms.

inclined to envy you if I came across any such. Be glad you have one at all!

I had no idea it was your first visit to Hamburg and to Chrysander, and was the more pleased to have your cheerful account.

But no more to-day except renewed thanks and kindest regards to you both.—Yours,

J. BR.

### 251. *Elisabet von Herzogenberg to Brahms.*

BERLIN, *October* 9, 1890.

DEAR FRIEND,—I have so often had the pleasure of showing you what an event a new piece is to me that I need not fear you will misunderstand my silent reception of your two children this time. Heinrich wrote to you recently that I had not been well. I have had great difficulty in breathing all this time, and felt almost paralyzed—not only in my physical movements, but mentally. This kind of oppression affects the Psyche within one, and her wings soon droop. If anything helped to pull me together, it was a glance into your scores, a walk through the sunny landscape of the new quintet,* which overflows with melodiousness, gentle loveliness, and heavenly peace. The 'old' quintet, the F major, affected me so powerfully again recently that the new one only found a footing with difficulty (old friends are fondest!); but my heart soon surrendered to the new-comer, and is prepared to admit its possibly greater beauty and benignity, its riper, sweeter vintage. Yet why compare them, when they are so eminently worthy to stand side by side!

* Quintet in G, Op. 111.

The very opening charmed me. I felt myself almost transported into the atmosphere of the G major sextet, and the acquaintance begun under such favourable auspices has at no point caused me any disillusion. How it meets one's comprehension halfway by its exquisite proportions, its compactness! How clear is the framework, thanks to the absence of everything superfluous, and how perfectly each part fulfils its allotted function! How much everyone might learn from it — everyone, that is, who does not choose simply to enjoy it; and how I wish I could hear it soon! It must sound so lighthearted, different again from the F major, which gives even our splendid players here all they can do to bring out its full brilliance. How charming the first motion is, and the melody for the 'cello! How insinuating the second subject, with its deft introduction !* Only the opening bars of the coda (H)† struck me as somewhat harsh; the imitation between fiddle and viola is hardly as insinuating in character as is obviously intended. But I will not weary you by telling you things you know so much better, and naming every bar that charmed me. I may just say how glorious I think the Adagio, however. The C sharp minor piece in the first quintet‡ is magnificent, but I rate this far higher, on account of its uniform character and continuity. Middle parts which are designed for contrast always hurt me a little, but here the colours are so blended as to enhance each other's brilliance, while the same even temper prevails throughout. A delicious movement! One is glad of the Allegretto, though, after so much solemnity. It relieves the

* P. 5, bar 7.                    † Letter H in the score.
‡ The second movement (*Grave ed appassionato*), Op. 88.—Tr.

strain without displaying—as do so many Allegrettos
—more sprightliness than is musically justifiable.
Laughter of that refined and witty order is becoming
enough.  And the coda in the Trio, with that adorable
*crescendo* before the *da capo* on the sustained D—you
knew well that your friends would exchange approving
nods at that point!  I cannot appreciate the Finale
thoroughly until I hear it, for it is not eye-music,
but rich, sonorous ear-music, too rich for my imagination to grasp *entirely*.  The rhythm and the line of the
melody remind me of the Scherzo in the B flat major
concerto :

It is even, perhaps, rather too striking a reminiscence
for anyone with such a store as yours to draw upon ;
yet children of the same parents do undoubtedly
resemble one another, and Nature's store is the most
inexhaustible!  So one concludes it had to be, and
that particular motif is only one of the many that
frolic together in this movement.  I could kiss the
second subject,† and all the sweet tangle after it.
It is so pretty the first time it comes, clever the
second, and irresistible after the development (which
one wishes had been longer), where it comes twisting
in again upon D.‡  What movement and swing there
is in it all; what a tempo in the development; and
how youthful and charming every detail!  The person
who invented it all must have felt very light-hearted.

\* Op. 111, p. 48, bar 9.            † P. 40, bar 15.
‡ Op. 111, p. 48, bar 9.

One feels you must have been celebrating—say, your thirtieth birthday!

*We* get pleasure out of it anyway, when you give us anything so charming, and rejoice that we have youthful hearts to enjoy what your youthful heart creates.

I was strangely affected by the old-new trio.* Something within me protested against the remodelling. I felt you had no right to intrude your mastertouch on this lovable, if sometimes vague, production of your youth. I decided it could not possibly be a success, because no one is the same after all that time, and I might have to sing a lament: '*Es war ein Duft, es war ein Glanz.*'†

I therefore made a point of not looking at the 'old' trio beforehand. I had forgotten many parts of it, and did not know where the new Brahms joined on, as I *never* notice what the papers say. However, I recognized your inset in the first movement *instantly,*‡ was completely disarmed, and played on in a transport of delight. It is *beautiful* in its present form, and I gladly leave it to the musical philologues to remonstrate with you. They are more concerned with the date of a thing than the thing itself—by which I mean no allusion to our quite unpetrified Spitta! The Adagio has gained wonderfully in smoothness by the contraction, and the glorious, stately stride of the principal subject has lost nothing of its fascination. In the Scherzo, where probably the least alteration has been made, we admire the amazingly clear accen-

---

* Op. 8 (*cf.* Letter 247, note).

† Quotation from the song *Heimweh* (Brahms, Op. 63, No. 9).

‡ P. 4, bar 8 of original edition. The principal alterations were made in the development section.

tuation of the original intention.  In short, who would not welcome this piece, with its wise face and its youthful complexion ?

> ' Nun kann man's zweimal lesen,
> Wie gut ist das gewesen !'

Farewell for to-day, dear, dear Friend, and let us thank you sincerely for letting us see your glorious things.  Do send them again soon—above all the quintet, *with the parts*—to Joachim as soon as possible.

Hermine Spies is said to have sung particularly well yesterday.  I see and hear nothing, but stay inside my shell, and do not grieve overmuch.  I find the most entertainment at home, after all.—Your old friend and admirer,

ELISABET HERZOGENBERG.

### 252. *Brahms to Herzogenberg.*

[VIENNA, *October* 27, 1890.]

As I am sending off a rather audaciously bulky letter, I will anticipate or follow it up by a few words to introduce young Prohaska to you.  I can recommend him warmly, although my own acquaintance with him is, unfortunately, very slight.

But you will soon see for yourself.  I hope he will prove a pupil after your own heart.

Please see in both pupil and parcel expression of my good-will.—With kindest regards,

J. BR.

INVOICE.*

To [musical notation] ρ—and—ρ—von—ρ †

Received herewith :

| | | | | |
|---|---|---|---|---|
| ~~As per bill~~ | ... | ... | ... | 1 Triolettchen |
| ~~Express~~ order... | ... | ... | |
| *On approval* | ... | ... | ... | 1 Quinkelei[1] |
| Further orders ? | ... | ... | |
| Copy for review !? | ... | ... | |

[1] Parts not available.


### 253. *Herzogenberg to Brahms.*

BERLIN, *October* 31, 1890.

DEAREST FRIEND,—Our delight at receiving such a glorious sign of life from you was indeed great, and would have been greater had we at least some hope and prospect of seeing the parts of the *exquisite* quintet.‡ As it is, we have to keep it to ourselves, and absorb it greedily *à deux.* You don't know what a pleasure it would have been to take it to Joachim at once. But, really, may he not have it for the *Kammermusik?* Won't you lend your sanction?— for our sakes and for his! His enthusiasm for your music is so young and vigorous. Only two days ago he gave his fine audience a perfect performance of

---

* The appended invoice was enclosed in a parcel of music containing the B major trio (*Triolettchen*) and the G major quintet (*Quinkelei*). The words crossed out in the left-hand column were scored through with blue pencil.

† 'To H. [German name for B natural] and E. von H.'—TR.

‡ Op. 111.

the F major quintet, displaying all its beauties more convincingly than ever.

This most affecting mark of your favour makes us uncomfortable in relation to him. Can nothing be done?

My wife intended playing the trio* yesterday, but the old breathing difficulty prevented her. We understand the scheme of the alterations now, though we silently mourn one or two lost favourites—the second subject in the first movement, for instance.

To-morrow I go to Leipzig to help to bury that dear little old lady, Frau Hauptmann.†

I have various things to do before then, and must leave my wife to finish. She will be eloquent in thanking you for the great pleasure you have given us.

I am most eager to see the new pupil. It so happens that I have just an hour free for him. Our natives are not good for much, so I welcome every foreigner.— Most sincerely yours,　　　　　HERZOGENBERG.


### 254. Brahms to Herzogenberg.

[VIENNA, December, 1890.]

Just the hastiest line for to-day! I may assume that you will be there when they try the quintet?

I want you to ask Joachim for my last letter to him, as my remarks and queries with reference to the beginning of the piece are addressed as much to you as to him. I should be very glad if you would listen critically, and write me frankly what you think.‡

* The revised trio in B, Op. 8.
† Widow of Moritz Hauptmann.
‡ It was a question of whether the 'cello, which has the principal subject in the first movement, would be heard clearly through the

And now a second hasty line to thank you for your
too kind letter, and the printed matter accompanying
it, which I have not yet read.\*

I wish I could express my thanks by showing you
my treasures from the Keller literary remains.†

I will enclose one small sample, which you can send
back after the rehearsals of the quintet.—Yours very
sincerely,

J. Br.

### 255. *Elisabet von Herzogenberg to Brahms.*

[Berlin] *December 16, 1890.*

Dearest Friend,—After the *Kammermusik* the other
day, where we heard your quintet, I begged Joachim for
another look at the score. It only came in the evening,
however, and I had to despatch it by the last post, so

---

semiquaver accompaniment (*forte*) of the other instruments, especially
as a counter-melody of some importance begins in the third bar.
The first performance of the piece was on November 11 in Vienna,
at one of Arnold Rosé's chamber-music evenings. Hummer, the
'cellist, despaired of making himself heard, in spite of the broad,
vigorous tone for which he was famous, and Sigmund Bachrich, the
first viola player, had the courage to point out to Brahms the necessity
for some modification in the tone of the others. After playing the
quintet in Berlin on December 11, Joachim wrote to Brahms: 'And
now the desired report as to the opening passage. After trying it in
various ways, we came back to your original version, except for a
slight modification of the *forte* from the end of the second bar,
increasing the tone again later.'

\* New compositions of Herzogenberg's.

† Professor Adolf Exner, successor to Jhering at Vienna University,
had handed over to Brahms the delightful correspondence between
Jhering, his sister Marie Frisch, and Gottfried Keller, to look through
before it was incorporated in Jakob Baechthold's *Life of Keller*
(vol. iii.). Brahms was so delighted with Keller's lively wit that he
would spend whole afternoons reading out extracts to his friends in
Vienna, and even copied out some for his own use.

could not, as I intended, write to you about it at once.
Instead of looking thoroughly into every detail that
had impressed me on hearing it, I employed the short
time I had in strumming bits of the glorious piece
and impressing the Adagio on my memory. How
beautiful, how impressive it is, how entirely satisfying
in *sound*, how luminously clear by virtue of its neat
proportions! It must take possession of all who have
ears to hear and hearts to feel. You know already
how we delight in the whole work, but you will not
be angry if I favour the two middle movements,
because I recognise in them such perfect unity of
emotion, vigour, and effect. I find it hard to accustom
myself to the sound of certain parts of the first movement, and had conceived of it as sunnier from reading
the score. The character of the principal theme hardly
seems to me to demand the tranquil treatment you
give it. A broken chord of the six-four is, after all,
nothing wildly uncivilized, and you make it so hard
for the poor 'cello to penetrate. Either the four others
make spasmodic efforts to restrain themselves for fear
of drowning the 'cello in his rôle as leader, or he must
scrape mercilessly to make himself heard, and the
effect is worse than ever. The original version is
undoubtedly the best, but the accompanying instruments must on no consideration exceed a *mezzo-forte*.
But could you not, dear master, make this passage
*more* beautiful? The continuation is so very beautiful.
Must we be *tested* a little before you dazzle us with
the second subject and its glorious introductory bars?*
The opening of the development is indescribably fine,
with its powerful Bach-like progressions: F, E♭, D♭,
C, and G, F, E♭, D. How Joachim and Hausmann

* Op. 111, p. 5, bar 3.

looked at each other there, and what a blissful moment
it was for us all! Later, at the close of the development,* the 'cello groans again—that is, Hausmann *never*
does (even though one hears all wood and no strings
after a time, which he is too hotly engaged to notice);
but the instrument itself gives signs of protest against
the exorbitant demands made on it. I venture to think,
in all humility, that a person like you ought to write
nothing which is not absolutely pleasing—not only to
the mind, but to the ear.

Please do not scold this saucy person! You did
send us a 'copy for review,' you know.† My gratitude
and my immense delight in this glorious new work
were marred *at times* by a certain disappointment in
the actual sound, not, of course, in the middle movements, which are moulded entirely out of silver and
gold; and as to the last—well, you *wanted* to be harsh,
witty, clever, and a trifle riotous there, and so the
occasional harshness in the sound is justifiable. But
the first movement! Reading it was like feeling
spring breezes; hearing it, they became equinoctial
gales, which you do get in March, it is true—but then
March is not spring!‡

Dear Barometer-Man on your Magic Island,§ do
show a little more clemency. Go over those few
places again with a soft stump, as if it were a charcoal
drawing, and smear it over, tone it down a little!

---

* P. 14, bar 3.
  † *Cf.* Letter 252, 'invoice.'
  ‡ '*Brahms on the Prater*' would be an ideal inscription for this
quintet, which smacks both of Vienna and the North. A friend
suggested it to Brahms after a rehearsal, and Brahms promptly
replied, 'You've hit it!' adding, with a sly smile, 'And all the pretty
girls there, eh?'
  § Title of a play by Ferdinand Raimund.

That high, scratchy part in F minor (I think), near
the end of the development,* really sounds anything
but beautiful.  It is so *laboured*, whereas *everything* in
this movement ought to sound beautiful.

Thank you for sending the enclosed poem, which
is very affecting.† By way of thanks, I should like
to send Heinrich's latest piece, which seems to me
particularly good.  It is a Latin Requiem for chorus
and orchestra‡—without solos, thank Heaven!  But
there is none of it here, as he is doing it in a concert
at Leipzig in March.  I flatter myself you would like
it, and am most anxious to hear your opinion.  Heinrich
wrote it this winter, in an incredibly short time, and
that is perhaps why it seems like the result of one
inspiration—flowing, melodious, and well written for
chorus singing, or so we hope!

Farewell for to-day, and thank you once more for
the strengthening, *precious* gift of the quintet.  I wish
I could close as effectively as you when you sing—

That F, coming in previously there, is too beautiful!
And so on!—Your admiring

E. H.

* Op. 111, p. 12, bar 9 (?).

† A poem by ——, which had been placed between the leaves of
the Adagio by the author, to whom Brahms had lent the score.  It
went to Berlin, and was returned in due course, Brahms's attention
being at last drawn to it by Frau von Herzogenberg.

‡ Herzogenberg's Requiem for four-part chorus and orchestra,
Op. 72.

§ Op. 111, Adagio, p. 27, bar 8.

## 256. *Brahms to Herzogenberg.*

[VIENNA, *January* 10, 1891.]

Forgive me if I only send this brief acknowledgment of your parcel to-day. I have long wanted to ask you to send me these tokens of your industry more frequently. I could really envy you your industriousness, your youth, your joy in life and in work! I hope you will thoroughly enjoy the Leipzig concert.*— Sincerely yours,

J. BR.

## 257. *Brahms to Elisabet von Herzogenberg.*

[VIENNA, *February*, 1891.]

DEAREST LADY,—I have not deserved a letter, and am not setting out to deserve one to-day, but you might have sent me a paper or a programme from which I could glean what manner of thing the *Königspsalm*† is! Also I should have been glad of a line to say whether you enjoyed Leipzig and the Leipzigers. I would dispense with other charming details, such as how many sandwiches were consumed during the rehearsal, how many stockings knitted (as under Riedel‡ of blessed memory!), what words of wisdom —let fall, etc.

What I really must know is whether Herr Astor is bestirring himself!§

* Herzogenberg's Requiem was performed at the Thomaskirche, Leipzig, on February 22, with great success.

† Herzogenberg's psalm, Op. 71, for chorus and orchestra, written in honour of the Kaiser's birthday, was performed on the same evening as the Requiem.

‡ Karl Riedel (1827-1888). *Cf.* Letter 121.

§ In bringing out Herzogenberg's compositions.

I look on at your wonderful energy and your pleasant circle of serious-minded, seriously-interested people with envious approval. Unfortunately, one or other of you is always having to lie up!

We do not follow your example in either respect here, but read and trifle away our spare time—witness the enclosed!*

But do let me hear something by one means or another.—With kindest regards, yours sincerely,

J. Br.

### 258. *Herzogenberg to Brahms.*

[Berlin, *February* 28, 1891.]

Dearest Friend,—I was on the point of dipping my pen to thank you for the trio and quintet† when your letter arrived with all the questions and the gay canons.

My wife's recovery is slower this time than ever before. She has been in bed six weeks, and the doctor cannot convince himself whether this inertia is a good or a bad sign. I will spare such a brilliantly healthy specimen as yourself a description of her symptoms, and will only say that they are of a serious, if not precisely dangerous, order. She sends kindest messages and many flattering remarks about my Requiem; the latter I am suppressing, as she is, for the first time in twenty-two years, inclined to depart from her usual impersonal standpoint. Those were delightful days at Leipzig, in spite of the melancholy nature of the piece and the anxiety I felt about my wife. You will

---

* The manuscript of *Thirteen Canons for Women's Voices*, published by Peters in 1891.

† The trio (B major) and quintet (G major) had been published in between by Simrock.

be most interested to hear that my perspiring efforts at all the rehearsals and performances were, to the surprise of my friends, as vigorous as could be desired, and were carried out with the endurance and ease of an acrobat. The performance was excellent. They say the acoustic properties of the new Thomaskirche* are splendid; indeed, Spitta and Hausmann are quite envious. The piece is too good to have good notices, but I would gladly send it you in one form or the other if by so doing I can squeeze from you another of those rare, precious, attar-of-roses drops with which I have periodically reprieved my artistic career. *Königs-psalm* is the title of a composition written for the Kaiser's birthday, such as every 'academic'† has to produce in his turn. I will not deny that I found a strong incentive in being commissioned to do something within a given time for once. It is a good index to the general level of one's productive powers. If it turns out passably well, one knows how one stands as regards technique.

That you should spot my furtive literary efforts‡ only proves the incredible range of your reading. You of course, like all musicians, will think me too learned, while learned people do me the greater compliment of thinking me too musical. So there I am, between two stools, a position I do not propose to maintain any longer than I am compelled.

The adaptability of the older to the younger Brahms in the 2nd, 3rd, and 4th movements of the trio is simply amazing. In the 1st I cannot get rid of the

* The old Thomaskirche had just been thoroughly renovated.

† An allusion to his election to membership of the Royal Academy of Arts.

‡ Herzogenberg had published an essay on Bischoff's *Harmonie-lehre* in the *Vierteljahrsschrift für Musikwissenschaft* (1891, p. 267).

impression of its being a collaboration between two masters who are no longer quite on a level. It is probably my own fault, for I still shed a tear each time for the dear departed E major subject.*

I wonder what you are meditating next. Can it be an opera, after all ? I must really ask ——.†—Kindest regards from us both. Your sincerest admirer,

HERZOGENBERG.

### 259. Brahms to Herzogenberg.

[VIENNA, April 29, 1891.]

. . . If I had not abjured letter-writing long ago, I would fire off a long epistle to Spitta, thanking him for his fine essay on the Requiem‡ and his last volume of Schütz, in which I am revelling. Do at least tell him that no one is more sincerely and gratefully appreciative of the fruits of his industry and learning than I.

My customary little grievance as to those confounded

clefs ▦▦▦ and ▦▦▦ § is mitigated this time

---

* Omitted by Brahms in the new edition.

† Some busybody, who professed to know all about Brahms and his plans.

‡ Spitta took Herzogenberg's Requiem as a basis for a historical critical essay on *Musikalische Seelenmessen*, afterwards incorporated in his book *Zur Musik* (Paetel, 1892).

§ Spitta, in his edition of the works of Heinrich Schütz (1585-1672), had retained the original clefs, thereby rendering the score more difficult to read. Brahms always advocated the use of the soprano, alto, and tenor clefs, and used them in his own vocal scores; but the mezzo-soprano and baritone clefs (as above) he considered obsolete, detesting them accordingly. He drew a sharp distinction between what he called 'antiquarian fads' and 'musical necessity.' A vocal score written in four clefs gave him a much clearer idea than the

by the possibility of transposing some of the numbers into readable positions, No. 7 into three sharps, and so on.

If you send a word in reply to this, add a good many on the subject of your dear wife's health. It is no good asking her.—With kindest regards to you both, yours,

J. Br.

### 260. *Herzogenberg to Brahms.*

Berlin, *April* 30, 1891.

. . . The Leipzig *Bachverein* is doing my Requiem for the second time on May 11th. What a pity it cannot be transferred to Brünn—when I should like someone I know to be present! Unfortunately, we cannot yet count on my wife's being able to go. Although she is much better on the whole, her condition is so uncertain that we cannot make any plans, and least of all run the risk of exposing her to the boisterous welcome of our Leipzig friends.

I shall pass on your kind and encouraging messages to Spitta at once. He can do with that sort of thing now and again. To me, too, this book of madrigals* seems much more accessible and interesting than many of the earlier ones. The things sound really exquisite; Adolf Schulze† is rehearsing them with the greatest care. You really learn to respect the

---

modern contraction of two (treble and bass), and he defended his preference even against his publishers, who would have preferred to meet the public convenience in the matter.

\* *Il primo libro dei Madrigali* (1611), by Heinrich Schütz.

† Adolf Schulze (b. 1835), singer, professor of singing at the *Hochschule*, Berlin.

26

man when you see him in his element conducting *a capella* choruses.

I don't know yet what we shall attempt this summer. I shall probably go—alone this time—to Sylt again for part of August. It has such a wonderfully strengthening and lasting effect on me. It would be charming if you could come. A silent ramble on the bare heath is so glorious.

My wife sends kindest messages.—Yours,

HERZOGENBERG.

### 261. *Brahms to Herzogenberg.*

[VIENNA, *May* 2, 1891.]

Mandyczewski* will be calling on you one day soon. I need not commend him to your kindness. I should be particularly glad if he could attend Schulze's choral class. They have no idea of that sort of thoroughness here, and Mandyczewski would be the man to turn it to profit for our school later, perhaps.—With kindest regards, yours,

J. BR.

### 262. *Brahms to Herzogenberg.*

[VIENNA, *May* 10, 1891.]

Many thanks for the parcel, which could not have arrived more opportunely. Wait a minute, though, that sounds as if I were ready for a Requiem myself! No, indeed, but my boxes are already packed for Ischl, and I can just lay it nicely on the top. Once there I shall be able to enjoy the fruits of your toil, while I remain blissfully idle myself. I hear your wife went

* *Cf.* Letter 150.

to Leipzig with you.   In *that* case she must be better, and you will have a delicious time together.   I should like to go to the North Sea with you, but my laziness will probably keep me at Ischl.

Kindest regards and best wishes for the summer from yours,

J. BR.

### 263. *Brahms to Herzogenberg.*

[VIENNA, January, 1892.]

MY VERY DEAR FRIEND,—I am too much with you in thought to be able to write.* It is vain to attempt any expression of the feelings that absorb me so completely.   And you will be sitting alone in your dumb misery, speechless yourself and not desirous of speech from others.

Be assured I am full of sorrow and profoundest sympathy as I think of you.   I could ask questions without end.

You know how unutterably I myself suffer by the loss of your beloved wife, and can gauge accordingly my emotions in thinking of you, who were associated with her by the closest possible human ties.

As soon as you feel at all inclined to think of yourself and others, let me know how you are, and how and where you intend to carry on your own life.

It would do me so much good just to sit beside you quietly, press your hand, and share your thoughts of the dear marvellous woman.—Your friend,

J. BRAHMS.

* Brahms had received the news of Frau von Herzogenberg's death (on January 7, 1892) by telegram.   No letters are in existence between May 10 and the present one.

### 264. *Herzogenberg to Brahms.*

[FLORENCE, *February* 2, 1892.]

MY VERY DEAR FRIEND,—It would indeed do me
good to have you sitting beside me. We have in
common so many memories of my precious wife.
Did we not always count the times when we were
all together our best? Leipzig, Carinthia, Salzburg,

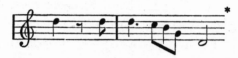

and the happy Christmas days you spent with us
at Zeitzerstrasse—wherever my thoughts wander, you
are woven into our lives at any point worth remembering. And how we lived on the memory of those
occasions! You took up so much more space in our
thoughts than in actual life.

All that we could talk over by the hour—but you
must spare me any account of those cruel last weeks.
Her sufferings hurt me even more now that I have
no hope to keep me up and deceive me. My suffering
has given me no time to realize my own position, and,
indeed, I have buried myself in work, hoping not to be
aroused from it again.

I shall stay on here into May, as this real hermit's
life suits me. I see Hildebrand now and then. He
was like a brother to me in those dark days. Did you
hear of my mother-in-law's death here a week before
my wife's? Neither knew of the other's condition. I

---

* Subject of the violin sonata, Op. 78, which Brahms brought with
him in manuscript to Salzburg in August, 1878 (*cf.* Letters 62
and 63).

kept it a secret from Lisl.  It was horrible, enough to drive one mad!

If you see Epstein, please tell him this, and remember me kindly to him.  I shall not feel like writing at present.

Are you not coming to Italy this spring?  I should be so glad to join you.—Keep a little friendship for yours ever,    HERZOGENBERG.

VIA DEI BARDI 22.

### 265. Brahms to Herzogenberg.

[VIENNA, March 6, 1892.]

In great haste—are you still at the same address? I may send you two small scores?* Peters sent them long ago, but I conclude they went to Berlin, and you never had them.  Forgive the intrusion, and look upon it merely as a means of conveying kindest greetings. —Yours ever,    J. BR.

### 266. Brahms to Herzogenberg.

[VIENNA, March 19, 1892.]

DEAREST FRIEND,—Thank you most sincerely for your parcel of yesterday.  How happy it must make you to distribute these beautiful, affecting pages among your friends!† What a host of questions

---

* Thirteen Canons, Op. 113.

† After her death Herzogenberg published Acht Klavierstücke, by Elisabet von Herzogenberg, dedicating each of the eight pieces to one or other of her friends, including Frau Emma Engelmann-Brandes, Frau Lili Wach (née Mendelssohn-Bartholdy), Frau Hedwig von Holstein, Fräulein Helene Hauptmann, Fräulein Johanna Röntgen, and Frau Clara Schumann.  No. 6 was left without a dedication, while No. 7 was dedicated to Frau Luise von Bezold-Engelmann by the composer before she died.

they raise!—the pieces in themselves and, for instance, the fact that I, for one, had no notion of their existence, although I had been told that one or other of your songs might be traced to your wife.

I look through them in vain (particularly the Servian songs), but cannot make up my mind as to the claims of any one above the rest.

It will, no doubt, have occurred to you to allow her friends to read extracts from her letters. I cherish those I have as, in the first place, one of the most precious memories of my life, and also for their intrinsic qualities of wit and temperament. But their appeal is personal to me. How I should like to see how she wrote to and of other people!

My spring plans are very much in the background this year. My thoughts hover about Florence, Siena, Orvieto, without awaking the smallest excitement in response; but if you were going too, I might rouse myself.

What do you propose for the summer? Will your family keep you in Austria?

Well, no more to-day.—Sincerest thanks and kindest regards from yours,

J. Br.

#### 267. Herzogenberg to Brahms.

ROME, PIAZZA DI PIETRA, PALAZZO CINI,
*March* 12, 1892.

MY VERY DEAR FRIEND,—Peters did send your latest solo quartets* and canons to San Remo,† but at such a time! You will, I know, forgive me for not reverting

---

* Six quartets for soprano, alto, tenor, and bass, with pianoforte accompaniment (Op. 112).

† It was at San Remo that his wife died.

to them.  Now I have something to look forward to
when I go back to Florence in a few weeks' time.  In
the end I did turn lonely and nervous, so came over
to Rome about a week ago, where my sister-in-law's*
family have very kindly taken me in.

I just missed making Billroth's daughter's† acquaintance at Dr. Fleischl's‡ the other day, but still hope to
meet her and Frau Quidde, who was also present,
sometime.  It was a large, dark, crowded drawing-
room, where I felt like a man in a dream.

Simrock has just sent the trio and quintet,§ so I
will not write any more to-day, but will fall to on the
music like a tiger.  Thank you for keeping me so well
in mind, you kind person!—Yours,

HERZOGENBERG.

### 268. Herzogenberg to Brahms.

ROME, PIAZZA DI PIETRA, PALAZZO CINI,<br>March 21, 1892.

MY VERY DEAR FRIEND,—To avoid 'dodging each
other round and round' (as in Leander's fairy-tales),‖
I will give you my plans for next month.  They are
open to variation here and there, but not where other
people's arrangements would suffer.

The beginning of April will find me in Florence
again, partly to see about the monument Hildebrand

---

* Frau Henry Bennet-Brewster.

† Fräulein Else Billroth, a talented amateur musician, pupil of
Stockhausen, living in Vienna.

‡ Otto von Fleischl, doctor in Rome.

§ Clarinet trio, Op. 114, and clarinet quintet, Op. 115, composed at
Ischl in the summer of 1891.

‖ Träumereien an französische Kaminen, by Richard Leander
(v. Volkman).

is designing,* partly to meet the Fiedlers, who are coming there in the spring. I shall be there the greater part of May also; go to Palanza, by way of San Remo, to see Frau Schumann at the end of the month, then higher up to Heiden,† to get my house arranged. There I remain until the autumn; I shall probably winter in Berlin.

How I should like to join you in your quiet excursions in Tuscany! Orvieto I don't know at all; Siena and Valterra only from flying visits. Although the world seems but a dream to me, it is, after all, a lovely dream—as, for instance, yesterday at Tivoli.

I am more glad than I can say that you approve of my publishing the piano pieces.‡ It was more a labour of love than anything I ever did. I had to reproduce some of them from memory, which cost me some far from easy but very affecting hours. The only one among my songs that Lisl wrote is Op. 44, No. 7. I had intended editing some of hers, but gave it up when I saw how much I should have to do to them. Some day I will show you them. There is a good deal of temperament in some of them, and the harmonies are clever and ingenious at times. The piano pieces were much more finished. I did practically nothing to them.

The two clarinet pieces are still growing on me. So far I fail to see why the quintet should be preferred to the trio; perhaps it was merely the fact of

* Hildebrand's fine monument is carried out in early Renaissance style, and represents St. Cecilia (with the features of Frau von Herzogenberg) seated at the organ.

† In the canton of Appenzell, on Lake Constance, where Herzogenberg had built a house, *Zum Abendrot.*

‡ *Cf.* Letter 266, note.

their appearing *simultaneously* that set everyone to work on these everlasting comparisons. I like them both equally much, and can imagine how splendidly the instruments must blend. It is so essentially *right*, too, that you should have assigned the clarinet an 'antiphonal' part. The effect must have justified you amply.

To-day the *De Sanctis** are giving us the F major Rasumofsky† by way of a novelty. They play it very decently, but, strange to say, with ever-increasing caution. Perhaps they are afraid to let themselves go.

Farewell, and be as nice to me as ever! I shall soon hear more of your plans, I suppose.—Always yours,

HERZOGENBERG.

### 269. *Brahms to Herzogenberg.*

[VIENNA, April 5, 1893.]

DEAR FRIEND,—I quite expect to be here still on the 10th, but that is the latest, I think, as I am to meet some friends at Genoa for Sicily.‡

Let me know soon precisely when you are coming, and where you will stay, so that I and some others

---

\* Probably a Roman quartet society.

† Beethoven's quartet, Op. 59, No. 1.—TR.

‡ This was Brahms's eighth and last Italian tour. He started on April 13, meeting his travelling companions, Josef Victor Widmann, of Berne, and Dr. Friedrich Hegar and the pianist Robert Freund, both of Zürich, at Milan, from whence they went to Genoa. The journey to Sicily was originally to have been made by boat, but Brahms did not care for long sea-journeys, and finally decided to go by train. On the way they stopped at Naples, Sorrento, Palermo, Girgenti, Catania, Syracuse, Taormina, Messina, Naples, and Venice. Brahms was back in Vienna on the 10th (*cf.* Widmann, *Johannes Brahms*, p. 163).

may look forward to it, and arrange for more pleasant meetings.

But you must put Utrecht out of your mind while you are here; I heard such a pleasant account of your visit there from the Engelmanns.

In any case, let me know soon. — With kindest regards,

J. Br.

### 270. *Herzogenberg to Brahms.*

BERLIN, *February* 14, 1894.

DEAR FRIEND,—I wanted to write as soon as I heard of Billroth's death,* but never got it done. I want you to *know* how much I thought about you; up to this you can at most only have guessed. I know what Billroth was to you. It was his personality which dominated—peopled—your whole world, for one can put up with practically everybody, given the consciousness of one deep friendship. And now, what a gap! Why not emigrate—to Berlin, where your banner is sturdily upheld by 'Seven Righteous Men'?†

I shall see Frau Schumann next Monday at Frankfurt, which I have a fancy to visit. They say she is very gay, and plays with all her former vigour and delight. God preserve this dear soul to us!

I have just seen Bülow's death‡ in the paper. He had many warnings, and must have been prepared; yet it came suddenly in the end, and in a strange country, which was hard on his poor wife! Poor comet! what will the orphaned comet's tail do without

* Theodor Billroth died February 6, 1894, at Abbazia.
† Title of one of Gottfried Keller's *Züricher Novellen.* The seven alluded to are probably Herzogenberg, Joachim, Hausmann, Spitta, Barth, Rudorff, and Adolf Schulze.
‡ Hans von Bülow died at Cairo on February 12, 1894.

its leader, who was, after all, a glorious compound of
talent and strength of will! He always put his whole
heart and soul into everything; even if the aim was
wrong, his motives were sincere. May he find rest!

I have at last purchased your glorious *Klavierstücke*,*
and ordered the entertaining fifty-one finger-torturers.†
I am looking forward to hearing Frau Schumann play
my favourites. She was singing their praises in the
summer at Interlaken. This set of pieces is apparently
easy, but we ordinary mortals find ourselves at a standstill once we have passed the reading stage. I really
felt as if I could play the GLORIOUS ballade‡ once or
twice, and do wish I could. Indeed, I spend my days
in silence now; if I did not keep up my old dull
routine of work, the neighbours might easily take me
for a painter or engraver, for all the noise I make.

Shall you not pass through here as you did last
year? Or at least through Heiden, where we shall
settle down in the beginning of May? My heart is
open to you.—Yours,                    HERZOGENBERG.


## 271. *Brahms to Herzogenberg.*

[VIENNA, *February* 14, 1894.]

DEAR FRIEND,—The rest another time—particularly
as you are just off on your travels! This is merely to
say that you need not buy my things; as it is, I behave
shabbily enough, considering the things you and Ritter
shower upon me. Who is responsible this time I
know not—Simrock is too good a man of business!

---

\* Op. 118 and 119.

† Finger exercises, published in 1893 without opus number
(*cf.* Letters 21, 77-79).

‡ Op. 118, No. 3.

Well, *bon voyage*, and remember me most kindly to Frau Schumann.

The supplementary and superfluous copies will come in nicely for one of your dear young ladies (Fräuleins Radecke or Spitta ?)—Ever yours,

J. Br.

### 272. *Brahms to Herzogenberg.*

[VIENNA, *February* 22, 1894.]

DEAR FRIEND,—I am again writing in haste merely to say that I was advised of the arrival of the first lot of my things which I sent to you at Florence, and have *not* had them returned through the dead letter office. So you see we are innocent. I am very glad that you should know it, and that you brought up the subject (in a shy, round-the-corner way).

Am I really so uncommunicative that it should be news to you when I say that it is not friends like Billroth who keep me here in spite of everything, who lead me to spend the summer in Austria instead of going to Switzerland; in spite of everything, I repeat, for I am frequently deeply conscious of all that I miss ?*
—Kindest regards. Yours,

J. Br.

### 273. *Herzogenberg to Brahms.*

BERLIN W. 62, *January* 30, 1895.

DEAR FRIEND,—We neither of us like being senti-mental, but we must not sacrifice another deeper emotion on that account, and thus deprive ourselves of the few precious moments life may offer. So I will

---

* Brahms was chiefly attracted to Austria and Vienna by the scenery, the city itself, and the people. He was never able to feel so much at home anywhere else.

make you a regular lover's declaration with regard to the two glorious flood-tide sonatas,\* and say, as my wife was so fond of saying, God bless you! They made me genuinely happy for a couple of days, and I almost felt again that life might be worth living.

I am positively haunted by lovely, original, spring-like melodies, without knowing to what they lead. At present they charm me, but I am looking forward to knowing and possessing them soon. Don't wait too long and let the manuscript paper get cold! You must know that we all want you. I most of all. Keep a little corner warm for me—'Tom's a-cold!'† —Yours,

HERZOGENBERG.

### 274. *Brahms to Herzogenberg.*

[ISCHL] *August* 8, 1895.

DEAR FRIEND,—I opened your parcel‡ this time with the greatest delight; in the first place because I had heard from Engelmann that you were at Graz with some eye trouble, but now that I have this message sent from your home, and in your own welcome writing, I hope I need not worry. I then discovered with renewed delight that you had not forgotten Eichendorff—the little god of most of us in our youth—in the midst of your strenuous life.

The songs (both music and words) are melancholy enough, certainly, but they sing the memory of such unforgettable charm and loveliness that one cannot feel sad or depressed.

\* Two sonatas for clarinet and piano, Op. 120.
† *King Lear*, Act III., Scene iv.
‡ Herzogenberg's *Elegische Gesänge* (words by Eichendorff) for soprano, Op. 91.

I should be glad of a few lines to say how you are, but an industrious man like you may always be said to have answered that question!

So good-bye. Kindest regards, and picture me happily engaged in leisurely appreciation.

J. BRAHMS.

### 275. *Herzogenberg to Brahms.*

HEIDEN, August 11, 1895.

MY VERY DEAR FRIEND,—I am delighted that my songs have procured me such a nice little letter. I should certainly have thought the oratorio,* by reason of its scope and treatment, more likely to arouse your comment, whether friendly, warm, frank, and encouraging, or the reverse. I confess I looked forward to it eagerly for a little time; then came this confounded inflammation, and I had to close my eyes patiently and examine myself from inside. I assure you it is not pleasant to feel the world growing 'drab as a dormouse' around you.

I should particularly enjoy having the clarinet sonatas to look at just now. If you should have thought of me with your usual kindness, the dear things may easily have stuck fast in Berlin. A hint from you, and they would fly hither. . . .

I hope I shall be well enough this year to visit Frau Schumann at Interlaken. Won't you go too, and get in a flying visit to Heiden?

I will undertake to bring you to her, incognito, via Rapperswyl and Brüning. I could envy you your

---

* Herzogenberg's *Die Geburt Christi*, Church oratorio for solos, mixed chorus, and children's voices, accompanied by harmonium, strings, oboe, congregational singing, and organ (Op. 90).

'leisurely enjoyment.'* For myself, I still labour under the delusion that there is work for me to do. Pray for me!—Yours sincerely,

HERZOGENBERG.

### 276. Brahms to Herzogenberg.

[ISCHL, *June*, 1896.]

DEAR FRIEND,—It is really a great pity that we hear so little of one another, but I can hardly expect to hear more when I am such a bad correspondent. However, I should like to have your summer address. I shall have a trifle to send soon, which may cause you to attack my unchristian principles in your new paper!† Other less compromising things, which are, however, not suitable for publication, I should very much like to have shown you at the piano.‡

But I suppose you will not be coming to Austria, not at least to Ischl?

In any case, your address, please. Kindest regards to yourself and dear companion.§—Yours,

J. BRAHMS.

* The tone of Brahms's letter (Letter 274)—in particular, perhaps the expression 'leisurely appreciation' (Brahms wrote '*behaglichsten Geniessen*' so indistinctly that Herzogenberg read '*behaglichen Genüssen*')—wounded Herzogenberg so deeply as to lead to a serious breach between the friends. It will be seen that there is an interval of ten months between this letter and the next.—TR.

† *Vier Ernste Gesänge*, Op. 121. Brahms had some qualms about publishing these songs, on account of the not only undogmatic, but in part incredible, texts to which they were composed. The new paper referred to is probably the *Monatsschrift für Gottesdienst und Kirchliche Kunst*, edited by Dr. Friedrich Spitta and Dr. Julius Smend, assisted by Herzogenberg.

‡ Probably the posthumous *Choralvorspiele* for organ.

§ Helene Hauptmann, daughter of Moritz Hauptmann, and an old friend of the Herzogenbergs, had undertaken to look after Herzogenberg and his house after his wife's death.

### 277. *Herzogenberg to Brahms.*

HEIDEN, NEAR RORSCHACH, SWITZERLAND,
*July* 1, 1896.

MY VERY DEAR FRIEND,—And is it Sunday to-day, that anything so charming should happen to me? A nice, nice letter from you and the thrilling prospect of some heathenish music—music of any sort indeed! Let me betray my hiding-place at once! We have been here since the beginning of June, composing much useless stuff, being incited thereto by Mother Nature, who must be held responsible.

The best way of sending music abroad is to label it 'Business papers, registered.' This by the way. The best way of all, however, is to bring it oneself by train. We should be quiet here all through August; why not come to Switzerland again? Towards the end of September I shall be returning to Berlin via Graz. Should I find you still at Ischl? I could easily arrange to go that much out of my way. Or should I find you in Vienna about September 29th?

As for my outburst of piety, let me remind you of the proverb : 'He who has no faith must have emotions.' I believe nothing, but experience emotions in consequence.

Particularly to-day !

All kind messages from Helene,* as from myself.— Yours,

HERZOGENBERG.

* Helene Hauptmann.

## 278. *Herzogenberg to Brahms.*

HEIDEN, *July* 15, 1896.

DEAR FRIEND,—Best thanks for the *Ernste Gesänge.*
You are indeed fruitful in surprises! Who but you
ever conceived the idea of composing Bible words in
this independent way, free from all the traditions of
Church and liturgy! What will the singers make of
it ? I can hear them singing in the drawing-room
after dinner of those who 'are yet able to receive meat,'*
for stupidity knows no bounds! But I ask myself
seriously how they are to be classified. All music
must be best suited to some occasion, after all. You
may shrug your shoulders, and take your pleasure in
advance at having created pieces of such glorious
depth ; I too, in my admiration of your powers of
technique and expression in No. 3 above all. How
blissfully one lingers over that E major part! Who
would not hope to pass away to the sound of such
rich, bittersweet, yearning harmonies. Then the
beautiful B major melody in No. 4, and the whole of
No. 2 ! Some parts are not to be taken in so quickly,
and that is just the best of it, for there will be new
beauties cropping up everywhere.

And so I may shrug my shoulders too, and leave it
to my friends the parsons to settle down again after
licking their lips in anticipation of a scandal.

Well, and where am I to see you—at Heiden, Ischl,
or in Vienna ?—As of old, yours very sincerely,

H. HERZOGENBERG.

* 'O Death, how bitter is the remembrance of thee to a man that
liveth at rest in his possessions . . . yea, unto him that is yet able
to receive meat' (Ecclesiasticus xli. 1).—TR.

27

### 279. *Brahms to Herzogenberg.*

[ISCHL, *July* 21, 1896.]

I was uncommonly glad to hear that my 'harvesters' revels'* met with your approval. I am afraid our meeting must be here or in Vienna, so please make inquiries before you start as to whether I am here or there. I should like to be able to look forward to a couple of days with you.—Kindest regards,

J. BR.

### 280. *Brahms to Herzogenberg.*

[KARLSBAD, *September* 15, 1896.]

DEAR FRIEND,—You will certainly not find me at Ischl. Just now I am here at Karlsbad, but have not succeeded in losing my touch of jaundice† so far. I *hope* to be in Vienna by the 28th. You are sure to be stopping there in any case? Otherwise I would write more definitely later.—Kindest regards. Yours,

J. BR.

### 281. *Herzogenberg to Brahms.*

BERLIN W. 62, KURFÜRSTENDAMM, 263,
*March* 26, 1897.

MY VERY DEAR FRIEND,—I have two habits which refuse to be shaken off: one is, that I still compose;

* The South German expression *Schnaderhüpfeln* is used to describe a lively song to which the harvesters dance at their festival. Brahms was fond of using it when alluding, either in speech or in writing, to his *Vier ernste Gesänge*, usually prefixing the adjective ' godless.'

† Brahms was taken ill at Ischl in June with jaundice, which proved to be a symptom of the more serious organic disease which eventually led to his death. The Karlsbad treatment did him more harm than good.

the other, that I ask—just as I did thirty-four years ago—'What will He say to it?'

'He,' I may say, is you. It is true you have had nothing to say to it for some years past—a fact I am at liberty to explain in my own way. It has certainly not affected my devotion to you, to which I propose to give expression by another dedication,* for which I claim your indulgence.

My thoughts are more than ever with you, now that I know you are ill. Let us hope spring will make a change of air possible. Even if the direct medicinal effect is not apparent, it refreshes and enlivens one mentally and physically, and no doctor will deny that that may lead to a cure.†—Your old friend and admirer,

H. HERZOGENBERG.

* Herzogenberg dedicated his second piano quartet, Op. 95, to Brahms.

† On the day when this letter was written, Brahms had gone to bed 'to rest a little.' He never got up again, but died on April 3. A letter to thank Herzogenberg for this dedication was dictated to Arthur Faber, but is, unfortunately, not now available.

# INDEX

THE END